ENVIRONMENTAL CRIME AND SOCIAL CONFLICT

GREEN CRIMINOLOGY

Series Editors:

Michael J. Lynch, *University of South Florida, USA*
Paul B. Stretesky, *University of Colorado, Denver, USA*

Now two decades old, green criminology – the study of environmental harm, crime, law, regulation, victimization, and justice – has increasing relevance to contemporary problems at local, national, and international levels. This series comes at a time when societies and governments worldwide seek new ways to alleviate and deal with the consequences of various environmental harms as they relate to humans, non-human animals, plant species, and the ecosystem and its components. Green criminology offers a unique theoretical perspective on how human behavior causes and exacerbates environmental conditions that threaten the planet's viability. Volumes in the series will consider such topics and controversies as corporate environmental crime, the complicity of international financial institutions, state-sponsored environmental destruction, and the role of non-governmental organizations in addressing environmental harms. Titles will also examine the intersections between green criminology and other branches of criminology and other areas of law, such as human rights and national security. The series will be international in scope, investigating environmental crime in specific countries as well as comparatively and globally. In sum, by bringing together a diverse body of research on all aspects of this subject, the series will make a significant contribution to our understanding of the dynamics between the natural world and the quite imperfect human world, and will set the stage for the future study in this growing area of concern.

Other titles in this series:

Environmental Crime and its Victims
Perspectives within Green Criminology
Edited by Toine Spapens, Rob White and Marieke Kluin

Exploring Green Criminology
Toward a Green Criminological Revolution
Michael J. Lynch and Paul B. Stretesky

Animal Harm
Perspectives on Why People Harm and Kill Animals
Angus Nurse

Environmental Crime and Social Conflict
Contemporary and Emerging Issues

Edited by

AVI BRISMAN
Eastern Kentucky University, USA

NIGEL SOUTH
University of Essex, UK

ROB WHITE
University of Tasmania, Australia

Routledge
Taylor & Francis Group

LONDON AND NEW YORK

First published 2015 by Ashgate Publishing

Published 2016 by Routledge
2 Park Square, Milton Park, Abingdon, Oxon OX14 4RN
711 Third Avenue, New York, NY 10017, USA

Routledge is an imprint of the Taylor & Francis Group, an informa business

British Library Cataloguing in Publication Data
A catalogue record for this book is available from the British Library

The Library of Congress has cataloged the printed edition as follows:
Environmental crime and social conflict : contemporary and emerging issues / [edited] by Avi Brisman, Nigel South, Rob White.
    pages cm. -- (Green criminology)
  Includes bibliographical references and index.
  ISBN 978-1-4724-2220-0 (hardback) 1. Offenses against the environment.
2. Criminology--Environmental aspects. 3. Social conflict. I. Brisman, Avi.
  HV6401.E585 2015
  364.1'45--dc23

                                                                2014037304

ISBN 9781472422200 (hbk)

Contents

List of Figures   vii
List of Tables   ix
Notes on Contributors   xi

1   Toward a Criminology of Environment-Conflict Relationships   1
       Avi Brisman, Nigel South and Rob White

PART I: CONFLICT OVER NATURAL RESOURCES POSSESSION

2   Mapping the Links between Conflict and Illegal Logging   41
       Tanya Wyatt

3   Gorillas and Guerrillas:
       Environment and Conflict in the Democratic Republic of Congo   57
       Richard Milburn

4   Land Uses and Conflict in Colombia   75
       David Rodríguez Goyes

5   With or Without a Licence to Kill:
       Human-Predator Conflicts and Theriocide in Norway   95
       Ragnhild Sollund

PART II: CONFLICT OVER DECLINING RESOURCES

6   The State-Corporate Tandem Cycling Towards Collision:
       State-Corporate Harm and the Resource Frontiers of
       Brazil and Colombia   125
       Bram Ebus and Karlijn Kuijpers

7   Somalis Fight Back:
       Environmental Degradation and the Somali Pirate   153
       Victoria E. Collins

PART III: CONFLICT THAT DESTROYS ENVIRONMENTS

8   Resource Wars, Environmental Crime, and the Laws of War:
      Updating War Crimes in a Resource Scarce World   177
      Aaron Fichtelberg

9   The Poaching Paradox:
      Why South Africa's 'Rhino Wars' Shine a Harsh Spotlight on
      Security and Conservation   197
      M.L.R. Smith and Jasper Humphreys

10   Weaponising Conservation in the 'Heart of Darkness':
      The War on Poachers and the Neocolonial Hunt   221
      Tyler Wall and Bill McClanahan

PART IV: CONFLICT OVER NATURAL RESOURCES EXTRACTION PROCESSES

11   The Hidden Injuries of Mining: Frontier Cultural Conflict   241
      Kerry Carrington, Russell Hogg and Alison McIntosh

12   On Harm and Mediated Space:
      The BP Oil Spill in the Age of Globalisation   265
      Nels Paulson, Kim Zagorski and D. Chris Ferguson

13   Environment and Conflict: A Typology of Representations   285
      Avi Brisman

Index   *313*

List of Figures

2.1   Conflict and illegal logging   48

6.1   A small-scale miners' community in Sur de Bolívar   126
6.2   A small-scale miner leaves the bocamina,
      the 'mouth of a mining shaft', with a cart full of minerals   130
6.3   Home of a riverine family on the Xingu River   132
6.4   Small houses in Altamira in an area that will be flooded by the
      Belo Monte dam   139
6.5   A miner working the oxygen poor mining shafts in Sur de Bolívar   142

List of Tables

2.1   Locations of conflicts where resources are an item in the conflict   44
2.2   Global illegal logging incidents   47

11.1   Estimation of Australia's resources sector workforce, 2012   258
11.2   Proportions of non-resident workers to the Moranbah
     resident population   259

12.1   Correlations among papers for reporting on a given day,
     controlling for the occurrence of a 'major event' in the first 100
     days after the Deepwater Horizon explosion   274
12.2   Correlations among papers for damages, origins, solutions, and
     risk, controlling for total number of articles on a given day and
     the occurrence of a 'major event' in the first 100 days after the
     Deepwater Horizon explosion   275
12.3   Risk reporting between the *Guardian* and *Financial Times* by per
     cent of stories   276

Notes on Contributors

Avi Brisman (MFA, JD, PhD) is an Assistant Professor in the School of Justice Studies at Eastern Kentucky University, USA. His writing has appeared in *Contemporary Justice Review*, *Crime, Law and Social Change*, *Crime Media Culture*, *Critical Criminology*, *International Journal for Crime, Justice and Social Democracy*, *Journal of Contemporary Criminal Justice*, *Journal of Criminal Justice and Security*, *Journal of Qualitative Criminal Justice and Criminology*, *Journal of Theoretical and Philosophical Criminology*, *Race and Justice*, *Social Justice*, *Theoretical Criminology*, and *Western Criminology Review*, among other journals. He is co-editor, with Nigel South, of the *Routledge International Handbook of Green Criminology* (2013), and co-author, with Nigel South, of *Green Cultural Criminology: Constructions of Environmental Harm, Consumerism, and Resistance to Ecocide* (Routledge, 2014).

Kerry Carrington is a Professor and the Head School of Justice, Faculty of Law, Queensland University of Technology, Australia. She is currently, Vice Chair of the Division of Critical Criminology (DCC), American Society of Criminology; Member of the Division of Women and Crime, American Society of Criminology; Co-Chief Editor of the *International Journal for Crime, Justice and Social Democracy*; Pacific Rim Editor of *Critical Criminology*; and an International Editorial Board member of *Criminology and Criminal Justice*. Described as 'one of Australia's most influential critical criminologists' (Walters 2003: 103), Professor Carrington's contributions to this field span 25 years and include *Feminism and Global Justice* (Routledge, 2014); *Who Killed Leigh Leigh?* (Random House, 1998); *Offending Girls: Sex, Youth and Justice* (Allen & Unwin, 1993); *Offending Youth: Crime, Sex and Justice* with Margaret Pereira (Federation Press, 2009); and *Policing the Rural Crisis* with Russell Hogg (Federation Press, 2006).

Victoria E. Collins is an Assistant Professor in the School of Justice Studies at Eastern Kentucky University, USA. Dr Collins' research and teaching interests include state crime, transnational crime, victimology, violence against women, and white collar crime. Dr Collins is currently working on a forthcoming book for Routledge, *State Crime, Women and Gender*. Some of her recent publications have appeared in journals such as *International Criminal Law Review*, *Critical Criminology*, *Contemporary Justice Review*, and *The Australian and New Zealand Journal of Criminology*.

Bram Ebus holds an MA in Global Criminology from the Utrecht University (The Netherlands). He has specialised in socio-environmental conflicts, especially caused by the mining industry, and has been active with Comité Académico Técnico de Asesoramiento a Problemas Ambientales (CATAPA) as a researcher and campaigner. He has conducted various studies on the mining industry in Guatemala, Peru, and his latest research pertains to the gold mining industry in Colombia and to state-corporate abuse of power.

D. Chris Ferguson is an Assistant Professor of economics at the University of Wisconsin-Stout and the Assistant Director of the Honors College. He earned his PhD in Economics from Indiana University. His research interests centre on public policy issues and the role of government in markets with externalities. His dissertation research examined human capital issues in the context of public policy and effects on long-term economic growth and inequality. His current research is focused on environmental issues relating to local watershed governance and phosphorus pollution mitigation.

Aaron Fichtelberg is an Associate Professor in the Department of Sociology and Criminal Justice at the University of Delaware. His primary research area is international criminal law and legal theory. He has a book forthcoming book, *Hybrid Tribunals: A Comparative Examinations*, with Springer Press.

David Rodríguez Goyes is a PhD Fellow at the Department of Criminology and Sociology of Law, University of Oslo. He holds a law degree and an MA in Law, Sociology and Criminal Policy from the National University of Colombia. He is co-author of *Determinantes científicas económicas y socioambientales de la bioprospección en Colombia* (2013). His research interests within the field of green criminology include biopiracy and the environmental impacts of the biomedical industry research practices. He is currently lecturer in criminology at the Antonio Nariño University of Colombia.

Russell Hogg is a Professor in the Crime and Justice Research Centre, Faculty of Law, Queensland University of Technology. He is the co-author of *Policing the Rural Crisis* with Kerry Carrington (Federation Press, 2006), *Rethinking Law and Order* with David Brown (Pluto Press, 1998), and numerous articles and book chapters on criminology and criminal justice.

Jasper Humphreys is Director of External Affairs of the Marjan Centre for the Study of War and the Non-Human Sphere in Department of War Studies, King's College, London. Formerly, he was a journalist with over 30 years of experience, writing for various newspapers that included *The Times* and the *London Evening Standard*. Some recent articles on wildlife and resource wars have appeared in *International Affairs*.

Karlijn Kuijpers holds an MA in Global Criminology and an MSc in Sustainable Development, both from Utrecht University (The Netherlands). Ms Kuijpers has specialised in state-corporate environmental crime and has conducted various research projects in the Brazilian Amazon. Her main fields of interest are corporate accountability and the concentration of power in the mining, energy and financial sectors. Ms Kuijpers currently works as a researcher for the Centre for Research on Multinational Corporations (SOMO) and as a research journalist for De Onderzoeksredactie, a Dutch organisation for investigative journalism.

Bill McClanahan is a Doctoral student in Criminology in the Department of Sociology at the University of Essex, UK. He holds a Master of Science degree in Criminology from Eastern Kentucky University and a Bachelor of Science degree in Criminal Justice and Criminology from Indiana University. His research interests include green, cultural, and visual criminologies, water justice, climate change, and wildlife crime.

Alison McIntosh (PhD) is a Senior Research Associate in the School of Justice, Faculty of Law, at Queensland University of Technology, and Managing Editor of the *International Journal for Crime and Justice and Social Democracy*. Dr McIntosh is a human geographer whose research focuses on issues which impact upon the well-being of persons living in regional and remote Australia. She has worked with the team led by Professor Kerry Carrington on a project funded by an ARC Discovery Grant which has examined impacts of FIFO/DIDO resource sector workers on those living in frontline mining communities. A number of joint international publications are based on this research.

Richard Milburn is a PhD candidate and Director of the Congo Research Group within the Marjan Centre for the Study of Conflict and Conservation, Department of War Studies, King's College London. His research focuses on the interaction of the environment and armed conflict in the Democratic Republic of Congo (DRC). He has worked with the International Gorilla Conservation Programme and is currently the UK Representative of the Pole Pole Foundation, a Congolese charity based in Bukavu that works to protect the eastern lowland gorilla and its habitat in the DRC and to promote the sustainable development of surrounding communities. His most recent publications are 'The roots to peace in the Democratic Republic of Congo: Conservation as a platform for green development', and 'Mainstreaming the environment into postwar recovery: The case for "Ecological Development"', both published in *International Affairs* in July 2014 and September 2012 respectively.

Nels Paulson is an Associate Professor of Sociology at University of Wisconsin-Stout. His research focuses on the environment and civil society with a global and comparative emphasis. Past research projects on civil society include disaster relief and religion, hunting as a substantive issue among international environmental organisations, and the place of indigenous groups in global environmental advocacy and governance. His work has appeared in *Conservation and Society*, *Nature and Culture*, and *Environmental Values*, among others. He is currently conducting research on phosphorus pollution in the Midwestern United States and the place of civil society in mitigating non-point source pollution.

M.L.R. Smith is Professor of Strategic Theory in the Department of War Studies, Kings College, London. He is also academic director of the Marjan Centre for the Study of Conflict and Conservation at Kings College, London where his main field of interest is in the militarisation of wildlife protection.

Ragnhild Sollund is a Professor in the Department of Criminology and Sociology of Law at the University of Oslo. She has conducted extensive research on police violence and racial profiling, and has engaged in in-depth study of refugees and labour migrants with a special emphasis on women. Over the past few years, Professor Sollund has focused on issues in green criminology, particularly crimes against endangered animal species. She has written, edited and coedited many works in English and Norwegian, including, *Global Harms: Ecological Crime and Speciesism* (Nova Science, 2008), and *Eco-Global Crimes: Contemporary Problems and Future Challenges* with Rune Ellefsen and Guri Larsen (Ashgate, 2012).

Nigel South is Professor in the Department of Sociology, University of Essex, UK. He has teaching and research interests in criminology, drug use, and health and environmental issues, and has written extensively on green criminological theory, environmental crime and the concept of ecocide. In 2013, he received the Lifetime Achievement Award from the American Society of Criminology's Division on Critical Criminology.

Tyler Wall is Assistant Professor in the School of Justice Studies at Eastern Kentucky University, USA. His research interests focus on the politics of security, police power, and state violence, primarily as related to the United States.

Rob White is a Professor of Criminology in the School of Social Sciences, University of Tasmania, Australia. His recent publications include *Environmental Harm: An Eco-Justice Perspective* (Policy Press, 2013) and *Green Criminology: An Introduction to the Study of Environmental Harm* with Diane Heckenberg (Routledge, 2014).

Tanya Wyatt is a Principal Lecturer in Criminology at Northumbria University. She teaches criminological theory, green crime and crimes of the powerful. Dr Wyatt's publications are featured in *Crime, Law and Social Change*, *Contemporary Justice Review* and the *Asian Journal of Criminology*, among others. Her book, *Wildlife Trafficking: A Deconstruction of the Crime, Victims and*

Offenders, was nominated for the 2014 British Society of Criminology's Book Prize. Other works include an edited collection with Reece Walters and Diane Solomon Westerhuis, *Emerging Issues in Green Criminology: Exploring Power, Justice and Harm*, and with Nigel South and Piers Beirne, a special issue on green criminology for the *International Journal of Crime, Justice and Social Democracy*.

Kim Zagorski is an Associate Professor of Political Science at the University of Wisconsin-Stout. Her research focuses on the intersections of political communication, policy making and social justice. Previous projects have studied the effect media portrayals of genocide, famine, and civil conflict have had on American foreign policy outcomes. Her current research is exploring the ways the voices of marginalised populations are included in debates over mineral extraction.

Chapter 1

Toward a Criminology of Environment-Conflict Relationships[1]

Avi Brisman, Nigel South and Rob White

Introduction and Overview

This collection includes chapters that range across a variety of forms or examples of conflict related to environmental matters.[2] This is deliberate in order to achieve several goals. First, we wished to pull together such disparate examples to provide a baseline resource for a criminology concerned with environment and conflict relationships. Although well explored in fields like political ecology, political science, geography and conflict studies, this is not a topic that has received much attention within criminology, despite the fact that crimes and harms of considerable seriousness and significance are intertwined with these conflicts. Second, we wanted to continue to highlight the international compass of a green or environmentally sensitive criminology (South and Brisman 2013; White 2010, 2011; White and Heckenberg 2014). The contributors to this volume exemplify this global engagement and they bring to bear on their chosen topics a keen intellectual interest, academic rigour and passionate concern. Finally, we wanted to explore our own thinking about a typology of environment-conflict relationships. In this introductory chapter, we start by outlining and filling out in a preliminary way what such a typology might look like. We then move to an overview of the chapters that follow.

A Typology of Environment-Conflict Relationships

At the outset, it should be acknowledged and emphasised that linkages between conflict and the environment are varied and not all are negative. Or, to put it another way, some factors, such as contested resource wealth, that in some circumstances

1   Portions of this chapter were presented by Brisman and South to the Department of Security and Crime Science, University College London (London, United Kingdom) on 21 May 2013. We are grateful to Ms Joanna F. Hill and Professor Shane D. Johnson for providing us with the opportunity to speak to their department. We thank them and other members of the audience for their questions, comments and suggestions.

2   We conceptualise 'conflict' specifically as *violence* or the *threat of violence* stemming from incompatibilities in stakeholders' interests, priorities, values or understandings.

may precipitate or support or subsidise conflict, may, in other circumstances, provide *a route out of*, or *insulation from*, conflict (see Butts and Bankus 2013; Conca and Dabelko 2002; see generally Gelling 2010; Greenberg 2010; Milburn this volume; Risen 2010; Romero 2009a). Muffett and Bruch (2011: 4), for example, observe that 'well-managed resources can help fund reconstruction efforts and help bring order from chaos', while Lujala and Rustad (2011: 19) argue that '[h]igh-value natural resources have the potential to promote and consolidate peace' and that valuable resources can help jump-start development, secure sustainable growth, raise living standards, and increase economic equality. While the notion that growth can be endlessly sustainable is contradictory (Ruggiero and South 2013), in the short term, it is true that such resources can serve as an important means of generating foreign currency for cash-strapped governments, can reduce dependence on international aid, and can support compensation and post-conflict relief for war-affected populations (see generally Polgreen 2009). Indeed, sometimes it is the prior conflict over resources, and disadvantages flowing from these, that provide the setting and impetus for later political and economic settlements. For instance, in the context of post-colonial relationships, it is notable that substantial benefits may occasionally accrue to formerly dispossessed or adversely affected parties through contemporary resource re-allocation. For example, in Australia such processes have resulted in the (albeit limited) hand-over of certain lands, rivers and iconic sites to indigenous people, such as Uluru – a massive rock that sits in the desert in the very heart of the nation – that local indigenous people now manage as park rangers and tourist guides.

Having made this point, we turn now to the main focus of this volume and of this introductory chapter: providing examples of conflicts that produce negative/ damaging environmental consequences. From those examples, it is our intention to create a typology of conflict-environmental relationships useful for green criminological research. We propose the following headings for our typology:

- conflict over natural resources possession;
- conflict over declining resources;
- conflict that destroys environments;
- conflict over natural resource extraction processes.

We flesh out and offer examples of each of these in turn, while stressing the fluidity of these categories and instances of overlap between them.[3]

---

3   We recognise that other formulations have been proposed and that other types of relationships have been described (see, e.g., Soysa 2000, for an overview and study of the linkages between natural resource abundance, scarcity and conflict; Eman et al. 2013: 20–23, who discuss different relationships between environment and security; Lee 2009, who distinguishes between two different conflict types stemming from climate change ('Hot Wars' and 'Cold Wars') and who recognises six future scenarios of climate change and conflict; Scheffran and Cannaday (2013: 262), who identify several types of energy-related conflicts).

Conflict over Natural Resources Possession

This type of conflict is concerned with issues of access to, control over and use of natural resources, including the abundance of natural resources and greed-motivated violence. There is, of course, nothing new about territorial disputes. The desirable nature of land owned by others may be based on ambitions to extend power, to improve or ensure security, to punish, or to repatriate, but almost always, there is a consideration regarding the resources that such land – or waterbodies – can yield. So, for example, currently, tensions between China and Japan may reflect a long history of rivalry, suspicion and conflict, dating back centuries and exacerbated during and since the Second World War. But they also have a forward-looking dimension spanning the next few decades and the rest of this century, anticipating a resource-hungry future in which competition will intensify. He (2007: 14–15) explains that, 'Territorial controversy over offshore islands is [a] major issue of bilateral contention. The phrase often used to describe the East China Sea separating China and Japan, 'a narrow strip of water', conveys the geographic proximity and thick cultural connections between the two countries. But recent years have seen an intensification of political disputes in this sea area, especially regarding the sovereignty of the Diaoyu/Senkaku Islands'. These disputes have a history, but the prospect of conflict over maritime resources in the East China Sea becomes ever more material in an age of resource depletion. According to He (2007: 15), 'China and Japan disagree on the delimitation of their Exclusive Economic Zones (EEZ), with China adhering to the principle of continental shelf and Japan regarding the midpoint as the boundary'. These tensions have continued and in late November 2013, 'China suddenly and unilaterally declared administrative control over a swath of airspace in the contested East China Sea, sparking an international crisis. Japan, South Korea and the US defied the rising superpower by spontaneously sending aircraft into its newly formed 'air defence identification zone'; China scrambled fighter jets in retaliation. Tensions are still simmering' (Kaiman 2013: 40; see also Takenaka 2014; see generally Buckley 2014; Wong and Ansfield 2014). The context is a need for resources as both populations and competition increase, as analysed by Xu (2014) in a report for the US-based non-profit Council on Foreign Relations:

> There are roughly half a billion people who live within 100 miles of the South China Sea coastline, and the volume of shipping through its waters has skyrocketed as China and ASEAN nations increase international trade and oil imports. The need for resources, especially hydrocarbons and fisheries ... has intensified economic competition in the region, particularly given the rapid coastal urbanization of China.

We keep these and others in mind in the process of outlining our typology and developing a criminology concerned with environment and conflict relationships.

Enormous oil and natural gas reserves are at stake and are, of course, of interest not just to China and Japan, but also to smaller nations, such as Malaysia, the Philippines, and Vietnam. Conflict, then, may be fuelled by competing claims: 'In December 2012, China's National Energy Administration named the disputed waters as the main offshore site for natural gas production, and a major Chinese energy company has already begun drilling in deep water off the southern coast. Competitive tensions escalated when India's state-run Oil and Natural Gas Corp announced it had partnered with PetroVietnam for developing oil in the disputed waters' (Xu 2014 [citing Perlez 2012; Reuters 2011]). Similar contests are apparent in other places as well, from the Arctic to Africa to the Timor Sea. For example, since its independence in July 2009, South Sudan and Sudan (from which the former country split) have been at loggerheads over how to share oil that is largely found in South Sudanese territory but which is pumped north through Sudan for export (see Kron 2012), while the newly independent country, East Timor (also known as Timor Leste or Timor-Leste), recently engaged in international court proceedings against Australia, accusing the latter of ruthlessly and unethically negotiating a mutual agreement over Timor Sea oil reserves by employing strong-arm tactics that included the coercive appropriation of confidential documents (see, e.g., AAP 2014; Allard 2014; Lamb 2014a, 2014b; Gearin 2014; International Court of Justice 2014).

Many other conflicts arise in relation to possession of natural resource wealth. Katunga (2006–07: 16) refers to the role of natural resources (specifically, minerals and forests) in the violence in the Democratic Republic of Congo (DRC) as 'engines of chaos'. There and elsewhere, the damaging and divisive exploitation and trade in diamonds, gold, timber and wildlife have generated funds that have spurred, supported and perpetuated internal conflicts, corruption and the externalising of economic surplus (Boekhout van Solinge 2008ab, 2010a, 2010b; Brack 2002; Brisman and South 2013b; Burnley 2011; Butts and Bankus 2013; Clark 2013; Duffy 2010; Elliott 2007; Gamba and Cornwell 2000; Green et al. 2007; McGrath, 2012b; Milburn, this volume; Romero 2011; South 2010; Soysa 2000; Wyatt this volume; see also Berdal and Malone 2000: 8; Chow 2013; Collier 2000: 106; Gelling 2010; Reno 2000: 57; Shearer,2000: 195). So, in countries such as Angola, Cambodia, Liberia, Madagascar, Nigeria, Sierra Leone, Venezuela and Zimbabwe, as well as in the DRC, rather than deriving broad benefit from resource wealth, local populations have instead suffered from sharp political discord, stunted growth and glaring inefficiencies – what has been called the 'resource curse' (see, e.g., Auty 1993; Herringsaw 2004; Le Billon 2011; Lujala and Rustad 2011; Romero 2009b; Soysa 2000; see generally Bearak 2010; Eviatar 2003; LaFraniere 2006; *The New York Times* 2004; Sullivan 2013a, 20103b; but see, for example, Laudati, 2013, who argues for a comprehensive 'economies of violence' analysis of the DRC's divergent natural-resource wealth, rather than a mineral-based explanation for conflict in the DRC).[4]

---

4   For an excellent overview of research in political ecology on the 'resource curse', as well as critiques thereof, see Pritchard (2013); for a brief description of the debates regarding the 'resource curse' in the DRC, see Cuvelier (2013: 135–6).

In the case of the DRC, rich in mineral resources such as coltan/tantalum, gold, tungsten and tin ore used for jewellery, mobile phones and laptops, the country has suffered ceaseless conflict for nearly two decades, as well as 'highly organised and systematic exploitation' of its resources (UN 2002: 10, 52; see also Butts and Bankus 2013; Cuvelier 2013; Duffy 2010; Lovgren 2006). Factional warfare between the Congolese army, 'defence forces' and 'rebel units', and genocide in neighbouring Rwanda have been devastating, with rebels and government forces profiting from the trades in mineral ores, subjecting civilians to massacres, rape and extortion, using forced labour and coercing children into the role of soldiers (Burnley 2011). The deaths caused by conflicts of this kind are not limited to combatants but include civilians, and in the DRC, it has been estimated that around 40 per cent of 'war casualties' have been women and children (Montague 2002; see also King 1993).

The combination of environmental resources and associated wealth can give rise to conflict and crime for various reasons, but as Kuijpers (2012) points out, one of the classic – and most basic – criminal motivations at work as a driver of conflict and war is greed. As Kuijpers (2012: 14) explains, 'Although it is often assumed that conflicts occur because of grievance, driven by high inequality, a lack of political rights, or ethnic and religious divisions ... many conflicts can better be explained by economic variables and ... greed is a better explanatory factor for conflict than grievance' (see also Peterson et al., 2011; Soysa 2000). Pečar identifies similar motivations for much environmental crime, asserting that 'environmental crime results from selfishness, which is determined by the need for profit associated with the control of nature' (1988: 116, cited in Eman, Meško and Fields 2009: 578). Similarly, Christy (2012: 38), in his investigative report on the illegal slaughter of elephants for ivory, remarks:

> Seen from the ground, each of the bloated elephant carcasses is a monument to human greed. Elephant poaching levels are currently at their worst in a decade, and seizures of illegal ivory are at their highest in years. From the air too the scattered bodies present a senseless crime scene – you can see which animals fled, which animals tried to protect their young, how one terrified herd of 50 went down together, the latest of tens of thousands of elephants killed across Africa each year. Seen from higher still, from the vantage of history, this killing field is not new at all. It is timeless, and it is now.

Yet, even this most basic of motives requires contextualisation. For instance, there is a need to ask: Whose greed and why? In our view, greed cannot be reduced simply to an essentialist notion of humanity or to a characteristic that applies to specific populations or to particular individuals;[5] rather, greed is socially and

---

5 For example, the drastic decline of Central African elephants has been attributed to poaching driven by 'the rising demand for ivory in Asia's rapidly growing economies' (Gettleman 2013b; see also Pitman 2013b, 2013c; see generally Associated Press 2013;

materially constructed, and it emerges as a significant motivation for specific reasons (see generally McGrath 2012a). Scarcity is certainly one factor influencing its manifestation, as is gender and particular constructions of masculinity, given the male dominated composition of the main protagonists (see Seager 1993a). So, too, is the way in which the 'free market' has been reshaping 'human nature' through its restructuring of opportunities on a world scale. An era in which greed flourishes has been grounded in concrete social, economic, political and military processes. Three decades of neo-liberalism basically sends a strong message to look after oneself first, to protect what you have and take what you can, because there is no collective solidarity and precious little welfare otherwise (see Brisman 2013; Giroux 2004, 2012; White 2014; cf. Ervine 2011, discussing market-based conservation). This is reinforced at a higher political level worldwide by the example of nation-states rushing to stake their claims over natural resources as quickly and ruthlessly as possible.

Conflict over Declining Resources

This type of conflict is concerned with issues of scarcity and the consequences of the broad degradation of environments in relation to conflicts and compromises over the use of resources. Michel (2009: 74), for example, warns that:

> Insufficient water supplies can impair agricultural production, endanger public health, strain established settlement patterns, and jeopardize livelihoods and social well-being. Where different countries (e.g., upstream and downstream) or different communities (e.g., rural and urban) share the same river, worsening climate pressures could engender sharpened competition or even violent confrontations to secure an increasingly scarce resource. Policymakers, pundits, and the popular press alike have openly worried that the coming century could witness the eruption of outright 'water wars'.

'Wars' per se, may not be the inevitable outcome of such resource pressures and, according to Michel, 'Closer inspection of global hydropolitics ... suggests

---

Pitman 2013a); 'China's booming economy' (BBC News 2012a; see also BBC News, 2012c); 'increased prosperity in China' (Gatehouse 2013); 'China's growing middle class' (Rosen 2012); and 'China, where new wealth means more people can buy ivory' (Joyce 2013; see also Joyce and Cornish 2013). But, as Benton (2007: 28) points out, 'material poverty ... drives people to destroy their environments out of desperation'. Only occasionally have reports revealed the complexity of the poaching problem, acknowledging how crippling poverty and the lack of other economic opportunities in many African nations can make the lure of illegal hunting of elephants and trafficking in ivory, where a pair of tusks may be a year's income to a subsistence peasant, too difficult to resist (Burnett 2012; Gettleman 2012a; see generally Cowell 2010).

that the more hyperbolic warnings of looming water wars are overblown' (2009: 74; but see Arsenault 2012). Indeed, water scarcity can lead to interstate collaborations or at least peaceful agreements. At the same time, there is no reason to suppose such arrangements will 'continue to prevail' (Michel 2009: 77). Nevertheless, as several researchers argue, water issues play an important role in modern ecological conflict. As Polgreen and Tavernise (2010: A1) note in their report on water disputes between India and Pakistan, '[w]ater has become a growing source of tension in many parts of the world between nations striving for growth. Several African countries are arguing over water rights to the Nile. Israel and Jordan have competing claims to the Jordan River. Across the Himalayas, China's own dam projects have piqued India, a rival for regional, and even global, power' (for examples of other interstate fights over water, as well as intrastate conflicts, see Arsenault 2012; Barringer 2011; Bichsel 2011; Boelens et al. 2011; Federman 2014; Gettleman 2009b; Hammer 2013). Ultimately, climate change is likely to produce differentiated social vulnerability to scarcity of both water and food, with competition and conflict being related risks (see, e.g., Agnew 2012a, 2012b; Brisman forthcoming; Cooper 2014; Hsiang et al. 2011, 2013; Kirby 2014; O'Loughlin et al. 2012; Rice 2012; South 2012; Waccholz 2007); some suggest that anthropogenic (human-caused) climate change *has already* contributed to instances of scarcity and conflict (or threat thereof) (see, e.g., Gettleman 2009a; Fussey and South 2012; Hulme 2009; see generally Ban 2008; Brisman 2008, 2013; Healy 2010; but see Kevane and Gray 2008).[6] Matters of environmental rights, human rights and environmental security will also coalesce around such circumstances and conditions (see Butts and Bankus 2013; Eman et al. 2013; Fussey and South 2012; Hall 2013a, 2013b; Hauck 2007; Mass et al. 2013; Scheffran and Cannaday 2013; Stack et al. 2013).

A further response to scarcity and contest is flight: so one pattern of response may be increased migration (see, e.g., Agnew 2012a, 2012b; Brisman 2013; Hall and Farrall 2013; Kramer and Michalowski 2012; Mares 2010; McNall 2011; Morrissey 2012; *The New York Times* 2012b; Sollund 2012; Waccholz 2007; White 2011, 2012b). Reuveny (2007: 657) provides hypotheses and data relevant to this scenario by providing insights into 'environmental migration' based on examination of the 'past effects on migration induced by environmental problems of the type climate change is expected to cause, and effects this migration had on conflict'. According to Reuveny, 'people can adapt to environmental problems in three ways: stay in place and do nothing, accepting the costs; stay in place and mitigate changes; or leave affected areas' (2007: 657). There is an important and sometimes rather overlooked point to be made here about how and why migration may be chosen, for this is not an easy decision to make and, even in the most

---

6   For a history of climate change and conflict, as well as predictions about the ways in which *anthropogenic* climate change may spur or contribute to conflict, see Lee (2009). For a brief discussion of how climate change has led to conflict for over 3,000 years and even the collapse of civilisations (see Cline 2014).

extreme circumstances where migratory flight might seem preferable to remaining in place, this is not always the option taken (see generally South 2012: 98). Reuveny (2007: 658) points out that the assumption is that:

> individuals decide to migrate if the net benefit (total benefit minus total cost) from migrating is larger than that from not migrating. Facing several possible destinations within and outside their countries, they choose the one that provides the largest net benefit. This model faces two problems. First, it assumes that people *choose* whether to migrate. Though people facing threats to their lives, including environmental threats, are, in a way, forced to migrate, migration is truly involuntary only if people are expelled; even people facing such threats can choose not to leave, hoping to survive ...

Reuveny (2007: 668) further argues that, '[e]nvironmental migration crosses international borders at times, and plays a role in conflict. Environmental migration does not always lead to conflict, but when it does, the conflict intensity can be very high, including interstate and intrastate wars'. From his examination of data relating to 38 cases of environmental migration, Reuveny concludes that '[i]n almost all the conflict cases, the receiving areas were underdeveloped and depended on the environment for livelihood. Other factors associated with conflict include resident emigrant ethno-religious tension and competition over resources and resource scarcity in the receiving areas' (2007: 668). Overall, evidence (Chen 2009) suggests that environmental degradation causes more internal conflict than international conflict; slow-start and slow-impact climate change events produce migrants, while rapid-start and rapid-impact events produce refugees (see also Morrissey 2012).

In the future, climate change(s) will impact food availability and 'food security' (Agnew 2012a; Butts and Bankus 2013; Hall 2013b; Kramer and Michalowski 2012; Mares 2010; Mass et al. 2013; McNall 2011; Scheffran and Cannaday 2013; Stack et al. 2013; White 2011, 2012b). But the significance of prospective change does not mean that the cumulative geo-political, pollution and cultural changes that have occurred over the past few decades should be overlooked. These have had – and continue to have – environmentally related impacts on population groups that also bring instances of physical and cultural conflicts. The conflicts that can occur about access to food resources can be complex where traditional diet, cultural symbolism and a way of life are bound together but opposed or undermined by interest groups and legal interventions (see, e.g., Duffy 2010; Hauck 2007; Walters 2005, 2011; see also Brown 2014; Cave 2009; Ervine 2011: 67 [citing McCarthy and Prudham 2004: 277]; Onishi 2011; Weeks 2012). This does not lead to conflict on the scale of wars and revolutions, but can certainly lead to cultural conflict and the extinction of a way of life with tragic consequences such as increased rates of suicide (Samson 2003; see also Brook 1998).

The hunting of seals and polar bears and other non-human animals provides a powerful example of *competing visions* of what it means to understand and defend animals, nature and the spirit of the wild (see, e.g., Kaufman 2011; Mooallem 2013; Sollund this volume). For example, O'Keeffe (2010) writes of the struggles and accommodations the Inuit of the Arctic have had to face as their environment has changed. This may sound strange. To many, the Arctic seems a place remote from environmental change or conflict. But nowhere on the planet is now truly too remote to avoid the impact of globalisation, modernity and the eradication of tradition (see, e.g., Brisman 2005; Walsh 2012). And here there is the nexus of a further form of environmental conflict: between modernisation and westernisation, on the one hand, and human spirituality, culture and tradition, on the other. According to O'Keeffe (2010):

> Inuit continue to survive in their northern homeland, but it has not been easy. Up until the middle of the last century, hunger and starvation were not uncommon during the long, dark winters, particularly for the more remote communities. As the Arctic became more accessible, after World War II, indigenous communities had greater access to reliable food supplies from the south, and the spectre of winter hunger started to disappear. But in its place have come other, more complex threats to Inuit food security and wellbeing, the product of decisions made far from the Arctic. The result is economic vulnerability, contaminated food and changes to the movement of the Arctic land and sea mammals – the source of traditional Inuit food.

> ...

> To understand the significance of food security for the Inuit, we must recognise that food security isn't simply reliable access to nutritious food. It is linked to climate change, wildlife management, pollution and economic vulnerability – and to cultural security ... In May 2008, the US Fish and Wildlife Service announced its decision to list the polar bear as a threatened species ... This decision was the outcome of a process which had seen environmental groups square off against the Inuit ... The Americans' move has been celebrated by environmental groups as a positive step in their campaign to pressure the nation's government into changing its position on climate change. For the Inuit, this represents a further erosion of their capacity to manage the resources that have sustained them through the centuries.

Polar bears and seals are endangered and must be protected. Indeed, the status, welfare and right-to-life of non-human animals generally is a source of controversy, contest and conflict (see, e.g., Beirne 1999, 2009, 2014; Benton 1998; Cazaux 1999; Nurse 2013; Sollund 2013, this volume; Yates et al. 2001). But human culture, traditions and ways of life may also become endangered, and thus merit consideration. Conflicts arising from declining 'resources' are complex matters with various dimensions, including actors, causes, context, dynamics, histories, interests (material and immaterial, such as livelihoods versus conservation aims), and possible resolution strategies (see Derkyi et al. 2014: 282; Hilhorst 2013: 5; see also Cuvelier 2013: 144) – something that a number of chapters in this volume demonstrate.

Conflict that Destroys Environments

This type of conflict is concerned with instances where environmental destruction and degradation are a result of war and other social conflict, where environmental destruction is used as a tactic or technique of war (or where the forces of nature are utilised as weapons), and where military activities and exercises in preparation for armed conflict have adversely affected the environment. As the author Andrew O'Hagan (2008: 42) has observed about the war zones that he has visited, 'one is often overwhelmed by the man-made mess. What you often witness is the detritus of war – the toxic, horrifying, poisonous litter, from field to hallowed field. Water is polluted, trees are uprooted, life is made less, endlessly less, and that's before you account for the loss of a single life' (see also Dilworth 2010; Mufffett and Bruch 2011; Rubin 2010). In fact, the Statute of Rome of the International Criminal Court (ICC) (Article 8(2)(b)(iv)) and the Geneva Convention 1949 (additional Protocol of 1978, Article 55) recognise that disproportionate military action causing long-term, widespread and severe damage to the natural environment should be prevented or criminalised as an offence under international law. Yet, as Wyatt (2010: 596–7) remarks, 'Serious and intentional damage to the natural environment in the context of armed conflict – ... "wartime environmental damage" – is, like war itself, regrettably no novelty in the history of humankind. Early examples of such environmental warfare can be found in the ancient strategy of "salting the earth" ... [and] large-scale burning ... frequently termed "scorched earth" tactics' (see also Maas et al. 2013: 203; Muffett and Bruch 2011: 4; Seager 1999: 165). As Wyatt (2010: 597–8) explains:

> In the period following World War II, armies moved beyond simple 'scorched earth' tactics to a more sophisticated and arguably more sinister species of environmental destruction, exemplified by the US bombing of Korean dams in the Korean War of 1950–1953 and, most significantly, by the array of environmental modification techniques carried out by the US military between 1961 and 1971 as part of the Vietnam War. Far from simply setting ablaze Vietnamese jungle in which the Vietcong were hiding (though this was also carried out with the incendiary weapon Napalm), from 1961 the United States began spraying twelve million gallons of highly toxic chemical agents over more than 6 million acres of crops and trees in an effort to preclude the growth of groundcover, and even endeavoured to influence weather patterns for military advantage by engaging in cloud seeding. Then, during the 1980s Iraq–Iran war, Iraqi bombers targeted Iranian oil installations in the Nowruz offshore field, sending enough smoke into the atmosphere to partially block out the sun for

days and enough oil into the Red Sea to create a slick of 12,000 square miles, with catastrophic consequences for wildlife, including endangered species in that region [internal footnotes omitted].

More recently, in the First Gulf War, the Iraq occupation army 'ignited about 150 Kuwaiti oil wells, sabotaged petroleum and natural gas processing facilities, opened oil pipelines, and discharged stored petroleum onto land and into the Persian Gulf' (Zilinkskas 1995: 237; see also Benton 1998: 151; Hall 2013b: 110, forthcoming; Maas et al. 2013: 203; Schofield 1999: 621 n.15; Seager 1999: 164; White 2013: 80). Iraq's 1990 incursion into Kuwait was subsequently presented as a reason for establishing a more overt and permanent US military presence in the oil-rich Persian Gulf region (Kramer 2012: 446 [citing Bacevich 2005; Klare 2004]; see also Byrne 2006; Dilworth 2010; Herbert 2005; Koppel 2006; Mouawad 2005), thereby demonstrating how conflict that destroys environments can lead to conflict over natural resources possession and declining natural resources (i.e., oil). Even more recently, in the case of the 2006 'Summer War' between Israel and Lebanon, drinking water systems and reserves were extensively damaged in Lebanon in violation of expectations of international humanitarian law (Zeitoun et al. 2014).

In another context and arena of conflict, beginning in the 1980s under the Reagan Administration, the United States has waged a global 'War on Drugs'. The United States – with other Western nations following suit – have usually found it more palatable to view this matter as more of a supply problem than a demand issue and hence favour seizure and crop eradication interventions (Coomber and South 2014). The latter actions are the focus of Rosa del Olmo's consideration of 'a type of crime committed on the pretext of preventing another crime', which is, as she wrote:

> A crime which has the characteristics of ecocide by virtue of making war with certain methods, systems, or prohibited weapons. Vietnam was a good example, with napalm and Agent Orange. Today the new war is on drugs and its weapons are toxic chemicals, especially herbicides prohibited in their place of origin for causing poisoning, contamination of food, and serious environmental problems, like *paraquat, gliphosphate* and *Agent Orange*. (del Olmo 1987: 30; see also del Olmo 1998: 273)

Crop eradication programmes have not won any drug wars but like other wars leave their legacy, including effects on the 'quality of life' and the health of local populations, especially when toxic chemicals are liberally used in aerial sprays that can be blown across a wide area (see del Olmo 1998; South 2007). del Olmo condemned this kind of state war on drugs as a:

> transnational crime of broad scope which we can call eco-bio-genocide. [This] involves the utilization of a whole complex of toxic chemicals ... which are

prohibited and/or restricted in the developed countries but have an unlimited market in Third World countries ... such chemicals are utilized widely in programs of drug eradication because the sole preoccupation is to destroy the marijuana and cocaine crops before they arrive in the United States in order to protect North American youth, regardless of the consequences for Third World youth. (del Olmo 1987: 31)

These policies and practices continue today, and not just in Latin America. del Olmo's work highlights the consequences of the conflict produced by the ongoing 'War on Drugs' and identifies these as important matters of environmental justice and as a denial of the rights of environmental victims of human-made harms. In general, as Hartmann (1999: 9) summarises:

Violence is ... a direct cause of environmental destruction. The German Institute for Peace Policy estimates that one-fifth of all global environmental degradation is due to military and related activities. Feminist geographer Joni Seager [1993b] argues that ... '[i]n modern warfare the environment has become a militarized target, and 'ecocide' provides another arena for the play of militarized manhood.' Even after the cessation of conflict, landmines and the lingering effects of scorched-earth policies and chemical warfare obstruct environmental restoration. [internal footnotes omitted]

Thus, the environment can be a casualty of actual wars (as described by O'Hagan [2008], above) and figurative ones (as in the case of the 'War on Drugs'). In addition, and as alluded to above, the environment can be used as a weapon of war. Here, we might try to differentiate between instances where the environment, itself, is a target (such as the deliberate contamination of agricultural water supplies or the destruction of farmland – a strategy pursued by the US during the Korean War), and cases where the environment is employed as a conduit for or instrument of violence and destruction, such as releasing chemical or biological weapons into the atmosphere (Schofield 1999: 620, 628; see also Eman et al. 2013: 27; Maas et al. 2013: 205, who distinguish between 'environment-as-target' and 'environment-as-tool'). But the distinction is far from clear. For example, in the aftermath of 11 September 2001, there have been concerns in the US that an attack on one of the country's chemical plants near a city or large town could unleash a toxic cloud endangering the lives of hundreds of thousands of people (Kocieniewski 2005; *The New York Times* 2009; see generally Lipton 2005). Such an attack might resemble the former, but have the effect of the latter. An attack on an oil facility or tanker or natural gas plant, to offer another example, could be intended as a means of generating a giant bomb or (given our fossil fuel reliance) as a means of creating an extreme economic crisis – much the way that the US, during the Korean War, recognised that bombing dams would hurt Korea's agrarian society (see, e.g., Arnold 2004;

Associated Press 2011; Banerjee 2004; Gorse 2010; Mouawad 2006; see also Green 2013; Temple-Raston 2013; Zarroli 2013).[7]

What about the US's activities during the Vietnam War? As noted above, the US eradicated vast areas of forests and vegetation in South Vietnam with Agent Orange and other defoliants in an effort to deny its enemy cover, mobility and sustenance (Schofield 1999: 621, 635; see also Kauzlarich and Awsumb 2012: 508; Maas et al. 2013: 203; South 2007: 244n.3; Stack et al. 2013: 163; White 2013: 18 [citing Al-Damkhi et al. 2009]; see generally Simon 2000: 641; Stephens 1996: 72). It also engaged in physical land-clearing, as well as a rainmaking programme designed to induce clouds to precipitate more rain than normal, in order to wash out bridges and river crossings and render roads unusable for the North Vietnamese (Zilinskas 1995: 243–4; see also Hulme 2009: 316, 2014: 73; Lee 2009: 156). While such tactics can be distinguished from the use of the environment as a conduit for destruction, such as the dissemination of a pathogen or biotoxin through the air or via a water supply, the damage caused by defoliation, land-clearing and rainmaking during the Vietnam War was widespread and long-lasting. Zilinskas (1995: 245) reports that 'about 12 percent of Vietnam's land area [was] damaged by defoliants and land-clearing', and that US operations resulted in four major long-lasting effects: nutrient dumping, species replacement, mangrove destruction, and land erosion. When we factor in the adverse human health impacts caused by the spraying of defoliants, herbicides, and other chemicals by US military forces in Vietnam (see Stephens 1996: 72; see also Seager 1993a: 59, 1999: 169), it may hardly seem to matter whether the forces of nature were (or are) used as weapons or whether the environment was (or is) manipulated and destroyed in the name of political or ideological zealotry; the end result was (and would be) the same: widespread, long-lasting and severe environmental damage and harm to human health.

We should also not forget the direct environmental impacts of running the war machine itself. Zilinskas (1995: 266) notes that 'most states are themselves guilty of undertaking, promoting, or condoning activities that harm the environment' (see also Osofsky, 2005: 1796), but here we point to the ecological costs of national security. As Baer and Singer (2009: 181; see also White 2011: 156, 2012a: 76) observe, 'the Pentagon is the single largest consumer of oil in the world. There are only 35 countries, in fact, that consume more oil than the Pentagon'.[8] Indeed, from greenhouse gas emissions to environmental degradation, the operational demands of the military are enormous. The US military relies heavily on energy-inefficient equipment and vehicles (see, e.g., Kramer and Michalowski 2012:

---

7 According to recent reports, small-scale attacks on a handful of the US's electric-transmission substations could bring down the entire country's power grid, causing prolonged coast-to-coast blackouts (Memmott 2014; Smith 2014).

8 According to King (2014), '[t]he US military is the country's single largest energy consumer, which comes with an annual bill of $20 billion. In Afghanistan alone it uses 9 million barrels of oil a year' (see also Seager 1999: 167).

78–9 [citing Sanders 2009]; Schweitzter 2005; cf. Friedman 2010; *The New York Times* 2012a; Rosenthal 2010), while at the same time has opposed wind projects on the grounds that turbine blades interfere with radar systems, thereby posing an unacceptable risk to training (Vestel 2010; cf. King 2014). It also extensively uses depleted uranium in weapons and armour (see White 2008, 2011, 2012a; see also Seager, 1999; Stephens, 1996) and rare earth elements ('REEs') or rare earth metals ('REMs') in military equipment (Krugman 2010; see also Kane and Brisman 2013). The methods employed to produce nuclear weapons (including the transportation and storage of radioactive and hazardous waste) have resulted in tremendous contamination of the environment (Kauzlarich and Kramer 1998; Seager 1999; Simon 2000).[9] US military training exercises have sparked fires and destroyed countless flora and fauna on land and at sea (see, e.g., Associated Press 2010a; Henkin 2011; McGuirk 2013; Navarro 2009a, 2009b; Seager 1993a; cf. Kaufman 2010),[10] while the Navy's use of sonar has caused harm to unknown numbers of whales and other marine mammals (Associated Press 2008; Earthjustice 2012; Gannon 2013; Goldbogen et al. 2013; Kaufman 2010; Liptak 2008a, 2008b, 2008c; *The New York Times* 2008a, 2008b; Yost 2008) – not to mention its use of dolphins and other cetaceans to locate mines (Hoare 2014; White 2007: 5, 216–17). The US's continued oil dependency increases the likelihood of military entanglements and threatens its national security (see, e.g., Bumiller 2006; Cooper 2007; Friedman 2004, 2005a, 2005b, 2005c, 2006a, 2006b, 2009; Gjelten 2012; Gore 2010; Krugman 2005; Leverett 2006; *The New York Times* 2005; Richter and Tsalik 2003; Romero 2004; Tierney 2006), while climate change will present new challenges to the US military, including an increased demand for humanitarian assistance and disaster relief (Brisman 2013; Talmadge 2012; Trauzzi 2014; see also Ahmed 2013, 2014; Davenport, 2014; Farrell 2014; Lee 2009; Krugman 2014; Mazzetti 2007; McNall 2011).[11] In addition, the social processes of war are themselves implicated in climate change. As Baer and Singer (2009: 39) succinctly put it, 'global warming and war are thus mutually reinforcing, with war and war production fuelling global warming and global warming pushing countries to war' (Baer and Singer 2009: 39; see also Lee 2009).

---

9   On the export of military waste to the Global South, see Stephens (1996); see also Pellow and Brulle (2005). For a discussion of military production of radioactive waste in the UK, see Walters (2007).

10   The US has not been alone in this regard. Seager (1993a: 63, 1999: 166, 182) notes nuclear weapons testing by the British and French in the South Pacific, while Low and Gleeson (1998: 4–6) discuss French nuclear tests in the Mururoa and Fangatauta atolls in the Pacific Ocean in the mid-1990s.

11   Hulme (2014: 25) adds that '[t]here is a close relationship, historically, between designations of emergency and the ever ready presence of the military to "assist" in the response. This has been seen in many cases of humanitarian emergency where the results of military intervention – however well-intentioned – have been ambiguous at best and destabilising at worst'.

Finally, it bears mention that US military personnel have recently become involved with conservation efforts, training park rangers in Africa in tactics to help fight against poachers and wildlife traffickers (Platt 2014). Given the increasingly militarised character of poaching (see BBC News 2012b; Chow 2013; Gettleman 2013a; Press Trust of India 2014; see generally von Essen et al. 2014) and the efforts to stop it (Duffy 2014; Gelling 2010; Gettleman 2012b; Smith and Humphreys, this volume; Wall and McClanahan, this volume), including the use of unmanned aerial vehicles (UAVs, commonly known as 'drones') (Kermeliotis 2013; Platt 2012; Rosen 2012; Steinborn 2014), the US military's participation in conservation efforts complicates – and perhaps obfuscates – the image of the military as perpetrators of environmental damage, destruction and harm. Indeed, as Hartmann (1999: 18) queried in her discussion of the US military's involvement in promoting 'sustainable development' in Africa and in assisting countries with fisheries management, game park preservation and water resource management, 'Isn't it a fundamental contradiction in terms to have the military engaged in "sustainable development" when it is [and] has been the cause of so much environmental devastation … ?'

Conflict over Natural Resource Extraction Processes

This type of conflict is concerned with issues pertaining to group conflicts over methods and techniques of, and the necessity for, certain types of resource extraction (including not just the 'raw resource', but also the infrastructure, such as transmission and transportation routes and pipelines (see Scheffran and Cannaday 2013)). For example, extraction of shale gas by use of fracking has become a contested topic and technique in many countries (see, e.g., Kane and Brisman 2014) and scientific opinion on energy benefits versus environmental harms can be torn. To illustrate, Batley and Kookana (2012: 425) present their findings in the following way:

> Coal seam gas reserves represent a major contribution to energy needs, however, gas recovery by hydraulic fracturing (fracking or fraccing), requires management to minimise any environmental effects. Although the industry is adapting where possible to more benign fracking chemicals, there is still a lack of information on exposure to natural and added chemicals, and their fate and ecotoxicity in both the discharged produced and flow-back waters. Geogenic contaminants mobilised from the coal seams during fracking may add to the mixture of chemicals with the potential to affect both ground and surface water quality.

This is a fairly neutral scientific assessment. Unsurprisingly, given the grounds for concern signalled, there are other more critical accounts of fracking operations and conflicts have arisen (see, e.g., Cleary 2012). Indeed, some writers have been able to point to attempts to coordinate global resistance and protest campaigns.

Franco, Martinez and Feodoroff (2013; see also Begos 2012) wrote of an international protest held on 22 September 2012 as 'the Global Frackdown Day where more than 100 events took place all around the world to protest against fracking. The day showed that citizens are awakening to the threat of this new corporate driven "golden age" of gas ... Anti-fracking activists have framed the campaign in terms of climate justice and their efforts have influenced local authorities of fracking-affected areas to take a strong stand against it'.

In other cases of contested mining and extraction processes, such as mountaintop removal (MTR), there are many instances of resistance to and protest and campaigns against the deleterious environmental and health impacts of such methods and practices (Stretesky and Lynch 2012; see also Brisman et al. 2014; McClanahan 2014). In some cases, local unease, as well as disease, go back centuries, with the persistence of the issues attributable to the dependence of the local economy on such industry at the same time as it devastates workers, communities and local spaces. In examining the balance of forces in these contests, economic interests are often the most powerful, not only when mobilised by mining companies, international or local, but also by local people concerned about jobs and security. So, for example, Cabrejas (2012), writing about MTR in Spain shows how critics and environmental protestors have been labelled as outsiders and troublemakers, and made unwelcome by a dominant narrative that stems from the region's history as one based on a tradition of coal mining. For over 15 years, illegal and legally subsidised MTR has provided jobs, but has also given rise to negative environmental and social problems despite the fact that this area is supposed to be protected under European environmental legislation. Conflict and divisions are now also arising because in 2018, the European Union (EU) will remove subsidy by the state for coal extraction. Environmentalists have been cast in the role of scapegoats and Cabrejas shows that, as in similar conflicts elsewhere, violence against critics of MTR, as well as a 'culture of silence' (Brisman 2012), have limited the effectiveness of campaigns to end use of this method of mining.

Elsewhere, the practice of forestry has been generating conflict for centuries and, of course, has also actually provided the weapons of war for much of this time. In the latter half of the last century, as Cullen (1987) noted, forestry and logging became a central concern in many environmental conflicts. Logging attracts protestors engaged in campaigns to preserve forests and the wilderness (see Cianchi 2013), but as with both mining and hunting, there is also a significant spectrum of voices that will be raised in support of logging and forestry for profit (see Satterfield 2002). This same scenario can be seen repeated in numerous contexts around the world and can also be extended to situations involving conflict over nuclear energy and hydropower and dam-building, as well as to conflict over measures to *prevent* the risks posed by climate change (Scheffran and Cannaday 2013; see generally *The New York Times* 2014a, 2014b).

There is no one-size-fits-all approach to preventing conflict over natural resources possession or extraction processes, to avoiding conflict over declining resources, or to ensuring post-conflict peace in resource-rich countries.

While efforts have been undertaken to limit the destruction of environments during conflict (see Fichtelberg this volume; Schofield 1999; Zilinskas 1995), the ongoing and expanding operations of the war machine continue to degrade the environment and present new challenges, as well as new forms of resistance (see, e.g., Brisman and South 2013a, 2014). Attention to context – what Muffett and Bruch (2011: 6) call 'situational awareness' – is crucial. This volume is an attempt to provide such context and in the next section, we outline how our contributors take us forward in this endeavour.

Summary of Chapters

This volume is divided into four parts reflecting components of the four categories in our typology. Part I: Conflict over Natural Resources Possession, begins with Tanya Wyatt's chapter, Mapping the Correlations between Conflict and Illegal Logging, which provides a global analysis of the environmental and social impacts of conflict over timber and the continued funding of conflicts with funds generated by illegal logging. In Chapter 3: Gorillas and Guerrillas: Environment and Conflict in the Democratic Republic of Congo, Richard Milburn uses the examples of deforestation and poaching by refugees to illustrate how conflict can cause harm to the environment, before turning to an examination of the ways in which the environment can provide resources for rebel and government forces that can fuel, exacerbate or extend conflict. While Milburn's focus is on how the living environment can be a casualty of conflict (e.g., deforestation by refugees in the Virunga National Park in the DRC) and how the living environment can exacerbate and perpetuate existing conflicts (e.g., illegal trade in ivory and charcoal to finance conflict), he concludes with a consideration of the impact that the environment can have in promoting peacebuilding and post-conflict recovery, a point we alluded to at the outset of this chapter.

Chapter 4: Land Uses and Conflict in Colombia, by David Rodríguez Goyes, documents the conflict in Colombia that is now more than 50 years old, describing how much of the conflict has stemmed from issues of land access and land use, and identifying the roles that improved agrarian infrastructure, increased social development in rural areas (health, education, shelter, and poverty eradication), increased funding for agrarian development, improved food security and different illicit drug crop substitution policies could have for enduring peace. Part I concludes with Ragnhild Sollund's chapter, With or Without a Licence to Kill: Human-predator Conflicts and Theriocide in Norway, which offers an in-depth analysis of 14 verdicts in Norwegian courts pertaining to the illegal killing of predators (brown bear, wolf, lynx and wolverine). Sollund criticises Norwegian policy, which favours the interests of hunters and farmers with livestock over the interests of predators to live and exist in their own right and challenges the very notion of *possession* – especially, possession of non-human animals – and the anthropocentric ecophilosophy underlying the ownership and domination of and violence towards non-human animals. Sollund would decry any conceptualisation that treats non-human animals as *resources* but given the endangered status of many of the predators she discusses, her chapter provides a helpful transition to Part II, Conflict over Declining Resources.

Part II: Conflict over Declining Resources, begins with Chapter 6: The State-Corporate Tandem Cycling towards Collision: State-Corporate Harm and the Resource Frontiers of Brazil and Colombia, by Bram Ebus and Karlijn Kuijpers. As the authors explain, due to the growing scarcity of natural resources and rising prices for energy and raw materials, multinational corporations are increasingly trying to access and gain control over the remaining resources – much of which are located in remote areas (often referred to as 'frontiers') – recently opened up to resource exploitation. Because gaining access to these areas and extracting the resources from them may displace groups of people already living in these areas or cause negative environmental impacts that adversely affect the survival of such groups, frontiers are often characterised by conflict and violence. Ebus and Kuijpers illustrate this through an examination of the activities of mining companies AngloGold Ashanti and Gran Colombia Gold in Colombia and the case of the Belo Monte hydroelectric dam in Brazil.

Chapter 7: Somalis Fight Back: Environmental Degradation and the Somali Pirate, by Victoria Collins, offers a permutation of the 'conflict over declining resources' theme. Here, the issue is not so much conflict *over* shrinking resources (and access thereto), but conflict *stemming from* diminishing resources and a degraded environment. Collins examines structural issues within the country of Somalia that have led to significant environmental degradation as more plausible and comprehensive motivators for piracy than connections with organised crime and international terrorist networks. As Collins reveals, environmental issues, such as drought and famine that have repeatedly plagued the country, as well as foreign interests engaging in toxic waste dumping and illegal fishing in Somalia's resource-rich waters, not only create conditions of economic desperation but make piracy a more viable option to ensure individual and industry survival.

According to Dilworth (2010: 397), 'the war drain on the natural wealth of the world has been terrific, taking a heavy toll on forests, oil and coal, as well as on iron and other metals, and adding to the already heavy depletion of soil resources' (footnote omitted). Our discussion above offers a number of examples of how conflict can and has resulted in serious environmental degradation, as well instances where the environment, itself, has been a target and ways in which the environment has been or could be employed as a conduit for violence and destruction. In Part III: Conflict that Destroys Environments, we begin with Aaron Fichtelberg's chapter, Resource Wars, Environmental Crime, and the Laws of War: Updating War Crimes in a Resource Scarce World. Fichtelberg's concern is not so much with documenting instances of conflict that result in environmental destruction (although he does touch on this), but on the ways in which the laws of war, and in particular those laws that describe *war crimes*, fail to adequately protect the environment from the sort of pillaging that has become a central component of recent warfare. Fichtelberg argues, as the chapters in Part I demonstrate, that many wars, can be characterised as *resource wars* – as wars where a group of states or rebels are intent upon securing control over a country's natural resources – and that the exploitation of natural resources is intimately bound up with the conduct of the war itself. Fichtelberg contends that despite the prevalence of resource wars over at least the last two centuries, the systematic exploitation of natural resources during the course of conflict or conquest is not adequately conceived as a war crime under modern international humanitarian law. Because the gap in international law leaves much of the globe's natural resources vulnerable to the vagaries of war and provides few significant legal protections for them, Fichtelberg maintains that the laws governing international war crimes are particularly ill-suited for the realities of modern war. To fill this lacuna, Fichtelberg suggests that the laws of war be revised to include the creation of a new international crime of war, which he refers to as *the criminal exploitation of natural resources in wartime*.

Fichtelberg's chapter, then, serves as an illustration of how we have and how we might *respond to* conflict over natural resource possession, conflict over declining resources and conflict that destroys environments. So, too, do Chapters 9 and 10, which also illuminate how the war machine's participation in conservation efforts confounds and clouds the picture of the military as perpetrators of environmental damage, destruction and harm. In Chapter 9: The Poaching Paradox: Why South Africa's 'Rhino Wars' Shine a Harsh Spotlight on Security and Conservation, M.L.R. Smith and Jasper Humphreys examine the effectiveness of the counter-poaching strategies in the 'Rhino Wars' in South Africa and consider whether such strategies run the risk of serving as an exercise in paramilitary 'pacification' and thus as supporting the interests of a minority elite (which in the case of rhinos in South Africa is related to the ranches and the tourism industry that are predominately run by the white population). In Chapter 10: Weaponising Conservation in the 'Heart of Darkness': The War on Poachers and the Neocolonial Hunt, Tyler Wall and Bill McClanahan, provide a critique of one nascent anti-poaching organisation, the International Anti-Poaching Foundation (IAPF), which takes as its project the 'securing' of African wildlife through the hunting down of African poachers and which includes the use of aerial surveillance drones (noted above). As the authors describe, the quite literal hunting of humans becomes the preferred conservationist technology to prevent the criminalised hunting of African wildlife. The IAPF's aggressive adoption of the language and practices of security, they argue, reflects the problematic logics of 'fortress conservation' – a process and practice that functions to defend local ecologies from the perceived threat of indigenous people. In the context of colonial history, anti-poaching security initiatives, such as the hunt for 'criminal poachers', can be seen to operate as tools to pacify local indigenous populations in an effort to fabricate a capitalist social order and further those processes of primitive accumulation essential to global capital associated with 'safari tourism' and 'big game hunting'. Their argument highlights how securitised conservation efforts in the 'war on poachers' may give rise to the construction of an African 'other' – in the form of the 'poacher' – and how this political construction emerges from the history of colonial power and primitive accumulation and extends these violent processes into the present.

Part IV: Conflict over Natural Resources Extraction Processes, contains two chapters. In Chapter 11: The Hidden Injuries of Mining: Frontier Cultural Conflict, Kerry Carrington, Russell Hogg and Alison McIntosh describe the harmful effects of mining on local communities and the environment. While mining has long been recognised as an agent of environmental harm, the authors illuminate how the global expansion of mining has contributed to localised patterns of violence, conflict, work and community life in mining towns in Australia. Chapter 12, On Harm and Mediated Space: The BP Oil Spill in the Age of Globalisation, focuses on international media coverage surrounding the 2010 Deepwater Horizon oil spill in the Gulf of Mexico, providing insight into the framing of conflict over natural resource extraction processes, including who benefits, who does not, and, most significantly, who is considered a legitimate actor in relation to such processes. The authors – Nels Paulson, Kim Zagorski and D. Chris Ferguson – investigate the ways in which disaster and harm are couched in the media, how this in turn is shaped by globalisation and national context, and ultimately what types of responses in risk management are most likely to occur as a result of media framing.

Chapter 12's consideration of media framings provides a nice segue to the volume's concluding chapter by Avi Brisman, entitled Environment and Conflict: A Typology of Representations. Drawing on the emerging perspective of green cultural criminology (Brisman and South 2013a, 2014), this final chapter of the volume examines fictionalised representations of environment and conflict. It begins by briefly describing four post-apocalyptic or dystopian novels and teasing out some commonalities and key differences between them in their depictions of the relationship between environment and conflict. With this literature as a point of comparison, Brisman's chapter then identifies four different categories of environment-conflict relationships in film – thereby offering a typology that bookends (but does not mirror the present chapter) – before turning to a consideration of the dangers and problems inherent in the messages communicated by these films. This chapter concludes by articulating the need for studying, examining and critiquing the depictions, representations and narratives in fiction and film of humans' relationship to the Earth and to each other. The chapter's hope, as with the chapters in this the volume more generally, is that we might find, in the words of Lovelock (2006: 153), a way to 'make a just peace with Gaia'.

References

AAP (Australian Associated Press). 2014. International Court of Justice bans Australia from spying on East Timor. 4 March. Available at: http://www.theaustralian. com.au/news/world/international-court-of-justice-bans-australia-from-spying-on-east-timor/story-e6f.rg6so-1226844389340. Accessed 7 January 2015.

Agnew, R. 2012a. Dire forecast: a theoretical model of the impact of climate change on crime. *Theoretical Criminology* 16(1): 21–42.

Agnew, R. 2012b. It's the end of the world as we know it: the advance of climate change from a criminological perspective. In R. White (ed.), *Climate Change from a Criminological Perspective*. New York: Springer, 13–25.

Ahmed, N. 2013. Pentagon bracing for public dissent over climate and energy shocks. *The Guardian* (UK), 14 June. Available at: http://www.guardian.co.uk/environment/earth-insight/2013/jun/14/climate-change-energy-shocks-nsa-prism. Accessed 7 January 2015.

Ahmed, N. 2014. Pentagon preparing for mass civil breakdown. *The Guardian* (UK), 12 June. Available at: http://www.theguardian.com/environment/earth-insight/2014/jun/12/pentagon-mass-civil-breakdown. Accessed 7 January 2015.

Al-Damkhi, A.M., Khuraibet, A.M., Abdul-Wahab, S.A. and Abdul-Hameed Al-Attar, F. 2009. Toward defining the concept of environmental crime on the basis of sustainability. *Environmental Practice* 11(2): 115–24.

Allard, T. 2014. Australia ordered to cease spying on East Timor by International Court of Justice. *Sydney Morning Herald*, 4 March. Available at: http://www.smh.com.au/federal-politics/political-news/australia-ordered-to-cease-spying-on-east-timor-by-international-court-of-justice-20140304-hvfya.html. Accessed 7 January 2015.

Arnold, W. 2004. As oil prices rise, a sense of alarm in Asia. *The New York Times*, 10 June, W1, W7.

Arsenault, C. 2012. Risk of water wars rises with scarcity. *Aljazeera*, 26 August. Available at: http://www.aljazeera.com/indepth/features/2011/06/2011622193147231653.html. Accessed 7 January 2015.

Associated Press. 2008. Navy settles lawsuit over whales and its use of sonar. *The New York Times*, 29 December, A15.

Associated Press. 2010. National briefing: Rockies: Utah: National Guard training starts wildfire. *The New York Times*, 21 September, A21.

Associated Press. 2011. Bin Laden files discuss attacking oil tankers. *The New York Times*, 21 May, A7.

Associated Press. 2013. Thailand's Prime Minister vows to end ivory trade. *Associated Press/The Jakarta Post*, 3 March. Available at: http://www.thejakartapost.com/news/2013/03/03/thailands-prime-minister-vows-end-ivory-trade.html. Accessed 7 January 2015.

Auty, R.M. 1993. *Sustaining Development in Mineral Economies: The Resource Curse Thesis*. London and New York: Routledge.

Bacevich, A.J. 2005. *The New American Militarism: How Americans are Seduced by War*. New York: Oxford University Press.

Baer, H. and Singer, M. 2009. *Global Warming and the Political Economy of Health: Emerging Crises and Systemic Solutions*. Walnut Creek, CA: Left Coast Press.

Ban Ki-moon. 2008. The right war. *Time* 171(17): 58.

Banerjee, N. 2004. Tight oil supply won't ease soon. *The New York Times*, 16 May, 1, 4.

Barringer, F. 2011. Indians join fight for an Oklahoma lake's flow. *The New York Times*, 12 April, A1, A13.

Batley, G. and Kookana, R.S. 2012. Environmental issues associated with coal seam gas recovery: managing the fracking boom. *Environmental Chemistry 9*: 425–8. Available at: http://dx.doi.org/10.1071/EN12136. Accessed 7 January 2015.

BBC News. 2012a. The illegal ivory trade threatening Africa's elephants. *BBC News*, 11 April. Available at: http://www.bbc.com/news/world-17675816. Accessed 7 January 2015.

BBC News. 2012b. Kenya rangers shoot dead five suspected poachers. *BBC News*, 21 April. Available at: http://www.bbc.com/news/world-africa-17798914. Accessed 7 January 2015.

BBC News. 2012c. WWF: Asia fuels illegal wildlife parts trade. *BBC News*, 23 July. Available at: http://www.bbc.com/news/world-asia-18950189. Accessed 7 January 2015.

Bearak, B. 2010. Tottering rule in Madagascar can't save falling rosewoods. *The New York Times*, 25 May, A1, A3.

Beirne, P. 1999. For a nonspeciesist criminology: animal abuse as an object of study. *Criminology* 37(1): 117–47.

Beirne, P. 2009. *Confronting Animal Abuse: Law, Criminology, and Human-Animal Relationships*. Lanham, MD: Rowman & Littlefield.

Beirne, P. 2014. Theriocide: naming animal killing. *International Journal for Crime, Justice and Social Democracy* 3(2): 50–67.

Begos, K. 2012. Global protests planned over gas drilling process. *Associated Press*, 21 September. Available at: http://finance.yahoo.com/news/global-protests-planned-over-gas-drilling-process-224202116.html. Accessed 7 January 2015.

Benton, T. 1998. Rights and justice on a shared planet: more rights or new relations? *Theoretical Criminology* 2(2): 149–75.

Berdal, M. and Malone, D.M. 2000. Introduction. In M. Berdal and D.M. Malone (eds), *Greed and Grievance: Economic Agendas in Civil Wars*. Boulder, CO: Lynne Reinner Publishers, 1–15.

Bichsel, C. 2011. Liquid challenges: contested water in Central Asia. *Sustainable Development Law & Policy* 12(1): 24–30, 58–61.

Boekhout van Solinge, T. 2008a. Crime, conflicts and ecology in Africa. In R. Sullund (ed.), *Global Harms: Ecological Crime and Speciesism*. New York: Nova Science Publishers, 13–34.

Boekhout van Solinge, T. 2008b. The land of the orangutan and the bird of paradise under threat. In R. Sullund (ed.), *Global Harms: Ecological Crime and Speciesism*. New York: Nova Science Publishers, 51–70.

Boekhout van Solinge, T. 2010a. Equatorial deforestation as a harmful practice and a criminological issue. In R. White (ed.), *Global Environmental Harm: Criminological Perspectives*. Devon: Willan Publishing, 20–36.

Boekhout van Solinge, T. 2010a. Deforestation crimes and conflicts in the Amazon. *Critical Criminology*, 18: 263–277.

Boelens, R., Bueno de Mesquita, M., Gaybor, A. and Peña, F. 2011. Threats to a sustainable future: water accumulation and conflict in Latin America. *Sustainable Development Law & Policy* 12(1): 41–5, 67–9.

Brack, D. 2002. Combatting international environmental crime. *Global Environmental Change* 12: 142–7.

Brisman, A. 2005. The aesthetics of wind energy systems. *New York University Environmental Law Journal* 13(1): 1–133.

Brisman, A. 2008. Crime-environment relationships and environmental justice. *Seattle Journal for Social Justice* 6(2): 727–817.

Brisman, A. 2012. The cultural silence of climate change contrarianism. In R. White (ed.), *Climate Change from a Criminological Perspective*. New York: Springer, 41–70.

Brisman, A. 2013. Not a bedtime story: climate change, neoliberalism, and the future of the Arctic. *Michigan State International Law Review* 22(1): 241–89.

Brisman, A. forthcoming. 'Multicolored' green criminology and climate change's achromatopsia. In Special Issue: Critical White Studies in Crime & Justice, *Contemporary Justice Review*.

Brisman, A. and South, N. 2013a. A green-cultural criminology: an exploratory outline. *Crime Media Culture* 9(2): 115–35.

Brisman, A. and South, N. 2013b. Resource wealth, power, crime and conflict. In R. Walters, D. Westerhuis and T. Wyatt (eds), *Debates in Green Criminology: Power, Justice and Environmental Harm*. London: Palgrave, 57–71.

Brisman, A. and South, N. 2014. *Green Cultural Criminology: Constructions of Environmental Harm, Consumerism and Resistance to Ecocide*. Oxford: Routledge.

Brisman, A., McClanahan, B. and South, N. 2014. Toward a green-cultural criminology of 'the rural'. *Critical Criminology* 22(4): 479–94.

Brook, D. 1998. Environmental genocide: Native Americans and toxic waste. *American Journal of Economics and Sociology* 57(1): 105–13.

Brown, C. 2014. Kayapo courage. *National Geographic* 225(1): 30–55.

Buckley, C. 2014. China calls Japan the aggressor in flybys over sea. *The New York Times*, 13 June, A8.

Bumiller, E. 2006. In visits to 3 states, Bush pushes energy alternative. *The New York Times*, 21 February, A16.

Burnett, J. 2012. Poachers decimate Tanzania's elephant herds. National Public Radio (NPR), 25 October. Available at: http://www.npr.org/2012/10/25/163563426/poachers-decimate-tanzanias-elephant-herds; transcript available at: http://www.npr.org/templates/transcript/transcript.php?storyId=163563426. Accessed 7 January 2015.

Burnley, C. 2011. Natural resources conflict in the Democratic Republic of the Congo: a question of governance. *Sustainable Development Law & Policy* 12(1): 7–11, 52–3.

Butts, K.H. and Bankus, B.C. 2013. Environmental change, insurgency and terrorism in Africa. In A. Maas, B. Bodó, C. Burnley, I. Comardicea and R. Roffey (eds), *Global Environmental Change: New Drivers for Resistance, Crime and Terrorism?* Baden-Baden: Nomos, 141–60.

Byrne, E.F. 2006. Leave no oil reserves behind, including Iraq's: the geopolitics of American imperialism. In T. Smith and H. van der Linden (eds), *Philosophy against Empire* (*Radical Philosophy Today*, vol. 4). Charlottesville, VA: Philosophy Documentation Center, 39–54.

Cabrejas, A.H. 2012. 'Laciana is black. Greens go away!' Environmentalists as scapegoats in a mountaintop removal conflict in Laciana Valley, Spain. *Organization and Environment* 25: 419–36.

Cave, D. 2009. New license law in Florida divides shore anglers. *The New York Times*, 7 August, A9.

Cazaux, G. 1999. Beauty and the beast: animal abuse from a non-speciesist criminological perspective. *Crime, Law and Social Change* 31: 105–26.

Chen, E. 2009. Climate induced migration and conflict: historical evidence, and likely future outlook. *Science 2.0*, 21 September. Available at: http://www.science20.com/alchemist/blog/climate_induced_migration_and_conflict_historical_evidence_and_likely_future_outlook. Accessed 7 January 2015.

Chow, D. 2013. Armed poachers reportedly raid African elephant sanctuary. *LiveScience/Yahoo!News*, 8 May. Available at: http://news.yahoo.com/armed-poachers-reportedly raid-african-elephant-sanctuary-151507614.html. Accessed 7 January 2015.

Christy, B. 2012. Ivory worship. *National Geographic* 222(4): 28–61.

Cianchi, J. 2013. I talked to my tree and my tree talked back: Radical environmental activists and their relationships with nature. PhD thesis, School of Social Sciences, University of Tasmania (Australia).

Cleary, P. 2012. *Mine-Field: The Dark Side of Australia's Resources Rush.* Collingwood, Victoria: Black Inc.

Cline, E.H. 2014. Climate change doomed the Ancients. *The New York Times*, 28 May, A21.

Collier, P. 2000. Doing well out of war: an economic perspective. In M. Berdal and D.M. Malone (eds), *Greed and Grievance: Economic Agendas in Civil Wars*. Boulder, CO: Lynne Reinner Publishers, 91–111.

Conca, K. and Dabelko, G.D. (eds). 2002. *Environmental Peacemaking.* Washington, D.C.: Woodrow Wilson Center Press.

Coomber, R. and South, N. 2014. Fear and loathing in drugs policy: risk, rights and approaches to drug policy and practice. In B. Labate and C. Cavnar (eds), *Prohibition, Religious Freedom, and Human Rights: Regulating Traditional Drug Use*. Springer: Heidelberg, 235–48.

Cooper, M. 2007. In speech, McCain intends to push for cap on emissions. *The New York Times*, 23 April, A16.

Cooper, R. 2014. The new IPCC climate change report makes it official: we are flirting with self-destruction. *The Week*, 31 March. Available at: http://theweek.com/article/index/259036/the-new-ipcc-climate-change-report-makes-it-official-we-are-flirting-with-self-destruction#axzz33Uy0sDfP. Accessed 7 January 2015.

Cowell, A. 2010. Ruling upholds international ban on ivory sales, rejecting moves by Tanzania and Zambia. *The New York Times*, 23 March, A4.

Cullen, P. 1987. Fighting over the forests: resolving conflicts in resource use. *Australian Forestry* [Online], 50, 3.

Cuvelier, J. 2013. Conflict minerals in Eastern Democratic Republic of Congo: planned interventions and unexpected outcomes. In D. Hilhorst (ed.), *Disaster, Conflict and Society in Crises: Everyday Politics of Crisis Response*. London and New York: Routledge, 132–48.

Davenport, C. 2014. Climate change deemed growing security threat by military researchers. *The New York Times*, 14 May, A18.

Derkyi, M., Ros-Tonen, M.A.F., Kyereh, B. and Dietz, T. 2014. Fighting over forest: toward a shared analysis of livelihood conflicts and conflict management in Ghana. *Society and Natural Resources* 27(3): 281–98.

Dilworth, C. 2010. *Too Smart for Our Own Good: The Ecological Predicament of Humankind*. Cambridge: Cambridge University Press.

Duffy, R. 2010. *Nature Crime: How We're Getting Conservation Wrong*. New Haven, CT, and London: Yale University Press.

Duffy, R. 2014. Are we hearing a 'call to arms' from wildlife conservationists? *Just Conservation*, 18 February. Available at: http://www.justconservation.org/are-we-hearing-a-call-to-arms. Accessed 7 January 2015.

Earthjustice. 2012. Navy training blasts marine mammals with harmful sonar. *Earthjustice* (Press Release), 26 January. Available at: http://earthjustice.org/news/press/2012/navy-training-blasts-marine-mammals-with-harmful-sonar. Accessed 7 January 2015.

Elliott, L. 2007. Transnational environmental crime in the Asia Pacific: an 'un(der) securitized' security problem? *The Pacific Review* 20(4): 499–522.

Eman, K., Meško, G. and Fields, C.B. 2009. Crimes against the environment: green criminology and research challenges in Slovenia. *Journal of Criminal Justice and Security* 11(4): 574–92. Available at: http://www.fvv.uni-mb.si/Varstvoslovje/Articles/VS-2009-4-Eman-Mesko-Fields.pdf. Accessed 7 January 2015.

Eman, K., Meško, G. and Fields, C.B. 2013. Environmental crime: a new security challenge. In A. Maas, B. Bodó, C. Burnley, I. Comardicea and R. Roffey (eds), *Global Environmental Change: New Drivers for Resistance, Crime and Terrorism?* Baden-Baden: Nomos, 15–35.

Ervine, K. 2011. Conservation and conflict: the intensification of property rights disputes under market-based conservation in Chiapas, México. *Journal of Political Ecology* 18: 66–80. Available at: http://jpe.library.arizona.edu/volume_18/Ervine.pdf. Accessed 7 January 2015.

Essen, E. von, Hansen, H.P., Nordström Källström, H., Peterson, M.N. and Peterson, T.R. 2014. Deconstructing the poaching phenomenon: a review of typologies for understanding illegal hunting. *British Journal of Criminology* 54(4): 632–51.

Eviatar, D. 2003. Can profits promote democracy in Africa? *The New York Times*, 4 December, A35.

Farrell, P.B. 2014. Climate science is a hoax: big oil, GOP, God say so. *MarketWatch*, 22 May. Available at: http://www.marketwatch.com/story/climate-science-is-a-hoax-big-oil-gop-god-say-so-2014–05–22. Accessed 7 January 2015.

Federman, J. 2014. Israel solves water woes with desalination. *Associated Press/Yahoo!News*, 30 May. Available at: http://news.yahoo.com/israel-solves-water-woes-desalination-053359192.html. Accessed 7 January 2015.

Franco, J., Martinez, A.M.R. and Feodoroff, T. 2013. *Old Story, New Threat: Fracking and the Global Land Grab*. Transnational Institute Agrarian Justice Programme. Available at: http://www.tni.org/sites/www.tni.org/files/download/fracking_old_story_new_threat_0.pdf. Accessed 7 January 2015.

Friedman, T.L. 2004. Dancing alone. *The New York Times*, 13 May, A27.

Friedman, T.L. 2005a. As Toyota goes. *The New York Times*, 17 June, A23.

Friedman, T.L. 2005b. Learning from Lance. *The New York Times*, 27 July, A25.

Friedman, T.L. 2005c. Too much pork and too little sugar. *The New York Times*, 5 August, A19.

Friedman, T.L. 2006a. The new red, white and blue. *The New York Times*, 6 January, A23.

Friedman, T.L. 2006b. Addicted to oil. *The New York Times*, 1 February, A29.

Friedman, T.L. 2009. The green revolution(s). *The New York Times*, 24 June, A29.

Friedman, T.L. 2010. The U.S.S. Prius. *The New York Times*, December 19, WK9.

Fussey, P. and South, N. 2012. Heading toward a new criminogenic climate: climate change, political economy and environmental security. In R. White (ed.), *Climate Change from a Criminological Perspective*. New York: Springer, 27–40.

Gamba, V. and Cornwell, R. 2000. Arms, elites, and resources in the Angolan Civil War. In M. Berdal and D.M. Malone (eds), *Greed and Grievance: Economic Agendas in Civil Wars*. Boulder, CO: Lynne Reinner Publishers, 157–72.

Gannon, M. 2013. Military sonar may hurt blue whales. *LiveScience/Yahoo!News*, 4 July. Available at: http://news.yahoo.com/military-sonar-may-hurt-blue-whales-141911253.html. Accessed 7 January 2015.

Gatehouse, G. 2013. African elephant poaching threatens wildlife future. *BBC News*, 14 January. Available at: http://www.bbc.com/news/world-africa-21018429. Accessed 7 January 2015.

Gearin, M. 2014. East Timor files seized in ASIO raid must be kept sealed, International Court of Justice orders Australia. ABC News (Australian Broadcasting Corporation), 4 March. Available at: http://www.abc.net.au/news/2014–03–04/icj-orders-australia-to-keep-east-timor-files-sealed/5296444. Accessed 7 January 2015.

Gelling, P. 2010. Indonesia tries to recast rebels as forest rangers. *The New York Times*, 7 March: 8.

Gettleman, J. 2009a. Ripples of dispute surround tiny island along watery border in East Africa. *The New York Times*, 17 August, A4.

Gettleman, J. 2009b. Lush land dries up, withering Kenya's hopes. *The New York Times*, 8 September, A1, A8.

Gettleman, J. 2012a. In Gabon, lure of ivory is hard for many to resist. *The New York Times*, 27 December, A8, A14.

Gettleman, J. 2012b. To save wildlife, and tourism, Kenyans take up arms. *The New York Times*, 30 December, 6.

Gettleman, J. 2013a. Isolated rangers in Chad encounter grim cost of protecting wildlife. *The New York Times*, 6 January, A14.

Gettleman, J. 2013b. Kenya: study details poachers' toll. *The New York Times*, 18 January, A8.

Giroux, H.A. 2004. *The Terror of Neoliberalism: Authoritarianism and the Eclipse of Democracy*. Boulder, CO: Paradigm.

Giroux, H.A. 2012. *Disposable Youth: Racialized Memories and the Culture of Cruelty*. New York and London: Routledge.

Gjelten, T. 2012. Energy independence for U.S.? Try energy security. *National Public Radio* (NPR), 25 October. Available at: http://www.npr.org/2012/10/25/163573768/energy-independence-for-u-s-try-energy-security; transcript available at: http://www.npr.org/templates/transcript/transcript.php?storyId=163573768. Accessed 7 January 2015.

Gleditsch, K.S., Salhyan, I. and Schultz, K. 2008. Fighting at home, fighting abroad: how civil wars lead to international disputes. *Journal of Conflict Resolution* 52(4): 479–506.

Goldbogen, J.A., Southall, B.L., DeRuiter, S.L., Calambokidis, J., Friedlaender, A.S., Hazen, E.L., Falcone, E.A., Schorr, G.S., Douglas, A., Moretti, D.J., Kyburg, C., McKenna, M.F. and Tyack, P.L. 2013. Blue whales respond to simulated mid-frequency military sonar. *Proc. R. Soc. B* 280(20130657): 1–8.

Gorse, M. 2010. Major oil slick flowing along Italy's Po River. *Agence France-Presse*, 25 February. Available at: http://www.tmb.ie/destinations/news.asp?title=Major-oil-slick-flowing-along-Italys-Po-River&id=176633. Accessed 7 January 2015.

Green, P., Ward, T. and McConnachie, K. 2007. Logging and legality: environmental crime, civil society, and the state. *Social Justice* 34(2): 94–110

Greenberg, P. 2010. Tuna's end. *The New York Times Magazine*, 27 June, 28–37, 44, 46, 48.

Greene, D. 2013. Algerian militants wanted to Create 'giant fireball'. National Public Radio (NPR)/Morning Edition, 4 February. Available at: http://www.npr.org/2013/02/04/171039684/algerian-militants-wanted-to-create-giant-fireball. Accessed 7 January 2015.

Hall, M. 2013a. Victims of environmental harms and their role in national and international justice. In R. Walters, D. Solomon Westerhuis and T. Wyatt (eds), *Exploring Issues in Green Criminology*. Basingstoke: Palgrave Macmillan, 218–41.

Hall, M. 2013b. *Victims of Environmental Harm: Rights, Recognition and Redress under National and International Law*. London and New York: Routledge.

Hall, M. forthcoming. *Interrogating Green Crime: An Introduction to the Legal, Social and Criminological Contexts of Environmental Harm*. Basingstoke: Palgrave Macmillan.

Hall, M. and Farrall, S. 2013. The criminogenic consequences of climate change: blurring the boundaries between offenders and victims. In N. South and A. Brisman (eds), *Routledge International Handbook of Green Criminology*. London and New York: Routledge, 120–33.

Hammer, J. 2013. Scarce tactics. *Smithsonian* 44(3): 18.

Hartmann, B. 1999. Population, environment and security: a new trinity. In J. Sillliman and Y. King (eds), *Dangerous Intersections: Feminism, Population and the Environment*. London: Zed Books, 1–24.

Hauck, M. 2007. Non-compliance in small-scale fisheries: a threat to security? In P. Beirne and N. South (eds), *Issues in Green Criminology: Confronting Harms against environments, Humanity and Other Animals*. Cullompton: Willan, 270–89.

He, Y. 2007. History, Chinese nationalism and the emerging Sino-Japanese conflict. *Journal of Contemporary China* 16(50): 1–24.

Healy, J. 2010. Bin Laden adds climate change to list of grievances against U.S. *The New York Times*, 30 January, A10.

Henkin, D. 2011. Era of mortars and artillery shells ends for Makua. *Earthjustice*, 17 February. Available at: http://earthjustice.org/blog/2011-february/era-of-mortars-and-artillery-shells-ends-for-makua. Accessed 7 January 2015.

Herbert, B. 2005. Oil and blood. *The New York Times*, 28 July, A23.

Herringshaw, V. 2004. Natural resources – curse or blessing? Accountability and transparency in the extractive industries. *New Economy* 11(3): 174–7.

Hilhorst, D. 2013. Disaster, conflict and society: everyday politics of crisis response. In D. Hilhorst (ed.), *Disaster, Conflict and Society in Crises: Everyday Politics of Crisis Response*. London and New York: Routledge, 1–15.

Hoare, P. 2014. Let slip the dolphins of war. *The New York Times*, 6 May, A25.

Hsiang, S.M., Burke, M. and Miguel, E. 2013. Quantifying the influence of climate on human conflict. *Science* 341(6151). DOI: 10.1126/science.1235367.

Hsiang, S.M., Meng, K.C. and Cane, M.A. 2011. Climate conflicts are associated with the global climate. *Nature* 476: 438–41. Available at: http://www.nature.com/nature/journal/v476/n7361/full/nature10311.html. Accessed 7 January 2015.

Hulme, M. 2009. *Why We Disagree about Climate Change: Understanding Controversy, Inaction and Opportunity*. Cambridge: Cambridge University Press.

Hulme, M. 2014. *Can Science Fix Climate Change?: A Case against Climate Engineering*. Cambridge: Polity Press.

International Court of Justice. 2014. Press: Questions relating to the seizure and detention of certain documents and data (*Timor-Leste v. Australia*): the court finds that Australia shall ensure that the content of the seized material is not used to the disadvantage of Timor-Leste. 3 March. Available at: http://www.icj-cij.org/docket/files/156/18076.pdf. Accessed 7 January 2015.

Joyce, C. 2013. Elephant poaching pushes species to brink of extinction. National Public Radio (NPR)/Morning Edition, 6 March. Available at: http://www.npr.org/2013/03/06/173508369/elephant-poaching-pushes-species-to-brink-of-extinction; transcript available at: http://www.npr.org/templates/transcript/transcript.php?storyId=173508369. Accessed 7 January 2015.

Joyce, C. and Cornish, A. 2013. 'Extinction looms' for forest elephants due to poaching. National Public Radio (NPR), 5 March. Available at: http://www.npr.org/2013/03/05/173559220/extinction-looms-for-forest-elephants-due-to-poaching. Accessed 7 January 2015.

Kaiman, J. 2013. Xi Jinping: Chinese ruler who's a riddle to the world. *The Observer* (London), 1 December, p. 40.

Kane, S.C. and Brisman, A. 2013. Technological drift and green machines: a cultural analysis of the *Prius Paradox*. *CRIMSOC: The Journal of Social Criminology*, Green Criminology Issue, Autumn 2013, 104–33. Available at: http://socialcriminology.webs.com/CRIMSOC%202013%20Green%20Criminology.pdf.

Kane, S.C. and Brisman, A. 2014. Water and climate change. *Anthropology News*, Available at: http://www.anthropology-news.org/index.php/2014/04/22/water-and-climate-change/. Accessed 7 January 2015.

Katunga, J. 2006–07. Minerals, forests, and violent conflict in the Democratic Republic of Congo. *Environmental Change and Security Program Report* 12: 12–19. Washington, D.C.: Environmental Change and Security Program, Woodrow Wilson International Center for Scholars. Available at: http://www.wilsoncenter.org/sites/default/files/Katunga12.pdf. Accessed 7 January 2015.

Kaufman, L. 2011. After years of conflict, a new dynamic in Wolf Country. *The New York Times*, 5 November, A9, A12.

Kauzlarich, D. and Awsumb, C.M. 2012. Confronting state oppression: the role of music. In W.S. DeKeseredy and M. Dragiewicz (eds), *Routledge Handbook of Critical Criminology*. London and New York: Routledge, 501–12.

Kermeliotis, T. 2013. Drone ranger: unmanned plane to spy on rhino poachers. *CNN*, 30 January. Available at: http://www.cnn.com/2013/01/30/world/africa/drone-poaching-ol-pejeta/. Accessed 7 January 2015.

Kevane, M. and Gray, L. 2008. Darfur: rainfall and conflict. *Environmental Research Letters* 3(3): 034006 (10pp). Available at: http://iopscience.iop.org/1748–9326/3/3/034006/pdf/1748–9326_3_3_034006.pdf. Accessed 7 January 2015.

King, E. 2014. Pentagon 'clear' climate change is a 'national security' Issue. *Responding to Climate Change*, 28 May. Available at: http://www.rtcc.org/2014/05/28/pentagon-clear-climate-change-is-a-national-security-issue/. Accessed 7 January 2015.

King, Y. 1993. Feminism and ecology. In R. Hofrichter (ed.), *Toxic Struggles: The Theory and Practice of Environmental Justice*. Philadelphia, PA: New Society Publishers, 76–84.

Kirby, A. 2014. Climate change 'makes violence likelier'. *Truthdig*, 31 March. Available at: https://www.truthdig.com/report/item/climate_change_makes_violence_likelier_20140331. Accessed 7 January 2015.

Klare, M. 2004. *Blood and Oil: The Dangers and Consequences of America's Growing Petroleum Dependency*. New York: Metropolitan Books.

Kocieniewski, D. 2005. Row of loosely guarded targets lies just outside New York City. *The New York Times*, 9 May, A1, A19.

Koppel, T. 2006. Will fight for oil. *The New York Times*, 24 February, A27.

Kramer, R.C. 2012. Curbing state crime by challenging empire. In W.S. DeKeseredy and M. Dragiewicz (eds), *Routledge Handbook of Critical Criminology*. London and New York: Routledge, 442–53.

Kramer, R.C. and Michalowski, R.J. 2012. Is global warming a state-corporate crime? In R. White (ed.), *Climate Change from a Criminological Perspective*. New York: Springer, 71–88.

Kron, J. 2012. South Sudan reports air attacks by Sudan. *The New York Times*, 24 April, A8.

Krugman, P. 2005. A pig in a jacket. *The New York Times*, 7 October, A31.

Krugman, P. 2010. Rare and foolish. *The New York Times*, 18 October, A35.

Krugman, P. 2014. Cutting back on carbon. *The New York Times*, 30 May, A25.

Kuijpers, K. 2012. The ambiguous effects of coltan mining in the Kivus. In M. de H.R. Ganzinga and K. Kuijpers (eds), The commodity chain of Coltan from the Democratic Republic of Congo, unpublished Master's, *Criminological Journal*, Utrecht University.

LaFraniere, S. 2006. In oil-rich Angola, cholera preys upon poorest. *The New York Times*, 16 June, A1, A14.

Lamb, K. 2014a. ICJ orders Australia to stop spying on East Timor. *SBS*, 4 March Available at: http://www.sbs.com.au/news/article/2014/03/04/icj-orders-australia-stop-spying-east-timor. Accessed 7 January 2015.

Lamb, K. 2014b. Timor-Leste v Australia: what each country stands to lose. *The Guardian* (UK), 23 January. Available at: http://www.theguardian.com/world/2014/jan/23/timor-leste-v-australia-analysis. Accessed 7 January 2015.

Laudati, A. 2013. Beyond minerals: broadening 'economies of violence' in eastern Democratic Republic of Congo. *Review of African Political Economy* 40(135): 32–50.

Le Billon, P. 2011. Bankrupting peace spoilers: what role for UN Peacekeepers? *Sustainable Development Law & Policy* 12(1): 13–17, 54–5.

Lee, J.R. 2009. *Climate Change and Armed Conflict: Hot and Cold Wars*. London and New York: Routledge.

Leverett, F. 2006. The race for Iran. *The New York Times*, 20 June, A21.

Liptak, A. 2008a. Justices return to work, with a less meaty docket for this term. *The New York Times*, 5 October: 33.

Liptak, A. 2008b. Court weighs concerns on whales and military. *The New York Times*, 9 October, A14.

Liptak, A. 2008c. Justices back navy in fight with environmentalists on sonar training. *The New York Times*, 13 November, A24.

Lipton, E. 2005. E.P.A. report finds lag in monitoring attacks. *The New York Times*, 25 March, A13.

Lovelock, J. 2006. *The Revenge of Gaia: Earth's Climate in Crisis and the Fate of Humanity*. New York: Basic Books.

Lovgren, S. 2006. Can cell-phone recycling help African gorillas? *National Geographic News*, 20 January. Available at: http://news.nationalgeographic.com/news/2006/01/0120_060120_cellphones.html. Accessed 7 January 2015.

Low, N. and Gleeson, B. 1998. *Justice, Society and Nature: An Exploration of Political Ecology*. London and New York: Routledge.

Lujala, P. and Rustad, S.A. 2011. High-value natural resources: a blessing or a curse for peace? *Sustainable Development Law & Policy* 12(1): 19–22, 56–7.

McCarthy, J. and Prudham, S. 2004. Neoliberal nature and the nature of neoliberalism. *Geoforum* 35(3): 275–83.

McClanahan, B. 2014. Film review: *Promised Land* and *The East*. *Contemporary Justice Review* 17(2): 306–10.

McGrath, M. 2012a. Python skin trade worth a billion – and often illegal. *BBC News*, 27 November. Available at: http://www.bbc.com/news/science-environment-20509720. Accessed 7 January 2015.

McGrath, M. 2012b. Wildlife crime profound threat to nations, says report. *BBC News*, 12 December. Available at: http://www.bbc.com/news/science-environment-20679454. Accessed 7 January 2015.

McGuirk, R. 2013. US drops bombs on Great Barrier Reef marine park. *Associated Press/Yahoo!News*, 21 July. Available at: http://news.yahoo.com/us-drops-bombs-great-barrier-reef-marine-park-014035736.html. Accessed 7 January 2015.

McNall, S.G. 2011. *Rapid Climate Change*. New York and London: Routledge.

Mares, D. 2010. Criminalizing ecological harm: crimes against carrying capacity and the criminalization of eco-sinners. *Critical Criminology* 18(4): 279–93.

Maas, A., Comardicea, I. and Bodó, B. 2013. Environmental terrorism – a new security challenge? In A. Maas, B. Bodó, C. Burnley, I. Comardicea and R. Roffey (eds), *Global Environmental Change: New Drivers for Resistance, Crime and Terrorism?* Baden-Baden: Nomos, 203–20.

Mazzetti, M. 2007. Bill proposes climate study focused on U.S. defense. *The New York Times*, 4 May, A18.

Memmott, M. 2014. Small-scale attacks could bring down U.S. power grid, report says. National Public Radio (NPR), 13 March. Available at: http://www.npr.org/blogs/thetwo-way/2014/03/13/289779344/report-small-scale-attacks-could-cause-national-blackout. Accessed 7 January 2015.

Michel, D. 2009. A river runs through it: climate change, security challenges, and shared water resources. In D. Michel and A. Pandya (eds), *Troubled Waters: Climate Change, Hydropolitics, and Transboundary Resources*. Washington, D.C.: Henry L. Stimson Center, 73–103.

Montague, D. 2002. Stolen goods: coltan and conflict in the Democratic Republic of Congo. *SAIS Review*, 22, 1: 103–18.

Mooallem, J. 2013. Law & order: endangered-species unit. *The New York Times Magazine*, 12 May, MM30–37, 46, 51, 57.

Morrissey, J. 2012. Rethinking the 'debate on environmental refugees': from 'maximalists and minimalists' to 'proponents and critics'. *Journal of Political Ecology* 19: 36–49. Available at: http://jpe.library.arizona.edu/volume_19/Morrissey.pdf. Accessed 7 January 2015.

Mouawad, J. 2005. Such good friends, again. *The New York Times*, 6 August, B1, B13.

Mouawad, J. 2006. Once marginal, but now kings of the oil world. *The New York Times*, 23 April, WK3.

Muffett, C. and Bruch, C. 2011. Introductory comments: the pervasive, persistent, and profound links between conflict and the environment. *Sustainable Development Law & Policy* 12(1): 4–6.

Navarro, M. 2009a. New battle on vieques, over navy's cleanup of munitions. *The New York Times*, 7 August, A10.

Navarro, M. 2009b. Navy's vieques training may be tied to health risks. *The New York Times*, 14 November, A14.

The New York Times. 2004. Editorial. Angola's elusive oil riches, 15 June, A22.

The New York Times. 2005. Editorial. Gas taxes: lesser evil, greater good, 24 October, A22.

The New York Times. 2008a. Editorial. Of whales and national security, 2 July.

The New York Times. 2008b. Editorial. The navy, whales and the court, 11 October, A22.

The New York Times. 2009. Editorial. You don't want to be downwind, 10 November, A34.

The New York Times. 2012a. Editorial. Cleaner energy, 28 May, A16.

The New York Times. 2012b. Editorial. Set, and left, adrift, 2 June, A20.

The New York Times. 2014a. Editorial. The koch attack on solar energy, 27 April, SR10.

The New York Times. 2014b. Editorial. The koch cycle of endless cash, 14 June, A24.

Nurse, A. 2013. *Animal Harm: Perspectives on Why People Harm and Kill Animals*. Surrey, UK: Ashgate.

O'Hagan, A. 2008. The legacy of war. *RSA Journal*, Autumn: 41–3.

O'Keeffe, A. 2010. Food security in the Arctic. *Griffith Review*, 27 February. Available at: http://griffithreview.com/edition-27-food-chain/food-security-in-the-arctic. Accessed 7 January 2015.

Olmo, R. del. 1987. Aerobiology and the war on drugs: a transnational crime. *Crime and Social Justice* 30: 28–44.

Olmo, R. del. 1998. The ecological impact of illicit drug cultivation and crop eradication programmes in Latin America. *Theoretical Criminology* 2(2): 269–78.

O'Loughlin, J., Witmer, F.D.W., Linke, A.M., Laing, A., Gettelman, A. and Dudhia, J. 2012. Climate variability and conflict risk in East Africa, 1990–2009. *Proceedings of the National Academy of Sciences* 109(45): 18344–9.

Onishi, N. 2011. Rich in land, Aborigines split on how to use it. *The New York Times*, 13 February: 6, 16.

Osofsky, H.M. 2005. The geography of climate change litigation: implications for transnational regulatory governance. *Washington University Law Quarterly* 83: 1789–855.

Pečar, J. 1988. 'Kriminološko' javno mnenje. *Zbornik znanstvenih razprav* 48: 105–25.

Pellow, D.N. and Brulle, R.J. 2005. Power, justice, and the environment: toward critical environmental justice studies. In D.N. Pellow and R.J. Brulle (eds), *Power, Justice, and the Environment: A Critical Appraisal of the Environmental Justice Movement*. Cambridge, MA: The MIT Press, 1–19.

Perlez, J. 2012. Disputes flare over energy in South China Sea. *The New York Times*, 5 December, A12.

Peterson, L., Lininger, J.C., Bergoffen, M., Snape, B. and Bradley, C. 2011. Natural resource 'conflicts' in the U.S. southwest: a story of hype over substance. *Sustainable Development Law & Policy* 12(1): 32–6, 61–3.

Pitman, T. 2013a. Ahead of CITES, pressure to ban Thai ivory trade. *Associated Press/News.net*, 2 March. Available at: http://www.usanews.com/article/178996/ahead-of-cites-pressure-to-ban-thai-ivory-trade/. Accessed 7 January 2015.

Pitman, T. 2013b. Group says Google shopping ads fuel ivory trade. *Associated Press/Yahoo!News*, 5 March. Available at: http://news.yahoo.com/group-says-google-shopping-ads-fuel-ivory-trade-062729114 – finance.html. Accessed 7 January 2015.

Pitman, T. 2013c. Online ivory trade threatens Africa's elephants. *Associated Press/Yahoo!News*, 5 March. Available at: http://news.yahoo.com/online-ivory-trade-threatens-africas-elephants-150550218.html. Accessed 7 January 2015.

Platt, J.R. 2012. Drones could help conserve endangered wildlife. *Mother Jones*, 2 October. Available at: http://www.motherjones.com/blue-marble/2012/10/drones-conservation-wildlife-endangered. Accessed 7 January 2015.

Platt, J.R. 2014. Elephant poachers have a new problem: U.S. Marines. *Takepart/Yahoo!News*, 24 May. Available at: http://news.yahoo.com/elephant-poachers-problem-u-marines-135420882.html. Accessed 7 January 2015.

Polgreen, L. 2009. Fishermen scoop up Sri Lanka's peace dividend. *The New York Times*, 31 July, A9.

Polgreen, L. and Tavernise, S. 2010. Water dispute raises tension between India and Pakistan. *The New York Times*, 21 July, A1, A6.

Press Trust of India. 2014. Rhino poacher killed in Kaziranga. *Business Standard*, 28 May. Available at: http://www.business-standard.com/article/pti-stories/rhino-poacher-killed-in-kaziranga-114052801707_1.html. Accessed 7 January 2015.

Pritchard, M. 2013. Re-inserting and re-politicizing nature: the resource curse and human-environment relations. *Journal of Political Ecology* 20: 361–75. Available at: http://jpe.library.arizona.edu/volume_20/Pritchard.pdf. Accessed 7 January 2015.

Reno, W. 2000. Shadow states and the political economy of civil wars. In M. Berdal and D.M. Malone (eds), *Greed and Grievance: Economic Agendas in Civil Wars*. Boulder, CO: Lynne Reinner Publishers, 43–68.

Reuters. 2011. China paper warns India against Vietnam oil deal. *Reuters*, 16 October. Available at: http://www.reuters.com/article/2011/10/16/china-vietnam-india-idUSL3E7LE1B420111016. Accessed 7 January 2015.

Reuveny, R. 2007. Climate change-induced migration and violent conflict. *Political Geography* 26: 656–73. Available at: http://www.csun.edu/~dtf46560/630/Misc/Reuveny-ClimateChangeMigration-2007.pdf. Accessed 7 January 2015.

Rice, D. 2012. Climate conflict: warmer world could be more violent. *USA Today*, 23 October. Available at: http://www.usatoday.com/story/weather/2012/10/22/climate-change-global-warming-violence-war/1649985/. Accessed 7 January 2015.

Richter, A. and Tsalik, S. 2003. Making sure the money goes where it's supposed to. *The New York Times*, 4 December, A25.

Risen, J. 2010. World's mining companies covet Afghan riches. *The New York Times*, 18 June, A4.

Romero, S. 2004. From pariah to belle of the oil ball. *The New York Times*, 20 July, C1, C8.

Romero, S. 2009a. An isolated village finds the energy to keep going. *The New York Times*, 16 October, A8.

Romero, S. 2009b. As blackouts hit energy-rich Venezuela, the President tells people to cut back. *The New York Times*, 11 November, A6.

Romero, S. 2011. In Colombia, rush for gold fuels conflict. *The New York Times*, 4 March, A1, A3.

Rosen, R.J. 2012. Google gives $5 million to drone program that will track poachers. *The Atlantic*, 11 December. Available at: http://www.theatlantic. com/technology/archive/2012/12/google-gives-5-million-to-drone-program-that-will-track-poachers/266133/. Accessed 7 January 2015.

Rosenthal, E. 2010. Military orders less dependence on fossil fuels. *The New York Times*, 5 October, A1, A13.

Rubin, A.J. 2010. Severed trees in Afghan orchards tell a story of nation. *The New York Times*, 11 July: 6.

Samson, C. 2003, *A Way of Life that Does Not Exist: Canada and the Extinguishment of the Innu*. London: Verso.

Sanders, B. 2009. *The Green Zone: The Environmental Costs of Militarism*. Oakland, CA: AK Press.

Satterfield, T. 2002. *Anatomy of a Conflict: Identity, Knowledge, and Emotion in Old-Growth Forests*. Vancouver, BC: UBC Press.

Scheffran, J. and Cannaday, T. 2013. Resistance to climate change policies: the conflict potential of non-fossil energy paths and climate engineering. In A. Maas, B. Bodó, C. Burnley, I. Comardicea and R. Roffey (eds), *Global Environmental Change: New Drivers for Resistance, Crime and Terrorism?*, Baden-Baden: Nomos, 261–92.

Schofield, T. 1999. The environment as an ideological weapon: a proposal to criminalize environmental terrorism. *Boston College Environmental Affairs Law Review* 26(3): 619–47.

Schweitzer, B. 2005. The other black gold. *The New York Times*, 3 October, A25.

Seager, J. 1993a. Creating a culture of destruction: gender, militarism, and the environment. In R. Hofrichter (ed.), *Toxic Struggles: The Theory and Practice of Environmental Justice*. Philadelphia, PA: New Society Publishers, 58–66.

Seager, J. 1993b. *Earth Follies: Coming to Feminist Terms with the Global Environmental Crisis*. London: Routledge.

Seager, J. 1999. Patriarchal vandalism: militaries and the environment. In J. Sillliman and Y. King (eds), *Dangerous Intersections: Feminism, Population and the Environment*. London: Zed Books, 163–88.

Shearer, D. 2000. Aiding or abetting? Humanitarian aid and its economic role in civil war. In M. Berdal and D.M. Malone (eds), *Greed and Grievance: Economic Agendas in Civil Wars*. Boulder, CO: Lynne Reinner Publishers, 189–203.

Simon, D.R. 2000. Corporate environmental crimes and social inequality: new directions for environmental justice research. *American Behavioral Scientist* 43(4): 633–45.

Smith, R. 2014. U.S. risks national blackout from small-scale attack. 12 March. Available at: http://online.wsj.com/news/articles/SB10001424052702304020 10457943367028406122O. Accessed 7 January 2015.

Sollund, RA. 2012. Introduction. In R. Ellefsen, R. Sollund and G. Larsen (eds), *Eco-global Crimes: Contemporary Problems and Future Challenges*. Farnham: Ashgate, 3–14.

Sollund, R. 2013. The victimization of women, children and non-human species through trafficking and trade: crimes understood through an ecofeminist perspective. In N. South and A. Brisman (eds), *Routledge International Handbook of Green Criminology*. London and New York: Routledge, 317–30.

Stephens, S. 1996. Reflections on environmental justice: children as victims and actors. *Social Justice* 23(4): 62–86.

South, N. 2007. The 'corporate colonisation of nature': bio-prospecting, bio-piracy and the development of green criminology. In P. Beirne and N. South (eds), *Issues in Green Criminology: Confronting Harms against Environments, Humanity and Other Animals*. Cullompton: Willan, 230–47.

South, N. 2012. Climate change, environmental (in)security, conflict and crime. In S. Farrall, T. Ahmed and D. French (eds), *Criminological and Legal Consequences of Climate Change*. Oñati International Series in Law and Society. Oxford and Portland, OR: Hart Publishing, 97–111.

South, N. and Brisman, A. (eds). 2013. *The Routledge International Handbook of Green Criminology*. London: Routledge, 448.

Soysa, I. de. 2000. The resource curse: are civil wars driven by rapacity or paucity? In M. Berdal and D.M. Malone (eds), *Greed and Grievance: Economic Agendas in Civil Wars*. Boulder, CO: Lynne Reinner Publishers, 113–35.

Stack, J.P., Fletcher, J. and Gullino, M.L. 2013. Climate change and plant biosecurity: a new world disorder? In A. Maas, B. Bodó, C. Burnley, I. Comardicea and R. Roffey (eds), *Global Environmental Change: New Drivers for Resistance, Crime and Terrorism?* Baden-Baden: Nomos, 161–81.

Steinborn, D. 2014. Drone, drone on the range. *Onearth*, 10 June. Available at: http://www.onearth.org/articles/2014/06/hi-yo-silver-the-drone-ranger. Accessed 7 January 2015.

Stretesky, P.B. and Lynch, M.J. 2011. Coal strip mining, mountaintop removal, and the distribution of environmental violations across the United States, 2002–2008. *Landscape Research*, 36(2): 209–30.

Sullivan, M. 2013a. As China builds, Cambodia's forests fall. *National Public Radio* (NPR), 29 January. Available at: http://www.npr.org/2013/01/29/170580214/as-china-builds-cambodias-forests-fall; transcript available at: http://www.npr.org/templates/transcript/transcript.php?storyId=170580214. Accessed 7 January 2015.

Sullivan, M. 2013b. China's insatiable demand for timber destroys Cambodia's forests. *National Public Radio* (NPR), 30 January. Available at: http://www.npr.org/2013/01/30/170691575/chinas-insatiable-demand-for-timber-destroys-cambodias-forests. Accessed 7 January 2015.

Takenaka, K. 2014. Japan condemns China fishing curbs: vows to defend islands. *Reuters/Yahoo!News*, 12 January. Available at: http://news.yahoo.com/japan-condemns-china-fishing-curbs-vows-defend-islands-080228487.html. Accessed 7 January 2015.

Talmadge, E. 2012. As ice cap melts, militaries view for Arctic edge. *Associated Press/Yahoo!News*, 16 April. Available at: http://news.yahoo.com/ice-cap-melts-militaries-vie-arctic-edge-072343565.html. Accessed 7 January 2015.

Temple-Raston, D. 2013. Algerian gas plant seizure may mark new stage in Al-Qaida evolution. National Public Radio (NPR)/All Things Considered. 22 January. Available at: http://www.npr.org/2013/01/22/170007513/seizure-of-algerian-gas-plant-could-be-next-stage-in-al-qaidas-evolution; transcript available at: http://www.npr.org/templates/transcript/transcript.php?storyId=170007513. Accessed 7 January 2015.

Tierney, J. 2006. Burn, baby, burn. *The New York Times*, 7 February, A25.

Trauzzi, M. 2014. CNA Corp's military advisory board calls climate change a 'catalyst for conflict'. (Interview by Monica Trauzzi, OnPoint, with Sherri Goodman, senior vice president and general counsel at CNA Corporation and former Deputy Undersecretary of Defense for Environmental Security.) *OnPoint/E&E Publishing*, 14 May. Transcript available at: http://www.eenews.net/tv/videos/1827/transcript. Accessed 7 January 2015.

UN (2002) *Interim Report of the Panel of Experts on the Illegal Exploitation of Natural Resources and Other Forms of Wealth of the Democratic Republic of the Congo*, United Nations Document S/2002/565/22 May, 1–19. Available at: http://www.unhcr.org/refworld/pdfid/3d0471ad4.pdf. Accessed 7 January 2015.

Vestel, L.B. 2010. On the radar, and that's the problem. *The New York Times*, 27 August: B1, B4.

Wacchholz, S. 2007. 'At risk': climate change and its bearing on women's vulnerability to male violence. In P. Beirne and N. South (eds), *Issues in Green Criminology: Confronting Harms against Environments, Humanity and Other Animals*. Cullompton: Willan, 161–85.

Walsh, B. 2012. Nature is over. *Time* 179(10): 82–5.

Walters, R. 2005. Crime, bio-agriculture and the exploitation of hunger. *British Journal of Criminology* 46(1): 26–45.

Walters, R. 2007. Crime, regulation and radioactive waste in the United Kingdom. In P. Beirne and N. South (eds), *Issues in Green Criminology: Confronting Harms against Environments, Humanity and Other Animals*. Cullompton: Willan, 186–205.

Walters, R. 2011. *Eco Crime and Genetically Modified Food*. New York: Routledge.

Weeks, L. 2012. Championing life and liberty for animals. *National Public Radio* (NPR), 25 October. Available at: http://www.npr.org/2012/10/25/158296711/championing-life-and-liberty-for-animals. Accessed 7 January 2015.

White, R. 2008. Depleted uranium, state crime and the politics of knowing. *Theoretical Criminology* 12(1): 31–54.

White, R. (ed.) 2010. *Global Environmental Harm: Criminological Perspectives*. Collumpton: Willan.

White, R. 2011. *Transnational Environmental Crime: Toward an Eco-Global Criminology*. London: Routledge.

White, R. 2012a. Climate change and paradoxical harm. In S. Farrall, T. Ahmed and D. French (eds), *Criminological and Legal Consequences of Climate Change*. Oñati International Series in Law and Society. Oxford and Portland, OR: Hart Publishing, 63–77.

White, R. 2012b. The criminology of climate change. In R. White (ed.), *Climate Change from a Criminological Perspective*. New York: Springer, 1–11.

White, R. 2013. *Environmental Harm: An Eco-Justice Perspective*. Bristol: Policy Press.

White, R. 2014. Environmental insecurity and fortress mentality. *International Affairs* 90(4): 835–52.

White, R. and Heckenberg, D. 2014. *Green Criminology: An Introduction to the Study of Environmental Harm*. London: Routledge.

White, T.I. 2007. *In Defense of Dolphins: The New Moral Frontier*. Malden, MA: Blackwell.

Wong, E. and Ansfield, J. 2014. China, trying to bolster its claims, plants islands in disputed waters. *The New York Times*, 17 June, A4, A12.

Wyatt, J. 2010. Law-making at the intersection of international environmental, humanitarian and criminal law: the issues of damage to the environment in international armed conflict. *International Review of the Red Cross*, 92(879): 593–646. Available at: http://www.icrc.org/eng/assets/files/review/2010/irrc-879-wyatt.pdf. Accessed 7 January 2015.

Xu, B. 2014. South China sea tensions. *Council on Foreign Relations*, 14 May. Available at: http://www.cfr.org/china/south-china-sea-tensions/p29790. Accessed 7 January 2015.

Yates, R., Powell, C. and Beirne, P. 2001. Horse maiming in the English countryside: moral panic, human deviance, and the social construction of victimhood. *Society and Animals* 9: 1–23.

Yost, P. 2008. Court rules for navy in dispute over sonar, whales. *Seattle Times*. 12 November. Available at: http://seattletimes.com/html/politics/2008381615_apscotusnavysonar.html. Accessed 7 January 2015.

Zarroli, J. 2013. Algeria attack raises security alarms for energy firms. National Public Radio (NPR), 22 January. Available at: http://www.npr.org/2013/01/22/170000601/algeria-attack-raises-security-alarms-for-energy-firms; transcript available at: http://www.npr.org/templates/transcript/transcript.php?storyId=170000601. Accessed 7 January 2015.

Zeitoun, M., Eid-Sabbagh, K. and Loveless, J. 2014. The analytical framework of water and armed conflict: a focus on the 2006 summer war between Israel and Lebanon. *Disasters* 38: 22–44.

Zilinskas, R.A. 1995. Preventing state crimes against the environment during military operations: the 1977 Environmental Modification Treaty. In J.I. Ross (ed.), *Controlling State Crime: An Introduction*. New York and London: Garland Publishing, 235–81.

PART I
Conflict over
Natural Resources Possession

Chapter 2

Mapping the Links between Conflict and Illegal Logging

Tanya Wyatt

Introduction

Inter-human conflicts that cost human lives and damage the environment are ongoing, even though at times they are largely invisible. Environmental destruction may (1) be an unintended consequence of conflict (i.e., 'collateral damage'); (2) be the cause of conflict; or (3) stem from efforts to fund and finance inter-human conflict. Indeed, these latter two categories – natural resource conflicts and the use of environmental and natural resources to fund existing conflicts – are areas that are beginning to receive international attention from inter-governmental agencies and are becoming topics of inquiry in the criminological community.

This chapter will explore the connection between reported inter-human conflicts and illegal logging. As Nellemann and INTERPOL (2012) and Global Witness (2002) claim, most illegal logging takes place in areas of inter-human conflict or corruption. This is an important connection to investigate as illegal logging is one of the main drivers of forest decline (Contreras-Hermosilla 2000) and can have significant consequences for people and the environment. The exploration undertaken in this chapter will be done by mapping conflicts in relation to the suspected locations of illegal logging in order to gauge the overlap between the two. Using data from the Heidelberg Institute for International Conflict Research (HIICR) conflict database, as well as reports from the International Tropical Timber Organization and academic literature on illegal timber, I will compare and map instances of conflict and illegal logging.

The chapter begins by considering the following questions: 'what constitutes "conflict" and "illegal logging"?' and 'where do these conflicts occur?' The relationship between the two phenomena (conflict and illegal logging) are then mapped and analysed. Underpinned by green criminological perspectives, the chapter considers the environmental and social impacts of conflicts over timber and the continued funding of inter-human conflicts with funds generated by illegal logging. This includes an exploration of the elements of environmental and species justice that are relevant to this green crime, which entails a discussion of the quality of both human and non-human animal life and the long-term health of these ecosystems.

What is Conflict?

The collecting and trafficking of natural resources such as wildlife and timber are prevalent yet understudied green crimes at the intersection of environmental and species justice and global security (Wyatt 2013b). Conservationists, the media and law enforcement speculate that groups engaged in conflicts in areas of high biodiversity and abundant natural resources fund their activities from the trafficking of these natural resources – timber, wildlife and/or minerals (Brisman and South 2013; South and Brisman 2013), but little concrete evidence has been obtained to fully verify this, particularly in regards to terrorism being funded through natural resource theft (UNEP 2009). Passas and Jones' (2006) research into 'blood' diamonds suggests that environmental commodities are connected to conflict, but the evidence and arguments are sometimes weak and contradictory (cf. Clark 2013; Mullins and Rothe 2008a, 2008b). A similar scenario exists for natural resources as a source of conflict, though this has been more rigorously documented in areas in the Congo Basin, where timber and other natural resources not only sustained the conflict financially, but were part of the reason for the conflict (Boekhout van Solinge 2008).

It is important that the term 'conflict' be clarified in relation to the range of confrontations, battles, wars and disputes that might be encapsulated by that term. There is no agreed upon definition and a full discussion of the nuances of the varying definitions is beyond the scope of this chapter (see Bartos and Wehr 2002 for a more complete discussion). The definition that is adopted here is that utilised by the HIICR in creating its database, which is an integral source of data for this comparison. This is primarily because it is one of the best sources for capturing political conflict. It is a fairly broad definition and is not limited to formal, declared, armed or large conflicts and includes conflicts that may transpire prior to any independent recognition by governments or inter-governmental bodies. Governments are sometimes slow to respond to conflicts or to identify them as conflict as evident in the international community's delayed discussion of and slow responses to the upheavals during the 'Arab Spring'. The West and the United Nations were hesitant to intervene in areas like Libya and Tunisia, although it was clear that 'conflict' had erupted.

This conceptualisation includes terrorism and insurgency, as well as local disputes isolated within regions with varying degrees of violence, but which have dynamics and activities that may link to global criminal markets, such as the trafficking of timber. Specifically then, the HIICR (2012: 20) defines 'conflict' as 'political conflict' or as:

> a positional difference, regarding values relevant to a society (the conflict items), between at least two decisive and directly involved actors, which is being carried out using observable and interrelated conflict measures that lie outside established regulatory procedures and threaten core state functions, the international order or hold out the prospect to do so.

'Conflict items', in turn, are 'material or immaterial goods pursued by conflict actors via conflict measures' (HIICR 2012: 120). While the HIICR's data is the predominant source for mapping conflict, other conflicts will be noted below.

The HIICR data categorises those conflicts in which 'the possession of natural resources or raw materials, or the profits gained thereof, is pursued' (HIICR 2012: 120). This definition captures two aspects of natural resources conflict: as a *funding source* and as a *reason for the conflict*. Clearly, then, the HIICR has found evidence to support the proposition that natural resources are used as both the cause of and catalyst for conflicts around the world. What is not always evident in those data is the resource involved in a particular conflict situation. Presumably, timber as a natural resource and therefore logging as the means to harvest the timber can be the reason for the conflict, but it can also be a conflict funding source. Either way – and as discussed below – the environment and people suffer as a consequence. Later sections of this chapter explore whether the illegal timber trade is in fact a reason and/or source of funding for conflict and the activities of terrorists and insurgents through transnational networks, as well as whether illegal timber plays a greater role in conflict than other natural resources (Fair Disclosure Wire 2011; UNEP 2009).

The reason for employing such a capacious conception of 'conflict' is to ensure comprehensive investigation of timber as a funding source and as a reason for conflict. In contrast, a narrow definition of conflict may exclude forms of exploitation that should be subjected to scrutiny. For instance, inter-tribal or ethnic conflicts not officially recognised in international conceptualisations of conflict such as the recent conflict in Darfur, have significant negative impacts. Thus, the application of a broad notion of 'conflict' may serve to uncover the ways in which timber is instigating tension and being used to finance and perpetuate conflict. In addition, a more inclusive definition of 'conflict' may help expose the human and environmental rights issues that arise in more isolated regions and between peoples in conflict situations that are not officially or widely recognised. Human and environmental injury can remain hidden if it is not formally declared or acknowledged and proper attention needs to be drawn to the suffering and damage in these areas.

Where is Conflict Happening?

In 2012, the HIICR documented 396 conflicts. Of these, 81 were connected to resources (although the specific resource was not always listed), making resource conflict the third most common cause of conflict after system/ideology and national power (HIICR 2012). Of these 81 resource conflicts, 35 were low intensity (non-violent), 32 were medium intensity (violent) and 14 were high intensity (war). What is not clear from this data is whether natural resource theft, such as illegal logging, is occurring to fund conflict or as the reason for it.

HIICR data also indicates that resource conflicts tend to be geographically clustered. Sub-Saharan Africa has the most conflicts related to resources (N = 27) and resources are the most frequent driver of conflict in that region (HIICR 2012). In the South Sudan and Sudan, for example, the conflict is over arable land. In other situations, it may be access to the sea, gas or claims over the Arctic. Table 2.1 displays a list of HIICR resource conflict locations.

As shown in Table 2.1, these conflicts are both inter- and intra-national and occur worldwide. While some are internal civil matters and others are occurring across borders, no region of the world is without some type of conflict over resources. A vast majority of the countries listed in Table 2.1 could be considered developing economies and to be part of the Global South. This is not always the case though, as is evident by both Norway's and the UK's involvement in resource-related conflicts in the Arctic and the Falkland Islands respectively. There are multiple conflicts in many of the countries, and these 81 conflicts occurred in 56 countries.

Table 2.1   Locations of conflicts where resources are an item in the conflict

In-country	Cross Border	In-country	Cross Border
Africa		*Europe*	
Angola	Angola – DRC		Cyprus – Turkey
Botswana	DRC – Rwanda		Russia – Kazakhstan
Chad	Equatorial Guinea – Gabon		Russia – Norway
DRC	Nigeria – Cameroon		Russia – Ukraine
Ethiopia	Sudan – South Sudan	*Middle East*	
Kenya	Uganda – DRC – Nigeria	Afghanistan	Syria – Israel
Niger		Iraq	
Nigeria		Israel	
South Sudan		Libya	
Sudan		North and South America	
Uganda		Brazil	Argentina – UK
Asia		Chile	Bolivia – Chile
Cambodia	Bangladesh – Myanmar	Colombia	Nicaragua – Colombia
China	China – Southeast Asia	Guatemala	Venezuela – Colombia
Indonesia	Indonesia – Timor-Leste	Honduras	
Kazakhstan	Japan – China	Mexico	
Kyrgyzstan	Myanmar	Panama	
Pakistan	Timor-Leste – Australia	Paraguay	
Papua New Guinea	Uzbekistan – Tajikistan	Peru	
The Philippines			

Source: HIICR 2012.

As noted, HIICR data does not always identify the resources that are being fought over or used to finance conflict. Timber is only specifically mentioned in relation to Cambodia where a journalist was killed while investigating the timber trade (HIICR 2012). Since the focus of this chapter is on illegal logging and resource conflict, it is necessary to define behaviours that constitute illegal logging.

What is Illegal Logging?

There is no standard or universal definition of illegal logging. According to the independent consulting firm, Seneca Creek and Associates (2004: 2), which has conducted one of the most comprehensive studies on illegal logging, the core of illegal logging is:

1. harvesting without authority in designated national parks or forest reserves;
2. harvesting without authorisation or in excess of concession permit limits;
3. failing to report harvesting activity to avoid royalty payments or taxes; and
4. violating international trading rules or agreements, such as export bans or CITES.

The International Tropical Timber Organization (ITTO 2014), an inter-governmental organisation that is a key stakeholder in global sustainable forestry management, simply defines illegal logging as the removal of wood in contravention of national laws. Thus, if a country's forestry regulation does not protect certain areas or species, it is not illegal to harvest them.

For present purposes, the harm-based approach of green criminology is applied (e.g., Brisman 2008; South et al. 2013; White 2011, 2013) to conceptualise illegal logging as entailing both logging that violates national or international law, as well as logging that is technically legal but which still causes harm to ecosystems and the biosphere. This conception also includes administrative and civil violations of licences and permits which, while technically not criminal, still result in deforestation and the accompanying environmental and social harms. A green perspective also considers harmful actions that are outside legal regulations. For instance, the recent Olympic Games in Sochi, Russia were preceded by drastic reduction of environmental protection laws to facilitate the building of Olympic venues (Chestin 2014). These venues were built inside a national park (so the construction would previously have been illegal) and involved the harvesting of endangered tree and shrub species (also once illegal; Chestin 2014). These clearly environmentally harmful actions, while legal and thus permissible, are also worthy of inclusion in a discussion of illegality due to their injurious impact.

Tacconi (2007) states that illegal logging encompasses a range of illegal activities that not only pertain to timber, but also to forest ecosystems, the forest industry and non-timber forest products. While these would also be included in this discussion, there is little research that documents this aspect of illegal logging and even less evidence, anecdotal or otherwise to connect it to conflict. Therefore, the focus here is upon illegal harvesting as it relates to conflict.

Illegal harvesting may be accomplished in a number of different ways but importantly it is generally tied to legal logging. This is evident through the use of falsified permits or bribes for permits that facilitate illegal harvesting (Nelleman and INTERPOL 2012). In addition, perpetrators will harvest beyond their concessions or mix in illegal timber with legal timber on the remote isolated logging roads (Nelleman and INTERPOL 2012). For example, in the remote regions of Russia Far East, illegally harvested timber is blended into the legal shipments that are crossing the isolated border check points into northern China (Wyatt 2014). In some cases, there have been instances of hackers stealing transport permits from government websites that allow for larger shipments of timber (Nelleman and INTERPOL 2012). While these tactics may be employed in conflict zones, there is also a problem of non-existent permits.

It is also important to identify the uses of profits from illegal logging, which Nelleman and INTERPOL (2012) claim go directly to conflict profiteers or are used to buy arms used in conflicts. Alternatively, guerrilla forces may impose taxes on timber companies and sell them false permits to harvest timber in conflict zones. One of the key tactics to gain profits from illegal logging is for conflict participants to control legal and/or illegal border points. The fees, taxes or bribes that are paid to cross the border fund the conflict and the timber is laundered into the legal market (Nelleman and INTERPOL 2012). There are also instances where opposing forces will agree with each other to non-combat zones, so that both sides can profit from the natural resources located in that area.

It is important to address the multiple reasons behind illegal logging, some of which are addressed here and later in the chapter when describing examples of the impact of the conflict–illegal logging connection. One of the important ecological consequences of illegal logging and timber trafficking is environmental degradation. It is estimated that deforestation, of which illegal logging is a significant portion, accounts for 17 per cent of global carbon emissions (Nelleman and INTERPOL 2012). This has obvious implications for climate change, particularly considering this amount of carbon emissions is one and a half times more than all the emissions from air, rail, road and sea travel (Nelleman and INTERPOL 2012). Unfortunately, 80 per cent of the global forests have been lost (Brack and Hayman 2002) and those remaining are under continuing pressure because of their instrumental value to human populations. The United Nations Environment Programme (UNEP) estimates that 30 per cent of global timber comes from illegal activities (Johnson 2012; Nelleman and INTERPOL 2012), which constitutes a black market estimated between US$30 billion annually (Melik 2012) and USD 100 billion (Nelleman and INTERPOL 2012). Overall, 50 to 90 per cent of the volume of forestry may be taken illegally (Nelleman and INTERPOL 2012). Additionally, Salo (2003) argues that the timber market plays a vital role in global political (de-)stabilisation because of its ties to conflicts and terrorism. So if there is competition over gaining access to timber (illegal or otherwise), this can lead to conflict, which may then contribute to the instability of governments.

Of course, it is difficult to know how much illegal logging takes place due to the isolated locations in which it occurs and lack of concern for the environment by illegal loggers, corporations and governments. While there are forests scattered around the globe, there are only four areas left with a significant forest cover (Brack and Hayman 2002). The Congo Basin in Central Africa is one of these areas (Brack and Hayman 2002), rendering it a key source of timber in the licit and illicit global markets. The Congo Basin has had ongoing conflicts and unrest and, as mentioned above, trafficking in timber plays a part in these conflicts (Boekhout van Solinge 2008). Because the greatest loss of forest cover (32 per cent according to Spector 2013) has been tropical timber, it is understandable that this dominates the forums regarding illegal logging (i.e., the International Tropical Timber Agreement). Equal concern, however, should be granted to the vast, isolated tracts of temperate forests in Eastern Russia (Wyatt 2014). In addition to the challenge of knowing how much illegal logging occurs, it is also difficult to know with any certainty how much deforestation and illegal logging is attributable to conflict. The discussion now turns to the question of where illegal logging takes place, followed by an examination of the correlations between the illegal logging and conflict.

Where is Illegal Logging Happening?

Arguably, illegal logging takes place anywhere where timber can be found. The incidences that are documented here are those that are substantial enough to provide profits that presumably could be utilised in instigating or funding conflicts. Table 2.2 collates data from the literature as to where illegal logging has been documented.

Table 2.2   Global illegal logging incidents

Africa	Asia	Europe	South America
Angola	Cambodia	Estonia	Bolivia
Cameroon	Indonesia	Latvia	Brazil
DRC	Laos	Russia	Colombia
Gabon	Malaysia		Guyana
Ghana	Myanmar		Paraguay
Liberia	Papua New Guinea		Peru
Republic of Congo	The Philippines		
South Sudan	Thailand		
Tanzania	Vietnam		
Zambia			

Sources: (ITTO/IUCN 2009; Nelleman and INTERPOL 2012; REDD Monitor 2009; Spector 2013; WWF Australia N.D.)

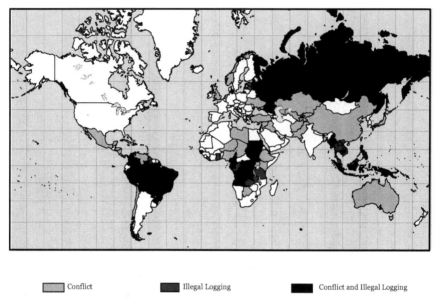

Conflict   Illegal Logging   Conflict and Illegal Logging

Figure 2.1   Conflict and illegal logging

There are 28 countries where illegal logging is a concern: 10 in Africa, 9 in Asia, 3 in Europe and 6 in South America. From these data, no noted illegal logging appears to be occurring in the Caribbean, Central America or North America. As discussed above, the tropics are the region that is most targeted for illegal logging with high prevalence in the Amazon and Congo Basins, as well as Southeast Asia. In terms of temperate forests, illegal logging occurs in Russia, Estonia and Latvia. Again, and as with conflict, the majority of countries challenged by illegal logging are economically developing countries mostly in the Global South.

Analysis

Figure 2.1 combines the two spheres of data. Light grey signifies countries where a conflict(s) has/have been identified, yet illegal logging has not been documented in the literature. Dark grey identifies countries that have incidents of illegal logging, but no documented ongoing conflicts. Finally, black identifies those countries where both conflict and illegal logging are known to take place. The overlap occurs in 16 of the 62 countries mapped (Angola, Bolivia, Brazil, Cambodia, Cameroon, Colombia, the Democratic Republic of Congo, Gabon, Indonesia, Myanmar, Papua New Guinea, Paraguay, Peru, the Philippines, Russia and South Sudan). While in Indonesia, for example, a connection between illegal logging and conflict has been substantiated (Boekhout van Solinge 2008), in other regions, there may be conflict and illegal logging, but the two may be independent. In other words, timber may not be the cause of the conflict and illegal logging may not be funding it. For instance, in Russia – a country plagued by illegal logging – the conflicts are over Arctic rights, gas and territory (HIICR 2012). Ongoing conflicts in the Central African Republic and Egypt, as well as in separatist regions of Moldova, Russia and Spain, to name a few, are not included in the 'Conflict Barometer' of HIICR in 2012. The wider definition employed in this chapter demands their inclusion. The Central African Republic is of specific interest as it is in the Congo Basin surrounded by neighbouring countries struggling with both conflict and illegal logging.

As might be expected, almost all of the countries experiencing conflict and illegal logging (with the exception of Russia) are economically developing nations in the Global South. Giordano and Giordano (2005) propose that conflict arises over resources when a resource is scarce and there is insufficient institutional capacity to properly regulate the use of the natural resource. If this is what drives conflict over resources, then it could be argued the illegal logging in areas with abundant timber must be fuelling rather instigating the conflict.

Historically, there are examples to support this proposition. The Khmer Rouge in Cambodia used the sale of illegally logged timber into Thailand (which generated as much as US$10 million every month) to survive for decades after having been removed from power (Salo 2003). Although the United Nations had banned exports of Cambodian timber, Thailand and Japan continued to purchase the timber because of its low cost. When the Khmer Rouge was given amnesty and its members integrated into the Cambodian army, timber companies filled the void and carried on illegal logging (Salo 2003) – a phenomenon that continues today (Nelleman and INTERPOL 2012).

Liberia is another example where abundant resource and high profits has fuelled conflict. Strictly speaking, industrial scale logging of Liberia by the Charles Taylor regime was not illegal because he determined what was criminal. This technicality does not mean that logging did not cause extensive human and environmental harm and, as such, a harm-based green criminological perspective would not exclude it from analysis. The timber profits from Liberia were used to purchase weapons that were sent to Sierra Leone during Sierra Leone's Civil War and also to pay the wages of militia that Taylor hired to maintain his own power in Liberia (Global Witness 2002). Timber cargo vessels coming from Southeast Asia brought weapons that were smuggled into Sierra Leone despite an international ban. Both the examples of the Khmer Rouge in Cambodia and the Charles Taylor regime in Liberia demonstrate that an abundance of valuable timber and a lack of governance and regulation are factors contributing to timber being used as a funding source in conflicts.

The investigation relating conflict and illegal logging through mapping has its limitations. As with all crime, the specific dynamics of illegal logging prevent an accurate estimation of the scale and scope of this form of green crime, which is further exacerbated by the remote locations of these crimes and the low priority given to prevention of environmental degradation by many governments, corporations and individuals. This means that the full extent of illegal logging is not known and therefore cannot be mapped. The same may be true for conflict, although human suffering and casualties tend to draw more public and international attention and are therefore more thoroughly recorded. Nevertheless, both datasets are likely to be incomplete in some fashion.

In addition, it is not always possible to connect illegal logging and conflict. This is by and large due to lack of data regarding both the extent and motivations of illegal logging and the ways in which conflicts are supported. This may be because of difficulty in investigating such green and violent crimes (as mentioned above with the assassination of a journalist in Cambodia) or, as indicated, lack of concern for the environment or for the conflicting parties. However, the lack of data does not necessarily mean that illegal logging and conflict are not in some way related (see Figure 2.1).

Despite these limitations, it is important to explore the linkages between illegal logging and conflict for several reasons. First, where there are overlaps, these conflicts may warrant further investigation as to the possibility of the exploitation of timber in the conflict. This is especially the case in those countries that possess similar geopolitical circumstances to those in Cambodia and Liberia. Identifying the conflict items and funding sources might aid in negotiating and brokering peace or in stopping the financial support that allows the conflict to continue.

Second, countries that are not highlighted but that fit the characteristics of, or are similar in geography and/or demographics to those that are highlighted, may warrant closer scrutiny. It is quite possible that they could be experiencing conflict and/or illegal logging and with hidden human and environmental victimisation. This seems a possibility in the Central African Republic, and countries in Central America and the Caribbean. Thus, the map offered in this chapter serves as a guide for further investigations. By identifying overlaps and gaps, it may become possible to identify where conflict and illegal logging may indeed be connected.

The Impacts of Conflicts Fuelled by Illegal Logging

The negative consequences of the theft of timber to fund and support conflicts range from environmental damage in various forms to negative impacts on human populations in these conflict zones. Illegal logging, whether for financing conflict or other reasons (e.g., as a tactical measure to literally remove the other side's cover), damages the environment in various ways. Boekhout van Solinge (2008) has documented how the environment may be used as a tool in conflict and forest fires can be employed as weapons to destroy resources that might be used by the enemy; how wildlife are displaced and killed as a result of conflict related destruction or to supply food for combatants in the bush; and how, when conflict forces people to move from one region to another, the environment may suffer as the displaced persons deplete its resources for food, fuel and shelter.

Widespread deforestation results in loss of biodiversity and species extinction, which can damage the health of ecosystems and lead to further biodiversity loss and extinctions. Areas of illegal logging activity may also attract wildlife poaching. According to the ITTO/IUCN (2009), illegal logging in the Congo Basin destroys the habitat of great apes. But loggers also poach great apes for bushmeat, contributing to decreasing populations and to the risk of extinction.

Deforestation also has implications for climate change. Trees and forests are one of the main carbon sinks for the planet. Losing them means that CO_2 that was once absorbed by the trees will linger in the atmosphere, contributing to a rise in global temperatures (Brack 2007). Loss of trees also takes a toll on the soil (EIA 2007). Root networks stabilise the soil. Their absence can lead to soil erosion and in turn nutrient depletion further damaging the environment. Soil erosion can also physically affect the integrity of rivers and the riparian ecosystems around them. River courses can change as can the topography around them, due to tree and soil loss and this, in turn, can affect which species can survive in that ecosystem. Forests can recover, but this takes decades if not hundreds of years, and there is no guarantee that the complexity and diversity of wildlife lost to illegal logging will return (ITTO/IUCN 2009).

An unhealthy environment has impacts upon the people in its vicinity who are supported by its natural resources. There are health, livelihood and financial ramifications to losing vital resources. Many people rely on non-timber resources for medicines and holistic therapies. For instance, there are over 4,000 plant species that are utilised in creating traditional medicines in Vietnam alone (Cao and Wyatt 2013). The loss of the forest means the loss of the ecosystem where such plants grow. Health is also impacted by the loss of food in the form of wildlife. In the Russian Far East, the harvesting of the protected cedar and oak trees has led to a decrease in the numbers of wild boar who rely on the acorns for food (Wyatt 2014). This, in turn, has impacted tiger populations (Wyatt 2014), as well as people who hunt boar as part of their subsistence lifestyle. Cooking fuel and heating sources from timber may also decrease as a result of illegal logging, thereby also negatively impacting human health. Many areas of the world rely on making and burning charcoal for cooking and warmth (Wyatt 2013a). In sum, loss of timber and a decrease in the health of forests can limit peoples' access to this life-sustaining natural resource.

Over half of the world's population are employed in fisheries, forestry and agriculture industries (United Nations Environment Programme 2004). The income of many is tied to forests. Illegal logging robs people of their means to support themselves and their families. Without a means of supporting oneself or one's family, desperate individuals may turn to crime. This certainly has financial implications (discussed below), but also has larger social consequences at the community and state level. For example, Veuthey and Gerber (2010) found that logging and natural resource extraction particularly disrupted the lives of women – a population that already, and disproportionately – bears the brunt of environmental degradation and disaster (see, e.g., Heckenberg and Johnston 2012; Wacholtz 2007).

The financial impact of illegal logging and timber trafficking is tremendous and represents a significant source of lost revenue for governments in nations with forestry sectors plagued by these crimes, such as Cambodia and Sierra Leone (Salo 2003; Boekhout van Solinge 2008). In countries like Indonesia where 50 to 80 per cent of logging is estimated to be illegal, the end result is a substantial loss of tax revenue that could and should have been paid to the state (Four Corners 2002). In Indonesia in 1998, the loss was estimated to be US$1.5 billion (Four Corners 2002). Such loss of tax revenue has huge implications for the funding of social services, such as schools and hospitals, and for other aspects of the national infrastructure. Lack of adequate schooling and educational opportunities limits the progress and opportunities of young people. Lack of medical care leads to undue suffering and preventable loss of life. Inadequate infrastructure, such as transportation, electricity grids and sanitation systems, further contributes to ill health and stymies development, which would improve the livelihoods of potentially millions of people in a country as populous as Indonesia. Instead of serving the population as a whole, timber is taken by insurgent groups and militias who sell it to unscrupulous companies and wood processors. The proceeds are then used to purchase food, supplies and weapons for soldiers. On other occasions, timber is traded directly for the food supply and weapons that these groups need. Either way, what the timber could have provided to the larger community is lost to the conflict.

Other negative social impacts can arise from conflict that is fuelled by illegal activity. Conflict zones obviously cost people their lives, so there is the physical insecurity for those who live in proximity to conflict. Such insecurity has major implications for foreign aid and international and domestic development. The international community does not always (or readily) wish to enter unsafe, dangerous areas with ongoing conflicts, regardless of how those conflicts are funded. Aid agencies may be unwilling to risk the lives of staff and foreign governments do not want to send money to areas where there is no guarantee about how the aid will be distributed. This can further isolate conflict areas, contributing to the invisibility of human victims, as well as to the hidden nature of environmental destruction.

Conclusion

As tropical timber continues to diminish, conservationists, governments and criminologists should anticipate increased conflict and the global community should prepare for the displacement of this green crime to those areas that still have forests that could be logged. This may well mean increased illegality in Eastern Europe and Russia, where governance and regulation may be weak. Isolated areas of North America may also fall prey to similar illegal logging. This chapter thus may serve less as a definitive answer to how conflict and illegal logging correlate and more as a tool for the future in planning further research and predicting the next instances of illegal logging as the source of conflict and a monetary resource to fund it.

Finally, and as suggested throughout this chapter, while illegal logging and conflict have various negative impacts independent of one another, they can also operate synergistically. Illegal logging and the resulting timber trafficking as a resource to fund and support conflict may be significant to the resilience of the conflict. Until recently, environmental degradation and crime have received little attention from law enforcement, academia or political agendas. While initiatives such as Forest Law Enforcement Governance and Trade (FLEGT) (a European Union trading scheme to certify sustainably harvested timber), legislation adopted by Australia and the US (the Australian Illegal Logging Prohibition Act and the US Lacey Act both ban the import of illegally harvested timber), and the growth of green crime scholarship hopefully indicate a change, environmental health remains low(er) on the list of priorities. As a result, conflicts funded by or over timber and other natural resources may continue with little or no intervention. This is in contrast to other funding sources, such as drugs, which usually elicit a quicker, more intense response costing billions of dollars. Until the connections between environmental well-being and human health are recognised and until the former becomes more valued, forests and the wildlife they support will continue to be the fodder that perpetuates inter-human violence – causing further damage to the environment, loss of biodiversity, species extinction and immense amounts of human suffering to those engaged in the conflict and those caught in its midst.

References

Bartos, O. and Wehr, P. 2002. *Using Conflict Theory*. Cambridge: Cambridge University Press.

Boekhout van Solinge, T. 2008. Crime, conflicts and ecology in Africa. In R. Sollund (ed.), *Global Harms, Ecological Crime and Speciesism*. New York: Nova Science, 13–34.

Brack, D. 2007. *Illegal Logging*. Chatham House Energy, Environment and Development Program EEDP/LOG BP 07/01.

Brack, D. and Hayman, G. 2002. *Illegal Logging and the Illegal Trade in Forest and Timber Products*. London: The Royal Institute of International Affairs.

Brisman, A. 2008. Crime-environment relationships and environmental justice. *Seattle Journal for Social Justice* 6(2): 727–817.

Brisman, A. and South, N. 2013. Resource wealth, power, crime, and conflict. In R. Walters, D.S. Westerhuis and T. Wyatt (eds), *Emerging Issues in Green Criminology: Exploring Power, Justice and Harm*. London: Palgrave Macmillan, 57–71.

Cao, A. and Wyatt, T. 2013. A green criminological exploration of illegal wildlife trade in Vietnam. *Asian Journal of Criminology* 8(2): 129–42.

Chestin, I. 2014. Sochi Olympics have left a trail of environmental destruction. *The Conversation*. Available at: http://theconversation.com/sochi-olympics-have-left-a-trail-of-environmental-destruction-23112. Accessed 23 February 2014.

Clark, R.D. 2013. The control of conflict minerals in Africa and a preliminary assessment of the Dodd-Frank Wall Street reform and consumer act. In N. South and A. Brisman (eds), *Routledge International Handbook of Green Criminology*. London and New York: Routledge, 214–29.

Contreras-Hermosilla, A. 2000. The underlying causes of forest decline. Center for International Forestry Research. Occasional Paper 30. Available at: http://webdoc. sub.gwdg.de/ebook/serien/yo/CIFOR_OP/30.pdf. Accessed 25 February 2014.

Environmental Investigation Agency (EIA). 2007. Attention Wal-Mart shoppers: how Wal-Mart's sourcing practices encourage illegal logging and threaten endangered species. Available at: http://www.eia-global.org/PDF/report-Walmart-forests-dec07.pdf. Accessed 1 February 2011.

Fair Disclosure Wire. 2011. House Committee on Foreign Affairs, Subcommittee on Asia and the Pacific holds a hearing on re-evaluating U.S. development assistance to China – Final. 15 November.

Four Corners. 2002. Consequences of illegal logging. *ABC Net*. Available at: http:// www.abc.net.au/4corners/content/2002/timber_mafia/resources/resources_ consequences1.htm. Accessed 26 February 2013.

Giordano, M. and Giordano, M. 2005. International resource conflict and mitigation. *Journal of Peace Research* 42(1): 47–65.

Global Witness. 2002. Logging off: how the Liberian timber industry fuels Liberia's humanitarian disaster and threatens Sierra Leone. September.

Heckenberg, D. and Johnston, I. 2012. Climate change, gender and natural disasters: social differences and environment-related victimisation. In R. White (ed.), *Climate Change from a Criminological Perspective*. New York: Springer, 149–71.

The Heidelberg Institute of International Conflict Research (HIICR). 2012. *Conflict Barometer 2012*. No. 21.

International Tropical Timber Organisation (ITTO). 2014. What is illegal logging and illegal trade? Available at: http://www.itto.int/feature06_01/. Accessed 23 February 2014.

International Tropical Timber Organisation/International Union for the Conservation of Nature (ITTO/IUCN). 2009. ITTO/IUCN guidelines for the conservation and sustainable use of biodiversity in tropical timber production forests. ITTO Policy Development Series PS-17.

Johnson, S. 2012. Interpol demands crackdown on 'serious and organised' eco crime. *The Guardian*, 29 March.

Melik, J. 2012. Interpol clamps down on illegal logging. *BBC News*, 10 September.

Mullins, C.W. and Rothe, D.L. 2008a. *Blood, Power and Bedlam: Violations of International Criminal Law in Post-Colonial Africa*. New York: Peter Lang.

Mullins, C.W. and Rothe, D.L. 2008b. Gold, diamonds and blood: international state-corporate crime in the Democratic Republic of the Congo 1. *Contemporary Justice Review* 11(2): 81–99.

NGI Knowledge Exchange. 2011. Big cats face extinction. 3 September.

The Nature Conservancy. 2014. China: A new agreement turns the tide on illegal logging. Available at: http://www.nature.org/ourinitiatives/regions/asiaandthepacific/china/explore/turning-the-tide-on-illegal-logging.xml#sthash.dfhPBbd5.dpuf. Accessed 21 February 2014.

Nellemann, C. and INTERPOL Environmental Crime Programme (eds). 2012. *Green Carbon, Black Trade: Illegal Logging, Tax Fraud and Laundering in the Worlds Tropical Forests*. A Rapid Response Assessment. United Nations Environment Programme, GRIDArendal.

Passas, N. and Jones, K. 2006. Commodities and terrorist financing: focus on diamonds. *European Journal on Criminal Policy & Research* 12: 1–33.

REDD Monitor. 2009. Forests, corruption and cars: why REDD has to be about more than carbon. Available at: http://www.redd-monitor.org/2009/06/05/forests-corruption-and-cars-why-redd-has-to-be-about-more-than-carbon/. Accessed 21 February 2014.

Salo, R. 2003. When the logs roll over: the need for an international convention criminalizing involvement in the global illegal timber trade. *The Georgetown International Environmental Law Review* 16: 127–46.

Seneca Creek and Associates. 2004. *'Illegal' Logging and Global Wood Markets: The Competitive Impacts on the U.S. Wood Products Industry*. Washington, D.C.: American Forest and Paper Association.

South, N. and Brisman, A. 2013. Critical green criminology, environmental rights and crimes of exploitation. In S. Winlow and R. Atkinson (eds), *New Directions in Crime and Deviance*. London: Routledge, 99–110.

South, N., Brisman, A. and Beirne, P. 2013. A guide to a green criminology. In N. South and A. Brisman (eds), *Routledge International Handbook of Green Criminology*. Oxford: Routledge, 27–42.

Spector, D. 2013. New maps show where Earth's forests are being destroyed. *Business Insider*. Available at: http://www.businessinsider.com/high-resolution-global-map-of-forest-change-2013–11#ixzz2tx1gbuUc. Accessed 21 February 2014.

Tacconi, L. 2007. The problem of illegal logging. In L. Tacconi (ed.), *Illegal Logging: Law Enforcement, Livelihoods and the Timber Trade*. Sterling, VA: Earthscan, 1–17.

United Nations Environment Programme (UNEP). 2004. Global Environment Outlook 4. Nairobi, Kenya.

United Nations Environment Program (UNEP). 2009. *Protecting the Environment and Natural Resources in Conflict Areas*. United Nations Environment Program.

Veuthey, S. and Gerber, J.F. 2010. Logging conflicts in southern Cameroon: a feminist ecological economics perspective. *Ecological Economics* 70(2): 170–77.

Wachholz, S. 2007. 'At risk': climate change and its bearing on women's vulnerability to male violence. In P. Beirne and N. South (eds), *Issues in Green Criminology: Confronting Harms against Environments, Humanity and Other Animals*. Cullompton: Willan, 161–85.

White, R. 2011. *Transnational Environmental Crime: Toward an Eco-Global Criminology*. London and New York: Routledge.

White, R. 2013. *Environmental Harm: An Eco-Justice Perspective*. Bristol: Policy Press.

World Wildlife Fund (WWF) Australia. (N.D.) Illegal logging. Available at: http://www.wwf.org.au/our_work/saving_the_natural_world/forests/threats/illegal_logging/. Accessed 21 February 2014.

Wyatt, T. 2013a. From the Cardamom Mountains of southwest Cambodia to the forests of the world: an exploration of the illegal charcoal trade. *International Journal of Comparative and Applied Criminal Justice* 37(1): 1–15.

Wyatt, T. 2013b. The security implications of the illegal wildlife trade. *Journal of Social Criminology* Autumn: 130–58.

Wyatt, T. 2014. The Russian Far East's illegal timber trade: an organized crime? *Crime, Law and Social Change* 61(1): 15–35.

Chapter 3

Gorillas and Guerrillas: Environment and Conflict in the Democratic Republic of Congo

Richard Milburn

Introduction

The Democratic Republic of Congo (DRC) has been endowed with a wealth of biodiversity and natural resources, including the world's second largest tropical rainforest, making it one of the two great 'lungs of the earth' along with the Amazon (Seyler et al. 2010). The country has also been blighted by almost two decades of armed conflict since the spill over from the Rwandan Genocide in 1994 led to an invasion of the DRC in 1996 (see Brisman and South 2013; South and Brisman 2013). Intra- and inter-state conflict has continued since then, including what has been termed 'Africa's World War' (Prunier 2009; Stearns 2011), as well as the recent M23 rebellion in North Kivu.

The DRC therefore makes an excellent case study to examine the interaction between the environment, natural resource wealth and conflict. While this interaction has attracted some headline news coverage, reporting has tended to focus on *natural resources* such as coltan, gold and diamonds, and far less so on *nature itself*, in the form of wildlife and forestry. The interaction of these living resources and conflict has generally been significantly overlooked. There is a need for the exploitation of 'nature' and of 'natural resources' to each be studied in their own right. The intention of this chapter is to examine specific issues relating to nature conservation and conflict in the DRC.

For too long, the living environment has taken a back seat in studies about conflict, and has usually received attention only from those with a conservationist focus, who have tended to examine the impact of conflict *on the environment*, rather than the role the environment could play *in contributing to* conflict (see, e.g., Brisman and South 2013; Clark 2013; Shambaugh et al. 2001). The emergence of green criminology and the growing appreciation of the security threat posed by the illegal wildlife trade and climate change have both helped to rectify this, but there is still a need to mainstream the study of the living environment into conflict studies (Milburn 2012).

The chapter begins with a more detailed explanation for the focus on the living environment before examining the different conflicts that have taken place in the DRC and their impacts. The chapter demonstrates that while such impacts have been predominantly detrimental, in some places, particularly with regard to forestry, conflict has simultaneously – and somewhat perversely – acted as effective means of conservation. The chapter then reviews the way in which environmental resources have sustained conflict in the DRC by providing the means for funding of rebel groups and creating incentives to maintain instability. Finally, the chapter examines an often-overlooked area – the impact the environment can have in promoting peacebuilding and post-conflict recovery. It evaluates the environmental peacebuilding work undertaken in the DRC to date and presents further potential approaches that could help to both improve security and protect the environment from unsustainable exploitation.

Nature, Not Natural Resources

The living environment is often relegated to a low position of importance, subsumed by resources such as diamonds whose role in contributing to conflict is well-known, well studied and well-reported (e.g., Brisman and South 2013; Clark 2013; South and Brisman 2013). Because the living environment does not seem to offer the same potential for monetary profit as some other sources of wealth, such as precious metals and minerals, it is often relegated to a lower position of importance and so the interaction of the living environment and conflict is overlooked.

While the living environment could simply receive further study in conjunction with the topic of natural resources, three key distinctions between the living environment and natural resources warrant a separate study focus: first, the renewable nature of the living environment that offers long-term value; second, the valuable ecosystem services provided by the living environment; and third, simply because the living environment has been overlooked for so long, it requires separate study to establish its importance in the study of conflict. These three distinctions are fleshed out below.

The first distinction is that the living environment is a renewable rather than non-renewable resource, and, as such, can provide valuable monetary and in-kind value in perpetuity. For example, a forest can provide revenue from the sale of timber as well as function as a habitat for wildlife that can in turn provide a source of protein to local communities in the form of bushmeat, and this can be maintained in the long-term if the forest is well-managed. In contrast, non-renewable resources, such as diamonds or coltan, provide income only from a one-off sale of the resource. As such, the living environment can be considered as an asset that pays ongoing dividends, providing a regular source of income while maintaining its underlying value. It is, therefore, crucial to managing the living environment to allow continued resource extraction in sustainable ways that prevents environmental degradation. While it is common to consider that non-renewable resources, such as gold or coal need to be carefully managed, the same is equally true of the living environment.

The living environment has another value in the form of ecosystem services. It provides both in-kind services, such as improved soil-fertility for farmers, as well as monetary benefit from the consumption of resources such as timber (Juniper 2013; Millennium Ecosystem Assessment 2005; ten Brink et al. 2012). In contrast, resources such as diamonds and coltan offer only a monetary benefit. Destruction of the living environment therefore has implications for the long-term ability of a country to recover and prosper in the post-conflict period (Millennium Ecosystem Assessment 2005). Given that the environment is the 'wealth of the poor', who are heavily dependent on it for their survival and prosperity, protection of the living environment is thus vital to enable a successful post-conflict recovery process (Mrema et al. 2009).

Finally, simply because the living environment has for so long been on the periphery of conflict study there is a need for specific study from a criminological and security perspective to effectively analyse the role that the living environment plays in conflict (Milburn 2012). In addition, far greater cooperation and coordination is required between conservation organisations and humanitarian and development organisations in regions of armed conflict in order to protect the living environment, both for its own sake and to preserve the ecosystem services for people living in these regions in the post-conflict period. Accordingly, work needs to be conducted to improve the perception of the importance of the living environment and subsequently to encourage cooperation between different agencies for its protection (Shambaugh et al. 2001).

Conflict in the DRC

The conflicts that have affected the DRC remain complex and the reasons behind them remain difficult to fully understand (Prunier 2009; Stearns 2011). A brief summary of the conflicts and most significant remaining rebel forces in the country is set out below.

The origins of conflict lie in the spill-over effects of the 1994 Rwandan Genocide, which led to the first invasion of the DRC by Rwandan and Ugandan-backed rebels who took control of the country under the new presidency of Laurent Kabila. A second conflict occurred soon after, which has been termed 'Africa's World War' (Prunier 2009; Stearns 2011) due to the number of African states involved in the conflict. This conflict ended with a 2003 peace accord, but since then, there has continued to be latent insecurity in eastern DRC. In particular, instability has plagued the North and South Kivu provinces, where the remnants of the génocidaires continue to operate in the form of the Democratic Forces for the Liberation of Rwanda (FDLR) rebel group and where Rwanda continues to exert its influence through the support of rebel groups, including the National

Congress for the Defence of the People (CNDP) and their most recent incarnation as the M23s.[1]

This range of conflicts had a significant effect on the environment in the DRC, including the devastation wrought on forests in the Kivus as a result of the refugee camps established there and the subsequent flight of refugees westwards. Accurate figures are difficult to come by and so the exact extent of the impact of conflict on the DRC is hard to measure, but some studies attempt to estimate the effects on the environment.

The Impact of Conflict on the Environment in the DRC

The effects of conflict on biodiversity in the DRC have been largely, but not wholly, negative. Poaching and deforestation – by armed groups as a source for funding and by communities for bushmeat and firewood – has wrought significant harm on a plethora of species and protected areas. Forestry has nevertheless remained largely well protected, with deforestation levels far below those of neighbouring countries or those experienced as a consequence of the civil war in Liberia and Sierra Leone. Some areas, however, have still been severely deforested as a result of the conflict, particularly those close to the refugee camps in the east of the country.

The Virunga National Park suffered especially from the influx of refugees from Rwanda after the genocide in the mid 1990s because the majority of refugees settled in camps in and around Goma, in close proximity to, or inside, the national park. At first, these refugees gathered deadwood from the forest. When this supply was exhausted, they started to cut down trees for firewood. Conservation efforts were futile, not only because of the sheer numbers of refugees, but also because the defeated Rwandan Army was regrouping and taking control of the camps and thus there was little the park rangers could do in the face of the threat refugees posed (Brauer 2009). The ongoing presence of camps around the park as a result of conflict and insecurity since then have continued to put stresses and strains on the park and it is estimated that at the peak of the crisis, 89 hectares of forest were being lost in the Virungas each day due to firewood harvesting (UNEP 2011).

The forest suffered, but the mountain gorilla population in the Virungas[2] has increased over the last two decades, although this appears to be more due to growth in the populations in Rwanda and Uganda than in the DRC (Brauer 2009). Congolese gorillas seem to have suffered far more from the Rwandan Civil War

---

1   The M23 rebels are made up of predominantly Tutsi soldiers who were reintegrated from the CNDP into the Congolese army after a 2009 peace agreement. The rebels deserted from the army in 2012, citing poor conditions and pay, and since then have been fighting the Congolese army and the UN's peacekeeping force (MONUSCO) in North Kivu.

2   The Virungas refers to three adjacent national parks that mountain gorillas inhabit: the Mgahinga Gorilla National Park in Uganda, the Volcanoes National Park in Rwanda, and the Virunga National Park in the DRC.

and genocide and the subsequent Congo War than those on the Rwandan side, who are generally better studied and protected (Brauer 2009). The threat of violence has restricted access to the gorillas in the DRC, whereas the greater security and successful tourist industry in Rwanda has provided far better access, infrastructure and financial incentives to carry out work to protect the gorillas and promote a growth in numbers. In contrast, several gorillas have been killed in the Congolese section of the gorilla habitat as retaliation for efforts by park rangers to limit the charcoal trade and its resulting deforestation (Nelleman et al. 2010).

Another protected area that has been badly affected by conflict has been the Kahuzi-Biega National Park. Much like in the Virunga National Park, refugees from the Rwandan Civil War and genocide set up camps in the Kahuzi-Biega National Park and soon began felling trees for building materials and firewood. One of the differences, however, is that for the Virunga National Park the invasion of Rwanda and the beginning of the first Congolese War provided some respite from the destruction wrought by the camps as the refugees were forced west across the country, whereas the Kahuzi-Biega National Park suffered immensely as refugees fled directly through the park, poaching elephants and decimating the gorilla population. It is estimated that as a result of this movement and the ongoing effects of conflict in the region, the elephant population has declined from 1,350–3,600 to almost zero, and the eastern lowland gorilla population has been reduced from 17,000 to 2,000–3,000 (Brauer 2009). The successful tourist industry has also been decimated by the war, as latent conflict and lack of stability has discouraged visitors to the Kahuzi-Biega National Park, resulting in a loss of funds and thus the ability to further protect against environmental degradation. Better facilities in the Virunga National Park, as well as interest in the popular and better-known mountain gorilla, has also contributed to the loss of interest in and protection for the eastern lowland gorillas in Kahuzi-Biega.

The Kahuzi-Biega National Park also faces mining problems, as is the case in many areas of the DRC. Illegal extraction of minerals, such as gold and coltan that occurred under the control of a militia, is frequently accompanied by the felling of trees and poaching of animals for bushmeat to feed those employed in the mines and as a secondary source of income through the provision of charcoal and meat to communities in the area (Nelleman et al. 2010). The presence of valuable natural resources in parts of Kahuzi-Biega National Park and elsewhere, therefore contributes to environmental harm, both from polluted water run-off and destruction caused by the mineral mines themselves, as well as the additional harm caused by the presence of workers there. Because the militias operating in these regions are armed and outnumber the limited number of Congolese Wildlife Service (ICCN) rangers working in these areas, it is especially difficult for the ICCN rangers to prevent the direct and associated environmental harms caused by mining activities.

Other protected areas and their wildlife have also suffered huge losses through the course of the conflicts described above. For example, while accurate numbers are difficult to obtain, it is estimated that the number of elephants in Garamba

National Park, in the Northeastern part of the DRC, has fallen from 20,000 in the 1970s to fewer than 2,000 today (Agger and Hutson 2013). The Okapi Faunal Reserve, to offer another example, has suffered losses as a result of the conflict as rebel forces have moved into the area, sacked the headquarters of the ICCN, and have started hunting for bushmeat and ivory, both for sale and to feed the soldiers based between Bunia and Kisangani (Beyers et al. 2011). The worst effects of the conflict in this reserve came between 2002 and 2004 as rebel militias fought in areas of high elephant density (Beyers et al. 2011). Since then, there have been periods of respite, as control of the territory has been largely regained by ICCN, with support from the Congolese Army (FARDC), but in 2009, there was another increase in poaching led by the FARDC (Beyers et al. 2011). Throughout the DRC as a whole, it is estimated that elephant populations have fallen from over 100,000 fifty years ago to fewer than 20,000 today, and their numbers continue to drop (Hart 2009).

It can therefore be seen that many protected areas have endured significant losses in wildlife and forestry as a result of the conflict and accompanying refugee crisis. But from a purely ecological perspective, conflict itself is not necessarily the only cause of ecological destruction and may in fact have had some protective consequences. While the forestry of the DRC has suffered the effects of conflict, deforestation has been far worse in other nations such as Liberia or Indonesia. In spite of the DRC's great swathes of forest, which are comfortably the largest in Africa, the current annual logging rate of 0.33 per cent remains far below other states in Central and West Africa, and this can be *attributed to the conflict* in the DRC, which has largely prevented mass forest exploitation in the country (Seyler et al. 2010). In other words, whereas some countries have experienced mass deforestation (due to a lack of other economic opportunities), conflict in the DRC has *prevented* deforestation from occurring at the same rate and on the same scale. The number of active timber companies in the DRC declined by around three-quarters and many sawmills have closed or reduced their capacity due to insecurity in the DRC and are instead waiting for stability to return to the region so that they can reengage their capital in timber exploitation. Most of the DRC's export timber is found in northern Equateur and Orientale provinces, both of which are controlled by rebel groups, and Kisangani was the main transfer site for moving it down river to Kinshasa. Somewhat ironically, armed conflict has served to protect some of DRC's forests by severely restricting the timber trade in some regions (Baker et al. 2003).In addition, the dilapidated state of infrastructure in the DRC has prevented the use of capital for logging and hindered the ability of companies or groups to export timber in great quantities, and rebel forces have been able to prevent transportation on the River Congo – the only other option in the country for transporting goods to markets. While rebel groups have felled trees and exported timber to assist in the funding of their campaigns, the overall effect of the conflict on the DRC's forests has not been that severe – at least in comparison to the timber exportation for four other African countries: Cameroon, Gabon, the Ivory Coast and Liberia. All four of these countries have a small fraction of the forestry that the

DRC contains, and yet each has exported more than double the amount of wood that the DRC has exported in the same time frame (Baker et al. 2003).

While overall rates of deforestation in the DRC have been low, conflict in the DRC has forced some companies to log in government-held areas and locations where rebels are absent in order to recoup their investments because they cannot carry on logging in rebel held areas. This has placed greater pressure on the Bas-Congo forest, which has been the worst affected area, because there is both easy access to the forest and it lies in close proximity to the port city of Matadi as well as Kinshasa. Furthermore, when government employees do not receive their wages, they are often instead paid with forest concessions. Additional deforestation and subsequent soil erosion and soil loss has been due to subsistence agriculture on steep slopes. The conclusion, then, is that conflict in some regions of the DRC has reduced deforestation for timber export in those regions, but in so doing has stressed those regions that are conflict-free; those conflict-free regions have experienced even further strain because of deforestation linked to economic instability (e.g., forest concessions in lieu of salary, felling trees for subsistence agriculture) (Baker et al. 2003).

While the conflict in the DRC has therefore served as an unfortunate but effective protection mechanism for much of the country's forestry, severe threats remain. As worldwide forestry declines, the DRC's well-preserved forests will be of increasing appeal to timber firms. If, as seems likely, the country continues to be afflicted by insecurity and weak and corrupt central and local governments, it will attract the most unscrupulous of logging firms, with little interest in sustainable logging practices. This increases the probability that the DRC's forests will start to be more adversely affected by logging, both in terms of the number of trees cut down and areas in which they are felled. Companies more interested in short-term profit than sustainable forestry and that are willing to pay bribes to increase their logging activities and exports will help entrench corruption and prevent a real change to forestry law and the enforcement thereof, thereby threatening the long-term vitality of the DRC's forests (Baker et al. 2003).

The DRC, therefore, epitomises an irony most succinctly expressed by McNeely (2002: 45): 'While war is bad for biodiversity, peace can be even worse ... Market forces may be more destructive than military forces'. Addressing the threats that peace may bring to the DRC is thus of critical importance from an ecological perspective, to say nothing of the negative effects of environmental degradation on human populations. I will return to this point later in the chapter. Before doing so, however, I will first examine another dynamic in the relationship between conflict and the living environment. Conflict can cause harm to the environment, as demonstrated above through the examples of deforestation and poaching by refugees, but the living environment can also fuel, exacerbate or extend conflict because it can provide resources to rebel and government forces. This role of the living environment as a *contributor* to conflict is an important consideration for those studying environment-conflict relationships. The following section explores the role the living environment has played, and continues to play, in fuelling and funding the ongoing conflict in the DRC.

The Impact of the Living Environment on Conflict in the DRC

The Illegal Ivory Trade

Perhaps the rebel group best known for its involvement in the ivory trade is the Lord's Resistance Army (LRA), due in part to the release of the Enough Project's[3] report on the matter (Agger and Hutson 2013). This report documented that Joseph Kony, the Uganda-born leader of the LRA, had ordered his soldiers to kill elephants and bring him their ivory, which was then exchanged for supplies such as food and weapons. Defecting soldiers and escapees have reported stories of carrying elephant parts out of the bush and helicopters arriving to take ivory away for sale outside the Garamba National Park, where much of the poaching is taking place (Agger and Hutson 2013). While the exact extent of this trading is unknown, ivory nevertheless is providing the LRA with a valuable resource to continue its ongoing campaign and is one of few funding sources they now have left.

Due to the ongoing instability in the DRC and the lack of government capacity and control over much of the territory, the Garamba National Park offers a safe haven for LRA fighters, providing them with a base from which to continue to launch attacks and a revenue stream in the form of ivory. It is unclear exactly how the ivory is traded, but it seems there may be middlemen operating out of the Central African Republic (CAR) and that ivory from the DRC is able to be transported into the CAR due to the ongoing weaknesses of the DRC state, and lax enforcement in the DRC and at the border between the DRC and CAR (Agger and Hutson 2013). This ivory trade provides financial support for the LRA, hindering US-supported efforts by the Ugandan Army to combat the LRA and find Kony.

The LRA, however, is not the only organisation involved in the ivory trade. It is believed that rogue factions of the Ugandan, Sudanese, South Sudanese and Congolese armies are also involved, seizing the opportunities afforded by porous borders and a lack of state authority in the region to engage in elephant poaching and the ivory trade (Gettleman 2012; Titeca 2013; see generally Brisman and South 2013). Recent evidence has suggested that the Ugandan Army is directly involved in poaching. Gettleman (2012) reports that a helicopter that was traced back to the Ugandan Army was operating in the area around which a parade of elephants were killed in a rather unusual manner – herded close together and then shot from the air. The Ugandan Army has denied involvement, but it is a concern that a force

---

3   The Enough Project is a research and advocacy organisation that aims to end genocide and crimes against humanity; its campaigns and initiatives have focused on the DRC, Sudan, South Sudan and Darfur (see www.enoughproject.org).

receiving international support, including by the United States, to combat the LRA threat may be using some of that support to engage in the ivory trade.

Aside from the LRA and the suspected involvement of the Ugandan Army, other organisations are also involved in the ivory trade coming out of the Garamba National Park, including the FARDC, further complicating the issue. Ongoing field research by Titeca (2013) suggests that the FARDC is using the presence of the LRA as a veil under which to operate its own poaching operations. Soldiers who are poorly paid and accustomed to a culture of corruption can all-too-easily fall into the trap of fast money from the ivory trade, and the cloak offered by the presence of the LRA allows them to carry on their operations with less hindrance. For example, a recent attack on rangers in the Garamba National Park, which was claimed to be an LRA attack, is believed to have in fact been the FARDC (Titeca 2013). Allegedly, this was retribution for an attack by ICCN rangers a few days before, when they came across soldiers poaching. It is thought the subsequent ambush was designed as a warning to the ICCN rangers to keep away from the FARDC's territory, much like the killing of gorillas in the Virungas described earlier in this chapter. For a wildlife service that has only a small number of rangers armed with little more than old, rusting rifles and machine guns, the threat posed by these militaries to them and the wildlife they are trying to protect seems insurmountable. In sum, the ivory trade funds both rebel groups and armies, and ongoing political instability and absence of strong state authority ensures these various groups will still profit from this illegal trade.

The role of the ivory trade in funding and perpetuating conflict is not peculiar to the DRC. For example, a similar phenomenon may be occurring in Somalia, where the ivory trade is believed to have funded the militant group, Al-Shabab, for its actions in Somalia and Kenya, as well as the Janjaweed in Darfur (Gettleman 2012). Taken together, we can see how political insecurity creates opportunities for rebel groups and armies, as well as terrorist outfits, in securing living environment resources for their own particular needs.

The Illegal Trade in Timber and Charcoal

There is a large market for charcoal in the DRC, as in many parts of the developing world, because so many Congolese people depend on charcoal as their primary source of fuel, which accounts for 85 per cent of domestic energy use in the DRC (Seyler et al. 2010). Gaining control of this business is therefore very lucrative and the FDLR has been shown to exploit this opportunity and utilise the charcoal trade as a source of funding for their continuing presence in the Kivus (IRIN 2009). It is estimated that the FDLR generates approximately US$28 million annually from charcoal sales (Nelleman et al. 2010).

Notably, the presence of the FDLR has been a source of contention for the Rwandan government ever since the organisation was born in the aftermath of the genocide, and the FDLR's continued presence in eastern DRC creates an ongoing security concern for Rwanda. This threat is used by the Rwandan government as a justification for its involvement in the Kivus in order to retain a sphere of influence in the region to protect the country from attack, which in turn contributes to strains in inter-governmental relations between Rwanda and the DRC as the Congolese government is seen as providing an ongoing safe haven to an enemy of the Rwandan state. The charcoal trade can therefore be seen to be playing a contributory role to the continuing insecurity in the DRC.

While the FDLR has been involved in the charcoal trade, the Congolese military is also accused of involvement, using the threat posed by military groups in the region as an excuse to venture into parts of the Virunga National Park and cut down trees, make charcoal, and poach (Lovgren 2007). To produce the charcoal, felled timber is placed in a 'kiln', which is often simply a rudimentary dome of larger branches covered with mud or other materials such as clay and sod, and is set alight. The aim is to minimise the amount of air so that the burning process removes water from the timber and what is left is mostly pure carbon, a process that can take several days (Wyatt 2013). The involvement of the FARDC in the charcoal trade is similar to the situation described earlier in this chapter of the ivory trade and the LRA, where the presence of a rebel group is used as a pretext by the Congolese military to launch its own poaching operations. As a consequence, the Congolese military has come into conflict with ICCN rangers in both parks, threatening the security of surrounding communities who suffer from the increasingly violent nature of the trade.

In addition to the funds generated from the charcoal trade, conflict timber has also been a source of funding for both rebel groups and the Congolese government. In some areas where natural resources such as coltan are being mined, logging is also occurring as a concurrent activity that adds to the financial resources of militias and provides materials and fuel for local communities and workers living and working in and close to the mines (Nelleman et al. 2010). For the rebel groups, this has been carried out on only a small scale, with mills commandeered and some logs exported for sale; in government-held territory, such operations have been more organised, with companies asked to fell trees and share the profits with the central government to help fund their war effort (Baker et al. 2003). Unlike the situation in Liberia, conflict timber has not been a main funding source for the government or armed groups in the DRC, but it has still contributed funds to both rebel groups and the government to assist in financing the ongoing conflict.

In addition to the direct security implications of the timber trade, there are also environmental consequences which subsequently negatively affect human populations. The loss of forests threatens the survival of ecosystems and associated ecosystem services, and the continued denuding of forest slopes risks destabilising the soil when heavy rains come, damaging farmland with mudslides. Furthermore, the production of charcoal remains inefficient and combines with deforestation to contribute towards climate change (Seyler et al. 2010). This impact on climate change potentially adversely affects not only the DRC, but the world as a whole, transforming a regional environmental problem into one with global consequences. Given the linkages between climate change and security, preventing mass deforestation is crucial to preventing environmental degradation and human harm on a national and international scale (Briggs 2012; Brown et al. 2007).

A Natural Peace

The previous section illustrated both how the living environment can be a casualty of conflict (e.g., deforestation by refugees in the Virunga National Park) and how the living environment can exacerbate and perpetuate existing conflicts (e.g., illegal trade in ivory, timber and charcoal to finance conflict). But what has yet to be examined is the impact of peace on the living environment and the role that conservation work can play in promoting and enabling a transition from conflict towards peace. The final section of this chapter will therefore begin by examining environmental peacebuilding theory and its application to the living environment through the emergence of the 'Peace Parks' movement. It will then examine how the living environment can be utilised to promote post-war recovery, and how the effects of recovery can be managed to try to prevent peace from having a more adverse impact on the living environment in the DRC than war.

Environmental peacebuilding theory (Conca and Dabelko 2002) emerged from research which found that many anticipated conflicts, particularly those over water, did not come to pass, and that opposing sides had chosen instead to cooperate over environmental resources. Environmental peacebuilding theory posits that cooperation over environmental management can provide neutral arenas for negotiation, help build mutual trust and develop collaborative mechanisms that could contribute towards a larger peacebuilding process (Conca and Dabelko 2002). One particular illustration is the emergence of 'Peace Parks' – transboundary protected areas (TBPAs) that are managed by a single, unified multinational authority and that either act as a symbol of peace between countries or are used as part of the peacebuilding process between countries in conflict with each other (Ali 2007).

Research has found that 'Peace Parks' have made positive contributions towards the peacebuilding process, but it remains difficult to effectively evaluate how significant and sustained that impact might be (Carius 2006). For example, in the Virungas, cooperation between Rwanda, Uganda and the DRC over protection of the gorilla habitat has achieved significant cross-country cooperation, even while formal diplomatic relations have been poor. While these three countries are in the second phase of a three-step process to create a TBPA in the region, communication between them remains limited (Martin et al. 2009). Although significant conservation successes have been achieved, including a revenue-sharing scheme to ensure that the DRC receives benefits from tourism, and although cooperation between the three countries has been obtained at a ministerial level, the TBPA and gorilla conservation remain a minor form of collaboration in a very specific context and geographical area. The TBPA process has had little effect on broader relations between the DRC and Rwanda, which continue to be strained, and the peacebuilding process has been minimal, as evidenced by continued insecurity in North Kivu, most recently involving the M23 rebellion.

That is not to say that environmental peacebuilding theory and 'Peace Parks' are totally without merit. As described above, successes have been achieved in the Virunga National Park and elsewhere. In addition, using conservation work as a tool for peacebuilding does offer some interesting potential solutions that warrant further investigation, such as how disarmament and reintegration programmes can be linked with conservation to aid the peacebuilding process (UNEP 2012). But at this point, it is too soon to determine the extent to which conservation in general, and 'Peace Parks' in particular, can play a significant role in the peacebuilding process (McNeely 2000). Further study and evaluation is required.

It is also worth noting that the M23 rebels have allowed ICCN staff into the gorilla habitat to monitor the gorillas even while they have been based there and engaged in the recent conflict with the FARDC (IGCP 2012). This is another example of how methods of communication or collaboration can be sparked by conservation initiatives. Recently – and relatedly – a proposal has been put forth to help convert M23 rebels into soldiers in a 'Yellow Berets' unit that would be charged with protecting the Virunga National Park. Conceived of as a variation on the Disarmament Demobilization and Reintegration (DDR) programmes, which are designed to reintegrate ex-combatants into the national army or civilian life, the 'Yellow Berets' would serve under the neutral command of either the United Nations or African Union. Aside from helping to improve security in the region, the 'Yellow Berets' would also assist in developing the infrastructure for sustainable natural resource extraction and export, as well as the renewal and expansion of the tourist industry in the DRC (Milburn 2012).

A similar idea was suggested by Mikhail Gorbachev, the former Soviet statesman, when he proposed the creation of the 'Green Helmets', a UN force much like the current 'Blue Helmets' peacekeepers, but with a mandate for environmental protection rather than peacekeeping. Given the proven inadequacies of UN peacekeeping forces in the DRC (Menondji 2013; Tull 2009; Vogel 2013), combined with ongoing difficulties obtaining the required funding and resources for peacekeeping operations, such as a lack of personnel, particularly from Western countries, and a lack of critical logistical support such as helicopters, a force designed for environmental protection stands little chance of success. A 'Yellow Berets' unit, in contrast, would be more cost-effective and a more viable means of protecting the environment because it would address a security problem (demilitarising the M23 rebels), improve conservation, and help stimulate the economy through sustainable natural resource extraction and tourism.

The notion of the 'Yellow Berets' unit is further supported by the recent success of the UN's Forward Intervention Brigade, a specially created force of just over 3,000 soldiers with an offensive mandate to actively engage with the M23 rebels, in contrast to the previous, far more defensive approach of MONUSCO. Rwanda and Uganda already have army units stationed close to the gorillas for protection of their tourist industry, so the precedent of using military forces for conservation protection is established in the region, as well as elsewhere, such as in South Africa. The 'Yellow Berets' would be an adaptation and extension of this concept and would not only addresses conservation concerns, but also the larger issue of border relations between Rwanda and the DRC.[4]

As previously suggested, the 'Yellow Berets' unit could help improve security in the region and set the foundation for economic recovery, as increased stability would bring more business and industry into the region, thereby creating wealth and providing an incentive for enduring peace. With greater security and stability, tourism could return to the region and sustainable timber extraction could also occur, although it would need to be managed effectively to prevent mass deforestation. Such a managed extraction process has been suggested for recovery in Liberia, where Blundell and Christie (2007) have suggested that thousands of jobs could be created in managing protected areas and through sustainable harvesting of forestry and of wildlife populations as sources of protein for local communities. In addition, work is underway to create a Civilian Conservation Corps, which will work to establish the infrastructure required to provide basic services such as education and healthcare to communities and to help kick-start economic development and, by linking these interventions to conservation, to improve the image of the protected areas and encourage communities to protect them. It is argued that through these processes, conservation can provide a platform for development and improve security in the region (Blundell and Christie 2007).

The UN is already working to reduce the impact of their forces on the environment, which is summarised in the paper, 'Greening the Blue Helmets' (UNEP 2012). In the DRC, the FARDC's choice to deforest, for security reasons, a migratory corridor used by elephants and buffalo in the Virunga National Park was identified as causing crop-raiding by elephants and buffalo in Rwanda and Uganda. Once this link was established, the deforestation was halted and conservation agencies were able to target their interventions to reduce the impacts of the crop-raiding on surrounding communities (Gray and Kalpers 2005 and Rainer et al. 2003). Actions such as these to reduce the impact of the military on the environment can help to prevent conflict between animals and people, and the broader process of integrating environmental considerations into military planning can help to reduce the impact of military operations and war on the environment. One needs to caution against idealism here, however. Militaries cannot be expected to significantly alter their approaches or tactics to prevent incidental environmental damage if doing so would negatively affect their capacity or objectives or otherwise threaten the lives of military personnel and/or civilian populations. But a greater appreciation of the value and importance of the environment can help in reducing

---

4 For a critical analysis of the militarisation of conservation and new forms of 'fortress conservation', see Smith and Humphreys (this volume) and Wall and McClanahan (this volume).

the impact of the military on the environment or, arguably, reduce the prolongation of military involvement in a conflict or a dispute.

Finally, as described earlier in the chapter, refugee and internally displaced persons camps can cause significant harm to the environment and so integrating environmental considerations into their planning and management is crucial. As with the military example above, it may sometimes be impossible; hundreds of thousands of people facing disease and starvation are unlikely to be moved to preserve a rare species of butterfly, for example. And, indeed, people new to a region may not even know whether their actions are adversely affecting local flora and fauna and, if so, which ones. Where changes, particularly at the planning stages, can be made however, an appreciation of the importance of the environment can help to ensure that the effects on the environment are reduced, strengthening the capacity of the region to recover from conflict. For example, placing camps further away from forests would be a simple change that would help avoid environmental degradation. Similarly, providing fuel-efficient stoves to those in camps or charcoal from other sites where it can be sustainably sourced can reduce the pressures on forestry, while also having positive impacts on public health by reducing fume inhalation. In contrast, if environmental degradation does take place as a result of displacement, migration and internally displaced person camps, it undermines the strength and capacity of the region to recover from conflict, which risks multiplying the threats in the post-war recovery phase and causing a return to conflict.

Conclusion

The DRC offers an excellent case study for examining the relationship between the living environment and conflict. This chapter has illustrated that while conflict can have devastating impacts on the living environment, it is not necessarily wholly negative as might be expected because insecurity can serve as a means of protection by preventing intensive exploitation – as demonstrated by the low deforestation level in certain regions of the DRC. It is important to remember, however, that these benefits are an unintended consequence; they do not stem from 'conservation' as such. As such, the prevailing relationships are ones in which the living environment can spur, support and perpetuate conflict, as demonstrated with examples of the living environment contributing to conflict through financing rebel groups and government forces (notwithstanding the danger of oversimplifying the poaching-financing dynamic or assuming that rebel forces are the only ones involved, as evidenced by the case of the LRA hunting for ivory). Finally, this chapter has offered an example of the impact of post-war recovery on the living environment, including both the threats posed by improved security and development in the absence of effective governance to limit environmental exploitation, as well as the role that conservation efforts can have in improving the post-war recovery process to simultaneously improve security and protect the environment.

Natural resources, such as diamonds and coltan, have tended to receive greater focus as factors in the conflict in the DRC, and indeed elsewhere, which has often led to the other aspects of the environment being overlooked. Consequently, there is a need to better differentiate and distinguish the ways in which the living environment can be both positively and negatively affected by conflict, as well as the mechanisms by which post-war recovery efforts can help ensure enduring peace and conservation. In sum, the living environment plays a significant, though often overlooked, role in the conflict in the DRC, and requires further study both to see how it can be utilised to improve security and ensure that if peace is achieved in the region, it does not contribute to or create conditions for environmental degradation that could, in turn, create conditions for the return to war.

References

Agger, K. and Hutson, J. 2013. Kony's ivory: how elephant poaching in Congo helps support the Lord's Resistance Army. *Enough Project.org*, 3 June. Available at: http://www.enoughproject.org/reports/konys-ivory-how-elephant-poaching-congo-helps-support-lords-resistance-army. Accessed 14 October 2014.

Ali, S.H. (ed.) 2007. *Peace Parks: Conservation and Conflict Resolution: Global Environmental Accord: Strategies for Institutional Innovation*. Cambridge, MA, and London: The MIT Press.

Baker, M., Clausen, R., Kanaan, R., N'Goma, M., Roule, T. and Thomson, J. 2003. *Conflict Timber: Dimensions of the Problem in Asia and Africa*, Volume 3. Burlington, VT: ARD, Inc.

Beyers, R.L., Hart, J.A., Sinclair, A.R.E., Grossmann, F., Klinkenberg, B. and Dino, S. 2011. Resource wars and conflict ivory: the impact of civil conflict on elephants in the Democratic Republic of Congo – The Case of the Okapi Reserve. *PLoS ONE* 6(11): e27129. doi: 10.1371/journal.pone.0027129.

Blundell, A.G. and Christie, T. 2007. Liberia: securing the peace through parks. In S.H. Ali (ed.), *Peace Parks: Conservation and Conflict Resolution: Global Environmental Accord: Strategies for Institutional Innovation*. Cambridge, MA, and London: The MIT Press, 227–38.

Brauer, J. 2009. *War and Nature: The Environmental Consequences of War in a Globalized World*. Plymouth, UK: AltaMira Press.

Briggs, C.M. 2012. Climate security, risk assessment and military planning. *International Affairs* 88(5): 1049–64.

Brink, P. ten, Mazza, L., Badura, T., Kettunen, M. and Withana, S. 2012. *Nature and its Role in the Transition to a Green Economy*. Available at: TEEBweb. org. Accessed 4 August 2014.

Brisman, A. and South, N. 2013. Resource wealth, power, crime, and conflict. In R. Walters, D.S. Westerhuis and T. Wyatt (eds), *Emerging Issues in Green Criminology: Exploring Power, Justice and Harm*. London: Palgrave Macmillan, 57–71.

Brown, O., Hammill, A. and McLeman, R. 2007. Climate change as the 'new' security threat: implications for Africa. *International Affairs* 83(6): 1141–54

Carius, A. 2006. *Environmental Cooperation as an Instrument of Crisis Prevention and Peacebuilding: Conditions for Success and Constraints*, Berlin: Adelphi Consult.

Clark, R.D. 2013. The control of conflict minerals in Africa and a preliminary assessment of the Dodd-Frank Wall Street reform and consumer act. In N. South and A. Brisman (eds), *Routledge International Handbook of Green Criminology*. London and New York: Routledge, 214–29.

Conca, K. and Dabelko, G. (eds) 2002. *Environmental Peacemaking*. Baltimore, MD: The Johns Hopkins University Press.

Gettleman, J. 2012. Rangers in isolated Central Africa uncover grim cost of protecting wildlife. *New York Times* [online]. Available at: http://www.nytimes.com/2013/01/01/world/africa/central-africas-wildlife-rangers-face-deadly risks.html?ref=ivory. Accessed 10 December 2013.

Gray, M. and Kalpers, J. 2005. Ranger based monitoring in the Virunga-Bwindi region of East-Central Africa: a simple data collection tool for park management. *Biodiversity Conservation* 14: 2723–41.

Hart J. 2009. *How Many Elephants are Left in D.R. Congo*? Available at: http://www.bonoboincongo.com/2009/02/01/how-many-elephants-are-left-in-dr-congo/. Accessed 12 December 2013.

IGCP 2012. *Back to the Business of Mountain Gorilla Monitoring*. Available at: http://www.igcp.org/back-to-the-business-of-mountain-gorilla-monitoring/. Accessed 6 December 2012.

IRIN 2009. *DRC: Charcoal Profits Fuel War in East*. Available at: http://www.irinnews.org/Report.aspx?ReportId=85462. Accessed 10 December 2013.

Juniper, T. 2013. *What Has Nature Ever Done For Us: How Money Really Does Grow on Trees*. London: Profile Books.

Lovgren, S. 2007. *Congo Gorilla Killings Fueled by Illegal Charcoal Trade*. Available at: http://news.nationalgeographic.com/news/2007/08/070816-gorillas-congo.html. Accessed 6 December 2013.

Martin, A., Rutagarama, E., Gray, M., Kayitare, A. and Chhotray, V. 2009. *Transboundary Natural Resource Management in the Greater Virunga: Lessons Learned from Regional Approaches to Conservation Facilitated by the International Gorilla Conservation Programme*. Rwanda: International Gorilla Conservation Programme Lessons Learned Initiative.

McNeely, J.A. 2000. War and biodiversity: an assessment of impacts. In J.E. Austin and C.E. Bruch (eds), *The Environmental Consequences of War*. Cambridge: Cambridge University Press, 264–96.

McNeely, J.A. 2002. Overview A – biodiversity, conflict and tropical forests. In R. Matthew, M. Halle and J. Switzer (eds), *Conserving the Peace: Resources, Livelihoods and Security*. Winnipeg: International Institute for Sustainable Development, 29–56.

Menondji, M.H.A. 2013. *Problematic Peacekeeping in the DRC: From MONUC to MONUSCO*. Available at: http://thinkafricapress.com/drc/problematic-peacekeeping-drc-monuc-monusco. Accessed 17 April 2013.

Milburn, R. 2012. Mainstreaming the environment into postwar recovery: the case for 'Ecological Development'. *International Affairs* 88(5): 1083–100.

Millennium Ecosystem Assessment 2005. Ecosystems and human well-being: synthesis. In A. Houdret and C. Roettger (eds), *Transboundary Natural Resource Cooperation in the Democratic Republic of Congo: Entry Points for Improving Regional Relations*. Berlin: Adelphi Consult, 20.

Mrema, E.M., Bruch, C. and Diamond, J. 2009. *Protecting the Environment during Armed Conflict: An Inventory and Analysis of International Law*. Nairobi: United Nations Environment Programme.

Nellemann, C., Redmond, I. and Refisch, J. (eds) 2010. *The Last Stand of the Gorilla: Environmental Crime and Conflict in the Congo Basin*. A Rapid Response Assessment. United Nations Environment Programme, GRID-Arendal. Available at: www. grida.no. Accessed 7 January 2015.

Prunier, G. 2009. *From Genocide to Continental War: The Congolese Conflict and the Crisis of Contemporary Africa*. London: HURST Publishers.

Rainer, H., Asuma, S., Gray, M., Kalpers, J., Kayitare, A., Rutagarama, E., Sivha, M. and Lanjouw, A. 2003. Regional conservation in the Virunga-Bwindi region. *Journal of Sustainable Forestry* 17(1): 189–204.

Rosen, G.E. and Smith, K.F. 2010. Summarising the evidence on the international trade in illegal wildlife. *Ecohealth* 7: 24–32.

Seyler, T.R., Thomas, D., Mwanza, N. and Mpoyi, A. 2010. *Democratic Republic of Congo: Biodiversity and Tropical Forestry Assessment (118/119) Final Report*. Available at: http://pdf.usaid.gov/pdf_docs/PNADS946.pdf. Accessed 9 December 2013.

Shambaugh, J., Oglethorpe, J. and Ham, R. (with contributions from Tognetti, S.) 2001. *The Trampled Grass: Mitigating the Impacts of Armed Conflict on the Environment*. Washington, D.C.: Biodiversity Support Program.

South, N. and Brisman, A. 2013. Critical green criminology, environmental rights and crimes of exploitation. In S. Winlow and R. Atkinson (eds), *New Directions in Crime and Deviance*. London: Routledge, 99–110.

Stearns, J. 2011. *Dancing in the Glory of Monsters: The Collapse of the Congo and the Great War of Africa*. New York: Public Affairs.

Titeca, K. 2013. *Ivory beyond the LRA: Why a Broader Focus is Needed in Studying Poaching*, African Arguments Online. Available at: http://africanarguments. org/2013/09/17/ivory-beyond-the-lra-why-a-broader-focus-is-needed-in-studying-poaching-by-kristof-titeca/. Accessed 9 December 2013.

Tull, D.M. 2009. Peacekeeping in the Democratic Republic of Congo: waging peace and fighting war. *International Peacekeeping* 16(2): 215–30.

UNEP 2011. *The Democratic Republic of the Congo Post-Conflict Environmental Assessment Synthesis for Policy Makers*. Nairobi: United Nations Environment Programme.

UNEP 2012. *Greening the Blue Helmets: Environment, Natural Resources and UN Peacekeeping Operations*. Nairobi: United Nations Environment Programme.

Vogel, C. 2013. *Congo: Why UN Peacekeepers Have a Credibility Problem*. Available at: http://www.theguardian.com/world/2013/aug/30/congo-un-peacekeepers-problem. Accessed 17 April 2013.

Wyatt, T. 2013. From the Cardamom Mountains of Southwest Cambodia to the forests of the world: an exploration of the illegal charcoal trade. *International Journal of Comparative and Applied Criminal Justice* 37(1): 1–15.

Chapter 4

Land Uses and Conflict in Colombia

David Rodríguez Goyes

Introduction[1]

Between 1 January 1958 and 31 December 2012 220,000 people were killed in Colombia as a result of internal armed conflict. Of these victims, 81.5 per cent have been civilians; the rest have been combatants. Since then, one out of every three violent deaths in the country has been related to continuing internal armed conflict. During this time, 5,700,000 people have been displaced by force (GMH 2013). The main actors involved are guerrilla groups (with its different branches), paramilitary groups, and the Colombian Army.

One paramount date in this conflict was 26 August 2012 when the FARC-EP (Revolutionary Armed Forces of Colombia), one of the main guerrilla branches, and the Colombian government, signed a conflict termination agreement. This agreement is not a peace treaty between both parties, but a starting point to discuss the conditions upon which the end of hostilities will be agreed and signed on. It consists of six points, which will be discussed below – two of which directly deal with land uses. In order to be supplied with inputs and proposals from citizen participation, the negotiating parties asked the United Nations and the National University of Colombia to arrange forums with representatives from all over the country to discuss the topics on the agreement. Since December 2012, forums have been taking place in Bogotá and San José del Guaviare in which 4244 communitarian and social representatives from all over the country have participated (PNUD 2012, 2013a, 2013b, 2013c).

This chapter intends to make use of the ideas expressed during these forums by the people directly involved in the conflict to broaden the understanding of

---

1   Because the main goal of this chapter is to give voice to the people who have directly suffered internal Colombian violence, many of the events described herein have been simplified. Regrettably, due to space restrictions, many atrocities perpetrated by all armed forces in the conflict have been reduced to numbers. For the same reason, the role of other important armed forces in the country, such as the M-19 or the ELN are not described in this chapter. It is my hope that readers interested in learning more about the history of violence in Colombia will consult the references at the end of this chapter. My deepest gratitude goes to Eva Magdalena Stambol, who supported me through the process of writing this chapter, and to Hanneke Mol, who as generously as always, took the time needed to carefully read and comment on the first draft of this chapter.

issues of land access and uses from the perspectives of the participants. As the intention of this chapter is to give voice to the people who have directly suffered the violence, data will be analysed using grounded theory[2] as described by Strauss and Corbin (2012). The main issues, which the forum participants have identified, are land access, land uses, land redistribution policies, land reserve zones, agrarian development policies, agrarian infrastructure, social development in rural areas (health, education, shelter, and poverty eradication), funding for agrarian development, food security and illicit drug crops substitution policies.

This chapter will illustrate how the Colombian government has continually treated indigenous peoples, raizales,[3] afro-descendants, peasants and rural women as second-class citizens. For too long, governmental policies in Colombia have favoured international trade commitments over the needs of its population, especially with respect to access to land. This chapter addresses how this privileging of the market over the needs of the population has resulted in environmental and socially harmful activities, such as detrimental forms of mining, large-scale industrial agriculture with the use of transgenic seeds, and extensive and intensive animal husbandry. All the while, people in rural areas are trying to survive amidst the hard conditions brought by war, illegal trafficking activities and new *legal*, yet impoverishing, transnational economic activities.

This chapter illustrates how conflicts over land access, use and exploitation can result in environmental crime, as different ethnic groups in search of survival end up pursuing innovative – and often harmful – ways of subsisting, such as burning or cutting forests and jungles or illegally trading wildlife (Sollund 2013). Similarly, it will illustrate that in Colombia, many of the traditional issues studied by criminology, such as drug issues, gender violence, white-collar crimes, and repressive state systems, are associated with or arise from the conflicts around land.

Through the chapter, the green criminology framework will provide valuable tools to understand the varied sources of conflict in Colombia. Attention will be paid to 'the geographical scale of environmental harm' (White 2012) by considering the social and environmental consequences of Colombia's national policies and transnational corporate activities on rural communities and ecosystems. The concept of *eco crime* (Walters 2011) will be of importance in understanding that in Colombia most of the destructive activities against ecosystems, biodiversity and communities are not recognised as illegal or illicit judicial categories. Finally, the critique of the concept of *sustainable*

---

2   Grounded theory is a methodology for developing theory that is grounded in data systematically gathered and analysed. 'Theory evolves during actual research, and it does this through continuous interplay between analysis and data collection' (Strauss and Corbin 1994: 273). It is based upon the assumption that all human beings have their perspectives and interpretations of their own and other actors' actions. As such, we, as researchers, are required to learn of their interpretations and perspectives. (Strauss and Corbin 1994).

3   Aboriginal communities from San Andrés, Providencia and Santa Catalina islands.

development (Riise 2012) will be fundamental to denouncing the paradox in which private corporations show interest over traditional knowledge, thereby clearly recognising its value, while at the same time they diminish the value attributed to traditional knowledge of indigenous communities by imposing farming methods and foreign technologies based on the argument of seeking the development of these communities.

In order to accomplish such goals, the chapter will briefly summarise the events of the Colombian internal armed conflict, including an account of the source and methodology of the forums taking place in Colombia as part of the current peace negotiations between the guerrillas and the government. Special attention will be devoted to what citizens have expressed in these forums concerning environmental crime and social conflict.

Colombian Internal Armed Conflict

Colombians have lived a life filled with violence. From its independence day (20 July 1810) to the present, internal violent conflict has been one of the distinguishing characteristics of this country.

Early in its history, the conflict was about the governmental system (centralism versus federalism). This soon gave rise to an ideological conflict between the Conservative Party and the Liberal Party, which began in 1849 and is better known as the 'war of conservatism against liberalism'. While the Liberals struggled to achieve ideological freedom for all people, irrespective of class, the Conservatives fought for the defence of Catholic values and beliefs. While Ferrell, Hayward and Young (2012) argue that all conflicts are, at their roots, ideological, this conflict was explicitly so: the Conservative Party was unanimously gathered around Catholicism, denying any acceptable form of plurality or multiculturalism (Sixirei Paredes 2011).

From this conflict, the infamous 'War of the Thousand Days' emerged. The left-wing party was backed by the governments of Ecuador, Honduras, Nicaragua and Venezuela, while the right-wing party was explicitly supported by the governments of the United States and France. One hundred thousand people were killed from 1899 to 1902, making it one of the most devastating wars in Colombian history. Even though both parties signed a peace agreement in the aftermath of the war, violent political actions between the two parties continued for five more decades.

On 9 April 1948, the nature and form of war and conflict in Colombia changed. Jorge Eliecer Gaitán, leftist leader and presidential candidate, was assassinated. People from all over the country reacted to this political murder. A new wave of violence began and guerrilla groups emerged as a significant force. This event initiated the period known as *la violencia*, which began in 1948 and ended in 1957 with the signing of the National Front agreement (Offstein 2003).

The Guerrillas are Born

With the death of Liberal front-runner Jorge Eliecer Gaitán, the Conservative leader Laureano Gómez was elected president of Colombia in 1950. As a result, many disappointed Liberal followers lost faith in the legal system and some launched a guerrilla war – an example of what Merton (2002) refers to as 'innovative divergent behavior'. The Liberal followers wanted to achieve political recognition, but employed illegal means.

This new stage in the Colombian internal conflict was structurally different from all former conflicts. While earlier clashes were between political parties and the goal of its combatants was to acquire the power to rule the state, this new phase of conflict was characterised by the use of war as a means to transform economic, social and political relations within the country. In other words, war was viewed as a revolutionary tool. To maximise their chances of success, guerrilla groups based their activities in locations (1) that were far from the strategic power positions of the Conservative ruling group; (2) where the inhabitants agreed with the revolutionary mission; and (3) where land was available to provide food for long periods of time for large groups of armed men (Medina Gallego 2010).

Although the guerrilla groups were initially under the command of the Liberal Party, they slowly started to operate independently, tracing a new (military) agenda separate from the Liberal Party's operations in the political arena. Importantly, the guerrilla groups were composed of peasants who had spent their lives fighting for their lands. These peasants adopted goals that extended beyond acquiring political power; they aimed to transform the structural conditions of the country (Medina Gallego 2010).

While this was happening inland, in Bogotá, the capital of Colombia, the leaders of the Conservative Party were having their own internal fight. Laureano Gómez, who was president of Colombia at the time (and who served in office from 7 August 1950–5 November 1951), was being threatened by a conspiracy led by Gustavo Rojas Pinilla, General Commander of the army. Pinilla had been given the task by the right-wing party of strengthening the Conservative regime but once he succeeded at taking over the government, he deviated from the commands received, and attempted to establish his own party. He succeeded at taking over the government between 13 June 1953 and 10 May 1957, but his actions evidently annoyed the Conservative Party, as well as the private companies, which felt jeopardised by the prospect of an alliance between Rojas Pinilla and the workers. On 10 May 1957, Conservatives, Liberals, private companies, students, representatives from the church and communists joined forces to overthrow Rojas Pinilla. They succeeded and consequently, the National Front agreement was established. One of the provisions of this agreement was that power should alternate between the Conservative Party and the Liberal Party, whereby one party would lead the country for four years, followed by a four-year period of rule by the other party (Medina Gallego 2009).

The first president selected under the National Front agreement was the Liberal, Alfonso Lleras Camargo. Having identified that a main cause of rural violence was land distribution, he tried to implement a plan for agrarian reform. The end-goal of this effort was to abolish large estates and to distribute these lands to smallholder peasants. But due to corruption and limited funds, this transformation was not accomplished. The frustration caused by the failure of agrarian reform helped to increase the strength of guerrilla groups, who were able to increase their numbers with the recruitment of disillusioned peasants who had lost faith in government and the rule of law, and who had come to believe that armed revolution was the only way to achieve land redistribution (Offstein 2003). It is for this reason that one could state the guerrillas were *always* fighting over land.

The Armed Revolutionary Forces of Colombia (FARC-EP) at the Head of Guerrilla Movements

Although the FARC was formally created in 1966, its roots can be traced back to the National Front agreement and to the struggles initiated by the Communist Party for land redistribution in the 1930s. Many of the former members of the Communist Party again embraced armed revolution after having been disappointed by the failed agrarian reform promised by Laureano Gómez. After the death of Jorge Eliecer Gaitán, the Liberal Party and the Communist Party joined forces to create the Self-defense Agrarian Forces (Autodefensas Agrarias) in 1951, whose main goal was to fight against abuse of power by the state. These agrarian forces were the early Colombian guerrillas that later would divide into the many guerrilla branches that would come into existence.

During the Tenth Colombian Communist Party Congress of 1966, the first seeds of a distinctive guerrilla branch were planted. This was a time when the United States was deeply involved in the Vietnam War and strongly committed to fighting communism. Thus, at this Congress, the Communist Party identified the need to arrange a distinctive revolutionary force, first, as a means of building upon lessons learned to give a definitive shape to guerrilla groups; and second, because of the perceived urgency of being able to fight against the threat of increased US imperialism. The Communist Party intended to create a group whose mission would be to create the material conditions that would lead to socialism as a step on the way to communism. In May of the same year, these plans would take on their definite shape when, in the course of the Second Conference of the Guerrillas from the South, the FARC was created.

One of the primary objectives of this group was to achieve agrarian redistribution, which would benefit the peasants. While the goal was to abolish large estates and grant land to poor peasants, the FARC expressed the desire to protect indigenous territories and to respect the lands of peasants who had farmed their own fields. Some of the other goals were to expel foreign armed forces from the country, to achieve reallocation of the funds spent on war in order to strengthen investment in health and education, and to reduce taxes paid by citizens.

Throughout its history, the relationship between the FARC-EP and civilians has been inconsistent. At the FARC's inception, it was often the only authority in rural areas where the state was not present. Later on, the state tried to impose its authority on those regions and challenged the guerrillas. As a result, some civilians backed the guerrillas, while others aligned with the state. Communities have, at times, also expressed disapproval of the justice systems adopted and imposed by the FARC in the territories under its authority.

As time passed by, dissidence appeared within the FARC. In 1978, the People's Army (Ejército del Pueblo or EP) joined with the FARC, becoming the FARC-EP. Along with this added name came a stronger confrontation strategy: the group would now use force for offensive, rather than just defensive, purposes. To do so, they sought to increase the number of combatants to 32,000 and to fight on 80 different fronts (including urban areas). But this caused some of the different sections of the guerrillas to accuse the Central Command of losing its foundational ideology and of wasting its monetary resources (Centro-Nacional-de-Memoria-Histórica 2013).

And Then the Paramilitaries

A new armed group joined the conflict in 1978: paramilitaries created by the government to squelch social and political protest.[4] While the government also attempted to suppress dissent by criminalising revolutionary political activities, the harshest means were through the creation of paramilitaries at the service of the government. These paramilitaries, however, did not operate within the law. Rather, they forcefully displaced peasants from their lands, engaged in drug trafficking, murdered leftists and social leaders, and undertook other activities consistent with their anti-communist ideals (Medina Gallego 2009).

Because the guerrillas were growing stronger, the government was desperate to resist them and, in the name of 'national security', rather than 'national defence', granted wide latitude to the paramilitaries. The use of exceptions to the law was another device intended to fight against the guerrillas. A 1968 law broadened the number of people who could possess self-defence weapons (formerly only permitted for the army) and approved the formation of self-defence militias. This relaxation of law was largely taken advantage of by the increasingly fearful and insecure Colombian oligarchy (Leal Buitrago 2011).

Drug trafficking was another phenomenon that contributed significantly to the formation and fortifying of the paramilitary forces. Drug trafficking cartels needed to be able to count on paramilitary structures to protect their commercial activities. In Colombia, the cartels of Medellín (of Pablo Escobar and Gonzalo Rodríguez Gacha) and Cali (of the Rodríguez Orejuela brothers) were directing what would come to constitute the strongest paramilitary groups. Carlos Castaño and Diego

---

4   The story of the paramilitaries is more complex than what I am able to describe here. For a further description and analysis see Ballvé (2012) and Grajales (2013).

Murillo, who had been in command of the cartel of Medellin army, feared that their former employers might soon have them killed (as had happened with others in similar positions) and decided to join forces and fight back.[5] After Pablo Escobar was killed, these paramilitary forces remained active in drug trafficking and in protecting the large landowners (Adams 2011).

Continued Efforts to Resolve the Conflict

In 1998, the Colombian government led by President Andrés Pastrana Arango, settled peace talks with the FARC-EP, commanded by Manuel Marulanda Velez. The latter required the demilitarisation of five Colombian municipalities. The peace talks were designated 'Caguán peace talks', after the municipality of San Vicente del Caguán in which they commenced. The government recognised the FARC-EP as a political party, but despite the demands from the guerrillas, civilians were not permitted to participate in these talks.

In January 1999, both parties resumed their peace negotiations. From November 2000 to January 2001, the dialogues were interrupted due to hostilities in other locations of the country, however, both parties agreed to continue to strive for a peace agreement. Sadly, on February 2002, President Pastrana decided to unilaterally end the peace talks, stating that the guerrillas were taking advantage of the armistice in the five municipalities to build infrastructure for drug trafficking. All hopes of resuming the peace efforts, which had developed over the previous three years (1999–2002), evaporated with the presidential election of Álvaro Uribe Vélez in 2002. Declaring a war on terrorism (following USA discourse after events on 11 September), Álvaro Uribe Vélez closed the door on new peace talks.

Somewhat incongruously, Álvaro Uribe Vélez did negotiate peace with the United Self-Defense Armies of Colombia (AUC), known to be the main paramilitary group in Colombia. As a result, the Peace and Justice Law was implemented in Colombia in 2005, which granted substantial benefits to paramilitary combatants who chose to demobilise. While the purported goal was to follow the truth, justice, reparation and guarantees of the non-recurrence frameworks of international war transition experiences (Uprimny Yepes, Saffon Sanín, Botero Marino, and Restrepo Saldarriaga 2006), the Peace and Justice Law provided that even though these combatants had committed atrocities, such as massacres and kidnappings, they would receive shorter sentences of five to eight years of imprisonment instead of the more than 40 years they could have received for these crimes. Although this law cannot be regarded as endorsing or condoning the atrocities committed by the paramilitary groups, in practice, the government backed a process in which truth was not achieved and the paramilitary groups were not dismantled (Uprimny Yepes 2011).

---

5   There is some speculation that they were supported in this by the United States' Drug Enforcement Administration (DEA).

The government asserted that the paramilitary groups were wiped out after the Peace and Justice Law. However, it has been proven that they are still operating under new names. Coined after the denomination *Bandas Criminales* (criminal gangs) used by the former Colombian president Álvaro Uribe Vélez, the United Self-Defense Armies of Colombia now operate under the generic name of BACRIM. These militias consist of roughly 9,000 combatants divided across 76 fronts, and are developing war operations in 25 of the 32 Colombian departments[6] (Reyes Quezada 2012).

All in all, both the peace process carried out from 1998 to 2001 between the government and the FARC-EP, and the peace agreement between the government and the AUC under the Peace and Justice Law of 2005, failed to lead to a change in the structural arrangement of the Colombian internal armed conflict. Six decades have now passed since Colombian guerrillas first took up arms and their original goals still have not been accomplished. Similarly, more than three decades have passed since paramilitary forces arrived on the scene and not only have they not been dismantled, but they keep taking advantage of the state's weaknesses to impose their rules and commit atrocities. New armed groups have entered the conflict, including both new guerrilla branches and new paramilitary groups. As stated in the Introduction to this chapter, 250,000 people have been killed in this period and 5,700,000 have been forcefully displaced. It can be expected that the dark figure of crime hide many others.

While these figures demonstrate the direct consequences of the internal armed conflict in Colombia, the country has also suffered a number of indirect material and cultural consequences. With respect to the former, institutional weaknesses have resulted in new injustices. For example, environmentally degrading mining activities carried out by foreign corporations have adversely affected peasants and indigenous populations (Toro Pérez 2012). In terms of cultural consequences, Colombia is nowadays suffering from what has been called a 'mafia culture', a product of the drug trafficking activities that have been the main fuel of the Colombian internal armed conflict. This mafia culture has stressed material luxury and ostentatious displays of wealth carry enormous social weight; as a result, 'easy money' is pursued, the execution of illegalities is taken as a sign of cleverness, and corruption within the government is accepted as a customary act (Mejía Quintana 2010).

A New Hope

From 23 February 2012 to 26 August 2012, delegates from the Colombian government and the FARC-EP met in Havana, Cuba, in order to engage in preliminary meetings that might move toward the signing of a general agreement for ending the conflict and the building of peace. This new process included

---

6   Colombia is a unitary republic formed by 32 departments. Departments are country subdivisions that are granted a certain degree of autonomy.

representatives of Norway and Cuba to help ensure the fairness and goodwill of both negotiating parties. As a result of their assistance, and as mentioned at the outset of this chapter, on 26 August 2012, a general agreement for ending the conflict and building a stable and long-standing peace was signed. This agreement included a plan for the discussion of six main topics that are regarded as the core issues to be dealt with in Colombia in order to achieve enduring peace:

1. comprehensive agrarian policy reform
2. political participation
3. conflict termination
4. solution to the problem of illicit drugs
5. victims reparation
6. implementation, verification, and popular countersignature of the final agreement reached by the parties.

The agreement stated as well that in order to guarantee the maximum participation of Colombian citizens in the dialogues, a procedure would be established whereby citizens could submit their proposals and suggestions regarding any of the discussion items. The method chosen to accomplish this goal was a formula somewhat similar to the 'consensus conferences' (Fischer 2003).[7] However, the structure of the system used in Colombia differed from the consensus conferences technique, in that there was no attempt to secure consensus. In it, representatives from all regions, communities, ethnicities, social and economic classes, productive sectors and political convictions within Colombia were called to take part in the event. They were chosen based on their knowledge of the specific topic to be discussed and for their ability to represent their background or provenance.

From late August 2012 until January 2013, the peace dialogue called for four different forums. All of these forums were conducted according to the terms

---

7   Developed by the Danish Board of Technology, the consensus conference is a method with the goal of integrating 'expert knowledge' with 'common knowledge' from the widest range of citizens possible (i.e., from citizens from different geographic regions and different social, economic and political groups). Such a process stimulates public discussion of the matters at stake and helps ensure that decision-makers at the negotiating table are provided with the most comprehensive information possible. This method usually begins by selecting participants who are familiar with the matter to be discussed. Later, a steering committee further narrows the topic to be discussed and the rules of the discussion; the idea is that every participant has the flexibility and freedom to define the topic through his/her own approach. The official conference begins with a panel of experts presenting their scientific account of the discussion theme to the attendants of the conference, a step whose objective is to supply participants with ideas for the subsequent debate. The participants are then encouraged to give their own opinions regarding the subject of interest. Based on the experts' accounts and participants' statements, a report is prepared, which reflects the range of views, concerns and interests expressed at the conference. Finally, this report is presented to the attendants and sent to the decision-makers.

defined by the peace dialogue. In total, these forums were attended by 4,244 people from 19 community-based organisations. Those attending represented peasants' organisations, indigenous peoples' organisations, women's organisations, victims' organisations, raizales organisations, youth organisations, afrodescendientes' organisations,[8] human rights activists, gay communities, churches, scholars, environmental activists, labour unions, private entrepreneurs, peace organisations, political parties, universities, community associations and experts on drug issues.

Panels of experts gave speeches to help start the debates that would take place over the following days. Subsequently, people were divided into groups of roughly 60 participants. In these groups, the participants expressed their opinions regarding the theme of the forum, which were recorded by rapporteurs, and at the end of the session, a report based on their statements was read to them and they were presented with the opportunity to amend the report. Afterwards, four of these reports were combined by the rapporteurs, and on the next day, a unified report was presented to the participants in all four groups. As with the previous stage, participants were given the opportunity to correct mistakes in the document. Finally, rapporteurs produced a unified report that was presented on the last day of the conference to all of the participants. The final document gathered all of the ideas presented during the respective forums. As noted above, no consensus was sought in that conflicting statements were included in the final report. The report was then sent to the dialogue table in Havana so that the representatives of the government and of the FARC-EP could use it as a basis for their negotiations.

What Do the People Who Have Suffered the War Have to Say?

During the forums, participants were at liberty to discuss any issues they regarded as important concerning the first, second and fourth categories listed above: comprehensive agrarian policy reform; political participation; and the solution to the illicit drugs problem. During the discussions, many participants expressed their concerns and proposed solutions. Disputes about land access and land use, however, were identified by the participants as the most important issues to be solved before a stable and long-standing peace could be reached in Colombia.

Land Access

The story told by coca growers of San José del Guaviare is a good example of how many conflicts in Colombia have stemmed from issues pertaining to land access. According to the coca growers, by the 1960s, large inequalities in access to land existed in the country. As a response to this, the government sent landless people to colonise the jungle. Upon their arrival, they cut trees and burned the jungle to

---

8　Communities formed by African descendants. In Colombia, they are mainly living in the Caribbean and Pacific coasts.

create land on which to grow crops. This was insufficient, however, given that the state did not provide means of transportation of the necessary infrastructure in order for them to market and sell their produce. When drug lords appeared and offered them large sums of money to grow coca, many accepted because it was a guaranteed source of income. Soon, guerrillas, paramilitaries and corrupt state agents all wanted a part of this lucrative business. These armed groups began fighting over control of the coca plantations, leading to the deaths and murders of many coca growers. Later, US-financed aerial fumigation efforts contaminated the land, and the growers and their families grew sick from the toxic effects of the spraying (see del Olmo 1998; Sanchez-Garzoli and Schaffer 2012).

Such an example demonstrates the linkages between land access and armed conflict in Colombia. Coca growers and other forum participants claimed that land access ensures their fundamental right of existence, and that violent conflict will continue until this issue is solved. Indeed, all of the forum participants identified agrarian reform as a *sine qua non* requisite for achieving peace. In addition, all the participants shared the belief that the amount of private property should be limited, that the land controlled or owned by someone who is not using the land effectively should be redistributed and that measures should be taken in order to prevent big estates from being owned by foreigners. Participants agreed that the process of land redistribution should be conducted based on each group's needs, demands, beliefs and knowledge, along with mechanisms for a harmonious multicultural coexistence.

During the forums, each of the represented cultural groups stated their claims regarding land access. Indigenous people and afro-descendants expressed a desire to be able to return to the lands from which they were originally expelled. Rural women asked for gender quotas to enable access to high quality lands. The *raizales* (aboriginal populations from the San Andrés and Providencia islands) demanded the return of lands that they considered were stolen for purposes of promoting tourism. Peasants requested that they be provided with productive lands, as well as a guarantee that they would not be driven away from them. The peasants also suggested changes to the ways in which property could be attained and, more specifically, recommended that peasant communities, indigenous communities and afro-descendant communities manage their lands as collective, rather than private, properties. Peasants pointed to the Peasant Enterprise Zones (PEZ), as a model for what they would like this new administration of property to be. PEZ are an arrangement where the communities themselves are in charge of agricultural activities, commercialisation activities and environmental protection.

Participants revealed at the forums that all along their history, the inequity in land access and the resulting struggles of the impoverished communities in order to secure land, has created conflicts among them and occasionally led to environmental harms as when the landless people seek to 'colonise' new lands in search of the means for their survival and end up deforesting and abusing nature. This vicious cycle born out of inequity is still going on and an example of it is the dispute over the natural reserves. The indigenous people claim that they are the only ones that should have access to the nature parks given that, according to their cosmology, they are the ones best suited to protect Mother Nature (by them entitled *Pacha Mama*). At the same time, the peasants keep requesting access to nature parks, because these areas are fertile and still without a private owner. It is not that peasants are unaware of the environmental impact that their farming activities might bring about. But their eco-philosophical orientation to the land is much more anthropocentric than that of the indigenous people (see White 2013). The peasants request arable land, and have threatened that if they are not granted such land, they will move to natural parks anyway.

Land Uses

Peasants associations assert that conflict in Colombia has not only resulted in loss of human life, but various environmental harms. As an example, they point to Fuquene Lagoon (one of the most important Colombian lagoons) whose areas have been reduced by more than 60 per cent due to invasive destruction by landowners. In addition, peasants find it somewhat hypocritical that peace negotiations are being held at the same time that neoliberal politics that degrade the environment are being implemented and political dissent is being violently repressed. Therefore, land *use* – how land is used or not used – is as much a concern and cause of harm as land *access*.

Afro-descendants, indigenous peoples and peasants demand that lands be used 'according to their nature' – that is to say, they demand that arable land be used for agriculture activities in order to nurture and sustain Colombian people, rather than in intensive and unsustainable ways, such as for mining, extensive animal husbandry, industrial farming, or tourism. At the core of the issue is the forum participants' critique of Colombian modes of production. Peasants denounce the capitalistic prioritisation of the health of the market over the lives of individual people and communities. They also accuse this system of allowing – and, indeed, facilitating – transnational biopiracy of Colombia's natural richness. For them, this system, in which production for export purposes is the primary goal, destroys communities' associativity and their cultural practices. Afro-descendants, indigenous peoples and peasants accuse the government of criminalising cultural and historical agricultural practices and confiscating their crops. For them, this demonstrates that the government is more interested in protecting the interests of multinational corporations than the needs of its own population. Given that this mode of production has failed to sustain the Colombian people, the peasants have demanded that decision-makers consider the realities of life in rural areas and the impacts that various national policies have had over the local economies – and that when decision-makers contemplate potential policies, they take into consideration the effects (or possible effects) of policies on rural areas and local economies. They also make a call for a renegotiation of free trade agreements in order for local production to be prioritised over foreign interests.

Indigenous populations, afro-descendants, peasants' and women's associations have identified megaprojects as particularly harmful. For them, agro-industrial megaprojects and mining megaprojects harm the environment, do not improve living conditions and undermine national sovereignty. These opponents note that when megaprojects are proposed, they are advertised and promoted as an economic stimulus – a means of improving the material conditions of local communities. What they neglect to reveal, however, is that these projects are accompanied by a wide range of environmental harms and that the profits from these projects go to foreign corporations, rather than being reinvested in the local communities. For this reason, indigenous populations, afro-descendants, and peasants' and women's associations argue that the communities should have the power to make decisions regarding the implementation of any megaproject.

Indigenous populations, afro-descendants, and peasants' and women's associations are particularly concerned about mining activities, which they denounce as undermining the peasants' economy, threatening their subsistence, damaging the environment and eroding Colombian social fabric. They voice concern about trading agricultural use of land for mining and demand that mining activities should be undertaken not only with regard to soil physiognomies, but to the dignity, rights and sovereignty of the populations of the areas where the mining is to occur.

Indigenous populations, afro-descendants, and peasants' and women's associations also reject extensive and intensive animal husbandry and industrial agricultural activities. In particular, they stress the need to protect the economy of local Colombian communities and the importance of promoting the national production of foods and its independence from the international markets. To this end, indigenous populations, afro-descendants, and peasants' and women's associations argue that local communities should be in charge of agricultural activities that use native seeds and farm in ecologically responsible ways, rather than turning over agricultural operations to multinational corporations, like Monsanto, that implement environmentally degrading agro-industrial processes.

The issue of 'crops for illicit use' is another activity identified as a deeply problematic land use issue.[9] Drug lords have displaced indigenous peoples, afro-descendants and peasants from their lands in order to grow 'crops for illicit use' – a phenomenon that, as noted earlier in this chapter, has led to the growth of paramilitary groups. The ensuing struggles over control of the drug trade have resulted in increased violent conflict, as many of the armed groups are sustained by the money that comes from drug trafficking.

What peasants, indigenous populations and afro-descendants condemn is not only the cultivation of 'crops for illicit use' but the governmental response. They

---

9   Participants at the forums insist that 'crops for illicit use' is a more appropriate term than 'the problem of illicit drugs'. For them, coca crops are sacred and beneficial, rather than problematic. What is 'illicit' is the use of coca for cocaine, not the coca as a crop. A common slogan among partakers was 'coca is not cocaine'.

claim that the government fails to recognise that coca is different from cocaine and that coca or the poppy crops can be used for cosmetic, medicinal, nutritional and religious purposes. Criminalising these crops as a whole, then, means criminalising these communities' culture, beliefs and identity. Prosecuting coca growers makes them scapegoats for a problem caused by drug lords, armed groups and corrupt state agents, who receive the economic benefits of the drug trade and threaten the farmers.

As noted above, all of the communities and their representatives have spoken out against glyphosate fumigations used to wipe out coca crops on the grounds that this means of eradication destroys life, poisoning flora and fauna. Such eradication through fumigation is also perceived by the afro-descendant communities as a direct attack because for them, the jungle is their 'pharmacy', and by destroying it in the process of fumigating coca crops, their right to health is being denied. Thus, the communities argue that manual eradication is the only acceptable method.

Finally, indigenous populations, afro-descendants, and peasants' and women's associations reject the presence of armed groups on their lands and demand an effective and real disarmament of paramilitary groups. Moreover, they question whether a military presence in rural areas is intended to protect the civilian population or to defend megaprojects of multinational corporations that are exploiting and looting the Colombian natural richness. Thus, for them, rural areas must be demilitarised in order for enduring peace to take hold. Similarly, indigenous populations request that in order to respect these groups' right to self-determination the removal of 'crops for illicit use' and substitution by legal ones should be carried out by the communities themselves, not by military forces.

What the People Perceive as Solutions to Their Conflicts

It is important to recognise that not all indigenous people, afro-descendants, raizales and peasant communities agree on what might be the proper solutions to the concerns expressed in the previous section. What one community or interest may consider a viable solution to its problems may not be appropriate or viable to another group or in another context. That said, many indigenous people, afro-descendants, raizales and peasants share many similar concerns, demands and hopes, all arising from their life experiences.

One central demand is to defend their right to food sovereignty. For them, this can be achieved only by considering who is cultivating, what is being planted, how it is being farmed, how much is being harvested and for whom food is being produced. As such, they demand their right to define for themselves the modes in which they produce food, the protection of their native cuisine, protection for their native seeds and the rejection of transgenic seeds seen as a source of profit for multinational corporations, but a cause of impoverishment for the communities and health problems for their populations.

For these communities, rural development should not be imposed on local communities from outside sources that ignore their interests, needs and cultural backgrounds, but should emanate from a process of dialogue. Indigenous people, afro-descendants, raizales and peasant communities are interested only in development that truly improves their (respective) quality of life and that recognises their cultural and environmental characteristics. To achieve such a goal, the traditional knowledge of each community should be honoured and used for the benefits of each respective community. This includes respecting communities' worldviews and permitting them to decide which new technologies to implement and which traditional means or mechanisms to maintain. For example, even when more efficient methods for obtaining water are available, the raizales have defended their traditional ways.

All of the communities taking part in the forums have requested subsidies from the state or easy access to loans. They have also stated that these funds should be used as the communities see fit rather than as dictated by the banks or the government and that the conditions of the loans should be such that default does not result in the immediate loss of small landowners' property to the banks. Peasants have also requested that the money currently being used in war and forced eradication be invested in rural development, and have proposed higher taxes should be imposed on larger estate owners. Indigenous peoples, afro-descendants and aborigines state that state subsidies should not be granted to large landowners to the exclusion of poor communities.

In order for their economies to be sustainable, indigenous people, afro-descendants, raizales and peasant communities have requested infrastructure improvements, such as transportation corridors and collection centres, in order to be able to meet market demand for their agriculture and produce. They have also stressed that such infrastructure improvements be implemented through a process of dialogue with the affected communities in order to avoid harmful impositions. For some of them, an undesirable example of infrastructural imposition is the *Initiative for the Integration of Regional Infrastructure in South America* (IIRSA), as it is seen to destroy the social fabric of the communities. IIRSA has as objective to promote regional connectivity by building infrastructure networks for physical integration progress. However, for the communities, the highways built through this project had a negative impact on their social dynamics by confronting them with entrepreneurs looking to establish business-operating bases within their territories, and who, at the same time, brought market logics in conflict with their traditional practices.

Finally, indigenous people, afro-descendants, raizales and peasant communities have emphasised the importance of environmental sustainability, including the protection of water sources and the preservation of fragile ecosystems, jungles and hydric zones. Admittedly, the different communities possess different environmental perspectives. While some have underscored the importance of environmental protection in order to defend the rights of future generations, others insist on defending nature for its intrinsic value. Regardless of the different eco-philosophies possessed by the different groups, all of them agree that the government is being too lenient with multinational corporations and that it is allowing a commitment to international trade agreements to take precedence over what should be a greater commitment to environmental protection.

Conclusion: The Need for New Tools to Pursue Peace

While harmful state activities that have led to environmental and social harm may be fruitfully examined through the state crime frameworks offered by Morrison (2006), Tombs and Hillyard (2004), and Ward (2004) among others, it is imperative that we not neglect the knowledge expressed by the people during the forums in order to get closer to peace. This proposition takes its inspiration from Ruggiero (2013), who has demonstrated that critical criminology's concepts are 'not a mad invention of some lunatic left-wingers', but ideas present throughout the history of Western thought. The same is true for the green criminology framework: it is not an invention of young, idealistic tree-huggers, but a perspective reflective of the orientation of long-standing communities who have relied on their 'traditional knowledge'[10] to live harmoniously with nature for centuries. Multinational corporations attempt to derive financial profits by exploiting the knowledge of ancestral communities (Barreda 2002; Carlsen 2003; Delgado Ramos 2001). By contrast, it is the ethical duty of green criminology to learn from this same knowledge in order to strengthen its defence of the Earth and to protect the integrity of these communities. A critical green criminology framework can help to move forward such a work by giving voice to the people commonly silenced and hearing what they have to say about environmental harms.

References

Adams, D. 2011. Vínculos entre paramilitares y drogas: antes y después de la desmovilización. In E.M. Restrepo and B. Bagley (eds), *La desmovilización de los paramilitares en Colombia. Entre el escepticismo y la esperanza.* Bogotá Universidad de los Andes, 69–87.

Ballvé, T. 2012. Everyday state formation: territory, decentralization, and the narco landgrab in Colombia. *Environment and Planning D: Society and Space* 30: 603–22.

Barreda, A. 2002. Biopiratería, bioprospección y resistencia: cuatro casos en méxico. *El Cotidiano* 18(110): 119–44.

---

10   Following Harding (1993), Swazo (2005) and Beltrán Barrera (2011), I disagree with the use of the term 'traditional knowledge', and consider it a way of discrediting the wisdom of aboriginal communities by suggesting that it is somehow 'second-rate knowledge'.

Beltrán Barrera, Y.J. 2011. *Colombia entre dos mundos: Un acercamiento a la relación entre investigadores de la biodiversidad y las comunidades*. (Magister en Biociencias y Derecho) Universidad Nacional de Colombia, Bogotá.

Carlsen, L. 2003. La Batalla por el Frijol amarillo: Un caso de Biopiratería en la frontera. In L. Carlsen, T. Wise and H. Salazar (eds), *Enfrentando la Globalización, Respuestas sociales a la integración económica de México*. Ciudad de México: Miguel Ángel Purrua, UAZ, Global Development and Environment Institute Tuts University, Red Mexicana de Acción Frente al Libre Comercio, 97–117.

Centro-Nacional-de-Memoria-Histórica. 2013. *Guerrilla y Población Civil. Trayectoria de las FARC 1949–2013*. Bogotá: Imprenta Nacional.

Delgado Ramos, G.C. 2001. La Biopiratería y la propiedad intelectual como fundamento del desarrollo biotecnológico. *Problemas del Desarrollo* 32(126): 175–209.

Ferrell, J., Hayward, K. and Young, J. 2012. *Cultural Criminology: An Invitation*. London: Sage Publications.

Fischer, F. 2003. *Reframing Public Policy, Discursive Politics and Deliberative Practices*. New York: Oxford University Press.

Foucault, M. 1977. *Historia de la sexualidad, La voluntad de saber* (18th edn, vol. 1). Ciudad de México: Siglo Veintiuno editores.

Foucault, M. 1991. *La verdad y las formas jurídicas* (E. Lynch, trans., 2nd edn). Barcelona: Gedisa.

Foucault, M. 1998. *Vigilar y castigar, nacimiento de la prisión* (27th edn). México D.F.: Siglo veintiuno editores.

GMH. 2013. ¡BASTA YA! Colombia: Memorias de guerra y dignidad. Bogotá: Imprenta Nacional.

Grajales, J. 2013. State involvement, land grabbing and counter-insurgency in Colombia. *Development and Change* 42(2): 211–32.

Harding, S. 1993. Rethinking standpoint epistemology: what is 'strong objectivity'? In L. Alcoff and E. Potter (eds), *Feminist Epistemologies*. London: Routledge, 49–82.

Leal Buitrago, F. 2011. Militares y paramilitares en Colombia. In E.M. Restrepo and B. Bagley (eds), *La desmovilización de los paramilitares en Colombia. Entre el escepticismo y la esperanza*. Bogotá Universidad de los Andes, 43–68.

Medina Gallego, C. 2009. *FARC-EP. Notas para una historia política (1958–2008)*. Bogotá: Universidad Nacional de Colombia.

Medina Gallego, C. 2010. *FARC-EP Y ELN. Una historia política comparada (1958–2006)*. (Doctor en Historia), Universidad Nacional de Colombi, Bogotá. Available at: http://www.bdigital.unal.edu.co/3556/1/469029.2010.pdf (3556). Accessed 7 January 2015.

Mejía Quintana, O. 2010. Cultura política y cultura mafiosa en Colombia: Elementos epistemológicos para una aproximación socio-cultural. In O. Mejía Quintana (ed.), *¿Estado y cultura mafiosa en Colombia?* Bogotá: Universidad Nacional de Colombia, 13–76.

Merton, R.K. 2002. *Teoría y estructura sociales* (F. Torner and R. Borques, trans., 4th edn). México D.F.: Fondo de Cultura Económica.

Morrison, W. 2006. *Criminology, Civilisation and the New World Order*. New York: Routledge.

Offstein, N. 2003. An historial review and analysis of Colombian guerrilla movements. *Documentos CEDE* (21): 1–50.

del Olmo, R. 1998. The ecological impact of illicit drug cultivation and crop eradication programmes in Latin America. *Theoretical Criminology* 2(2): 269–78.

PNUD. 2012. Balance foro política de desarrollo agrario integral – Enfoque territorial. Available at: http://www.pnud.org.co/sitio.shtml?x=67369#. UqjtcvTuIik. Accessed 7 January 2015.

PNUD. 2013a. El foro sobre participación política. Available at: http://www.pnud. org.co/sitio.shtml?x=70942#.UqjrmfTuIik. Accessed 7 January 2015.

PNUD. 2013b. La Universidad Nacional de Colombia y la Organización de Naciones Unidas Informan. Available at: http://www.pnud.org.co/sitio. shtml?apc=i1 – – &x=73644#.Uqjt7PTuIik. Accessed 7 January 2015.

PNUD. 2013c. ONU y Universidad Nacional de Colombia concluyen foro sobre la solución al problema de las drogas ilícitas en San José del Guaviare. Available at: http://www.pnud.org.co/sitio.shtml?apc=b-a-1 – &x=73726#.UqjtqPTuIik. Accessed 7 January 2015.

Reyes Quezada, L.F. 2012. *El desmonte parcial de las AUC y la reconfiguración del fenómeno paramilitar*. (Magister en Sociología), Universidad Nacional de Colombia, Bogotá. Available at: http://www.bdigital.unal.edu.co/7908/ (7908). Accessed 7 January 2015.

Riise, I.H. 2012. Natural exploitation: the shaping of the human–animal relationship through concepts and statements. In R. Ellefsen, R. Sollund and G. Larsen (eds), *Eco-Global Crimes, Contemporary Problems and Future Challenges*. Farnham: Ashgate, 133–56.

Ruggiero, V. 2013. Critical criminology, power and systemic conflicts. *European Group for the Study of Deviance and Social Control Newsletter*, 22–4. Available at: http://www.europeangroup.org/links/. Accessed 7 January 2015.

Sanchez-Garzoli, G. and Schaffer, A. 2012. Ineffective U.S. fumigation policy adversely affects Afro-Colombians, *WOLA*. Available at: http://www.wola. org/commentary/ineffective_us_fumigation_policy_adversely_affects_afro_ colombians. Accessed 7 January 2015.

Sixirei Paredes, C. 2011. *La violencia en Colombia (1990–2002). Antecedentes y desarrollo histórico*. Vigo: Universidad de Vigo.

Sollund, R. 2013. Crimes against animal life. In G. Bruinsma and D. Weisburd (eds), *Encyclopedia of Criminology and Criminal Justice*. Tasmania: Springer, 758–69.

Strauss, A. and Corbin, J. 1994. Grounded theory methodology. In N.K. Denzin and Y.S. Lincoln (eds), *Handbook of Qualitative Research*. Thousand Oaks, CA: Sage Publications, 273–85.

Strauss, A. and Corbin, J. 2012. *Bases de la investigación cualitativa* (E. Zimmerman, trans.). Medellín: Editorial Universidad de Antioquia.

Swazo, N.K. 2005. Research integrity and rights of indigenous peoples: appropriating Foucault's critique of knowledge/power. *Studies in History and Philosophy of Science Part C: Studies in History and Philosophy of Biological and Biomedical Sciences* 36(3): 568–84.

Tombs, S. and Hillyard, P. 2004. Towards a political economy of harm: states, corporations and the production of inequality. In P. Hillyard, C. Pantazis, S. Tombs and D. Gordon (eds), *Beyond Criminology: Taking Harm Seriously*. London: Pluto Press, 30–54.

Toro Pérez, C. 2012. Geopolítica energética: minería, territorio y resistencias sociales. In S. Coronado, L.T. Roa Avendaño, J. Ferro Morales and C. Toro Pérez (eds), *Minería, Territorio y Conflicto en Colombia*. Bogotá: Editorial Universidad Nacional de Colombia, 17–58.

Uprimny Yepes, R. 2011. Las leyes de Justicia y Paz. In E.M. Restrepo and B. Bagley (eds), *La desmovilización de los paramilitares en Colombia. Entre el escepticismo y la esperanza*. Bogotá: Universidad de los Andes, 91–121.

Uprimny Yepes, R., Saffon Sanín, M.P., Botero Marino, C. and Restrepo Saldarriaga, E. 2006. *¿Justicia transicional sin tansición? Verdad, justicia, reparación para Colombia*. Bogotá: Ediciones Antropos.

Walters, R. 2011. *Eco Crime and Genetically Modified Food*. Abingdon: Routledge.

Ward, T. 2004. State harms. In P. Hillyard, C. Pantazis, S. Tombs and D. Gordon (eds), *Beyond Criminology: Taking Harm Seriously*. London: Pluto Press, 84–100.

White, R. 2012. The foundations of eco-global criminology. In R. Ellefsen, R. Sollund and G. Larsen (eds), *Eco-Global Crimes, Contemporary Problems and Future Challenges*. Farnham: Ashgate, 15–31.

White, R. 2013. *Environmental Harm: An Eco-Justice Perspective*. Bristol: Policy Press.

Chapter 5

With or Without a Licence to Kill: Human-Predator Conflicts and Theriocide in Norway

Ragnhild Sollund

Introduction

Conflicts between humans and predators have century long traditions and many causes – from humans' wish to protect their livestock to culturally based practices and prejudices as reflected in fairy tales like Little Red Riding Hood (e.g., Kohm and Greenhill 2013). Underlying factors include anthropocentrism (whereby humans position themselves at the centre of the world, thinking that everything and everyone, whether nature or nonhuman species, *exist for them*, rather than *in their own right*) and speciesism (humans' discrimination and prejudice against nonhuman species) (Benton 1998; Beirne 1999; Nibert 2002; Sollund 2008). These phenomena imply that humans think their own species is more *valuable* than other species, thus giving them the *right* to exploit the others. The most evident dogma in the human–nonhuman animal relationship (or lack thereof) is that *power gives right* (Sollund 2014).

In this chapter, the notion that *power gives right* will be illuminated through an analysis of verdicts in Norwegian courts concerning the illegal killing of predators in order to demonstrate how the Norwegian judicial system punishes such acts. These crimes are assessed in the light of state predator policy and whether this, too, may legitimise such killings by shaping peoples' and especially hunters' attitudes towards these kinds of nonhuman species.

In the chapter I will present the Norwegian predator policy and the situation for Norwegian predators. Next, I will describe the verdicts in brief before I turn to a discussion of the content of these verdicts ending with the logic implied (i.e., the lack of individual animal rights versus the animals' value as part of biodiversity). This chapter begins by defining some central concepts and identifying the parties, including the animals, involved in what we may call human-predator conflicts in Norway. I employ the term 'theriocide' (Beirne 2009, 2014; Sollund 2014) to refer to the act by which a human causes the death of an animal; theriocide is analogous to homicide. In the material presented below, theriocide also implies wilful intent, though the motivation behind such intent will vary. I will also refer to these acts as killing. I also apply the term 'theriocider' to refer to the individual who causes the death of an animal; theriocider therefore being analogous to murderer/killer. I use 'who' rather than 'it' or 'that' when referring to nonhuman animals to emphasise that they are individuals with interests, rather than objects (Regan 1999).

The chapter is situated in the framework of green criminology in the way it is sketched out by Beirne (2007) and South, Brisman and Beirne (2013: 33) insofar as it intends to 'discard legalistic definitions of crime and, instead base inquiry on notions of harm, inequality, social exclusion, suffering and pain'. I will explore whether legislation relevant for predator theriocides, like animal welfare legislation and 'wildlife' laws, serve to protect nonhuman animals, or other interests. I adopt a socio-legal approach (Brisman 2008) and thus I consider harms, whether or not they are criminalised, and focus on *acts* of theriocide, which may or may not be illegal. A socio-legal approach includes an environmental justice perspective, although I conceptualise environmental justice such that it does *not* exclude nonhuman species, which is often the way environmental justice is usually defined (Sollund 2013; White 2013).

By 'conflict', I imply that the parties involved have *adverse interests*, to an extent that can lead one to kill another, but also to punish one another. Conflict may also lead parties to attempt to avoid direct confrontation, for example, when predators try to escape from human hunters, or when humans try to frighten rather than kill predators. There are many dimensions, roles and parties involved in predator conflicts in Norway:

1. Humans as (a) owners of livestock, (b) hunters, (c) predator protectors, including the state. Farmers seek to protect their livestock to prevent predators from eating the livestock (before the livestock is eventually killed for human consumption). Predators constitute a threat to hunters' dogs, and hunters disapprove of predators taking 'their prey'. Thus, here, predators are killed by hunters because of their diet. The state has a multidimensional role: it has to protect farmers and their animals, ensure that public norms are respected and laws are obeyed, while also respecting national legislation and international conventions, such as the Bern Convention, which is intended to protect endangered species. As a consequence, the state kills *and* the state protects the predators. Public norms (local community norms), the Bern Convention (and the Norwegian legislation which is committed to the convention) are often based on *conflicting* interests.
2. Predators, such as wolves, lynx, bear and wolverines, to which the state may have adverse interests because of its obligations towards farmers and decisions made in the *Stortinget* (the parliament) which direct the ways in which predator populations are controlled in Norway.
3. Animals who are 'owned' by humans and who may be prey of predators, such as sheep, reindeer, who have adverse interests to predators who may want to kill and eat them.
4. Animals who are not under human ownership and who are natural prey for predators e.g., deer, hare, moose all have adverse interests to the predators

in that they would prefer to live than to serve as food. They also indirectly play a part in hunters' conflicts with predators over prey.

5. There are adverse interests between humans as owners of nonhuman animals destined to become food or other commodities, and these animals who would rather live than be killed and eaten. This deserves mention (but will not be pursued) as humans' exploitation of nonhuman animals as meat is the basis for much of the human-animal conflict in Norway.

6. Finally, the conflict over predators has also become a conflict between rural and urban areas (Hagstedt and Korsell 2012; see also Nurse 2013), although conflict lines are not always that clear-cut (Skogen et al. 2013).

As human populations increase and expand, they encroach upon the habitats of predators and other nonhuman animal species. Although humans may express a desire for biodiversity, they have a greater interest in living virtually everywhere, and in Norway, this may include practices whereby farmers let their livestock out in the summer, usually unherded. The stated policy of the Norwegian political party, *Senterpartiet*, the centre party (formerly the farmers' party, which was part of the previous coalition government 2008–12), is to exterminate wolves in Norway. This demonstrates how the party favours the interests of farmers with livestock and hunters over predators (Christensen 2013). The argument was precisely the conflict between predators (Christensen 2013) and farmers with livestock but also the conflict between hunters and predators. *Senterpartiet*'s political programme states:

> Hunting, outdoor recreation is reduced when the density of predators increase. This affects the life quality of those who use nature. The grazing industry, both farming and reindeer husbandry and harvesting [*sic*] through hunting and fishing must have priority before the predators.[1]

Still, according to the NGO *Foreningen våre rovdyr* in 2008, the Directorate for Nature Management, now The Norwegian Environment Agency, formulated the values which direct the state management of predators in Norway:

> In Norway, as a principle, no one owns wildlife. In this principle is the recognition that wildlife has intrinsic value and the right to existence. Therefore we have the responsibility for conservation in our legislation and we permit only interventions in the populations when these do not conflict with conservation.[2] (translation by author)

---

1   http://www.senterpartiet.no/getfile.php/Bildegalleri/Fellesfiler/endelig%20 utkast%20f.ra%20programkomiteen%20-%20august%202012%20med%20f.orside.pdf.

2   http://fvr.no/fvr_page/om-forvaltning.html.

I will see if these values are transparent in the verdicts concerning the illegal killing of predators. Through the analysis of these verdicts, it will also become clear what motivates predator theriocides and how they typically can be categorised. Underlying topics in this analysis include legal versus illegal killing, state-licenced versus self-initiated killing, and the human-predator conflict and its causes.

Norwegian Predator Policy and Nonhuman Animal Predators in Numbers

In Norway, there are four species of big predators: brown bear, wolf, lynx and wolverine. Although they are all protected, the degree of protection depends on the species' degree of vulnerability. Despite Norway's international obligations, the state, through the Norwegian Environment Agency licences hunting on a regular basis. An agreement was made in *Stortinget* (the National Assembly) in June 2011, renewing an agreement from 2004 (Tønnessen 2013), providing that predators can settle only within designated zones. Predators either wandering or trying to establish themselves outside these zones may be killed because they may be a threat to sheep. Unfortunately, the predators do not possess maps showing them where humans allow them to settle and where they will be subject to hunting, and some of these areas are natural habitats for them (e.g., rich in moose and deer). The state thus determines *how many* lynx, wolves, bears and wolverines shall be allowed to live in the country. It also determines *where*, depending on where farmers keep livestock, usually sheep but also reindeer and pigs.

Wolves

For centuries, the killing of these predator species was rewarded through bounties; now, they are protected. In Norway, killing wolves was criminalised in 1973 (Tønnessen 2010), *after* wolves were considered extinct (Skogen, Krange and Figari 2013). The species was and still is not extinct, but it is still listed as *critically threatened* on the Norwegian list of endangered species. In 2013, there were approximately 30–35 wolves in Norway; if one includes wolves that cross the border between Norway and Sweden, the number increases slightly to 80,[3] and if one includes all of Scandinavia, the number rises to 380. Because they are so few wolves, they are genetically homogeneous; in fact, they are all bred from only three wolves (Grønli 2005). This reduces reproduction and means low survival rates among pups.

The Norwegian predators, especially the wolves, are under complete human control, being labelled and collared with heavy devices causing them pain and

---

3   All numbers of existing individuals are from Rovdata, the Norwegian database for predator species (http://www.rovdata.no/).

discomfort (Cazaux 2007; Tønnessen 2010). This labelling may also facilitate illegal theriocide as the devices may be used to track them. They are subject to helicopter hunts and forced sedation under which blood samples are taken. This regime has led many to ask how 'wild' the Norwegian wolves actually are (Tønnessen 2013).

Because they are all labelled, except when the body is hidden and the collar removed, it is easy to establish how each individual dies. Between 10 February 2013 and 5 February 2014, a total of 18 wolves were killed:[4] one was killed in self-defence (*nødverge*),[5] one was hit by a car, one was presumably killed by a train, and seven were killed by hunters; the deaths of the remaining eight were categorised as *skadefelling*.[6] As of 11 February 2014, eight wolves have been killed by the state or by an individual with a licence from the state. Two of these – a couple – were killed on 5 February and 8 February from a helicopter. This theriocide was committed by *Statens naturoppsyn*, the operative part of the Norwegian Environment Agency. It was justified on the grounds that these wolves were settling in a zone close to sheep and that the killing was necessary to prevent them from breeding and settling and subsequently posing a potential future threat to sheep. The couple had settled in the same area where another couple was killed on licence in April 2013.

Lynx

From 1845 to 1980, there was a bounty on lynx and there were no limits to hunting them. Today, lynx are listed as *vulnerable* on the Norwegian red list. As of February 2014, there are around 350 lynx in Norway and there are annual hunting quotas in different areas of Norway although in western Norway it is a free hunt during the hunting period but across the country the hunt will stop when the total quota is reached.[7] In 2014, the quota for 1 February to 31 March was for 79 lynx.

---

4   All numbers of deaths of wolves, lynx, wolverines and bears come from Rovbasen, the database of the Norwegian Environment Agency (http://www.rovbase.no/Contentpages/InnsynDodeRovdyrSokeresultat.aspx?Arbeidsomrade=InnsynDodeRovdyr).

5   'Self-defence' can mean either in defence of the human or in defence of the human's livestock; it refers to instances where there is a direct threat or an emergency. In this particular situation, it is not clear whether the death resulted from a human protecting himself/herself or from a human protecting his/her livestock. In most verdicts, however, nødverge refers to a killing in defence of livestock.

6   *Skade* means damage, injury; *felling* means to 'make fall'. *Skadefelling* means these were shot because they had threatened or killed livestock. *Skadefelling* is more deliberate than *nødverge* and it refers to situations where permission is given to kill an individual because it has killed livestock (or may do so). 'Licenced killing' is when predators are outside designated areas. There are three categories of legal killing: ordinary hunt (e.g., lynx and bear, every year), *skadefelling*, and licenced hunt.

7   This is according to the Norwegian Environment Agency. http://www.miljodirektoratet.no/no/Nyheter/Nyheter/2014/Januar-2014/Kan-felle-79-gauper-under-arets-kvotejakt/.

Seventy were killed in the hunt.[8] According to *The Norwegian Environment Agency* numbers of lynx in Norway are in decline because of the hunt. Between 4 January 2013 and 6 February 2014, 85 lynx were categorised as dead due to *hunting* (usually killed with a shot gun or a rifle), one was killed in a trap, one was 'shot not included in quota' and five were categorised as *skadefelling*, seven were hit by train or car, and three died for unknown reasons.

Wolverine

There were around 350 adult wolverines in Norway in 2013, a decline from 395 in 2012. During the seventeenth and eighteenth centuries, a wolverine fur was very valuable and there was a bounty on wolverine until its protection in 1973 in Southern Norway and since 1982 across the country. The wolverine is listed as *critically endangered* on the Norwegian red list. As the state's goal for total numbers of wolverine is reached, wolverines are killed on state-licenced hunts. Between 1 January 2013 and 5 February 2014, a total of 100 registered wolverines died; 97 were shot, two died for unknown reasons and one was run over by a car. Of these 97, 40 are listed as *skadefelling* and the rest were categorised as hunted, with two killed by the use of traps.

Brown Bear

Brown bear is listed as *very threatened* on the Norwegian red list. In 2012, on the basis of DNA analysis, it was established that there were 137 brown bears, of whom 51 were females and 86 males. The goal now is to have 13 cub litters annually. Four bears were killed in 2013; two of these were categorised as *skadefelling*, two as hunted. Licences were issued to kill 18 bears in August 2013, according to the Norwegian Environment Agency.[9]

The Norwegian licence to hunt for predators is not without controversy, and there are several organisations fighting for the animals' right to live. The Norwegian Environment Agency has been accused of and brought to trial for permitting licenced hunting, which is a breach of law. In other words, it is argued that the state-issued licences to kill are a breach of the Law of biodiversity and the Bern Convention. The following cases have been about the basis for this legalisation. One case in 2000, involved the killing of five wolves in Hedemark. The NGO

---

8   http://www.miljodirektoratet.no/no/Nyheter/Nyheter/2014/April-2014/70-gauper-felt-under-kvotejakta-/.

9   http://www.miljodirektoratet.no/no/Nyheter/Nyheter/2013/August-2013/17-bjorner-kan-felles-i-lisensjakta/.

that brought the suit lost,[10] both at the trial level *Oslo tingrett*[11] and in the appeals court (*Borgarting lagmannsrett*), and the wolves were killed.[12] In another case from 1999,[13] however, the state was convicted for illegally licensing the killing of a wolf couple. In explaining its verdict, the court stated that Norway is obliged through the Bern Convention to protect wolves regardless of the total number of wolves living in Sweden (and on the Norwegian-Swedish border areas). When this decision to kill the wolf couple was made, there were only 20 wolves in Norway. The decision was also a breach of the Wildlife law, §1.[14] This verdict is interesting in that it also states that about 250,000 sheep and reindeer are released to graze every year and that (in 1999) 125,000 died – 20 per cent of which are assumed to have been killed by predators, 500 of which were killed by wolves. The court further stated that:

> 150 years ago, the same number of live stock were out, but the number of predators was much larger, approximately 3000 bears and considerably more wolves and wolverines. Back then, livestock were protected from predators by shepherds and they were collected at nighttime.

Today, sheep are usually allowed to graze freely and seldom herded. Although they may be kept in enclosures, these are intended to prevent predators from entering rather than to stop sheep from leaving. Sheep are bred to produce more meat, which makes them less capable of escaping predators and also makes them vulnerable when they get stuck in marshes (Børresen 1996). Thus, most of the sheep die for reasons unrelated to predators – i.e., for reasons for which the farmers may be

---

10   The case was brought by a coalition of NGOs: Foreningen våre rovdyr, WWF Norway and Norges naturvernforbund (which translates as the Norwegian Environmental Protection Association).

11   TOSLO-2005-18299 and LB-2007-14564-RG-2008-577. The letters and numbers preceding verdicts identify the cases and pertain to the different courts in the Norwegian judicial system. These verdicts are registered in *Lovdata*: (http://lovdata.no/info/information_in_english). While all verdicts from the Supreme Court (Høyesterett) are registered, only those verdicts from appeal courts that are considered to be of special importance are registered. As such, I may thus have missed verdicts that either were not appealed or that were appealed and not registered.

12   Court decisions from *Lovdata*: LB-2007-14564-RG-2008-577 and LB-2006-23415 – RG-2006-1197.

13   RG-2000-1125 (153–2000).

14   http://lovdata.no/dokument/NL/lov/1981-05-29-38#KAPITTEL_1 Lov om jakt og fangst av vilt [[Law about hunting and catching wildlife] [The wildlife law]: http://lovdata.no/dokument/NL/lov/1981-05-29-38#KAPITTEL_1 §1, [The purpose of the law. Wildlife and the habitats of wildlife shall be managed in accordance with the Law of biodiversity to ensure nature's productivity and biodiversity. Within this framework 'wildlife' can be harvested [*sic*] for the benefit of agriculture and leisure] (my translation).

regarded as responsible. I will not examine these verdicts further but rather keep them as part of the framework for the others with which I will deal.

On the basis of 22 verdicts from different Norwegian courts, in addition to the four mentioned about predator management, I will attempt to discern the motivations for theriocide of predators that have *not* been licenced by the state. These verdicts represent all the ones I could locate in the Norwegian database, *Lovdata*, relating to breaches of the wildlife law concerning predator theriocides (except those concerning eagles and hawks). Several of the verdicts concern cases that have been appealed through all levels of the judicial system, and thus there are, on occasion, several verdicts pertaining to the same case. There is often cross-referencing between the different verdicts as verdicts create precedent, especially those from the Supreme Court (*Høyesterett*).

The Verdicts

Verdicts contain theriocide or attempted theriocide in three cases for wolves, eight cases for bears, three cases for wolverines, and two cases for lynx. In total, 13 nonhuman animals were killed; these 16 cases also included chasing wolves with a car without killing them. These killings were a relatively small number, however, when compared to the large number of predators killed under state licensing (e.g., 208 in 2008). In other words, legal killings far outnumber illegal killings, and this highlights how the state or its subordinates (when given a licence to kill) are responsible for the killing of many large predators in Norway.

Those who have been convicted have usually breached § 56 or § 17 of the Viltloven (Lov om jakt og fangst av vilt), which translates as the 'Wildlife law' (law about hunting and catching wildlife).[15] For self-defence to apply, other means

---

15   Viltloven (Lov om jakt og fangst av vilt) [Law about hunting and catching wildlife. LOV-1981-05-29-38]. Section 56.*(strafferegler)* provides (in English translation):

Those who breach rules stated in this law will be punished with fines or prison up to 1 year, unless the act is punishable under a stricter law. Prison sentence up to 2 years may be applicable under very aggravating circumstances. If the breach also concerns the Law of biodiversity, the § of punishment in this act shall be applied. Breaches of this law are a minor offence. Attempts are punished as completed acts. (Translation by author.)

Section 11, concerning the right to kill predators attacking livestock, was suspended on 19 June 2009 and therefore sentences concerning the claim of self-defence after that date relate to §17 in the 'Law on nature biodiversity', and other laws, depending on the circumstances revolving around each specific crime.

Naturmangfoldsloven. http://lovdata.no/dokument/NL/lov/2009-06-19-100. § 17 ... Vilt kan avlives når det må anses påkrevd for å fjerne en aktuell og betydelig fare for skade på person. Eieren, eller en som opptrer på vegne av eieren, kan avlive vilt under direkte angrep på bufe, tamrein, gris, hund og fjørfe ... [Wildlife can be killed when necessary to remove an actual and considerable danger of harm to

than theriocide must have been attempted, such as to scare the predator away. The Animal Welfare Act is also applied, although rarely.

In the paragraphs that follow, I provide a brief overview of the cases and the opinion of the judges. Five of the cases (10, 11, 12, 13 and 14) are particularly relevant and thus will be presented in more detail than the rest to provide further insight into the motivations of theriociders. They concern different species and different types of modus operandi.

Case 1: TOVRO-2012-30478

Wolf theriocide: Man shot wolf at 84 m. distance. The wolf was 25 m. from electric enclosure for sheep, but it was difficult to determine whether the wolf would attack sheep. Claimed but not justified self-defence. Serious breach of Law of biodiversity. Verdict: 120 days prison, confiscation of rifle, withdrawal of hunting rights for two years.

Case 2: LE-2001-246, HR-2001-1436 – Rt-2002–258

Attempted wolf theriocide: Two men put out poisoned bait in order to kill wolves who were settling in the area. Appeal case: 1st instance verdict: 1st offender, 30 days suspended prison, 13,000 NOK fine, 2nd offender, 30 days suspended prison,[16] fine of 15,000 NOK. Appeal court, *Lagmannsretten*: verdict: 1st offender, 21 days prison sentence (proved guilty as fingerprints were found on plastic bag covering the bait), withdrawal of hunting rights for two years; 2nd offender, acquitted. On appeal, the judge emphasised general deterrence and the use of unethical hunting methods. Appeal to the Supreme Court: Appeal was rejected, the verdict upheld and the judges reasoned this by the need for harsh punishment for general deterrence.

Case 3: Appeal Case LE-1995-1493

Bear theriocide: Man shot bear during moose hunt. 1st instance verdict: 21-day suspended prison, rifle confiscated, and withdrawal of hunting rights for three years. 2nd instance: same sentence.

---

person. The owner or anyone acting on the owner's behalf can kill wildlife directly attacking cattle, pig, reindeer, dog and birds] (my translation).

16   In suspended prison sentences, the suspension is for two years meaning the offender will not go to prison if s/he does not commit any crimes during this period. If s/he commits other crimes and misdemeanours within this period, then the old sentence is added to the new one.

Case 4: Appeal Case 5 LE 1997-455-RG-1998-1977 (157-198)

Bear theriocide: Man shot and killed bear while collecting sheep, bear approached group of people and sheep. Shot at 50 m. distance. Claimed self-defence. Verdict: 1st instance: convicted. Ordered to pay a fine of 6,000 NOK (and administrative costs, 2,000 NOK). 2nd instance: acquitted for the theriocide, but convicted with a fine of 1,000 NOK for not reporting the killing.

Case 5: Appeal Case LE-2004-70950-RG-2005-1454

Bear theriocide: The hunt was licenced but the offender did not have the licence to kill and was not part of the hunting team, thus interfered with the hunt and injured the bear without reporting it. First instance: acquitted. Second instance: acquitted for the theriocide but convicted for not reporting it. 30 days suspended prison, 10,000 NOK fine, withdrawal of hunting rights for one year.

Case 6: TSOST-2009-103124 and LE-2010-12617

Bear theriocide: Appeal case: Five men chased bear with dogs and car and ended up killing (shooting) him. They used a device with a sender and a receiver attached to the dog's collar that can communicate with mobile phones and a unit in 1st offender's car. The court found there were very aggravating circumstances, because of the dog and the cars. Final court decision: 1st offender: 90 days prison, withdrawal of hunting rights for three years, confiscation of weapons (rifle and shotgun), 30,000 NOK compensation to the wildlife fund, 4,000 NOK administrative costs. 2nd offender: 45 days prison (of which 30 days suspended), withdrawal of hunting rights for two years, confiscation of rifle, 20,000 NOK confiscation of value of car used in the crime, 4,000 NOK administrative costs. 3rd offender: 10,000 NOK fine, 4,000 NOK costs. 4th offender: 5,000 NOK fine, 4000 NOK costs. 5th offender: Prison 45 days of which 21 days suspended prison, withdrawal of hunting rights for 2 years, 10,000 NOK fine, 4,000 NOK administrative costs.

Case 7: Appeal Case LE -2006-142925-RG-2008-129

Bear theriocide: Man shot and killed bear in bear zone, under aggravating circumstances. A bear had killed a sheep; the dead sheep was left on the ground. The bear came to eat and was shot. 1st instance verdict: 45 days suspended prison, 7,500 NOK fine and withdrawal of hunting rights for two years. Second instance, verdict upheld. Appeal to the Supreme Court rejected.

Case 8: Appeal Case HR-1992-42-B-Rt-1992-346

Wolverine theriocide: Two men killed two wolverines using traps. There were aggravating circumstances. Traps were illegal during breeding season, the killing was deemed indiscriminate because more animals could have been killed. 1st instance verdict: 60 days suspended prison, confiscation of trap. Final Supreme Court verdict: In addition to verdict from previous instance, a fine of 30,000 NOK and withdrawal of hunting rights for two years.

Case 9: Appeal Case 19 LE -2002-357

Attempted theriocide on lynx: An illegal lynx trap was not supervised during two weeks (must be checked twice every 24 hours). Defendant failed to report the trap, did not place his name on the trap, and hunted lynx out of season. Verdict: a 20,000 NOK fine and withdrawal of hunting rights for one year.

Case 10: TNOST 2010-57617

Bear theriocide (A) and wolf chasing (B): One man was convicted with 36 days suspended prison sentence, in addition to a fine of 7,000 NOK, confiscation of rifle, and withdrawal of hunting rights for two years for hunting and killing bear with dog, and grossly negligent animal abuse for chasing a pack of four wolves over a long distance with a car. The offender claimed the bear was on his way to take sheep. Court rejected this claim, but found no aggravating circumstances.

A) Bear theriocide: The offender was convicted of, under aggravating circumstances, to have chased, caught, killed or injured protected wildlife, being a breach of the Wildlife law. He was also convicted for a breach of the Animal Welfare Act. He committed these crimes on two occasions. On 20 June 2009 at 11.10 p.m., he chased a bear with his dog and then shot the bear. The offender was informed that a bear was seen near his sheep. He went to the described location and let his dog (trained to pursue bear) out and followed the dog. The bear, he claimed, was 140 metres from the enclosure with his 6–7 sheep. The offender had a rifle in his car because in the two preceding days, and he had been hunting a wolf on a licenced hunt. He brought the rifle when he went looking for the bear. When he located the bear, he went down on his knee and shot and injured the bear. The dog pursued and chased the bear down towards a lake. They could hear the bear growl and then saw the bear in the lake. The offender returned to his car and drove down to the lake and fired two shots at the swimming bear. After the second shot, which apparently went through the bear's head, the bear, still alive, turned and swam towards the shore and towards the offender's dog; after a few strokes, he submerged and died. The bear, it is stated in the verdict, was a young wandering male and thus not one of the 'most protectable individuals. This is the kind of animal it is easiest to get permission to kill' (p. 6). The bear was approaching the offender's sheep and the man claimed self-defence – an argument that was *not* accepted by the Court. By the same token, the offender's misjudgement of the situation was not regarded as severe negligence [*grov uaktsomhet*]. As such, the Court determined that there were no aggravating circumstances. The Court found it likely that the bear was scared by the dog and the car and would have withdrawn to the forest rather than attacking the sheep. Furthermore, the Court stated in its verdict that the offender, as a member of the predator hunting team of the local community and as member of the wildlife committee [*Kommunal viltnemd*], had an interest in and experience with hunting and therefore special understanding of the rules. He was therefore found to be punishable for negligence (although, as noted above, not for severe negligence). The verdict states that the offender, who previously had documented on video how easy it is to scare bears by making sounds, should have known that the bear would run away if he had fired in the air, or if he had shouted or clapped his hands. He tried none of these alternatives.

B) Chasing pack of wolves with car: During January or February 2009, the offender pursued a pack of four wolves with his car along the road in Rendalen. At times, he drove so close to them that the wolves could not be seen from the front seat from where he was trying to film the wolves while pursuing them. The wolves escaped by running off the road. The offender stopped the car and one of the wolves who was not able to keep up with the rest of the pack returned to the road upon which the offender continued the chase with the car, so close, in fact, to the wolf that he nearly drove over him/her. The Court found this constituted 'injuring' wolves and possibly 'life threatening animal abuse', and thus found the offender guilty of grossly negligent animal abuse and a breach of the Animal Welfare Act § 3: 'Animals have intrinsic value independent of the use value they may have for humans. Animals shall be treated well and not subjected to unnecessary strain and stress'. An expert witness experienced in sedating predators stated in Court that when it comes to pursuing wolves with a helicopter, a wolf can suffer lasting injury if he/she is chased for more than three minutes.

Case 11: TNAMD-2003-619, LF-2004-3583, HR-2005-769-A LF-2005-80106-RG-2006-690

Appeal case: Bear theriocide. Two men – a sheep owner and a shepherd – were acquitted in the first court instance. The case was appealed. In the second court instance, both were again acquitted. The prosecutor appealed the case to the Supreme Court, which suspended the sentence from the previous court. The reason for the suspension was that the Court did not accept that the bear had attacked the men, thus this Court reviewed the applicability of the conditions for emergency right to self-defence in paragraph 11 of the Wildlife law. A new trial in *Lagmannsretten* resulted in conviction with a penalty of a 60-day suspended prison sentence for the 1st offender and a 10,000 NOK fine, and a 45-day suspended prison sentence for the 2nd offender with a 10,000 NOK fine.

The underlying facts of the case are as follows: On Thursday, 10 July 2003, a sheep owners and a sheep herder were accused of killing a female bear with three cubs under especially aggravating circumstances. The men had heard that a bear had been observed and therefore brought their rifles and a Karelean bear dog to look for cadavers and the bear. Witnesses who had seen the bear said she was not aggressive to humans, despite having cubs. Both offenders had been competitive shooters and had several decades of experience as moose hunters. The shepherd also had much experience with bears. The men went looking for the bear and saw her as she was walking along the fence to the enclosure of about 150 acres with 150 sheep. They then saw her enter. The men then went through another gate towards a salt stone to look for sheep there, hoping to cut her off, when they heard the bells from the sheep at some distance. Shortly thereafter, the bear appeared at the edge of the forest with her three cubs just behind her. The distance from the men was 140 metres. The bear galloped but not with maximum speed. She approached the men while increasing the distance from her cubs behind her. When she was about 90 metres from the men, both aimed at her with their rifles. Both fired to kill her, but missed. The bear then changed her course and ran 17 metres before they shot at her again. She then changed course again, and the sheep owner then shot again, now at a distance of 104 metres. At the autopsy, the coroners found only one shot, which had entered her body on the right side, pierced both lungs and exited on the left side. The shepherd explained that he believed that she was injured by the first shot from the first offender.

The defence of the men in the first court instance claimed that killing her was necessary to prevent her from suffering after the first shot, thus something they had to do according to the Animal Welfare Act. This argument, however, was rejected by the Court, as the bear exhibited no sign of have been wounded. Rather, she increased her speed and changed direction in her attempt to escape her killers.

Case 12: Appeal Case LH-2004-7591 LH-2004-99118 – RG-2005-1367

Bear theriocide: Bear shot while eating. Claimed self-defence. 1st instance verdict: acquitted. 2nd instance verdict: acquitted. Appealed to the Supreme Court. At the Supreme Court, the verdict from the appeal court was suspended and there was a new treatment of the case in *Lagmannsretten*. The final verdict was a 21-day suspended prison sentence, a fine of 1,000 NOK, and confiscation of the offender's weapon. The Court found that there were no particularly aggravating circumstances.[17]

On 5 August 2003 at 00.30 a.m. a 43-year-old man intentionally shot and killed a bear who was eating from his pigs' trough in a pigpen. The pigs and 80 dairy cows were on grazing land and the pigpen was located in this area.

---

17 The procedural history of this case is a little complicated: The judges in the Supreme Court suspended the previous verdict for procedural reasons. The issue was about the applicability of the law regarding emergency right. The Supreme Court thus suspended the previous verdict and a new trial was set.

The bear had been there twice before, but had not harmed the pigs on previous visits. On his third and final (fatal) visit, the bear did not attempt to hurt any of the 14 pigs. There were six persons present, including a biologist who for many years had conducted research on bears and who had assisted the authorities as an adviser. He had long experience in bear observations and was an adviser for wildlife (predator) authorities. At the time of the theriocide, he was seated in his car nearby and he could have been consulted regarding the bears' behaviour. The biologist had unsuccessfully tried to contact the authorities regarding the bear's presence and also to warn that it might be necessary to take measures against him the following day. The group agreed to form a guard during the night. At 10.15 p.m., the biologist observed the bear jump into the bin without attacking any of the pigs. The bear went to the trough and ate from it for 30 minutes, pausing only to stand up on his hind legs to watch and listen. At 10.50 p.m., the theriocider came in his car and scared the bear, who ran off to the forest. The theriocider exchanged a few words with the biologist and learned that the bear had been there. He charged his rifle and went into an office in the barn to keep watch. At 00.30, he heard a car and thought this might make the bear move and thus positioned himself with his rifle aimed at the pigpen. After a short while, he witnessed the bear in the pen with the pigs, who were anxious and squealing. The bear was calm and went towards where (the accused claimed that) the pigs were. The bear then proceeded to the trough, stood up to listen a couple of times, and then started eating. After a couple of minutes, the accused shot the bear in the breast intending to kill him. The shot threw the bear backwards; the bear disappeared over the fence out of view. The accused initiated a search for the bear and he was found dead outside the pen.

The offender claimed an emergency right to protect the pigs, but this excuse was not accepted by the court, which found beyond reasonable doubt that the pigs were not under direct attack when the accused shot and killed the bear. Objectively, there was no cause for emergency, according to the Wildlife law, §11. The bear was standing still and calmly eating, not caring about the pigs, who were walking around in the bin. There were no concrete indications that an attack would take place. The conditions for conviction for killing protected wildlife were thereby present, according to the verdict (p. 4). The minority of the Court[18] voted against conviction, and therefore he was acquitted, but sentenced to 21 days suspended prison on appeal.

---

18   The Court was *lagmansrett* (appeal court). There were seven judges in the panel, including four lay judges (*meddommer*). The majority (three professional judges and one lay judge) voted in favour of a conviction for negligence, whereas three lay judges voted for acquittal. Procedural law (*Straffeprosessloven*) § 35 requires five votes to convict in *Lagmansretten*. Therefore, he was acquitted. Lay judges are usually locals from the community who may share the offenders' interest in killing bears and protecting sheep. Whether this influenced the verdict is not clear.

Case 13: Appeal Case LE-2004-1152, HR-2005-162-A- Rt-2005-76

Wolverine theriocide: Verdict 1st instance: acquitted for emergency rights.[19]

Verdict 2nd instance: all offenders received a 30-day suspended prison sentence, were deprived of hunting rights for two years, and had their rifles and snow scooters confiscated. Verdict at the Supreme Court: all received a 21-day prison sentence and were deprived of hunting rights for two years.

Four men killed a wolverine in his nest. They saw his tracks in the snow, followed them with a snow scooter and found the nest. They dug him out and shot him when he came out as he lost his cover. The theriociders claimed emergency rights, but this defence was rejected by the court. The court stated that they had plenty of time to consider the situation, both when they discovered the tracks and when they found the nest. They had a mobile phone and could have contacted the wildlife authorities. It was not an acute situation; there were no sheep grazing. The head of the court found there were very aggravating circumstances, an argument not accepted by the majority of the lay and professional judges in Court, who held that the wolverine was killed with the same methods usually applied by the state; what was aggravating was only the vulnerability of the species. The Court, however, emphasised when setting the punishment that wolverine is rare, not threatened or vulnerable. The offenders had had a licence to kill the wolverine a couple of months earlier but had failed to kill him. They also tried to hide the crime by dumping the dead body in a lake. The men owned sheep and used to send their sheep to the mountains to graze. In 2001, a wolverine appeared and started taking sheep. The farmers were sad and frustrated by watching the suffering of the lambs, who on occasion were found torn and mutilated, but not dead. The state's animal welfare commission in the district (Dyrevernsnemda) had previously stated that to protect the sheep, they could not continue to graze in the mountains, thus creating problems for the farmers who were in danger of losing their grazing land. It is stated in *Lagmannsretten* in favour of the offenders that: 'It has been a central element in all husbandry to protect livestock against predators as long as livestock has been held' (p. 8). The offenders had good reason to worry about wolverine attacks and the Court accepted this rationale.

The Court further opined that prison sentences must be applied for killing protected predators, because illegal hunting makes wildlife authorities' management of predators difficult. Prison sentences should be applied because there are persons who disagree with the authorities in protecting predators, and in addition, Norway has international obligations to protect certain species; no ameliorating circumstances could alter this. The theriociders acted deliberately and determinedly against authorities. As noted above, the verdict in the second instance entailed a 30-day suspended prison sentence for all four offenders, withdrawal of hunting rights for two years, and confiscation of rifles and snow scooter.

---

19 Pursuant to § 48 of the Penal law, emergency right, a punishable act is not to be punished if the act is committed as emergency protection.

In the appeal case in the Supreme Court, however, all offenders were convicted with unsuspended prison sentences for 21 days. This verdict was unanimous among the five judges of the Supreme Court.

Case 14: TFOLL-2006-104417

Lynx theriocide: A lynx was caught in a trap as part of a research project. The offender killed her/him, subsequently hid the body, requested a taxidermist to stuff the body as a trophy and later pretended s/he was killed as part of a licenced hunt. Verdict: 15 days prison, withdrawal of hunting rights for three years, confiscation of knife, shotgun and pistol.

The theriocider worked as a volunteer for a research project between 2001 and 2005 and was responsible for the supervision of three lynx traps. He was a hunter with hunting grounds. On 2 February 2005, he called the predator contact for *Statens naturoppsyn* (*State nature surveillance*), Tveter, and reported that he had shot a lynx. Tveter suspected this was a breach of the rules of the ongoing licenced lynx hunt to kill three individuals. By the label on the lynx's ear, s/he was identified as being from an area other than where the offender claimed to have killed her/him. S/he also appeared to have been frozen and bloodstains and a tooth from the lynx were found in the trap. The biopsy showed s/he had been shot in the breast and also had wounds from stabbing. What caused her death, according to the verdict (p. 5), was a combination of shock and pneumothorax (in which air comes into the chest) caused by perforation. It entails a collapse of the lungs and strangulation. The Court stated (p. 9) that the lynx was in a stressful situation during the attack because she was trapped, and that the way she was killed appeared *brutal and inhumane*.

Confronted with these facts, the offender changed his statement. He said that when he came to inspect the lynx trap in January 2005, s/he was trapped, with one leg stuck. He claimed to have lifted the trapdoor to release her/him from the trap and said he tried unsuccessfully to contact the research manager. He then returned to the trap and stabbed the lynx repeatedly with a knife on a stick until s/he died. He confessed to killing the lynx and also to have tried to conceal the theriocide by simulating a hunt. He later changed his confession, claiming emergency: he had killed the lynx to stop her suffering caused by a broken leg. Later on, he changed this explanation again, admitting to having decided to kill the lynx when he could not reach the research manager. The theriocider said he shot her to pretend she was killed during the hunt and broke her leg post-mortem, which would enable him to claim that the fracture was caused by the trap, and thus the killing was permissible under the Animal Welfare Act. These stories were contradicted by the autopsy. The Court found proof beyond a reasonable doubt that the offender killed the lynx in the trap by stabbing her numerous times with a knife. The motive was to have the lynx stuffed to keep her/him as a trophy. Furthermore, he knew the lynx was protected and killing her was illegal. He acted intentionally. As an active hunter and volunteer in the lynx project, he was well aware of how lynx should be 'humanely' killed. Therefore, the circumstances of this killing were particularly aggravating. The Court found that the first part of Wildlife Law §56 applied: under very aggravating circumstances, a two-year prison sentence may be imposed. The Court, however, pointed out that lynx are *not entirely* protected, that hunting quotas are licenced, and that the degree of threat to the species is different from, for example, the wolverine. He was further convicted for not safely keeping his pistol.

The Court also stressed (on p. 10 of its opinion) the importance of general deterrence, as per Wildlife Law §56 1st part §3, in imposing its sentence. The case had been delayed in the judicial system – a circumstance that repeatedly leads to a more lenient sentence in the case of wildlife crimes (because it is regarded as an extra burden for the offenders to wait so long for their case to be settled), which are seldom prioritised. The Court stated that the media attention to the case had been difficult for the defendant and that as a result, a 15-day prison sentence would be more appropriate than a 21-day sentence. Strong public interest also indicated that he should not be allowed to hunt and he therefore lost hunting rights for three years, in addition to confiscation of his shotgun, pistol and knife.

Discussion of the Offenders' Motivations Based on the Verdicts

This section examines the motivations offenders had for killing the predators in a less anthropocentric perspective than that presented in the verdicts. There was a conflict situation in Case 10, between the offender, and the bear and wolves where the victims' species are crucial. It is likely the offender's ownership of the sheep further accentuated the underlying conflict because of his assumption that he and his victims, especially the bear, would *share* interest in killing the sheep. The offender claimed to have killed in order to protect his sheep and stated that he wanted to film the wolves to establish whether they wore a collar, to ascertain whether they were part of the Osdalpack. The theriocider was an experienced hunter, who knew a lot about the behaviour of bears. This raises the question of whether he actually sought to protect the sheep. His ownership of sheep could have simply been a pretext for doing what he had tried to do with impunity the day before – kill a critically endangered wolf – or what he had done habitually – kill moose or unprotected animal species. It is clear in the verdict that killing animals is an acceptable practice per se, but that the offender killed under the wrong circumstances. While ignorance of the law is never an excuse, the Court found that the defendant's status as a hunter should make him extra aware of what these circumstances are.

The Court emphasised the offender's lack of empathy in Case 10: 'That the accused continued to pursue the (fourth) wolf after her return to the road had no purpose according to the explanation of the accused, and is therefore particularly bad'. It is interesting then, that even though the Court found the abuse served no purpose, it was characterised as severe *negligent* abuse rather than *deliberate* abuse.

Unless an act or omission is proscribed by law, courts do not consider animal rights (Benton 1998; Pellow 2013) or species justice (White 2013: 111–43) perspectives. An animal rights or species justice perspective would have found the killing of a female bear with three cubs unacceptable. This, however, was not an issue for the Court. There is no indication in the verdict of concern for the three cubs who witnessed their mother being killed, while she tried to escape her theriociders. And while the court did consider the circumstances of the mother bear's death, it did not contemplate whether the cubs could, would or did survive without her. The court did not consider how from a biodiversity viewpoint, killing an individual of a protected species who is a mother increases the threat to the species threefold.

Both Cases 13 (wolverine) and 14 (lynx) exemplify the cruelty that humans can exhibit towards nonhuman animal – especially Case 14 where the lynx who was trapped was subsequently stabbed to death. In both Case 13 and Case 14, the theriociders killed helpless animals who could not escape and there were no immediate actions from their side that justified the attacks. The wolverine (Case 13), despite being suspected of have previously killed sheep, was, at the time of the theriocide, in his nest. He was not a threat to either humans or sheep, yet, he was awakened and killed in cold blood. In this case, these theriociders were motivated by their purported desire to protect their sheep, claiming they killed in an emergency. They had previously been licenced to kill him, but had failed. Nevertheless, they interpreted the initial licence to kill the wolf as an open-ended invitation to do so – in their minds, both a precautionary act and probably also a vindictive one.

In the Cases 8 and 12, the men seem excited by the hunt and to have acted in what Norwegians refer to as *blodtåke* (*blood fog*). The men may have been seduced by the thrill of chasing the bear and killing him (in Case 8) or pursuing the tracks of the wolverine to his nest and killing him (in Case 12) (Nurse 2013; Sollund 2014). That there were several men colluding in these acts may also have reinforced the lack of sober reflection and the determination to kill, which in Case 8 continued for at least four hours.

Excitement and thrill may have also been an issue in Cases 13 and 14, where the men may have been fuelled by the powerlessness of the potentially dangerous predators and by their own power. In Case 13, the description of the men rushing to the nest and digging out the wolverine suggests that they may have been driven be adrenaline and emotion. This may have given them a desirable sensation of control often witnessed in violent crimes between humans (Sollund 2001).

In Cases 10, 11, 13 and 14, there is a striking lack of empathy with the victims and a seeming will to carry out abuse. The absence of emergency in these cases renders them different from several of the others and makes them appear even more cruel. Neither the offenders nor the Court in Case 13 pay attention to the *individual* victim: the *wolverine*'s loss of life is not mentioned, only international obligations to protect endangered *species*. In the first verdict of Case 13, the Court states that the method of theriocide did *not* differ from that applied by the authorities when killing wolverine, thereby suggesting that killing is acceptable; it was only bad timing (after the licence to kill had expired). In Case 14, the lynx's pain from the repeated stabbings and her inability to escape the attack must have caused her great fear and suffering. When reading about the gruesome details of this theriocide, what emerges is a sense of a total absence of empathy and a determined will to kill for a trophy (as was stated in the verdict). The offender's behaviour in Case 14 also indicates a strong degree of alienation and social distance, which may be perceived as requisites for animal abuse (Sollund 2008, 2011, 2013), together with techniques of neutralisation, especially the denial of the victim (Agnew 1998; Nurse 2013; Sollund 2012).

There may also have been an element of hatred in Case 14. Hatred has been found to be one motivation for the killing of large predators in Sweden (Hagstedt and Korsell 2012). It is possible, then, that a combination of motivators were at play in Case 14: the opportunity to kill a lynx, hatred of the lynx (or lynx, more generally), power, and the chance to obtain a trophy which would establish or reinforce the hunter's/killer's reputation as a hunter. Likewise prejudices against wolves may have inspired the hatred which may have been an underlying factor in the wolf theriocide and chase (Cases 1, 2 and 3); as stated by Skogen et al. (2013: 18): '... peoples' images of the wolf and its place in Norwegian nature guide actions which have big consequences for wolf management and for the wolf'.

In Case 12, we observe not a genuine conflict between the theriocider and the bear, but an *assumed* conflict. The theriocider explained that he believed the bear wanted to kill 'his' pigs, even though the bear showed no such intent. To the offender, the bear's expected or anticipated behaviour – 'all bears are battle bears' – mattered more than what the bear was actually doing (or not doing) at that particular moment. What the bear did was not to attempt to kill the pigs, but to steal their food. The Court's verdict demonstrates that the theriocider's trust in his own prejudices was given more weight than the bear's actual behaviour and the threat the bear may have presented. This case (and others) lends strong support to the claim that predators will kill only when necessary; in this case, the bear had a choice between food in the pigs' trough or the pigs, themselves, *as food*. The bear opted for the former, but the offender anticipated the latter and killed the bear. In many ways, then, bears differ from humans who kill even when they do not need to.

Men Killing for What?

A common feature of the cases presented is that all offenders are *men* who kill and that they do so *frequently* and *for pleasure*. In most of the cases, the offenders are hunters who kill moose, foxes, deer and birds. Under other circumstances, some have also been licenced to kill predators. This is particularly relevant in the two Cases (5 and 13) where licences had been issued to kill wolverine and bear, but the hunters had failed to kill wolverines within the time given and the theriocider who killed the bear was not part of the hunting bear team. Killing was legal, but the offender in these cases did so under illegal circumstances. In other words, in some of these cases, the 'crime' is not *the killing*, but *the circumstances* under which the killing occurs: wrong person (killer without a licence); wrong species; wrong place (in predator zone); wrong time of year/expired licence. Licenced hunting and hunting rights both legitimise and encourage theriocides and make them righteous (Katz 1986) because it reflects the belief that animals are 'resources', that killing them is a leisure activity, or that they are enemies who can easily be 'taken out'. Weak law enforcement of predator crimes and the few demands of evidence of predator killings to receive compensation for dead livestock further legitimise it as predators are made scapegoats for what is most often human lack of care for their livestock, so that they die for a number of other reasons (Tønnessen 2010).

Hunters have the opportunity and skills and, as it appears from some of the verdicts, the desire to kill. When the theriociders are inspired to kill – or when they perceive predators' (potential) attack on their sheep or pigs – they may feel they are defending the primordial good (Katz 1986; Tønnessen 2010: 70). This 'good' may be defended in cold blood, with what Børresen (1996) calls 'hunter (predator) aggression', an instinct which instantly removes the capacity for any potential empathy with the victim. Another emotion involved is rage, which is categorised as effective aggression (Børresen 2006: 50) (Cases 11, 13, 14).

What offenders claim in police interviews and in Court possibly does not reveal all of their reasons. Hatred is an emotion that is never mentioned in the dry language of the verdicts. But when a man decides to chase, trap, poison, shoot, or stab an animal to death without consideration for the pain, horror and suffering this entails, it is reasonable to believe that such emotions may be involved. It is also probable that such bloody attacks and confrontations are consequence of what the theriociders may experience as a 'conflict', which, in turn, gives them a moral right to kill.

As noted above, it is hardly a coincidence that *all* offenders in the verdicts are male. According to Nurse (2013: 135, 136), 'Many wildlife crimes also involve appropriate male behaviours such as aggression, thrill-seeking, or having an adventurous nature … [W]hile masculinities may not be the cause of all animal harm, it is certainly a factor to be taken into account in some wildlife crimes and some companion animal abuse'. In Norway, of the 456,000 registered hunters in 2012/13, 12 per cent were women. Less than 3 per cent of all Norwegian women, but 19 per cent of all Norwegian men are registered in the Hunters register (*Jegerregisteret*).[20] This is a quite substantial number of people who enjoy killing, and it also demonstrates the normative climate for such acts: hunting is perceived as tradition, sport, and leisure, further solidifying its acceptability and desirability (see also Nurse 2013). That the number of women in the hunter community in Norway is increasing may be due to Norwegian standards for gender equality, through which, in this case, women adjust to masculine standards rather than the opposite.

20　According to Statistics Norway, https://www.ssb.no/jegerreg/.

The offender characteristics and their motivations for committing these theriocides are varied, but interlinked. First, many are hunters killing for leisure, thus fitting the category of *lifestylers* found in a Swedish study (Hagstedt and Korsell 2012: 217). Second, many of the killers are animal owners, and have access to and knowledge of how to use weapons. Third, some killers are motivated by hatred (Hagstedt and Korsell 2012; Olsen in Tønnessen 2010) and status, as in case 14, where the lynx theriocider sought possession of a predator trophy. Fourth, in several cases, the hunts and theriocides seem to have brought about feelings of excitement, mastery and pleasure (see also Nurse 2013, Skogen et al. 2013: 210) – feelings that they may have previously experienced during other, legal hunting outings. Finally, the hunters frequently exhibit a lack of empathy for their victims, which again must be produced by speciesism and social distance, through which animals are not regarded as having intrinsic value and hunters cannot or will not try to position themselves in a nonhuman animal's situation (Sollund 2008).

Intrinsic Value versus Biodiversity Value

As mentioned throughout this chapter, theriocide is seldom given weight in the verdicts and it is not regarded as objectionable per se. Theriocide is punishable under specific circumstances and the animals enjoy rights to live only on the condition that they do not breach rules set for them by the Norwegian state regarding where they go, where they settle, and what (who) they eat. If they breach these rules or if they are not protected because their species is insufficiently vulnerable or threatened, they will be subject to state-licenced theriocide. Furthermore, if the species is not critically threatened, then the Court will not find any aggravating factors that would enhance the punishment. Consequently, in the verdicts, killing a wolf illegally is a more serious crime than killing a lynx. This is a serious breach of species justice, as for the individual nonhuman animal, the species s/he belongs to is of subordinate interest to her own survival (see Regan 1999; Sollund 2014). It is clear in the verdicts that biodiversity is far more appreciated than the intrinsic value of the predators. Nowhere in any of the verdicts is there any consideration for the animals' own interest in living (Regan 1999) and only seldom is there any mention of the pain and suffering caused by the theriociders. Only in Case 10, involving the wolves who were chased, and in Case 14, involving the lynx, is the Animal Welfare Act applied. The Animal Welfare Act was *not* applied in the chase and theriocide of the bear in Case 10, however. The bear is rather regarded as being *less* important for biodiversity and there is little consideration for the bear's intrinsic value. Consequently, the crime is regarded as less severe. It is clear, then, that the Wildlife law and the Law of biodiversity have priority over the Animal Welfare Act: the first two are concerned with species survival and ecosystems, the third with individuals. As White (2013: 107) puts it, 'While occasionally reference is made to intrinsic values, it is human benefit that is a key driver in environmental law enforcement and regulation'.

For the bear himself; this may be looked upon differently. Not only was he chased by a dog and a car, both supposedly very stressful, but he was further shot and injured, again and again, trying to swim away from his theriocider before finally dying. There is no doubt that human and nonhuman animals have the same capacity to feel fear and pain (Hessen 2013). We can thus safely assume that he suffered during the hunt and the killing. This must consequently be characterised as animal abuse (see Agnew 1998; Beirne 1999).

It is of further interest that the offender in Case 10 already had a rifle in his car because he had been participating previously in the legal hunt of a wolf. This wolf should possess the same inherent value as the wolves who were chased and settled outside the wolf zones, yet this wolf was to killed because s/he was causing 'damage' (supposedly to livestock).

The verdicts thus demonstrate the lack of acceptance of animals as individuals with intrinsic value (Regan 1999), and they show that nonhuman animals are protected not for *who* they are, but only for *what* they are – *part of* a protected species. The trials and the subsequent verdicts represent ongoing conflicts between the authorities and their predator management, and the people who object to living with the predators (Hagstedt and Korsell 2012; Skogen et al. 2013; Tønnessen 2010). The number of killed livestock, which every year is compensated for economically by the state, exceeds many times the number of actual predator victims; consequently, the predators take the blame and thereby are constructed as legitimate enemies, even when 'innocent'. They become scapegoats sacrificed to amend this conflict.

When the state acts as an executioner – when the state decides how many individuals of a species are permitted to live and how many shall be killed, where and when – it exhibits a bureaucratic approach to the predators that reflects a lack of feeling or regard for the individuals. The individual animals are thus also victims of a system that makes them invisible as individuals mainly because they are nonhumans and consequently not regarded as 'victims' (Sollund 2008, 2012). When criminalisation does occur, it often reflects very limited anthropocentric notions of what is best for humans; 'nature' and 'wildlife' are simply and mainly regarded as resources for human exploitation, while the intrinsic value of specific ecological areas and species tends to be downplayed or ignored (White 2012: 24). Although killing is central in all the verdicts, the question 'Why do people kill animals?' is never raised.

The General Deterrent Effect of the Verdicts

Although general deterrence is used as a rationale in many of the verdicts, most offenders receive short suspended prison sentences. One can assume that these short sentences undercut any deterrent effect, especially given that risk of being detected in the first place is minor. In order for a punishment to serve a generally deterrent effect, the public must be aware of the risk of punishment, the punishment must come with certainty, and the punishment must outweigh the possible intended benefits to the would-be offender (Andenæs 1974; Jacobsen 2004).

In the cases discussed in this chapter, it is unclear how rational the offenders were during the commission of their crimes – a question whose answer depends, in part, on the circumstances surrounding and the offender(s) motivation(s) for his/their crime(s). Some cases describe a contact (though remote) between predators and livestock in which the theriocide is committed without the predator having precipitated this act through her physical proximity to livestock. Defence situations, whether realistic or not, may lead the theriocider to be less rational and thus engage in less of a calculus of the benefits of the action and risks of apprehension and punishment, and consequently the argument about general deterrence weakens.

In several Cases (2, 4, 6, 8, 10, 13, and 14), from what appears in the verdicts – for example, when the offenders stop their pursuit to discuss how to proceed before continuing – the theriociders (or attempted theriociders) could have weighed their actions, yet deliberately followed a plan to kill the predators. If hatred against the predators is an explicit emotion in these theriociders (or would-be theriociders), a lenient sentence – such as a short two-year suspended prison sentence suspended – will probably have little deterrent effect if they also consider the low risk of detection. Withdrawal of hunting rights and confiscation of weapons and additional fines may constitute a far more severe punishment for a person who enjoys killing.

That the general deterrent effect of punishment for killing wolves in Norway and Sweden is not particularly strong may be illustrated by a study from 2009 establishing that 50 per cent of Scandinavian wolves die in illegal hunts (Liberg et al.). Biologist Petter Wabakken states that the Scandinavian stock would have been *four times* bigger were it not for illegal hunting – 990 individuals rather than 263 in 2008/2009 (Rønning 2011). As mentioned above, the maximum sentence for breaches of the Wildlife law is two years in prison. As we have seen, however, the harshest sentence so far is four months in prison (in Case 1, wolf theriocide). In both Cases 13 and 14, general deterrence is used as an explanation for the sentence, however, the prison sentences are short and I wonder what kind of circumstances would be regarded as sufficiently aggravating for the maximum prison sentence to be applied, when it was not used in these cases.

In some of the cases, the judge specifically seeks to avoid conflict between the judicial system and the local communities in distributing sentences that are too severe, although it is important that the people in the local community in predator districts understand and agree to state predator control and management (e.g. Case 8); there must be accordance between the norms of the population and norms signalled by the law and punishment for breaching the laws (Aubert 1954). Other verdicts (like Case 6), exhibit less of a need for balance in the sense that local communities may disagree with the law and protection of predators, making it important for courts to convey strong signals that killing predators (outside state management) is strictly forbidden and will be punished.

Conclusion

This chapter has attempted to illuminate the conflict over the right to kill – predators' right to kill for food versus farmers' right to have their sheep and livestock killed under the circumstances that they dictate (e.g., as food for humans) rather than having them eaten by predators and humans' concomitant right to kill predators in defence of their right to kill their own sheep and livestock for human consumption. For example, the mother bear in Case 11 does *not* have the right to kill, even though she needs to feed herself and her cubs. For wolves, lynx, bears and wolverines, killing is a necessity; for humans it is luxury.

Even though the cases described above contain guilty verdicts, the anthropocentrism underlying the legislation concerning 'wildlife' crimes is quite clear. Killing predators is illegal not out of respect or sanctity for individual life, but in the interests of biodiversity. Speciesism is central, implying that humans, whether individual hunters or represented by the state, have the right to kill animals and the state has the right to authorise or deprive people of this right.

The lenient punishments in all of these cases shows that even though the predators have protection in law, this protection is minor and linked to their behaviour: if they act too much like the predators that they are – if they are too 'predator-like' by settling in un-wanted areas, eating animals that humans let out to graze, or reproduce too successfully – they will be killed. The lenient punishments imposed by the courts also signal that despite the protection that free-born animals (including predators) have due to the Wildlife law, Bern Convention and the Animal Welfare Act, breaches of these laws are not regarded as serious crimes. Rather, they are treated as misdemeanours. As a result, the image of predators as enemies of people in general, and of hunters, farmers and livestock, in particular, continues to be maintained.

State management of the predator populations in Norway historically was, and unfortunately still is, characterised by ecocidal tendencies (Agnew 2013; Boekhout van Solinge 2008; Larsen 2012; South 2010). The consequences of the crimes described above are comparable to the consequences of wildlife trafficking in destroying habitats, and the laws have little effect in preventing this ecocide (South 2010: 233). The harms and crimes committed against predators in Norway, whether legal and state authorised or illegal, have detrimental effects for the *individual* predators, for the *species* of which they are a part, and for other *animal species indirectly involved*, as well as *ecosystems* (such as in the case of overpopulation of moose and deer, which in turn, 'must be taken out' by hunters). It is also a great harm to all *humans* who appreciate nonhuman animals for the richness they provide for and to nature and who prefer to let nonhuman animals, including predators, live where they naturally belong, rather than exploit them for their own selfish purposes.

References

Agnew, R. 1998. The causes of animal abuse: a social psychological analysis. *Theoretical Criminology* 2(2): 177–210.

Andenæs, J. 1974. *Punishment and Deterrence*. Ann Arbor, MI: The University of Michigan Press.

Aubert, V. 1972. *Om straffens sosiale funksjon*. Oslo: Universitetsforlaget.

Beirne, P. 1999. For a nonspecisiest criminology. Animal abuse as an object of study. *Criminology: An Interdisciplinary Journal* 37(1): 117–49.

Beirne, P. 2007. Animal rights, animal abuse and green criminology. In P. Beirne and N. South (eds), *Issues in Green Criminology*. Cullompton: Willan, 55–83.

Beirne, P. 2009. *Confronting Animal Abuse*. Plymouth: Rowman & Littlefield.

Beirne, P. 2014. Theriocide: naming animal killing. Special issue of *International Journal for Crime, Justice and Social Democracy* 3(2): 49–66.

Benton, T. 1998. Rights and justice on a shared planet: more rights or new relations. *Theoretical Criminology* 2(2): 149–75.

Boekhout van Solinge 2008. Crime, conflicts and ecology in Africa. In R. Sollund (ed.), *Global Harms: Ecological Crime and Speciesism*. New York: Nova Science, 13–35.

Børresen, B. 2006. *Den ensomme apen. Instinkt på avveie* [The lonely ape. Instincts gone astray]. Oslo: Koloritt forlag.

Brisman, A. 2008. Crime-environment relationships and environmental. *Seattle Journal for Social Justice* 6(2): 727–817.

Cazaux, G. 1999. Beauty and the beast: animal abuse from a non speciesist criminological perspective. *Crime, Law and Social Change* 31: 105–26.

Cazaux, G. 2007. Labelling animals: non speciesist criminology and techniques to identify other animals. In P. Beirne and N. South (eds), *Issues in Green Criminology*. Cullompton: Willan, 87–114.

Christensen, T.B. 2013. *Kampen om de norske ulvene. Natur og miljø*. Available at: http://naturvernforbundet.no/naturogmiljo/kampen-om-de-norske-ulvene-article28279–1024.html. Accessed 7 January 2013.

Francione, G. 2008. *Animals as Persons: Essays on the Abolition of Animal Exploitation*. New York: Colombia University Press.

Grønli, K.S. 2005. Innavl blant skandinavisk ulv. *Forskning*. No. 28, January. Available at: http://www.forskning.no/artikler/2005/januar/1106765 810.44. Accessed 7 January 2015.

Hessen, D. 2013. Hvor unikt er mennesket [How unique is man]. In R. Sollund, M. Tønnessen and G. Larsen (eds), *Hvem er villest i landet her?* Oslo: Spartacus SAP.

Hobbs and Håkan Sand 2011. Shoot, shovel and shut up: cryptic poaching slows restoration of a large carnivore in Europe. *Proceedings of the Royal Society B: Biological Sciences*, 32. Available at: http://rspb.royalsocietypublishing.org/content/early/2011/08/08/rspb.2011.1275.full/. Accessed 7 January 2015.

Jacobsen, J. 2004. Om allmenprevensjon og straff. *Nordisk Tidsskrift for Kriminalvidenskab [Nordic Journal for Science of Crime]* 91(4): 311–20.

Kohm, S. and Greenhill, P. 2013. 'This is the North where we do what we want': popular green criminology and 'Little Red Riding Hood' films. In N. South and A. Brisman (eds), *Routledge Handbook in Green Criminology*. London and New York: Routledge, 365–79.

Larsen, G. 2012. The most serious crime: eco-genocide concepts and perspectives in eco-global criminology. In R. Ellefsen, R. Sollund and G. Larsen (eds), *Eco-Global Crimes: Contemporary Problems and Future Challenges*. Aldershot: Ashgate, 33–57.

Nibert, D. 2002. *Animal Rights, Human Rights: Entanglements of Oppression and Liberation*. Lanham, MD: Rowman & Littlefield.

Nurse, A. 2013. *Animal Harm: Perspectives on Why People Kill and Harm Animals*. Aldershot: Ashgate.

Pellow, D.N. 2013. Environmental justice, animal rights, and total liberation: from conflict and distance to points of common focus. In N. South and A. Brisman (eds), *Routledge International Handbook of Green Criminology*. London and New York: Routledge, 331–46.

Regan, T. 1999. *Djurens rättigheter. En filosofisk argumentation*. Falun: Bokförlaget Nye Doxa. [The case for animal rights. Berkeley University Press 1983.]

Skogen, K., Krange, O. and Figari, H. 2013. *Ulvekonflikter. En sosiologisk studie* [Wolfe conflicts. A sociological study]. Oslo: Akademika.

Sollund, R. 2001. Political refugees' violence in Norway. *Journal of Scandinavian Studies in Criminology and Crime Prevention* 2(1): 84–103.

Sollund, R. 2008/11. Causes for speciesism: difference, distance and denial. In R. Sollund (ed.), *Global Harms: Ecological Crime and Speciesism*. New York: Nova Science, 109–31.

Sollund, R. 2012. Specieisism as doxic practice, or valuing plurality and difference. In R. Ellefsen, R. Sollund and G. Larsen (eds), *Eco-Global Crimes: Contemporary Problems and Future Challenges*. Aldershot: Ashgate, 91–115.

Sollund, R. 2014. Animal abuse, animal rights and species justice. Paper presented at Presidential panel about green criminology at the ASC meeting in Atlanta, November 2013. Available at: https://asc41.com/Annual_Meeting/2013/Presidential%20Papers/Sollund%20Animal%20Abuse.pdf. Accessed 7 January 2015.

South, N., Brisman, A. and Beirne, P. 2013. A guide to a green criminology. In N. South and A. Brisman (eds), *Routledge International Handbook in Green Criminology*. London and New York: Routledge, 27–42.

South, N. 2010. The ecocidal tendencies of late modernity: transnational crime, social exclusion, victims and rights. In R. White (ed.), *Global Environmental Harm: Criminological Perspectives*. Cullompton: Willan, 288–49.

Sykes, G. and Matza, D. 1957. Techniques of neutralization: a theory of delinquency. *American Sociological Review* 22(6): 664–70.

Tønnessen, M. 2010. The legality and ethical legitimacy of wolf hunting in Scandinavia. In Conference report of the Nordic Council for Criminology, 65–72. Available at: http://www.nsfk.org/portals/0/research_seminar_report_52.pdf. Accessed 7 January 2015.

Tønnessen, M. 2013. Hvem er villest i landet her? Et ulveliv. In R. Sollund, M. Tønnessen and G. Larsen (eds), *Hvem er villest i landet her?* Oslo: Spartacus SAP.

White, R. 2012. The foundations of eco-global criminology. In R. Ellefsen, R. Sollund and G. Larsen (eds), *Eco-Global Crimes: Contemporary Problems and Future Challenges*. Aldershot: Ashgate, 15–33.

White, R. 2013. *Environmental Harm: An Eco-Justice Perspective*. Bristol: Polity Press.

PART II
Conflict over Declining Resources

Chapter 6

The State-Corporate
Tandem Cycling Towards Collision:
State-Corporate Harm and the
Resource Frontiers of Brazil and Colombia

Bram Ebus and Karlijn Kuijpers

Due to the growing scarcity of natural resources and rising prices for energy and raw materials, multinational corporations are increasingly trying to access and gain control over the remaining resources – much of which are located in remote areas, often referred to as 'frontiers' – recently opened up to resource exploitation (McLellan et al. 2012; Yellishetty et al. 2012). As Rivero and Cooney Seisededos (2010: 57) explain, a 'frontier' is the border that divides a known or organised space from another space that is as yet unknown or viewed as worthy of exploration and exploitation. 'More than just a theoretical concept, the frontier is a powerful metaphor that establishes the space of transformation, change, and conquest'. In order for a particular venture to be profitable, multinational corporations frequently need or require exclusive access to these resource-heavy areas; once obtained, the extraction processes are usually intense. Because gaining access to these areas and extracting the resources from them may displace groups of people already living in these areas or cause negative environmental impacts that adversely affect the survival of such groups, frontiers are often characterised by conflict and violence (Langfur 2006). This chapter discusses conflict over natural resources on three frontiers by examining the activities of mining companies AngloGold Ashanti and Gran Colombia Gold in Colombia and the case of the Belo Monte hydroelectric dam in Brazil.

In this chapter we analyse the conflicts over natural resources using state-corporate crime theory, which will be shortly commented on here. Much of what is considered an environmental justice issue can be understood as state-corporate crime, as states in many cases permit or facilitate environmental crimes (Zilney et al. 2006). Using the lens of state-corporate crime enables one to see the mutually beneficial relations between a small elite of state and corporate actors who, acting in concert, exploit natural resources. As this chapter will demonstrate, state-corporate interactions facilitate corporate access to natural resources (Ruggiero and South 2013; White 2013). Despite numerous adverse impacts of these projects, state actors often frame these controversial activities as 'motors for

Figure 6.1   A small-scale miners' community in Sur de Bolívar
Source: Photographer: Bram Ebus.

economic development' and therefore extensively support these projects (Deheza and Ribet 2012; Seoane et al. 2005). In Colombia, the energy-mining sector is one of the five 'locomotives of development' (DNP 2010). In Brazil, mining is also one of the most important economic sectors and hydroelectric dams are being constructed to attract mining corporations and other investments to frontier regions such as the Amazon (Kuijpers et al. 2014; Vargas 2013). But in both countries, this development policy faces serious opposition. On several occasions in 2013, hundreds of thousands of Colombians took to the streets in nationwide protests against the government's national development plans (BBC 2013), expressing anger and concern about current and future environmental, social and economic impacts related to the extractive industry. Brazil has also witnessed various protests against the government's development policy, the adverse social, environmental and economic impacts, and related corruption (Saad-Filho 2013).

As the state has subsumed corporate interests in its national development policy, both state and corporate actors become mutually dependent and have an interest in the rapid exploitation of natural resources. State and corporate actors can and do combine their different powers to concentrate control over natural resources in the hands of a few corporate actors through a process of accumulation by dispossession. As this chapter will explain, by privileging the interests of multinational corporations and consequently denying local communities' access to natural resources they are highly dependent upon, state actors virtually ensure that severe social conflict will ensue. This conflict is facilitated and exacerbated by many legal advantages that are granted by the state to corporate actors to create an attractive atmosphere for (foreign) multinationals, such as easy licensing processes, military and police support for these enterprises, tax advantages, and weak enforcement of state regulations. Furthermore, state actors repeatedly fail to properly protect human rights or the environment, which is especially important on frontiers, as these areas are often characterised by a range of adverse environmental and social impacts.

As Michalowski and Kramer (2000) argue, 'great powers and great crimes are inseparable. When economic and political powers pursue common interests, the potential for harm is magnified further'. This is clearly the case in the projects analysed, as this chapter will describe in further detail. But in order to keep on rolling-out the above-described economic development policy, it is in the interest of state and corporate actors to hide or otherwise distract attention from the serious adverse impacts of these projects and shape an image that suggests these projects foster local development. Large-scale mining and energy projects are therefore often developed under the guise of Corporate Social Responsibility (or CSR). CSR is commonly regarded as a duty of every corporate body to protect the interest of the society at large (Holme and Watts 1999). Nevertheless, we argue that CSR cannot be regarded as a generous form of well-doing, but as a capitalist tool to increase profits (Banerjee 2008; Fooks et al. 2013; Gatto 2002). The so-called 'voluntary' implementation of CSR often leads to better social and political acceptance of the projects, which serves companies and government actors that want to continue developing them (Fooks et al. 2013). CSR is no guarantee of any decrease in adverse impacts and can often be better regarded as a public relations tool or device for managing regulatory environments (Fooks et al. 2013) or as a profit-based, strategic calculation as a response to the bad reputation of industry (Dashwood 2012). Taking this perspective, it seems that not much has changed since Friedman's (1970) famous statement, 'the one and only social responsibility of business is to increase its profits'.

Our chapter takes a critical stance towards the concept of CSR and other corporate neutralisation techniques more generally. Sykes and Matza (1957) identified various techniques used by delinquents to justify their illegitimate actions: denial of injury, denial of responsibility, denial of the victim, condemnation of the condemners, and appeal to higher loyalties. We analyse the techniques used by corporations in the cases studied and discuss why these are illegitimate, based on the internationally accepted UN Guiding Principles on Business and Human Rights (UNGPs) which stipulate corporate responsibilities for adverse human rights impacts and are one of the most authoritative and inclusive normative frameworks on business responsibilities for human rights (Aaronson and Higham 2013; Frankental 2012; Kemp and Vanclay 2013; Lindsay et al. 2013). This UN Framework is unanimously endorsed by the UN Human Rights Council.

The case descriptions are based on fieldwork that we conducted in the affected areas between April and November 2013. Data have been obtained through semi-structured interviewing of affected groups, and corporate and state actors who are involved in these developments. Additional data have been collected through scientific literature review and analysis of government, corporate and NGO documents.

AngloGold Ashanti: A New Epoch of Violence

AngloGold Ashanti (AGA), the world's third-largest gold mining multinational, has set its sights on Colombia's gold reserves. The South African company has already obtained 424 land concessions covering an area of 763,337 hectares (ha) in Colombia, which will add up to 865,649 ha when 625 additional outstanding applications are granted (Colombian Mining Database 2013). AGA engaged in questionable methods to obtain the lion's share of these concessions. Rather than march in and try to acquire them as AGA, which could have raised public concern and opposition, AGA used its subsidiaries, Kedahda S.A. and Kedahda Segunda Ltda., to procure the concessions, allowing the parent company to maintain a low-profile in Colombia while stockpiling its grand total (Idárraga et al. 2010). A mutually beneficial situation between company and state arose when former employees of the Ministry of Energy and Mines charged with granting mining titles (AGA controls 59 per cent of these titles, together with the company Mineros S.A. with whom AGA has a joint venture (Portafolio 2012) found new jobs with AGA after serving the national government (La Silla Vacía 2011).

Despite the elaborate CSR strategy that the mining company is implementing internationally, it suffers from a bad image. For example, AGA won the 2011 Public Eye award for most irresponsible multinational because of water contamination it caused in Ghana (Public Eye Awards 2014). Six years earlier, Human Rights Watch (2005) discovered that AGA had made payments to paramilitary groups in the Democratic Republic of Congo. While AGA tries to gain a better name in Colombia, its practices again reveal the true nature of the company.

The adverse impacts of future mining operations of AGA in Colombia are already manifesting themselves in various ways. The megaproject 'La Colosa', which is – according to the company – targeting one of Latin America's biggest gold reserves, has entered the exploratory phase. Illegal drilling in forest reserves (Ministerio de Ambiente, Vivienda y Desarrollo Territorial 2010) and the illegal use of water have been reported (Colombia Solidarity Campaign 2013) and suggest that if the company is already neglecting the law in the pre-exploitation phase, it will likely continue to do so once the project commences. Apparently, AGA's disregard for the law is not limited to drilling and water use. Colombia's Contraloría (comptroller) has raised red flags about the mining company, pointing out that AGA has not paid surface levies in the amount of 3.9 million USD, which would make the company guilty of tax evasion (Contraloría General de la República 2013).

Representatives of the national ombudsman, environmental authorities, and the Contraloría have expressed concern about adverse economic and environmental impacts, and human rights problems which are beginning to emerge. For example, an adversary of AGA's megaproject 'La Colosa' was killed in front of his children in September 2013. As a result, an Early Day Motion (a means of drawing attention to an issue) was tabled in the British Parliament to urge the Colombian authorities to undertake a thorough and independent investigation of this murder (Parliament.uk 2013). Another individual was killed in Cauca on 30 September 2013. The victims' entire municipality is the subject of an application for large-scale mining concessions (National Mining Agency 2013) and she had spoken out publicly against the company's interest in the region. Although it is unknown who committed the murder, AGA has had prior contact with paramilitaries in other operations abroad (HRW 2005) and the mining industry in Colombia has an extensive track record of killing activists (Ramirez Cuellar 2005). While it would seem that the *adversaries* of AGA are in need of projection, AGA has signed various agreements with the Ministry of Defence and a number of military bases have deployed forces for the protection of AGA. According to Goodland (2011), this is not the best way to solve security issues: 'At the moment, a full 30 percent of the budget of the Ministry of Defense is spent on protecting foreign mining corporations from impacted communities. This waste of money could be greatly reduced by following Colombian law and best practices to prevent damaging impacts that lead to conflict and violence. Prevention is better than cure'. Ivan Cepeda, representative in the Colombian Chamber, worries about the military aid for foreign multinationals and calls it paradoxical that communities in the same mining zones were excluded from extra military help when receiving threats from illegal armed groups. It should come as no surprise then, that AGA pays 1.9 million USD to the Ministry of Defense (El Colombiano 2014).

AGA participates in the CME (mining-energy committee) – a business-initiated, business-regulated and business-ruled platform that works on the implementation of the UNGPs, and advises for example on how to relate to the military for self-protection. Sanctions after violation of the UNGPs are not given (CME 2013). According to a representative from an international human rights organisation, there is no place for NGOs in the platform; it is ruled solely by the extractive sector and the Colombian government. AGA publicly promotes its concern for human rights through its participation in the CME. But its involvement in various curious cases and its repeated denial of responsibility – for which the company has emerged unscathed – call into question the credibility of the platform (Interview, 15 October 2013).

Figure 6.2   A small-scale miner leaves the bocamina, the 'mouth of a mining shaft', with a cart full of minerals

Source: Photographer: Bram Ebus.

Sur de Bolívar

The arrival of AGA in Sur de Bolívar (first under the name of Kedahda S.A.) in 2003 was badly received by most of the local population. The development pretext used by the Anglo-South African multinational seems more of a myth to the miners from Sur de Bolívar. According to the local miners union large-scale mining does not have anything to offer for their members. Their job security diminished significantly after a new mining code was implemented in 2001, facilitating the increased acquisition of their territories by foreign multinationals such as AGA. The most noticeable change after AGA (amongst others) bought their mining titles in the region is the aggravated security situation for small-scale miners, social activists and unionists.

One of the most startling examples is the death of a community leader and miner from Sur de Bolívar in 2006. According to a first-hand witness (Interview community leader, 18 September 2013), this community leader was murdered under the false pretext of being a member of Colombia's second largest guerrilla group, the ELN (National Liberation Army). Interviewees all claim that he had nothing to do with the ELN although he was known for his publicly stated opposition to the entry of multinational corporations. Nevertheless, the army fabricated a fictitious relationship between the community leader and the insurgency movement. A month before the assassination of this local leader, a *guerrillero* from the ELN was murdered in a battle with the army that was, according to one informant, a staged fight. The body of the *guerrillero* was left in front of the community leader's door with the threat 'next time it will be you', a threat that was followed through.

More formal grounds for suspecting the community leader of involvement with the ELN followed later when the army made a document discussing a relationship between the victim and the ELN (Informe Inteligencia Batallón Nueva Granada 2006) specifically referring to the victim's presence in a community meeting in March 2006 that was organised to block the entrance of AGA and Kedahda S.A. in the community. Only a half year later, on 19 September 2006, he was murdered.

The witness interviewed was walking fewer than 100 metres behind the victim and saw how he encountered a group of soldiers from the nearby battalion, was engaged in a staged fight and the victim was abused though not killed at this point. Quickly entering a house to alert a nearby family, the witness heard seven or eight shots as a killing under false pretext took place. The victim's body was collected by family members on the next day from the military base. The battalion officially stated that their target was killed in a fight with members of the 'narco-terrorist organisation' ELN. A human rights lawyer (Interview, 12 September 2013) claims the battalion Nueva Granada is known for its role in protecting the interests of AGA – a sentiment that is confirmed by various other interviewees.

It is impossible to ascribe the violence directly to the newly entered multinationals. As stated above, AGA has agreements with the Colombian Ministry of Defense, and military battalions are deployed for their 'safety and security'.

Figure 6.3   Home of a riverine family on the Xingu River
Source: Photographer: Karlijn Kuijpers.

Moreover, paramilitary human rights violations, including abductions, death threats, torture and murder closely accompanied the arrival of the mining multinational. While Colombia is on the verge of becoming a mining-dominated country, the 'arrival decade' of mining companies seems to suggest some of the possible impacts of the multinational mining industry in conflict-ridden Colombia.

Gran Colombia Gold's Business in Segovia

Another newcomer to Colombia is the company Gran Colombia Gold (GCG), headquartered in Canada and listed on the Toronto Stock Exchange. According to the company, GCG is currently the largest underground gold- and silver-extracting company operating in Colombia (GCG 2013). In 2012, GCG extracted 100,895 ounces of gold (GCG 2013), mostly from its operation in Segovia – mining gold veins that have been exploited since the Spanish conquest (Echeverry Castañeda 2009). Most inhabitants of the municipality work in the mines or have jobs linked in some way to mining, which is why Segovia can be considered a traditional mining community. Gold mining is a way of life for the local population, essential for their livelihoods. As mining methods developed, the implementation of the poisonous mercury in the extraction process brought about negative environmental and health consequences. Due, in part, to the irresponsible use of mercury in places like Segovia, Colombia is now the world's largest per capita mercury polluter (Veiga 2012). But, aside for the mercury pollution, Segovia is a tough place to live for other reasons.

Over the years, the high concentration of gold has triggered considerable conflict in the region as various armed groups have sought to gain control over the local natural resources. Periods of (paramilitary) violence are not unknown to the local population. For example, one of the most extreme cases of violence occurred in 1988. An indiscriminate daytime attack by one of the many paramilitary groups that still roam Colombia took 43 lives in the central village square of Segovia. This massacre was directed against the growing local influence of the legalised political party UN (Unión Patriótica) which had its origin in the armed revolutionary forces (las Farc). According to Uekert (1995), the massacre was 'an attempt to physically eliminate UP members and by doing so, to create an atmosphere of terror among all persons associated with the UP party'. This act of violence cannot be separated from the conflict over the Segovian gold reserves and territorial control.

Paramilitary presence and violence is still reported in Segovia, with a slight change in the political character. According to the Colombian magazine Semana (2013), some of the 200 miners who work in the area under the control of GCG made payments to criminal groups linked to the paramilitary chief 'El Macaco' Carlos Mario Jiménez, currently incarcerated in the US (United States Department of Justice 2011). An interviewee (Representative Frontino syndicate, 12 July 2013) stated that the paramilitaries continue to threaten the local population, but according to him, they currently act on behalf of the Canadian mining multinational. The representative of the syndicate of the previous owners of the Segovian mines – Frontino S.A. – reports that several of his co-workers were abducted and murdered in the last few years. One of his colleagues is still recovering from the effects of a 2010 shooting in which five bullets hit him in the stomach. The interviewee himself is unable to work in Segovia because of ongoing death threats. Although he no longer lives in Segovia proper, he still feels it a necessary precaution to change accommodation every two or three days. 'It is certainly the case that groups outside the law pressure us small-scale miners to not continue working within the title of Gran Colombia Gold. If we continue to work without a permit of Gran Colombia Gold; they will kill us'.

GCG's Legal Land Grab

The local community's problems concerning GCG began around 2010 when the administration of Colombia's ex-president Álvaro Uribe Vélez provided GCG with mining titles of a former British mining company active in Segovia, Frontino S.A. Frontino had gone bankrupt in 1979. In order to compensate Frontino's former miners and retirees, an act was drawn in New York that provided for the transfer of the mining rights to the Frontino labour union and its (former) workers. This act was approved by the Colombian consulate, the Ministry of Labour, and the superintendent of Frontino, but was concealed until, by chance, a trade unionist discovered the existence of the document in 2000 (Langlois and Mariani 2011). Since then, the former employees have claimed to be the legal owners of the Segovia mine, which was confirmed by the labour court in Medellín and the Supreme Court in 2007. Yet in spite of these legal decisions, GCG has continued its operations in the area.

In 2010, former President Uribe transferred the mining rights of Segovia to GCG, denying the rights of the small-scale miners and retirees in Segovia (Langlois and Mariani 2011). Subsequently, a few of Uribe's former government employees began working for GCG (La Silla Vacía 2012). Former campaign manager Mario Pacheco, Ernan Martinez, ex-minister of Mines and Energy, and María Consuelo Araujo, ex-minister of Culture, all found high-placed positions within GCG (La Silla Vacía 2012).

Uribe, who now is under investigation by the Colombian congress for his relations with the paramilitary (InsightCrime 2013), grew up in Antioquia, the province where Segovia is located. According to the union's representative, he had a large role in the Frontino-GCG transfer. In the 12 years after the 2001 mining code, 1.5 million ha have been sold to large-scale mining companies (Portafolio 2012). Uribe was president during eight of these years and a group of his political elite found its way to high positions within the same companies who benefited from his term in power.

Not implementing the Act of New York did not only mean the syndicate's workers and pensioners missed out on the already more than 30 years' worth of gold exploited in Segovia. It also meant a rise in forced displacement of the small-scale miners, along with many threats and human rights abuses for those who remained. This 'legal robbery' – the disregard of a legal agreement – has favoured a group of former government leaders and a large corporation, while causing a new period of human suffering for everyone else. As a local unionist said: 'Gran Colombia Gold has also had a history of poor socially responsible practices on its mining site in Segovia, Antioquia. The multinational's presence has contributed to the instability of the area by outsourcing the production process and avoiding its responsibility to provide effective protection measures for local miners, who are blackmailed and threatened by local paramilitaries' (US Office on Colombia 2013).

Involvement in Causing Crime

The accusation that a great deal of paramilitary violence in and around Segovia in recent years is linked to GCG is not a unique case of multinational-paramilitary connections in Colombia. Captain Cardenas, the former director of SIJIN-Urabá (Judicial Investigations and Intelligence Service), has stated that 'the paramilitaries ... favour the interests of the multinationals in Colombia, and they are in charge of cleansing the terrain of people who represent a challenge to their interests, such as unionists or popular leaders, who disappear or are being killed' (CINEP, 'Deuda-General del Río' 6, in Hristov, 2009). His statement is consistent with an argument made by the president of Colombia's mining union Sintraminercol, Ramirez Cuellar (2005): 'the forced displacement caused by paramilitary groups has a high correlation with resource-rich areas where mining companies settle and develop plans'.

An interviewee (Representative Frontino syndicate, 12 July 2013) explained how a part of GCG's 'legal robbery' functions: the company offers money to local miners in order to buy their mine shafts, based on the present concentration of gold. The interviewee says that GCG manipulates the gold concentration studies in order to offer less than half the value for the mines. When people do not agree with the price, state forces are put into action by the company to evict the miners. This practice stands in sharp contrast to the strategy GCG claims to have with its Artisanal Miner Partnership Model, which it describes as follows: 'By integrating artisanal miners into our mining operations, Gran Colombia has created a social and economic model that has attracted positive attention from business, governmental and social/humanitarian organisations around the world' (GCG 2012). Their slogan 'Be a positive agent of change for our communities' is difficult to swallow; state agents are ordered to forcefully evict miners from their operations and unionists face life threats and violence related to their campaigning activities against the interests of GCG. For years this area has become the operation zone of illegal armed groups with an interest in the production of gold: from the paramilitaries of the 'Bloque Central de Bolívar' under command of 'Macaco', to their heirs of the post-demobilisation structures (CITpax 2012).

Even if the company is not directly responsible for the violence and threats directed at local miners by paramilitary units, it is not actively opposing such measures and should recognise its role in the conflict being fought for control of resource-rich areas. Because GCG benefits from these human rights violations, it bears a *moral* responsibility. Michalowski and Kramer (2000) describe the 'plausible deniability' of crimes, when direct responsibility for specific crimes is denied. Nevertheless, they argue that a political culture and organisational framework can be created that ultimately leads to heinous acts that would not occur without that culture and those frameworks – exactly the case in Segovia.

In situations where corporations benefit from human rights violations, the company sometimes has little impetus to take reasonable steps to stop those reprehensible activities (Gatto 2002). In the present example, GCG benefits from armed violent groups operating outside the law, chasing out small-scale miners and threatening Frontino unionists. While one would hope that a company claiming to engage in CSR would investigate whether violent groups are violating human rights in the company's interest, GCG has failed to do so. In fact, two representatives from the headquarters of GCG in Canada (5 December 2013), made the following statements in an interview: 'We know for sure that there was a lot of conflict before we arrived. You know, there was, also there is today.

But there is still a lot of money to be made from gold mining. And I guess the statistics are proving that there's more to be made from gold mining than that there is cocaine nowadays'. Another corporate representative stated, 'I don't think that a company has to be in charge of fixing a problem that the government has to resolve ... The government has to be the one to take care of that. We can help indirectly but we cannot solve this as a company'.

According to the UNGPs, companies have an obligation to prevent any contribution to adverse human rights impacts (UNOHCHR 2011). Under the UNGPs, companies should refrain from the engagement in projects situated in conflict zones where contributing to human rights violations is inevitable. These obligations should be based on a moral and ethical stance towards society, even though they still fit in the voluntary approach (UNOHCHR 2011). The risk of CSR is that it is often regarded as a tool for inclusive, sustainable and ethical conduct of business, but fails to focus on the possibilities it offers to cover up misconduct.

When summing up the allegations, it appears that GCG's CSR does not tackle their involvement in violent practices, environmental degradation, social harm and the adverse impacts on the livelihoods and futures of small-scale miners. For a small-scale miner, an already harsh life can become unbearable and tragic when it is accompanied by displacement and violence and the destruction of a way of life.

Belo Monte or Belo Monstro

'Belo Monte continues to be developed with norms from the military dictatorship. With the same behaviour of disrespecting laws, with human rights violations, with disrespect of socio-environmental rights, disrespecting all types of laws' – Public Defender and Researcher University of Pará, 26 July 2013.

'Belo Monte will be constructed, by fair means or foul' – Former President Luiz Inácio Lula da Silva. (Hall and Branford 2012)

'They are conducting crimes using public money'– Local resistance leader, 2 August 2013.

The Belo Monte Dam, which will be the third-largest hydroelectric dam in the world, is currently being installed in the Brazilian Amazon on the Xingu River in the state of Pará (Stickler et al. 2013). The first plans for the construction of the dam date back to 1975 and led to a lot of resistance in the subsequent period. In 1989, when the government wanted to put the plans for the dam into practice, the first Encounter of the Peoples of the Xingu with more than 3,000 participants was held. Shortly after this encounter, two local leaders protesting against the dam were killed. As a result of the continuing protests and the controversial nature of the size, location and potential impacts, the plans were stalled (Fearnside 2006; McCormick 2011).

But under the Lula government (2003–10) – and specifically, under the federal government's Program for Accelerated Economic Growth (PAC), a large infrastructure program aimed at accelerating economic growth in Brazil (Domingues et al. 2009; Erber 2009) – plans for constructing the Belo Monte Dam were revived. In 2008, a Second Encounter of the Peoples of the Xingu was convened and further protests in following years underlined continuing antagonism to Belo Monte and the development paradigm that it symbolised for many people (Hall and Branford 2012). Despite these protests, the dam is currently being built by Norte Energia, a consortium of public and private enterprises.

The controversy surrounding the Belo Monte Dam is not unusual. Rather, it is a typical situation in which control over natural resources is concentrated in corporate hands through a process of accumulation by dispossession. Due to the technical design of the Belo Monte Dam, the flow of the Xingu River will be drastically changed (Hall and Branford 2012). Canals will be built to cut off the Big Bend of the Xingu River and most of the river's runoff will be led through these canals so that the Big Bend will see an 80 per cent reduction in river runoff (see Figure 6.1) (Cunha and Ferreira 2012; Jaichand and Andrade Sampaio 2013; Hochstetler 2011).

The Xingu River is essential for the subsistence of the riverine communities, as fish is their most important source of protein and rivers are the only mode of transport in these isolated areas (Forsberg et al. 1993). The reduced river runoff will likely decimate fish stocks and it will become impossible for indigenous communities to reach the nearby city of Altamira to trade products (Barthem et al. 1991; Bunn and Arthington 2002; Schwartzman et al. 2013). Furthermore, the formation of small, stagnant pools of water in the original riverbed will provide a breeding ground for malaria and other waterborne diseases (Gorayeb 2009). The lowering of the water table will also destroy the agricultural production of the region and will affect water quality and the rainforests in a much larger area (de Sousa Júnior and Reid 2010). As a result, between 20,000 and 40,000 people, including 1,400 indigenous people from 10 different communities, will be forced to move and most of them will receive no compensation (de Sousa Júnior and Reid 2010; Schwartzman et al. 2013; Interview Public Defender Altamira, 2 August 2013). Further upstream, the lands of forest and riverine communities will be flooded. At the time of writing, most of the affected people have already left the region and have moved into nearby cities or villages which are facing rapid urbanisation but whose public services are ill-equipped to handle such an influx (see generally Brisman 2012). Furthermore, various types of crimes, such as human trafficking, forced prostitution, violence and theft are on the rise in these cities (Interview Human Rights Advocate, 25 July 2013; Globo Pará 2013).

The Belo Monte Dam has faced serious protests because of its anticipated adverse social and environmental impacts, and because of serious allegations of corruption surrounding the project (MPF 2007, 2009). Nevertheless, a number of interviewees claim that the current protest movement is weaker than in the 1980s. According to these interviewees, protests on the construction site have been criminalised. As these interviewees claim, the police are threatening individuals from non-governmental organisations and have had an excessive presence at every local protest (Interview Human Rights Advocate, 25 July 2013; Interview Local Leader Altamira, 2 August 2013). As a human rights advocate explains, the police impede protesters' access to the construction site, threaten them with arrests, and, when arrests do occur, sometimes confiscate individuals' possessions, such as clothes or documents, without returning them (Interview Human Rights Advocate, 25 July 2013). In 2012, various local leaders were imprisoned after a peaceful protest at the construction site (MXVPS 2012). Interviewees also report strong discrepancies between the capacities of non-governmental organisations and corporations in court cases related to protests. As an human rights advocate (Interview, 25 July 2013) explains, corporations have a group of advocates ready to open court cases when people protest against the project. The interviewee claims that these advocates have well-prepared denunciations even before the protests start. During the protests, they make the denunciations so that the police can close the case even before human rights advocates can react to the denunciations, which creates an uneven playing field in court. In addition, various local labour unions or environmental organisations have been paid by Norte Energia and various opposition leaders have been offered government positions in an effort to weaken these organisations or make them less critical (Interview Local Leader Altamira, 2 August 2013; Interview President Agricultural Union Altamira, 6 August 2013; Interview Member Instituto Socioambiental, 30 July 2013). Despite these difficulties, various (indigenous) groups continue to protest against the dam.

The Inter-American Commission on Human Rights has called upon the Brazilian government to halt the licensing process for the dam on the grounds that it would constitute a violation of the right to life and physical integrity (IACHR 2011; Veçoso and Do Amaral Jr. 2011). Also the International Labour Organisation (ILO) and the UN have expressed concerns about adverse human rights impacts related to the dam (ILO 2012; UNHRC 2013, 2010). The public prosecutor has filed 20 court cases concerning adverse social and environmental impacts and serious allegations of corruption by Norte Energia and construction companies involved (MPF 2007, 2009, 2013; Interview Public Prosecutor Belém, 21 July 2013). Nevertheless, the construction of the dam started in 2011. As a result, numerous (indigenous) people have been displaced without proper compensation, and further human rights violations will occur when the plans are pursued (Jaichand and Andrade Sampaio 2013; MPF 2011). Despite these concerns and the lively protest of affected groups, the Brazilian government supports the project in various ways.

Figure 6.4   Small houses in Altamira in an area that will be flooded by the Belo Monte dam

Source: Photographer: Karlijn Kuijpers.

State Support for the Belo Monte Dam

The Brazilian state supports the Belo Monte project through applying a licensing process that repeatedly favours corporate interests. The Environmental Impact Assessment (EIA) that forms the basis of the licensing procedure has grave faults and omissions (Barbosa Magalhães Santos and Del Moral Hernandez 2009; Vieira Lisboa and Carvalho Zagallo 2010). For example, most people who will have to leave the area as a result of the dam have not been considered 'directly affected' in the EIA and therefore have received no compensation. Nevertheless, the Brazilian environmental authorities have accepted the EIA and have allowed for the construction of the dam without any compensation for most people living in the Big Bend, all of whom will have to leave or have already left their territories because of the drop in water levels of the river they highly depend on (Interview Public Defender Altamira, 2 August 2013). In other words, the drop in river levels has forced their evictions – a type of forced displacement and migration that contravenes various human rights instruments (UNOHCHR 2013).

The Brazilian government further facilitates the quick construction of the dam by neglecting the right to Free, Prior and Informed Consent, as stipulated in the United Nations Declaration on the Rights of Indigenous Peoples (UN 2008) and ILO Convention 169 on Indigenous and Tribal Peoples (1989). The affected indigenous communities have the right to give their consent over decisions that affect their territories, but as Jaichand and Andrade Sampaio (2013) argue, 'it can be concluded beyond doubt that the dialogues established with indigenous peoples did not comply with the obligation to consult them in a free, prior, and informed manner'. Former president Luiz Inácio Lula da Silva did not seem willing to take into account the interests and opinions of minorities such as indigenous groups. As he said, 'fifteen or twenty thousand people cannot impede progress for 185 million Brazilians' (Leroy et al. 2009). By saying so, Lula undermined the self-determination of affected people by appealing to a higher loyalty of nationwide development.

As part of the licensing procedure, IBAMA (environmental authority) and FUNAI (authority for indigenous peoples) did set 40 conditions that had to be met before a construction licence could be granted. These conditions were meant to remediate the adverse impacts of the dam (Fearnside 2012). The Norte Energia consortium, responsible for building the dam, did not fulfil these conditions (MPF 2012). A number of IBAMA officials who had refused to give the licence were then forced to leave office (Galindo da Fonseca and Bourgoignie 2011). Finally, a 'partial licence' was given, unprecedented in Brazil and regarded by many as a way to circumvent official licensing procedures (Fearnside 2012). The dam currently is under construction, and most of the conditions still have not been met (IBAMA 2013). Nevertheless, Norte Energia and other corporations involved present these obligatory conditions as CSR projects and use them to show that 'the dam brings development to the region'. The conditions are thus being used as a neutralisation technique by appealing to higher loyalties, such as local (economic) development, better education, better health care and employment. The development of these projects is not just a form of CSR that companies can flout without penalty, but are legal obligations that still have not been met (IBAMA 2013).

Brazil's public prosecutor has opened 20 court cases concerning the illegality of the Belo Monte Dam, various of them directed against the Brazilian state or state institutions (MPF 2013). According to various interviewees, including some Public Prosecutors, most of these court cases have foundered in a judicial system that mainly serves corporate interests (Interview Public Prosecutor Belém, 21 July 2013; Interview Human Rights Advocate, 25 July 2013). None of the court cases has been concluded, although some of them commenced more than 10 years ago (MPF 2013). Lawyers have halted construction of the dam several times, but these injunctions have been repeatedly reversed by the decisions of other judges within a few days (BBC 2011; Oliveiira 2013; Sibaja and Clendenning 2010). Many interviewees claim that judges are very partial and biased. A human rights advocate (25 July 2013) claims: 'the judge is totally biased. Biased, biased, biased. The judges are strongly linked to the local power. The power of Norte Energia is superior to all, including the local public power. The judges are fully linked to Norte Energia's practices. We know that judges use practices that favour the company'. As a public prosecutor in Belém (21 July 2013) claims:

'Judges are financially supported by enterprises, so the public prosecutor can't compete with these forces'. A local resistance leader (2 August 2013) claims that 'Brazil's current judicial system acts in concordance with the corporate interests. The judicial system does not accredit and investigate court cases opened by the Public Prosecutor. There are some ethical judges, but only some. But they are being paralysed by the important judges who are in favour of these crimes. The majority of the judges are an instrument of the state to realise its objectives of economic development'. The local resistance group, Movimento Xingu Vivo Para Sempre, has reported several cases where judges speaking against Belo Monte have subsequently been intimidated with threats and political pressure (MXVPS et al. 2010). Because Brazilian judges have failed to properly try and punish the responsible actors, they have facilitated the denial of harms and victims and illegality related to Belo Monte.

In 2011, the Inter-American Commission on Human Rights (IACHR) called upon the Brazilian government to stop the licensing process for the dam, as several human rights would be violated as a result of the construction of the dam (Veçoso and Do Amaral Jr. 2011). The Brazilian government reacted by calling back its ambassador to the IACHR and threatening to freeze payments to the commission. Subsequently, the Organization of American States (OAS) called upon the IACHR to revise its statement and the commission did so (Hall and Branford 2012; Jaichand and Andrade Sampaio 2013). The Brazilian state has denied the adverse human rights impacts and has placed pressure on official bodies, such as the IACHR, to neglect the adverse impacts. This has enabled corporations to keep on denying the adverse impacts and present the project as 'responsible' or 'sustainable'. As the mining company, Vale, a member of the Norte Energia consortium, claims: 'We think that Belo Monte is a sustainable project in all aspects. Vale does not cause any human rights violations in its projects nor in consortiums in which it takes part' (Email contact Vale, 6 August 2013).

Despite the grave problems related to the Belo Monte Dam, the Brazilian state has supported the dam through the publicly owned BNDES, the Brazilian Development Bank. This bank, that in total gives out twice as many loans as the World Bank, awarded the project with the largest loan in the bank's history – a stunning 10.8 billion USD – about 85 per cent of the total project costs (BNDES 2012). BNDES did not set any environmental or social conditions for the project (BNDES 2012). BNDES is closely linked to Belo Monte, as the director of BNDES is also a member of the administrative council of the mining company Vale, which is a member of the Norte Energia consortium and one of the corporations that will benefit significantly from the energy generated by Belo Monte (Kuijpers et al. 2014; Vale 2013).

The Brazilian state further supports the project with police and military support (Ribeiro 2013; Sposati 2013). According to many interviewees, the military police has strong links with corporate actors and repeatedly favours business interests by intimidating and attempting to silence people who are critical about the dam.

Figure 6.5   A miner working the oxygen poor mining shafts in Sur de Bolívar

Source: Photographer: Bram Ebus.

As a human rights advocate claims, 'civil and political rights are extremely violated in cases related to Belo Monte'. According to a number of interviewees, Norte Energia provides food and housing for military police, which is regarded as a strategy to make them act in favour of the Belo Monte Dam and suppress local protest. The blurred division between the company and governmental authorities becomes clear when looking at the police passing by in Altamira: they all have the company's logo on their cars. As a public prosecutor in Altamira claims, 'the interests of the federal government are the same as those of the companies. There is no clear separation between the two'.

It is clear that the Brazilian government supports the quick construction of the dam, and that the interests of government and corporate actors are interwoven, as the state is dependent on the corporate actors for the realisation of its economic development policy and the corporate actors are reliant on a state willing and able to facilitate its corporate development goals. As a result, the Brazilian state fails to protect human and indigenous rights, and uses judicial, legislative, police and military powers to support the construction of the dam. As an interviewee from Instituto Socioambiental (30 July 2013) explains, 'the federal government is commanded by the construction companies. Or the other way around: construction companies can also be a tool through which politicians can reach their political goals'.

As a result of the strong interlinkages between state and corporate actors, the neutralisation technique of denial of responsibility is often used. According to many interviewees, Norte Energia shirks various responsibilities to state actors (Interview human rights advocate Belém, 25 July 2013; Interview resistance leader Altamira, 2 August 2013), and members of the consortium shirk responsibilities to each other (Email contact Vale, 6 August 2013; Email contact BNDES, 30 July 2013). Nevertheless, according to the UNGPs, 'the responsibility to respect human rights is a global standard of expected conduct for all business enterprises wherever they operate. It exists independently of States' abilities and/or willingness to fulfil their own human rights obligations, and does not diminish those obligations'. Furthermore, 'the responsibility of business enterprises to respect human rights applies to all enterprises regardless of their size, sector, operational context, ownership and structure' (UNOHCHR 2011). Every corporation thus has a responsibility to respect human rights, a responsibility that is being undermined when using the neutralisation technique of denial of responsibilities.

Conclusion

Resource frontiers are integral to the realisation of both corporate and state objectives: corporations try to gain control over frontier resources and states often try to attract these corporations to the frontiers to increase investment and economic growth. The wealth of resource frontiers can only be exploited through control of territories, politics and people, which only can be achieved by actors with the political and monetary means to do so. The cases described in this chapter demonstrate that both corporate and state actors are eager to manoeuvre themselves into positions of 'control'. In theory, governments are expected to regulate and control corporate actors, holding them accountable for harmful activities, while ensuring and protecting its citizens' human rights, the nation's well-being, and the health and future of its environment and natural resources (UNOHCHR 2011). But in practice, state actors often fail to do so, as the overlapping interests of states and corporations are often exploited to create mutually beneficial relationships that seem to benefit an elite group of corporate and state actors and rely on crimes, harms to people and nature, and land grabbing. State actors deny problems by ignoring violations, fail to enforce the law, and create lax licensing procedures (or sidestep onerous ones) and repeatedly give benefits to corporate actors, through illegally transferred titles, support of violent state forces (Hristov 2005), or contracts or new laws that are highly beneficial for these corporate actors. By doing so, state actors facilitate corporations, and the law-breaking behaviour by those 'partners in crime' therefore fits the terminology of state-corporate crimes.

Because these harmful projects are essential in economic development policies and corporate strategies, both state and corporate actors have an interest in neutralising adverse impacts related to the projects. The premise of local and national (economic) development is being used either to ignore or justify the harms and crimes related to the projects. CSR is further used to enhance the image of the harmful projects. Attention is being drawn away from serious problems by focusing on projects with a development character. Nevertheless, these projects are not a simple form of righting wrongs or compensating victims or offsetting harm, but should rather be regarded as a strategy to neutralise or hide harmful practices. According to the internationally accepted UNGPs, this strategy is invalid: 'a failure to respect human rights in one area cannot be cancelled out by a benefit provided in another' (UNOHCHR 2012).

The present study shows that risks for adverse environmental and social impacts on resource frontiers are especially high when the interests of corporate and state actors overlap or merge. Various neutralisation techniques, as described by Sykes and Matza (1957), are being used to cover up the adverse impacts. Given the increasing scarcity and rising prices of natural resources and because various Latin American governments continue to build their economic development policies on the exploitation of natural resources (Seoane et al. 2005), this pattern is likely to continue in the future.

References

Banerjee, S.B. 2008. Corporate social responsibility: the good, the bad and the ugly. *Critical Sociology* 34(1): 51–79.

Barbosa Magalhães Santos, S.M.S. and Del Moral Hernandez, F. (eds) 2009. Painel de Especialistas. Análise Crítica do Estudo de Impacto Ambiental do Aproveitamento Hidrelétrico de Belo Monte. Belém, September 2009.

Barthem, R.B., de Brito Ribeiro, M.C.L. and Petrere Jr, M. 1991. Life strategies of some long-distance migratory catfish in relation to hydroelectric dams in the Amazon Basin. *Biological Conservation* 55(3): 339–45.

BBC. 2011. Brazil dam company wins Belo Monte appeal. Available at: http://www.bbc.co.uk/news/world-latin-america-16228680. Accessed 20 December 2013.

BBC. 2013. Colombian government to negotiate with striking farmers. Available at: http://www.bbc.co.uk/news/world-latin-america-23850074. Accessed 15 October 2013.

BNDES (Banco Nacional de Desenvolvimento Econômico e Social). 2012. BNDES aprova financiamento de R$ 22,5 bilhões para Belo Monte. Available at: http://www.bndes.gov.br/SiteBNDES/bndes/bndes_pt/Institucional/Sala_de_Imprensa/Noticias/2012/e nergia/20121126_belomonte.html. Accessed 8 July 2013.

Brisman, A. 2012. Urbanization. In W.R. Miller (ed.), *The Social History of Crime and Punishment in America: An Encyclopedia, Vol. 4*. Thousand Oaks, CA: Sage Publications, 1847–52.

Bunn, S.E. and Arthington, A.H. 2002. Basic principles and ecological consequences of altered flow regimes for aquatic biodiversity. *Environmental Management* 30(4): 492–507.

Chan, L. 2012. Toxic gold rush. *UBC Reports* 58(2), 1 February 2012.

CITpax Colombia. 2012. *Actores Armados Ilegales y Sector Extractivo en Colombia*. V Informe 2012

Colombia Solidarity Campaign. 2013. La Colosa: a death foretold. Alternative Report about the AngloGold Ashanti Gold Mining Project in Cajamarca, Tolima, Colombia. London, Colombia Solidarity Campaign.

Colombian Mining Database. 2013. *Catastro Minero Colombiano*. Available at: www.simco.gov.co/Inicio/CatastroMineroColombiano/tabid/107/Default.aspx. Accessed 15 October 2013.

Comité Minero Energético (CME). 2013. *Qué no es el CME*. Available at: http://cmecolombia.co/que-no-es-el-cme/. Accessed 5 January 2014.

Contraloria General de la República. 2013. *CGR detectó 12 hallazgos fiscales por 7 mil millones al evaluar fiscalización minera a AngloGold*. 22 April 2013. Available at: www.contraloriagen.gov.co/. Accessed 3 May 2013.

Cunha, D.A. and Ferreira, L.V. 2012. Impacts of the Belo Monte hydroelectric dam construction on pioneer vegetation formations along the Xingu River, Pará State, Brazil. *Brazilian Journal of Botany* 35(2): 159–67.

Dashwood, H. 2012. *The Rise of Global Corporate Social Responsibility: Mining and the Spread of Global Norms*. New York: Cambridge University Press.

Deheza, E. and Ribet, U. 2012. Latin America's mining boom. The socio-environmental and security dynamics in the case of Colombia. *The RUSI Journal* 157(5): 22–31.

Departamento Nacional de Planeación. 2010. Plan nacional de desarrollo 2010–2014. Available at: https://www.dnp.gov.co/LinkClick.aspx?fileticket=4-J9V-FE2pI%3D&tabid=1238. Accessed 22 August 2013.

De Sousa Júnior, W.C. and Reid, J. 2010. Uncertainties in Amazon hydropower development: risk scenarios and environmental issues around the Belo Monte dam. *Water Alternatives* 3(2): 249–68.

Domingues, E.P., Magalhães, A.S. and Faria, W.R. 2009. Infraestrutura, crescimento e desigualdade regional: uma projeção dos impactos dos investimentos do Programa de Aceleração do Crescimento (PAC) em Minas Gerais. *Pesquisa e Planejamento Economico* 39(1): 121–58.

Echeverry Castañeda, S., Cárdenas Vera Alan, F., Ordónez Carmona, O. and Muñoz Aguare, O. 2009. *Aspectos estructurales y relaciones de algunos sistemas vetiformes del distrito minero Segovia-Remedios*. Boletín Ciencias de la Tierra. No. 26.

El Colombiano. 2014. *Cepeda cuestiona contratos de seguridad entre el Estado y multinacionales*. Available at: http://www.elcolombiano.com/BancoConocimiento/C/cepeda_cuestiona_contratos_que_protegen_a_multinacionales/cepeda_cuestiona_contratos_que_protegen_a_multinacionales.asp. Accessed 9 January 2014.

El Tiempo. 2012. Oro en Segovia, Antioquia refleja problemática social. Available at: http://www.eltiempo.com/colombia/medellin/ARTICULO-WEB-NEW_NOTA_INTERIOR-12422502.html. Accessed 15 September 2013.

Energia S/A e IBAMA. Belém, MPF. Available at: http://www.prpa.mpf.mp.br/news/2012/arquivos/Belo_Monte_cautelar_Condicionantes.pdf/at_download/file. Accessed 17 May 2013.

Erber, F.S. 2009. As convenções de desenvolvimento no governo Lula: um ensaio de economia política. *Revista de Economia Política* 31(1): 31–55.

Fearnside, P.M. 2006. Dams in the Amazon: Belo Monte and Brazil's hydroelectric development of the Xingu River Basin. *Environmental Management* 38(1): 16–27.

Fearnside, P.M. 2012. *Belo Monte Dam: A Spearhead for Brazil's Dam Building Attack on Amazonia?* GWF Discussion Paper 1210. Canberra: Global Water Forum.

Fooks, G., Gilmore, A., Collin, J., Holden, C. and Lee, K. 2013. The limits of corporate social responsibility: techniques of neutralization, stakeholder management and political CSR. *Journal of Business Ethics* 112(2): 283–99.

Forsberg, B.R., Araujo-Lima, C.A.R.M., Martinelli, L.A., Victoria, R.L. and Bonassi, J.A. 1993. Autotrophic carbon sources for fish in the Central Amazon. *Ecology* 74(3): 643–52.

Friedman, M. 1970. The social responsibility of business is to increase its profits. *New York Times Magazine*, 13 September 1970. Available at: http://www. colorado.edu/studentgroups/libertarians/issues/friedman-soc-resp-business. html. Accessed 10 January 2014.

Galindo da Fonseca, P. and Bourgoignie, A. 2011. The Belo Monte dam case. *National Affairs* 41(2): 104–7.

Gatto, A. 2002. *The European Union and Corporate Social Responsibility: Can the EU Contribute to the Accountability of Multinational Enterprises for Human Rights?* Institute for International Law Working Paper No. 32, September 2002. Available at: https://www.law.kuleuven.be/iir/nl/onderzoek/wp/WP32e. pdf. Accessed 20 December 2013.

Globo Pará. 2013. Conselho Tutelar denuncia rede de tráfico humano no sudoeste do Pará. Available at: http://g1.globo.com/pa/para/noticia/2013/02/conselho-tutelar-denuncia-rede-de-trafico-humano-em-altamira-pa.html. Accessed 29 December 2013.

Goodland, R. 2011. Best practice mining in Colombia. Presented at a Best Practice Mining forum.

Gorayeb, I. 2009. Considerações sobre a problemática com insetos hematófagos vetores de doenças. In S.M.S. Barbosa Magalhães Santos and F. Del Moral Hernandez (eds), *Painel de Especialistas. Análise Crítica do Estudo de Impacto Ambiental do Aproveitamento Hidrelétrico de Belo Monte.* Belém, September 2009.

Hall, A. and Branford, S. 2012. Development, dams and silma: the saga of Belo Monte. *Critical Sociology* 38(6): 851–62.

Hochstetler, K. 2011. The politics of environmental licensing: energy projects of the past and future in Brazil. *Studies in Comparative International Development* 46: 349–71.

Holme, R. and Watts, P. 1999. *Corporate Social Responsibility.* Geneva: World Business Council for Sustainable Development.

Hristov, J. 2009. *Blood and Capital: The Paramilitarization of Colombia.* Ohio: Ohio University Press.

Human Rights Watch. 2005. *The Curse of Gold, Democratic Republic of Congo.* New York: Human Rights Watch. Available at: http://www.hrw.org/sites/default/files/reports/drc0505_0.pdf. Accessed 24 February 2014.

IACHR (Inter-American Commission on Human Rights). 2011. PM 382/10, ch. III. Indigenous Communities of the Xingu River Basin vs. Brazil. Available at: http://www.oas.org/en/iachr/docs/annual/2011/TOC.asp. Accessed 13 July 2013.

IBAMA (Instituto Brasileiro do Meio Ambiente e dos Recursos Naturais Renováveis). 2013. Análise do 3o Relatório Consolidado de Andamento do PBA da UHE Belo Monte. PAR. 004933/2013. Brasília, IBAMA.

Idárraga Franco, A., Muñoz Casallas, D.A. and Velez Galeano, H. 2010. *Conflictos socioambientales por la extracción minera en Colombia: Casos de la inversión británica.* Bogotá, Censat Agua Viva – Amigos de la tierra Colombia.

ILO (International Labour Organization). 2012. *Report of the Committee of Experts on the Application of Conventions and Recommendations. Report III (Part 1A). General Report and Observations Concerning Particular Countries.* Geneva: International Labour Office.

ILO (International Labour Organization). 1989. C169 – Indigenous and tribal peoples convention. International Labor Organization, Geneva. Available at: http://www. ilo.org/dyn/normlex/en/f?p=1000:12100:0::NO::P12100_INSTRUMENT_ID: 312314. Accessed 22 October 2012.

Informe Inteligencia Batallón Nueva Granada, 2006.

Jaichand, V. and Andrade Sampaio, A. 2013. Dam and be damned: the adverse impacts of Belo Monte on indigenous peoples in Brazil. *Human Rights Quarterly* 35(2): 408–47.

Kuijpers, K., van Huijstee, M. and Wilde-Ramsing, J. 2014. A normative-empirical analysis of state duties and corporate responsibilities related to adverse human rights impacts on the Amazonian minerals-energy frontier. *Journal of Cleaner Production* (DOI 10.1016/j.jclepro. 2014.02.049).

La Silla Vacía. 2011. Los expertos de la administración Uribe se cotizan en las empresas mineras. 23 marzo de 2011. Available at: http://lasillavacia.com/ historia/los-expertos-de-la-administracion-uribe-se-cotizan-en-las-empresas-mineras-22761. Accessed 9 October 2013.

La Silla Vacía. 2012. María Consuelo Araújo. Available at: http://lasillavacia.com/ perfilquien/40636/maria-consuelo-araujo. Accessed 2 December 2013.

Langfur, H. 2006. *The Forbidden Lands: Colonial Identity, Frontier Violence, and the Persistence of Brazil's Eastern Indians, 1750–1830.* Stanford, CA: Stanford University Press.

Langlois, R. and Mariani, P. 2012. Por Todo El Oro de Colombia. Woow & Canal + Production. Documentary available at: http://vimeo.com/43866542. Accessed 1 April 2013.

Leroy, J.P., Acselrad, H., Santos Souza, A.P., do A. Mello, C.C., Malerba, J., Laschefski, K. and Novoa Garzon, L.F. 2009. Por avaliações sócio-ambientais rigorosas e responsáveis dos empreendimentos que impactam o território e as populações. In S.M.S. Barbosa Magalhães Santos and F. Del Moral Hernandez (eds), *Painel de Especialistas. Análise Crítica do Estudo de Impacto Ambiental do Aproveitamento Hidrelétrico de Belo Monte.* Belém, September 2009.

McCormick, S. 2011. Damming the Amazon: local movements and transnational struggles over water. *Society & Natural Resources: An International Journal* 24: 34–48.

McLellan, B.C., Corder, G.D., Giurco, D.P. and Ishihara, K.N. 2012. Renewable energy in the minerals industry: a review of global potential. *Journal of Cleaner Production* 32: 32–44.

Michalowski, R. and Kramer, R. 2000. *State-Corporate Crime: Wrongdoing at the Intersection of Business and Government.* London: Rutgers University Press.

Ministerio de Ambiente, Vivienda y Desarrollo Territorial. 2010. Resolución 1481. 30 Jul 2010. Available at: www.minambiente.gov.co/documentos/normativa/ gaceta_ambiental/2010/res_1481_300710. Accessed 7 January 2015.

MPF (Ministério Público Federal). 2007. Ação Civil Pública C/C Ação de Responsabilidade por Ato de Improbidade administrativa com requerimento de medida liminar em face de Aloisio Marcos Vanconcelos Novais, Rogério da Silva, Construções e Comércio Camargo Corrêa S/A., Construtora Andrade Gutierrez, Construtora Norberto Odebrecht S/A. Belém, MPF.

MPF (Ministério Público Federal). 2009. *Executivos de empreiteiras são denunciados por fraude a licitação e formação de cartel.* Available at: http:// www.prba.mpf.mp.br/mpf-pdf. Accessed 17 May 2013.

MPF (Ministério Publico Federal). 2011. Ação Cautelar Inominada com pedido de liminar em face de Norte Energia S/A e Instituto Brasileiro do Meio Ambiente e dos Recursos Naturais Renováveis (IBAMA). Available at: https://bit.ly/ Integra-Belo-Monte-15. Accessed 5 December 2013.

MPF (Ministerio Público Federal). 2012. Ação Cautelar Inominada com pedido de liminar Norte noticias/patrimonio-publico-e-social/executivos-de-empreiteiras-sao-denunciados-por. Accessed 5 August 2013.

MPF (Ministerio Público Federal). 2013. Processos caso Belo Monte. Available at: http://www.prpa.mpf.mp.br/news/2013/arquivos/Tabela_de_ acompanhamento_atualizada_23–10–13.pdf. Accessed 10 December 2013.

MXVPS (Movimento Xingu Vivo Para Sempre), Terra de Direitos, CIMI (Conselho Indigenista Missionário), SDDH (Sociedade Paraense de Direitos Humanos), Justiça Global, Comitê Metropolitano do Movimento Xingu Vivo, Prelazia do Xingu, CPT Pará (Comissão Pastoral da Terra), Rede FAOR, Associação de Defesa Etno-ambiental- Kanindé. 2010. Letter to Ms. Gabriela Carina Knaul de Albuquerque e Silva, Special Rapporteur of the Human Rights Council on the Independence of Judges and Lawyers, Office of the UN High Commissioner for Human Rights. Curitiba & Altamira, 10 May 2010.

MXVPS (Movimento Xingu Vivo Para Sempre). 2012. ONGs denunciam à ONU perseguição da polícia a manifestantes contra Belo Monte. Available at: http:// www.xinguvivo.org.br/2012/06/28/ongs-denunciam-a-onu-perseguicao-da-policia-a-manifestantes-contra-belo-monte/. Accessed 6 January 2013.

National Mining Agency. 2013. Actualización del Catastro Minero del Cauca, abril 15 de 2013, Hoja de reporte RT-0176-13. Bogotá: National Mining Agency.

Oliveiira, M. 2013. TRF determina retomada das obras da usina de Belo Monte, no Pará. Available at: http://g1.globo.com/pa/para/noticia/2013/12/ trf-determina-retomada-das-obras-da-usina-de-belo-monte-no-para.html. Accessed 20 December 2013.

Parkinson, C. 2013. Colombian judge orders investigation into Uribe's paramilitary ties. *InsightCrime.* Available at: http://www.insightcrime.org/ news-briefs/colombia-judge-calls-for-investigation-into-uribes-paramilitary-ties. Accessed 2 February 2014.

Parliament.uk. 2013. British Parliament: early day motion 746, assassination of environmental campaigners in Colombia. Available at: http://www.parliament. uk/edm/2013-14/746. Accessed 19 November 2013.

Portafolio. 2012. 30% de áreas tituladas la tienen 18 grandes mineras. Available at: http://www.portafolio.co/economia/30-areas-tituladas-la-tienen-18-grandes-mineras. Accessed 2 January 2014.

Public Eye Awards. 2014. Hall of shame. Available at: http://publiceye.ch/en/hall-of-shame/. Accessed 4 April 2013.

Ramirez Cuellar, F. 2005. *The Profits of Extermination: How US Corporate Power is Destroying Colombia*. Monroe, ME: Common Courage Press.

Ribeiro, L. 2013. Força Nacional reforça segurança de Belo Monte. Available at: http://exame.abril.com.br/brasil/noticias/forca-nacional-reforca-seguranca-de-belo-monte. Accessed 3 October 2013.

Rivero, S. and Cooney Seisdedos, P. 2010. The Amazon as a frontier of capital accumulation: looking beyond the trees. *Capitalism Nature Socialism* 21(4): 50–71.

Ruggiero, V. and South, N. 2013. Toxic state–corporate crimes, neo-liberalism and green criminology: the hazards and legacies of the oil, chemical and mineral industries. *International Journal for Crime, Justice and Social Democracy* 2(2): 12–26.

Saad-Filho, A. 2013. Mass protests under 'Left neoliberalism': Brazil, June–July 2013. *Critical Sociology* 39(5): 657–69.

Schwartzman, S., Villas Boas, A.,Yukari Ono, K., Gesteira Fonseca, M., Doblas, J., Zimmerman, B., Junqueira, P., Jerozolimski, A., Salazar, M., Prates Junqueira, R. and Torrés, M. 2013. The natural and social history of the indigenous lands and protected areas corridor of the Xingu River basin. *Philosophical Transactions of the Royal Society* 308: 1–12.

Semana. 2013. Oro y crimen: minería ilegal. Available at: http://www.semana. com/nacion/articulo/oro-crimen-mineria-ilegal/338107-3. Accessed 28 December 2013.

Seoane, J., Taddei, E. and Algranati, C. 2005. *The New Configurations of Popular Movements in Latin America*. Buenos Aires: Consejo Latinoamericano de Ciencias Sociales.

Sibaja, M. and Clendenning, A. 2010. Judge overrules decision that would block Amazon dam. Available at: http://www.pressherald.com/news/nationworld/ judge-overrules-decision-that-would-block-amazon-dam-_2010–04–17.html. Accessed 20 December 2013.

Sposati, R. 2013. Justiça determina reintegração de posse do canteiro de obras de Belo Monte. Brasil de Fato. Available at: http://www.brasildefato.com.br/ node/12853. Accessed 19 December 2013.

Stickler, C.M., Coe, M.T., Costa, M.H., Nepstad, D.C., McGrath, D.G., Dias, L.C.P., Rodrigues, H.O. and Soares-Filho, B.S. 2013. Dependence of hydropower energy generation on forests in the Amazon Basin at local and regional scales. *PNAS* 110(23): 9601–6.

Sykes, G.M. and Matza, D. 1957. Techniques of neutralization: a theory of delinquency. *American Sociological Review* 22(6): 667–70.

Uekert, B. 1995. *Rivers of Blood: A Comparative Study of Government Massacres.* Westport, CT: Praeger.

UNHRC (United Nations Human Rights Council). 2010. *Report by the Special Rapporteur on the Situation of Human Rights and Fundamental Freedoms of Indigenous People.* James Anaya, cases examined by the Special Rapporteur (June 2009–July 2010). A/HRC/15/37/Add.1. New York and Geneva: United Nations.

UNHRC (United Nations Human Rights Council). 2013. *Report by the Special Rapporteur on the Situation of Human Rights Defenders.* Margaret Sekaggya, observations on communications transmitted to Governments and replies received. A/HRC/22/47/Add.4. New York and Geneva: United Nations.

UNOHCHR (United Nations Office of the High Commissioner for Human Rights). 2011. *Guiding Principles on Business and Human Rights: Implementing the United Nations 'Protect, Respect and Remedy'.* New York and Geneva: United Nations.

UNOHCHR (United Nations Office of the High Commissioner for Human Rights). 2012. *Interpretive Guide for the Corporate Responsibility to Respect Human Rights.* Available at: http://www.ohchr.org/Documents/Issues/Business/RtRInterpretativeGuide.pdf. Accessed 12 July 2013.

UNOHCHR (United Nations Office of the High Commissioner for Human Rights). 2013. *Forced Evictions.* Available at: http://www.ohchr.org/EN/Issues/Housing/Pages/ForcedEvictions.aspx. Accessed 3 October 2013.

United States Department of Justice. 2011. Colombian paramilitary leader sentenced in Miami to 33 years in prison for drug trafficking and narco-terrorism. Available at: http://www.justice.gov/opa/pr/2011/November/11-crm-1475.html. Accessed 5 January 2014.

US Office on Colombia. 2013. Large-scale mining in Colombia: human rights violations past, present and future. Available at: http://www.usofficeoncolombia.org/docs/large-scale-mining-full-report.pdf. Accessed 24 February 2014.

Vale. 2013. Conselho de Administração. Available at: http://www.vale.com/PT/aboutvale/leadership/board/Paginas/default.aspx. Accessed 26 June 2013.

Vargas, M. 2013. IIRSA-COSIPLAN and European Capital's Responsibility. In M. Vargas and B. Brennan (eds), 2013. *Impunity Inc. Reflections on the 'Super-Rights' and 'Super-Powers' of Corporate Capital.* Amsterdam: Transnational Institute.

Veçoso, F.F.C. and Do Amaral Jr., A. 2011. The inter-American system a new grossraum? Assessing the case law of the Inter-American Court of Human Rights. *ESIL Conference Paper Series* 1(1): 1–21.

Veiga, M. 2010. Antioquia, Colombia: the world's most polluted place by mercury: impressions from two field trips. UNIDO – United Nations Industrial Development Organization.

Vieira Lisboa, M. and Carvalho Zagallo, J.G. 2010. Relatório da Missão Xingu. Violações de Direitos Humanos no Licenciamento da Usina Hidrelétrica de Belo Monte. Relatoria Nacional do Direito Humano ao Meio Ambiente, Plataforma Brasileira de Direitos Humanos Econômicos, Sociais Culturais e Ambientais.

White, R. 2013. Resource extraction leaves something behind: environmental justice and mining. *International Journal for Crime and Justice* 2(1): 50–64.

Yellishetty, M., Mudd, G.M. and Ranjith, P.G. 2012. The steel industry, abiotic resource depletion and life cycle assessment: a real or perceived issue? *Journal of Cleaner Production* 19(1): 78–90.

Zilney, L.A., McGurrin, D. and Zahran, S. 2006. Environmental justice and the role of criminology: an analytical review of 33 years of environmental justice research. *Criminal Justice Review* 31: 47–62.

Chapter 7

Somalis Fight Back: Environmental Degradation and the Somali Pirate

Victoria E. Collins

This chapter provides an in-depth examination of the structural issues within the country of Somalia as they relate to the significant environmental degradation experienced by the Somali people. Informed by literature from green criminology, this chapter will highlight the environmental issues that are central to the economic desperation that plagues the country. The goal is to demonstrate that piracy can be viewed as a more viable option to ensure individual and industry survival than more traditional forms of employment that are viewed as more legitimate within the broader socio-political global order. Before describing the origins and causes of environmental degradation in Somalia, I will first provide a brief overview of the issue of piracy in Somalia and the literature on green criminology, as it will be applied here.

Piracy in Somalia

Piracy in Somalia has been the topic of increased media and political attention for more than a decade (Barling 2003; Borger 2008; Collins 2012; The White House 2007; World Food Programme 2007; van Ginkel and Landman 2012). Individuals engaged in piratical acts have been depicted as violent and predatory, cruising both Somali and international waters for vulnerable ships to hijack (Alexander and Richardson 2009; MacAskill 2011; Rice 2008). Often described as 'savage' (Rice 2008), 'dangerous' and 'gruesome characters' (O'Sullivan 1999: 3), with connections to both organised crime and Islamist terrorism (Doyle 2005; Mackay 2005; Norton-Taylor 2008; Silverstein 2005; Singh and Bedi 2012), pirates are said to be 'spill[ing] into the Gulf of Aden' (Lacey 2001: 2) for the purpose of 'turn[ing] supertankers into floating bombs' (Barling 2003: 12). More recently, pirates in Somalia have become the subject of Hollywood entertainment with the release of blockbuster movie *Captain Phillips*. Based on the failed-real life hijacking attempt of US cargo ship *Maersk Alabama,* the film portrays the four young Somali men who embark on the attack as greedy villains, armed with assault rifles and rocket propelled grenade launchers, trawling the seas for innocent seafarers

(Collins 2014; Gettel 2013). Predicated on this discourse, an understanding of piracy in Somalia has evolved that has led to the initiation of anti-piracy responses that include the deployment of between 30–40 military vessels to the region for the purposes of deterring future attacks (van Ginkel and Landman 2012).

Beyond the media hype and political rhetoric that propagates the dominant understanding of piracy in Somalia, there has been little policy attention paid to the etiological factors for piracy in the region (see Collins 2012; Panjabi 2010; Rothe and Collins 2011). Although there is some acknowledgement from scholars from varying disciplines that the motivations for piracy in Somalia stem from economic and structural conditions within the country itself (Panjabi 2010; Rothe and Collins 2011) rather than from a desire to launch terrorist attacks, there has been little in-depth discussion of the relationship between these economic and structural conditions and environmental degradation, that together have pushed individuals to commit acts of piracy.

Green Criminology: A Lens for Analysis

There is a large body of literature from environmental, green, conservation or ecological criminology that examines varying corporate, state, state-corporate, and illicit practices that result in environmental harm (Beirne and South 2007; Boekhout van Solinge 2010; Clifford and Edwards 2012; Lynch and Stretesky 2010; South and Brisman 2013; Walters 2006; Walters et al. 2013; White 2010a). Much of this literature examines specific harms caused to the environment, what Carrabine and colleagues (2004) refer to as 'primary' forms of environmental harms. These practices, which include deforestation (Boekhout van Solinge 2010) and mining (Rothe and Collins 2014), have direct environmental, social and political consequences, as well as indirect impacts on ecosystems, including human and non-human species (Beirne 2007; Lynch et al. 2010; Lynch and Stretesky 2010, 2013).

A second body of literature focuses on 'crime that grows out of the flouting of rules that seek to regulate environmental disasters' (Carrabine et al. 2004: 318), termed 'secondary' forms of environmental harm. Examples include toxic waste dumping (Heckenberg 2010; Shuqin 2010), the trade and abuse of endangered animals (Beirne 2012; Herbig 2010; Wellsmith 2010), state perpetrated violence against oppositional groups as has been the case in localised conflicts over resources (Brisman and South 2013; Carrabine et al. 2004; Potter 2012; Ross 2003), and the disregard and/or circumvention of regulatory laws by both corporate and state interests (Kluin 2013; Walters 2010). As noted by Potter (2012: 2), however, the study of environmental harm should not be limited to the above two typologies of harm as green criminology can be further extended to provide insight into broader issues of crime, justice and social harm, including examining 'environmental harm as a *cause* of crime'.

In taking Potter's (2012) approach, criminological inquiry can draw on green perspectives to better understand large scale violence that arises due to conflict over scarce resources, massive social and environmental harms that result due to harmful, often unintentional, practices of international financial institutions (Friedrichs and Friedrichs 2002; Friedrichs and Rothe 2012; Rothe and Collins 2014), crime committed as a result of environmental harm, such as protests, both peaceful and violent (Potter 2012), as well as threats of violence and acts of environmental destruction (Schwartz 1998). This is particularly relevant here, as it is through this perspective that piracy in Somalia will be viewed as a crime motivated by the environmental harm perpetrated against the Somali people. Although there has been some attention paid to the etiological factors that motivate individuals towards committing piracy in Somalia (Bahadur 2011; Collins 2012; Eichstaedt 2010; Panjabi 2010; Rothe and Collins 2013), there has been no attempt within the criminological literature to situate the issue of piracy in Somalia within an environmental harms framework linking it to larger issues of environmental degradation. Prior to delving into the case at hand, it is first necessary to provide a brief contextual overview of the historical events that have shaped Somalia as a country and intersect with, and in some instances have helped facilitate, the perpetration of environmental harms.

Structural Conditions within Somalia: A History

The region known today as Somalia has a long history of divisiveness and conflict which can be traced back to its occupation by colonial powers. The northern region of the country was colonised by Britain, the southern region of Somaliland by Italy, and regions in the West were occupied by Ethiopia and France (Ahmed and Green 1999; Cliffe 2005; Rothe and Collins 2011). Although the northern and southern regions were unified in 1960, outbreaks of localised violence between opposition groups have continued to plague the country until this day. After independence, efforts to unite the region occurred solely in a geo-political sense, as the nation remained divided economically and socially along deeply embedded ancestral lines (Murphy 2011; Rothe and Collins 2011).

In 1969, President Abi Rashid Ali Shermarke was assassinated; this allowed General Siad Barre, with the assistance of the Supreme Revolutionary Council (SRC) – a group of ex-combatants, military and police officers – to take control of the country in a bloodless coup (Rothe and Collins 2011). Barre made promises to 'cure all the country's ills' (Lewis 1994: 150), and initially gained support from the country's people who welcomed the possibility of change (Africa Watch Committee 1990). The Barre regime, however, became increasingly corrupt, marred by political favouritism and oppression, with Barre placing himself in control of all aspects of power, and in effect creating an autocratic security state (Amnesty International 1990; Human Rights Watch 2007).

Despite Barre's efforts to preserve and expand his power, his regime came to an end in 1991 when opposition groups formed a coalition (including the Somali National Movement (SNM), the United Somali Congers (USC), and the Somali Patriotic Movement (SPM)) and ousted Barre from power (Davies 1994). The vacuum created by Barre's departure resulted in intense internal fighting for political and economic power in the country's capital, Mogadishu (Africa Watch and Physicians for Human Rights 1992). The fighting continues to this day despite numerous unsuccessful efforts at peace agreements and efforts from the international political community (IPC) to institute a Transitional Federal Government (TFG) to stabilise the country.

The decades-long hostility has had many adverse consequences for the Somali people, including torture, executions, and indiscriminate killings (Human Rights Watch 2012), as well as civil and external conflicts and a war with neighbouring Ethiopia (Rothe and Collins 2011). This has left much of the country in a state of humanitarian crisis which has been further compounded by three significant environmental harms: (1) illegal fishing; (2) toxic waste dumping in Somali coastal waters, which have depleted the already overfished marine resources; and (3) drought and subsequent famine that plagued the country in 2011. I consider each of these in turn.

Fishing Somalia's Seas

Somalia is, and historically has been, a pastoral society, but prior to 1991 there also existed a small fishing industry. This is related to the fact that Somalia has the longest coastline in all of Africa stretching over 3,330 kilometres (United Nations Security Council 2011b), an area that is equal to the eastern seaboard of the United States. During Barre's regime, funds were provided for the purposes of expanding the fishing industry by encouraging nomadic families to settle along the coast. Funding was also provided for the purchasing of vessels and fishing supplies, and as a result the fishing industry developed dependent on Somali's resource rich waters (Murphy 2011). Following the ousting of Barre in 1991, the fishing industry became largely unorganised and unprotected (Eichstaedt 2010). The absence of a legitimate government and the country's weak institutional controls left the waters vulnerable to illegal fishing (United Nations Security Council 2011b).

Somali coastal waters are one of the most resource rich fishing grounds in the world, and because of the presence of a continental shelf, Somali waters are an important breeding ground for many migratory fish species. As a result, fishing constitutes the country's second largest industry (Achieng 1999). It has therefore increasingly been targeted for illegal and unlicenced fishing (Panjabi 2010), with reports of approximately 700 unlicenced fishing trawlers traversing Somali waters in 2005 alone. Countries known to have engaged in this practice include, but are not limited to, China, France, Germany, Honduras, India, Italy, Japan, Kenya, Pakistan, Portugal, Saudi Arabia, Spain, Thailand, the United Kingdom, and

Yemen (Achieng 1999). In 2002, the University of British Columbia found that of the 60,000 tons of fish caught in the Somali waters, 50 per cent were taken by foreign vessels (United Nations Security Council 2011b). Thus, the problem is large in scale and engaged in with little thought of the long-term sustainability of the marine species being plundered (Tharoor 2009).

Many ships have not only been engaged in illegal fishing but also been caught utilising fishing techniques that are known to cause considerable damage to the fragile marine environment. For example, Achieng (1999) draws attention to foreign vessels engaged in the illegal practice of dropping dynamite into the water damaging the coral reef, knowingly destroying endangered marine species, such as turtles, orcas, baby whales and sharks. Such practices not only cause initial damage, but have long-term effects on the fishing industry, as well as on the marine ecosystem itself.

Unlicenced and illegal fishing in Somalia coastal waters have gone largely unmonitored and without sanction, contributing to the reduction in legitimate opportunities for the Somali people to earn a living. Furthermore, it has fuelled Somali anger and frustration towards those states and their vessels that are plundering the Somalia waters and stealing their fish. Despite this, there is little acknowledgement of the harm caused by such practices, which undermines the seriousness of both the illegal fishing and the environmental degradation that results. For example, at the international level, claims of illegal fishing in Somali waters continue to be marginalised, and in some instances, have been dismissed by the IPC for being 'not verified' (United Nations Security Council 2011b: 12). This is in direct contradiction to numerous reports from Somali fishermen that have, since the 1980s, maintained that foreign vessels continue to exploit their marine resources. For example, in an interview in 2010 with journalist Peter Eichstaedt (2010: 30), a man called 'Ismail' asserts, 'They collected our animals from the seas'. 'When we tried to fish', he continues, 'we didn't get anything, we became very angry. Everyone was coming. Where can we get our fish?' This issue of illegal fishing is often coupled with that of toxic waste dumping in Somali waters, which I consider next.

Toxic Waste Dumping

Ninety per cent of the world's hazardous waste is generated by industrial countries that do not have the capacity or the technology to dispose of it at a rate equal to, or consistent with, its production (United Nations Environment Programme 2006). As a result, less industrialised countries often agree to import and dispose of this waste from more developed countries, a process often referred to as 'toxic colonialism' (Panjabi 2010). These countries are particularly vulnerable to this practice due to political instability, conflict, and the lure of the economic benefit of accepting the waste. It is important to note that the companies engaged in dumping toxic waste in less developed nations also benefit financially as estimates indicate that it costs approximately $2.50 per ton to dispose of waste in African states, which is drastically less than the $250 per ton it costs in Europe (United Nations Environment Programme 2005b). Somalia has been particularly vulnerable to the dumping of hazardous waste because of the aforementioned long period of civil unrest. For example, following the ousting of Barre in 1991, reports emerged that Swiss and Italian firms had entered into contracts for waste disposal with various Somali warlords. In many instances, warlords and businessmen in Somalia would accept the toxic waste in exchange for weapons and ammunition (Mohamed 2001). This was later confirmed five years later by a United Nations Environmental Programme (UNEP) investigation that found European companies were taking advantage of the instability caused by the ongoing conflict and political turmoil in the country by dumping toxic waste.

Other reports indicate that as far back as the early 1980s, the types of waste being dumped in Somali waters has included 'uranium radioactive waste, lead, cadmium, mercury, industrial, hospital, chemical, leather treatment and other toxic waste' (United Nations Environment Programme 2005b: 134). The majority of the waste is carelessly dumped on the beaches and coastal waters in poorly sealed barrels and large tankers that easily leak (United Nations Environment Programme 2005b). Further evidence of the extent of the waste dumping in Somali waters was illuminated by the 2004 tsunami.

In December 2004, an earthquake off the island of Sumatra in the Indian Ocean generated a tsunami that had devastating effects, causing flooding in coastal states from Somalia to Indonesia. The waves swelled to heights of 10 to 30 metres or more as they hit Somalia's shore, destroying much of the country's fishing industry (United Nations General Assembly 2005), and washing up on the county's beaches large amounts of debris, including toxic waste. The tsunami 'stirred up rotting containers and leaking drums full of toxic substances that were previously dumped off the coast' (Hussein 2010: 7). As indicated by the United Nations Environment Programme (2005a), 'Somalia's coastline has been used as a dumping ground for other countries' nuclear and hazardous wastes for many years as a result of the long civil war and, thus, the inability of the authorities to police shipments or handle the wastes'. Throughout the dumping, there appears to have been little regard for the significant environmental degradation and devastating health impacts on the local population.

Although it is impossible to estimate the full impact of toxic waste dumping in Somali waters, effects that have been acknowledged include deaths resulting from local populations opening barrels washed up on the beaches (United Nations Environment Programme 2005b), as well as contamination of the country's water and food supplies, including ground water and Somali's rich marine life (Mohamed 2001; United Nations Environment Programme 2005a). According to the BBC, in 2002, thousands of dead fish washed up on the shores of both Somalia and Kenya. Experts indicated that this was caused by the large amounts of toxins entering the water from hazardous waste (BBC News 2002). In addition, it has been suggested that increased deaths in livestock that have occurred in recent years are connected to toxic waste dumping (Mohamed 2001).

Further harms suffered by human populations include complaints of unusual health issues, such as 'acute respiratory infections, heavy dry coughing, mouth bleeding, abdominal haemorrhage and unusual chemical skin reaction[s]' (United Nations Environment Programme 2005b: 134). Hussein (2010: 11) notes that medical professionals have reported that there have been considerable increases in cases of cancer, as well as 'unknown diseases, spontaneous miscarriages of the pregnant women and child malformation' in coastal populations. As indicated by Dr Pirko Honenen, a doctor for the United Nations Children's Fund (UNICEF) 'a new unknown disease is killing people in Bardale [a small town in the Bay region of Southern Somalia] in high numbers ... [T]here were already more than 120 victims in two months ... and the symptoms are high fever, trembling, nose and mouth haemorrhage' (Hussein 2010: 12). Considering the poor infrastructure in the country itself, in all likelihood, the extent of the damage mentioned here represents only a small glimpse of the human and environmental damage caused by illegal waste dumping practices.

Despite these devastating effects, there is little formal acknowledgement from the IPC of the relationship between illegal waste dumping and piracy. When it is broached as a possible motivating factor – that of local populations protecting their coastal waters from foreign trawlers – its seriousness is both marginalised and kept separate from the popular understanding of the issue. For example, in 2011, the United Nations Secretary General issued a special report on the protection of Somalia's natural resources and waters. This report attempted to address the allegations of both illegal fishing and toxic dumping that 'have been used by pirates to justify their criminal activities' (United Nations Security Council 2011b: 1). In this report, the Secretary General emphasised that States are 'required to take all measures necessary to prevent, reduce and control pollution of the marine environment from any source, including pollution by dumping' (United Nations Security Council 2011b: 9). This report also acknowledged that there has been a long history spanning at least 20 years of allegations of dumping different types of waste including 'radioactive, hazardous and medical, on land and in Somali waters' (United Nations Security Council 2011b: 12). As is the case with illegal fishing, however, the Secretary General asserted that these allegations cannot be confirmed (United Nations Security Council 2011b), despite the first-hand accounts from local fishermen, and numerous reports from credible, international and regional organisations, including those mentioned above and INTERPOL, indicating illegal dumping continues to occur (INTERPOL 2008, 2009).

The environmental degradation in Somalia is not limited to the devastating consequences of illegal fishing and toxic waste dumping in the country's coastal waters, but extends to larger humanitarian crises. The most apparent, and arguably calamitous, is Somalia's history of drought and famine. The recent drought of 2011, which I consider next, has been described as the 'worst humanitarian disaster in the world' (Guterres 2011).

Famine and Drought

In the summer months of 2011, the Horn of Africa experienced one of the worst droughts to hit the region in 60 years. For the four years preceding the drought, there had been little rainfall, which led to poor annual crops, the death of livestock, and a spike in food prices (Food Security and Nutrition Analysis Unit 2011). This situation led to a famine that had devastating effects not only on the already weak and failing Somali economy but also on the civilian population. In 2011, the United Nations Office for the Coordination of Humanitarian Affairs reported that 3.7 million people were in crisis with approximately 30 per cent of children in the region being extremely malnourished. Mortality rates increased to three times the number that constitutes a state of emergency (Muhumed and Kemenade 2011). In addition, during this time period, over 2 million Somali's were displaced from their homes, and a further 4 million were estimated to be in need of food aid (United Nations Office for the Coordination for Humanitarian Affairs 2012).

Those displaced from their homes were without the most basic services and necessities, such as water, food, and access to sanitation, which significantly increased their risk for disease. For example, 80 per cent of the Somali population was without safe drinking water (Internal Displacement Monitoring Centre 2012), leading to dehydration as one of the leading causes of death in Somalia (United Nations Children's Fund 2012). Many displaced persons sought refuge in displacement camps set up in neighbouring Ethiopia and Kenya, and at the height of the crisis, as many as 2,000 people were crossing into Ethiopia each day. In order to get to the camps, many people walked for days risking death, victimisation and violence at the hands of local militant groups on their way. Furthermore, because of the large influx of people, many of the camps were quickly filled leaving many of those who had journeyed in search of aid without the requisite food and water they desperately needed (Muhumed and Kemenade 2011). As stated by Jerome Souquet of Doctors Without Borders, 'We can treat the severely malnourished children, but they will definitely come back to us underfed because there is not enough food and almost all of them suffer from diarrhea' (Muhumed and Kemenade 2011).

As indicated by the UN, the famine itself resulted from the intersection of severe drought, poor governance, ongoing and prolonged fighting, as well as dramatic increases in the prices of food and water. The World Food Programme reported that due to this crisis, it expected approximately 10 million people in the Horn of Africa to require food aid (Muhumed and Kemenade 2011). These conditions echo those that provided the catalyst for the famine of 1992, which resulted in approximately 1.5 million people facing starvation and 5 million being dependent on food aid. During the 1992 famine, it is estimated that almost one-third of Somali children died of starvation (Clark 1992). Many people left Somalia between 1995 through 2010 for neighbouring countries in search of security and a better life. For those that remained, traditional coping mechanisms were eradicated and internal displacement was common.

These conditions of poverty, lack of government infrastructure, healthcare, education, sanitation, and prolonged periods of drought and famine, as well as continued conflict (Rothe and Collins 2011) have created a criminogenic environment where piracy becomes a fiscally viable option for survival. In addition, illegal fishing and toxic waste dumping in the region have compounded the deprivation, creating multilayered motivations for piracy extending beyond the popular understanding of the issue – that of terroristic or predatory actors targeting vulnerable ships.

Environmental Degradation and the Somali Pirate

Somalia has long been a victim of environmental harm, some of which can be directly attributed to vulnerability to the exploitative practices of more powerful and developed states. Other harms have resulted not only from the multiple environmental disasters that have impacted the region (droughts, famines and tsunami), but because of the poor state infrastructure that provides very limited assistance to the Somali people in response to such disasters. Although there has been some political and media attention paid to the more than 20-year conflict that has plagued the region and its connection to piracy (United Nations Security Council 2000, 2001, 2007, 2008a), due to the significant vacuum of governmental, social and legal control over both Somalia's sovereign territory and its population, this focus eclipses other long standing environmentally harmful practices that provide more plausible motivations for the crime. While the effect of conflict, disorder, warring factions, and lack of state infrastructure has been acknowledged as a contributing factor in motivating individuals to commit acts of piracy, little attention has been paid to the crimes of toxic waste dumping and illegal fishing that are also motivated and facilitated by the same structural conditions.

As noted by Green and Ward (2009), weak and failing states may be conducive to the perpetration of crimes of opportunities, which lead to the redistribution of wealth. In situations where state control mechanisms have collapsed, periods of conflict persist, and social disorganisation increases, opportunistic crimes become more common (Rothe and Ross 2010). Here, we see that the conflict within Somalia has provided two types of opportunistic crimes. First, vessels have been able to trawl Somali waters for fish and dump hazardous waste with relative impunity, as the ongoing conditions of social disorganisation in Somalia facilitate the exploitative practices of more powerful states at the cost of weaker more vulnerable states.

Second, the Somali people have not only suffered the consequences of internecine fighting and instability in their country, but they have been deprived of a legitimate source of income – that of fishing. As institutional control mechanisms have become significantly degraded and legitimate sources of income have been removed, alternate opportunities arise as individuals and groups form to provide structures for criminal behaviours (Mullins and Rothe 2008).

The perpetration of environmental harms in Somalia has created a setting favourable to the perpetration of opportunistic crimes, including piracy and hijacking for ransom (Hastings 2009). As noted by the United Nations Security Council (2010), the motivations for Somali piracy are the economic and structural conditions within the country itself. The connection between environmental degradation, the economic conditions and lack of governance within the country, the desperation of the Somali people to obtain what is necessary to meet their basic needs, with the pull of piracy as a fiscal opportunity, appear to be more plausible explanations for the motivations behind for piracy than politically or religiously inspired terrorism. As noted by scholars of organised crime (Clinard and Yeager 1980; Green and Ward 2009; Hashim 2006), economically driven crimes have benefits that extend beyond the individual to groups and even to communities. It is likely that the funds from piracy are distributed to surrounding communities in Somalia (United Nations Office on Drugs and Crime 2010: 1), providing buffers against the poor conditions and the dying fish industry. This is again supported by the fact that initial increases in piracy attacks were focused in part on targets that contained food supplies (World Food Programme 2007). Although these environmental harms have significant economic implications, to reduce the motivations for piracy to just economic hardship, ignores the political motivations for piracy.

Motivations for piracy extend beyond the opportunistic and provide political motivations, separate and distinct from the ideological motivations of terrorism, in what Green and Ward (2009: 1) would term a 'dual purpose' crime. Local fishermen, angry and frustrated at the foreign trawlers plundering their fish and destroying their livelihood with toxic waste, began to organise to defend their waters. This is reflected by the establishment of a volunteer coastguard by local fishermen to patrol Somali waters using speedboats to try to dissuade the dumpers and trawlers, or at least levy a 'tax' on them (Hari 2009). The coastguard resulted from the banding together of local fishermen in efforts to defend their livelihoods, as indicated by Jeylani Shaykh Abdi: 'They are not only taking and robbing us of our fish, but they are keeping us from fishing ... They have rammed our boats and cut our nets' (Johnson 2009). Initial instances of piracy in the early 1990s indicate that these operations were poorly organised and not very sophisticated with fishermen targeting foreign vessels, demanding replacement nets, fuel and even fish from them rather than money. Ironically, it was the foreign fishermen who first introduced financial incentives, as they began to offer payments in advance, to ensure entrance into Somali waters (Murphy 2011). Therefore, these quasi-political motivations can be associated with a desire to retaliate against the foreign interests that have stolen Somali resources as a way of fighting back. As indicated by Hari (2009: 2), 'European ships have been looting Somalia's seas of the greatest resource: seafood. More than 300 million [USD] worth of tuna, shrimp and lobster are being stolen every year by illegal trawlers ... We have destroyed our own fish stocks by overexploitation – and now we have moved on to theirs'.

The feelings of anger and frustration, as displayed by the local fishermen, have been exacerbated by the militarised anti-piracy response. For example, in 2011, the President of the Puntland Non-State Actors Association (PUNSAA) stated that the military forces involved in the war on piracy are 'protecting illegal fishing vessels but not protecting fishermen' (Noor 2011). Levett (2008: 18), to offer another example, argues that 'there are now warships from India, Malaysia, Britain, the US, France, Russia, Spain, and South Korea in the region shepherding merchant shipping and pursuing pirates but largely ignoring the illegal foreign fishers'.

The distinction between fishermen and pirates is also blurred in many instances because, as suggested by the United Nations Office on Drugs and Crime, '[t]he majority of apprehended 'pirates' are released at sea, in part because you never know if naval interceptions are of regular fishermen' (Mangan 2011). The irony here is that many of the states engaged in the fight against piracy are also involved in illegal fishing in Somali coastal waters.

There was little attention paid to the problem of illegal fishing by the IPC until 2011, when Special Advisor to the Security Council on issues related to piracy off the coast of Somalia, Jack Lang, began advocating for the need to address the underlying causes of piracy especially as they relate to the economic development of both Somaliland and Puntland (United Nations Security Council 2011a). Although Lang has drawn attention to illegal fishing as one of the reasons for the development of piracy in the region motivated by the 'Somali population to protect its territorial waters and marine resources against illegal fishing', he has also undermined the credibility of his assertion by stating that 'the nexus between piracy, on the one hand, and illegal fishing ... on the other, continues to be invoked without having been proven to date' (United Nations Security Council 2011a: 12). This marginalisation of illegal fishing is in direct contradiction to the numerous first-hand accounts from self-professed pirates claiming that the motivation for piracy is to prevent foreign interests trawling for fish in Somali territorial waters.

In a similar vein, local fishermen have organised to protect their seas and their livelihoods against toxic waste dumping. Following the tsunami in 2004, local fishermen became angry and frustrated at the harm that was being caused to their coastal waters. This, coupled with the increased reports of previously mentioned health issues impacting the local population, mobilised local fisherman to fight back against those perpetrating harm against them. As stated by pirate leader Junana Ali Jana, 'The Somali coastline has been destroyed. We believe this money is nothing compared to the devastation we have seen on the seas' (Johnson 2009). Through this lens, the illegal dumping and fishing in Somali waters can be viewed as a "resource swap' with Somalis taking $100 million annually in ransoms while Europeans and Asians poach $300 million in fish' (Jasparro 2009: 2).

In examining patterns of environmentally harmful practices, it has also been widely recognised that they reflect broader geo-political structures that promote the corporate and state interests of the most powerful over weaker states and peoples (Brisman and South 2013; Gaardner 2013; White 2010b, 2013). As noted by

White (2013: 245), 'the biggest threat to environmental rights, ecological justice, and non-human animal well-being are system-level structures and pressures that commodify all aspects of social existence via the exploitation of humans, animals and natural resource'. Here, the coastal waters have been commodifed by more powerful countries, who benefit economically from both stealing fish and using the area to cheaply depose of their industrial waste. In addition, corporate and state interests of the most powerful states are centred on protecting the global shipping lanes in efforts to protect capital tied up in world trade (Collins 2012). Therefore, the etiological factors that motivate individuals to commit acts of piracy, both economic and political, are secondary to the interests that promote profit making. As suggested by President Ahmed Hussen of the Canadian Somali Congress in an interview with CBC News (2009):

> When you see the coverage of piracy, in most of the national media, you don't hear much about the $300 million annually that's lost by Somali fishermen in illegal fishing done by foreign interests. You also never hear about the cost that cannot be estimated, the negative costs of toxic waste ... What is hard to comprehend is why the outside world [is] turning a blind eye to foreigners fishing illegally in Somali waters and poisoning them with toxic waste. And as can be expected, the starving people who've been robbed have retaliated with some countering of their own. The attacks on foreign ships, Somalis say, started as a reaction to foreign pillages trying to put their fishermen out of business.

The economic and political motivations for the real causes of piracy in Somalia are absent from the policies that have been created, enacted and enforced in response to the 'problem' of the Somali pirate. The anti-piracy policies, predicated on the risk of a maritime terrorism attack and dangerous actors plaguing the seas (Collins 2012), involve over 50 different actors, including at least 20 individual states deploying military forces 'to take part actively in fighting piracy' (United Nations Security Council 2008b: 3). These warships are actively patrolling the Gulf of Aden, but there has yet to be one vessel stopped or detained for dumping toxic waste (Johnson 2009). In addition, the militarised response to the piracy in Somalia has been extremely costly to states, insurance companies, and corporations with a total cost of $6.6 billion USD in 2011 alone. When compared to the direct cost of piracy (in the form of ransoms) for the same year, the cost totalled only US$160 million (Oceans Beyond Piracy 2011). It is clear that the response has not only become more expensive than piracy itself but it grossly exceeds the amount spent on the humanitarian crisis within the country. For example, in 2011, US$4.5 million was dedicated to addressing issues associated with the humanitarian situation in Somalia (Rinehard 2012). Furthermore, the large amount of money spent on fighting piracy does nothing to address the illegal fishing, toxic waste dumping, or conditions of drought and famine that have contributed to the growth of piracy in the region. As indicated by Geoffrey Egbide, the brother of a man kidnapped by pirates, who spoke to an investigative journalist, 'When a man is destitute, he will do anything to survive. It is a desperate situation in Somalia. It is a place where might makes right. In Somalia, if they can hijack a ship and get 1 million dollars, then it is something right for them to do' (Eichstaedt 2010: 99).

The current response has failed to address the root causes of the problem, i.e., the environmental degradation, conflict, and resulting structural conditions within Somalia, and instead has advanced the interests of those engaged in piracy. As indicated by Jasparro (2009: 1), the policies on piracy, '[m]ask deeper problems of unfairness in international economic order ... Of the countries that contributed naval vessels to the anti-piracy operation, half are nations engaged in fishing in the Indian Ocean with a vested interest in deterring piracy'. The irony is that the problem of piracy in the Gulf of Aden is not likely to disappear until a more holistic approach to the problem is advanced. This would include acknowledging and addressing the long history of wrong-doing perpetrated by powerful states against Somalia – including the exploitation of the country's marine resources and the long-lasting harms caused to humans, non-human animals, and ecosystems as a result of illegal dumping of toxic pollutants. These harms need to be acknowledged and given legitimacy in conjunction with addressing larger-scale humanitarian needs resulting from both environmental disasters (droughts, famines, tsunami) and the ongoing conflict.

Conclusion

Contrary to popular understandings of the issue, piracy in Somalia is not about the threat of maritime terrorism or gruesome characters terrorising the seas. Interestingly, there were no reports of Somali piracy prior to 1992 (Collins 2012), and it is only after the ousting of Barre that piracy becomes a problem with the number of attacks steadily increasing to its peak in 2011, with 237 attacks (International Maritime Bureau 2011). Therefore, the 'problem' of piracy coincides with the internecine fighting, the decline of the fishing industry and the humanitarian situation within the country itself (see Collins 2012 for a more holistic overview of the development of the current anti-piracy response). As this chapter has attempted to explain, piracy in Somalia is an opportunistic criminal phenomenon driven by basic economic needs situated in global inequities that promote the interests of powerful states over those of weaker states. The issue of piracy in Somalia cannot be accurately understood by solely examining the acts of individual perpetrators, instead, it is best understood within the broader global, political and economic context in which it occurs. Political economic analysis is not only relevant to the issue of piracy, but exposes some of the core motivations of both the perpetrators and the controllers of this behaviour. From this vantage point, Somali fishermen are angry and frustrated at the destruction of the fishing industry and the continued practice of dumping hazardous waste in their waters. Those engaged in piracy do not view themselves as criminal actors. Instead, they refer to themselves as 'saviours of the seas', arguing that those stealing their fish are the real pirates (Bahadur 2011: 15). By taking to the seas, the pirates of Somalia are able to simultaneously act to protect their interests, as well as fill an economic need caused by the bleak conditions within the country itself.

By marginalising the impact of the environmental harm and the conditions within the country itself, media and political coverage of the problem negates the seriousness of the environmental abuses suffered by the people of Somalia. The lack of acknowledgement by politically and economically stronger countries has led to a situation where there is nothing left to lose for the Somali people. Coastal communities are affected not only by the immediate impact of toxic waste dumping on their fish but also have to deal with lasting and serious health effects, contaminated water and the contamination of their food supply. Therefore, living in conditions of prolonged conflict, poverty and humanitarian crisis, piracy becomes not a predatory act but a desperate act of survival. As noted by the East African Seafarer's Assistance Program, Andrew Mwangura, 'desperate people take desperate measures … most [pirates] don't know how to swim, yet they go two hundred miles out to sea' (Eichstaedt 2010: 118). In response to these multifaceted harms perpetrated against the Somali people, they have mobilised in efforts to fight back, engaging in acts of piracy, to reclaim their right to life.

References

Achieng, J. 1999. *Environment – Somalia: Local Fishermen Battle Foreign Trawlers.* Available at: http://www.somwe.com/fishmen.html. Accessed 1 November 2013.

Africa Watch Committee. 1990. *Somalia: A Government at War with its Own People.* New York: Human Rights Watch.

Africa Watch and Physicians for Human Rights. 1992. *No Mercy in Mogadishu: The Human Cost of the Conflict and the Struggle for Relief.* Available at: http://www.hrw.org/reports/1992/somalia/. Accessed 7 January 2015.

Ahmed, I.I. and Green, R.H. 1999. The heritage of war and state collapse in Somalia and Somaliland: local-level effects, external interventions and reconstruction. *Third World Quarterly* 20(1): 113–27.

Alexander, Y. and Richardson, T.B. (eds) 2009. *Terror on the High Seas: From Piracy to Stategic Challenge.* Santa Barbara, CA: ABC-CLIO, LLC.

Amnesty International. 1990. *Somalia: Report on an Amnesty International Visit and Current Human Rights Concerns.* New York: Amnesty International.

Bahadur, J. 2011. *The Pirates of Somalia: Inside their Hidden World.* New York: Pantheon Books.

Barling, R. 2003. Terrorism at sea poses new threat: increasingly ruthless piracy against ever bigger ships in southeast Asian waters has given rise to fears that extremists will turn supertankers into floating bombs. Russell Barling Reports. *South China Morning Post*, 23 November, 12.

BBC News. 2002. Mysterious East African fish deaths. *BBC News*, 31 January. Available at: http://news.bbc.co.uk/2/hi/africa/1793838.stm. Accessed 1 December 2013.

Beirne, P. 2007. Animal rights, animal abuse and green criminology. In P. Beirne and N. South (eds), *Issues in Green Criminology: Confronting Harms against Environments, Humanity and Other Animals.* Abingdon: Routledge, 55–86.

Beirne, P. and South, N. (eds). 2007. *Issues in Green Criminology: Confronting Harms against Environments, Humanity and Other Animals.* Abingdon: Routledge.

Boekhout van Solinge, T.B.V. 2010. Equatorial deforestation as a harmful practice and a criminological issue. In R. White (ed.), *Global Environmental Harm: Criminological Perspectives.* Cullompton: Willan, 20–26.

Borger, J. 2008. Piracy and ransom payments: risky business – safe transactions. *Guardian*, 14 November. Available at: http://news.bbc.co.uk/2/hi/africa/1793838.stm. Accessed 2 December 2013.

Brisman, A. and South, N. 2013. Resource wealth, power, crime and conflict. In R. Walters, D. Westerhuis and T. Wyatt (eds), *Emerging Issues in Green Criminology: Exploring Power, Justice and Harm.* New York: Palgrave Macmillan, 57–71.

Carrabine, E., Cox, P., Lee, M., Plummer, K. and South, N. 2004. *Criminology: A Sociological Introduction.* New York: Routledge.

CBC News. 2009. President Ahmed Hussen of the Canadian Somali Congress. Pirates in Somalia. *CBC News.* Montreal, Radio Canada: CBC News.

Clark, J. 1992. *Famine in Somalia and the International Response: Collective Failure.* Arlington, VA: US Committee for Refugees.

Cliffe, L. 2005. *Armed Violence and Poverty in Somalia: A Case Study for the Armed Violence and Poverty Initiative.* Bradford, UK: Centre for International Cooperation and Security.

Clifford, M. and Edwards, T.D. (eds) 2012. *Environmental Crime.* Burlington, MA: Jones and Barlett.

Clinard, M.B. and Yeager, P.C. 1980. *Corporate Crime.* New York: Macmillan.

Collins, V.E. 2012. Dangerous seas: moral panic and the Somali pirate. *Australian and New Zealand Journal of Criminology* 45(1): 106–32.

Davies, J.L. 1994. *The Liberation Movements of Somalia.* Available at: http://www.civicwebs.com/cwvlib/africa/somalia/1994/lib_movments/lib_movements.hm. Accessed 14 November 2013.

Doyle, L. 2005. Terror temperature rises in Somalia as PM survives an attack. *The Independent*, 1 December, p. 25.

Eichstaedt, P. 2010. *Pirate State: Inside Somalia's Terrorism at Sea.* Chicago, IL: Lawrence Hill.

Food Security and Nutrition Analysis Unit. 2011. *Famine Continues: Observed Improvements Contingent on Continued Response.* Nairobi: Food Security and Nutrition Analysis Unit.

Friedrichs, D.O. and Friedrichs, J. 2002. The World Bank and crimes of globalization: a case study. *Social Justice* 29(1–2): 1–12.

Friedrichs, D.O. and Rothe, D.L. 2012. Crimes of globalization as a criminological project: the case of international financial institutions. In F. Packes (ed.), *Globalization and the Challenge to Criminology.* New York: Routledge Press, 45–63.

Gaardner, E. 2013. Evading responsibility for green harm: state-corporate exploitation of race, class, and gender inequality. In N. South and A. Brisman (eds), *Routledge International Handbook of Green Criminology.* New York: Routledge, 272–81.

Gettel, O. 2013. 'Captain Phillips': Tom Hanks on 'skinniest, scariest' co-stars. *Los Angeles Times.* Available at: http://www.latimes.com/entertainment/envelope/moviesnow/la-et-mn-captain-phillips-envelope-screening-series-tom-hanks-skinniest-scariest-costars-20131223,0,4548624.story#axzz2pSO3gs4M Accessed 2 November 2013.

Green, P. and Ward, T. 2009. The transformation of violence in Iraq. *British Journal of Criminology* 49(5): 609–27.

Guterres, A. 2011. Interview with *Huffington Post.* In M.M. Muhumed and L.V. Kemenade (eds), *Somali Drought is 'Worst Humanitarian Crisis':* *U.N.* Available at: http://www.huffingtonpost.com/2011/07/10/somalia-drought-worst-humanitarian-crisis-_n_894072.html. Accessed 28 November 2013.

Hahim, A.S. 2006. *Insurgency and Counter-Insurgency in Iraq.* London: Hurst.

Hari, J. 2009. Johann Hari: you are being lied to about pirates. *The Independent,* 5 January. Available at: http://www.independent.co.uk/opinion/commentators/johann-hari/johann-hariyou-are-being-lied-to-about-pirates-1225817.html. Accessed 4 November 2013.

Hastings, J.V. 2009. Geographies of state failure and sophistication in maritime piracy hijackings. *Political Geography* 28(4): 213–23.

Heckenberg, D. 2010. The global transference of toxic harm. In R. White (ed.), *Global Environmental Harm: Criminological Perspectives.* Cullompton: Willan, 37–61.

Herbig, J. 2010. The illegal reptile trade as a form of conservation crime: a South African criminological investigation. In R. White (ed.), *Global Environmental Harm: Criminological Perspectives.* Cullompton: Willan, 110–31.

Human Rights Watch. 2007. *Shell-Shocked: Civilians under Siege in Mogadishu.* New York: Human Rights Watch.

Human Rights Watch. 2012. *Somalia: Country Summary.* Available at: http://www.hrw.org/world-report-2012/world-report-2012-somalia. Accessed 1 November 2013.

Hussein, B.M. 2010. *The Evidence of Toxic and Radioactive Wastes Dumping in Somalia and its Impact on the Enjoyment of Human Rights: A Case Study.* Geneva: Human Rights Council. Available at: http://somalitalk.com/sun/toxic_waste_dumping_somalia.pdf. Accessed 15 December 2013.

Internal Displacement Monitoring Centre. 2012. *New Displacement and Worsening Humanitarian and Protection Crisis for IDPs.* Available at: http://www. internal-displacement.org/8025708F004CE90B/(httpCountries)/02EE5A59E 76049F5802570A7004B80AB?opendocument. Accessed 15 December 2013.

International Maritime Bureau. 2011. Annual report on piracy and armed robbery against ships. *International Chamber of Commerce (ICC) Commercial Crime Services.* Available at: http://www.iccwbo.org. Accessed 11 December 2013.

INTERPOL. 2008. *The Waste Transport Checks Manual: AUGIAS.* Lyons: INTERPOL.

INTERPOL. 2009. *Electronic Waste and Organized Crime: Assessing the Links.* Lyons: INTERPOL.

Jasparro, C. 2009. Piracy offers lessons on global governance. *Yale Global.* Available at: http://yaleglobal.yale.edu/content/somalia%E2%80%99s-piracy-offers-lessons-global-governance. Accessed 12 November 2013.

Johnson, R. 2009. Somali pirates began as volunteer Coast Guard. *People's World,* 22 April. Available at: http://www.peoplesworld.org/somali-pirates-began-as-volunteer-coast-guard/. Accessed 7 January 2015.

Kluin, M.H.A. 2013. Environmental regulation in chemical corporations: preliminary results of a case study. In R. Walters, D. Westerhuis and T. Wyatt (eds), *Emerging Issues in Green Criminology: Exploring Power, Justice and Harm.* New York: Palgrave Macmillan, 145–72.

Lacey, M. 2001. Pirate militias from Somalia spill into the Gulf of Aden. *New York Times,* 12 September, p. 2.

Levett, C. 2008. Fishing fleets are pirates too. *Sydney Morning Herald,* 24 November.

Lewis, I.M. 1994. *Blood and Bone: The Call of Kinship in Somali Society.* Lawrenceville, NJ: Red Sea Press.

Lynch, M., Burns, R. and Stretesky, P. 2010. Global warming and state-corporate crime: the politicalization of global warming under the Bush Administration. *Crime, Law and Social Change,* 54(3): 213–39.

Lynch, M.J. and Stretesky, P.B. 2010. Global warming, global crime: a green criminology perspective. In R. White (ed.), *Global Environmental Harm: Criminological Perspectives.* Cullompton: Willan, 62–84.

Lynch, M.J. and Stretesky, P.B. 2013. Green criminology. In F.T. Cullen and P. Wilcox (eds), *The Oxford Handbook of Criminological Theory.* New York: Oxford University Press, 625–48.

Macaskill, E. 2011. Somali pirates kill four Americans: US military says hostages shot on board Quest before Navy rescue attempt. *The Guardian,* 22 February. Available at: http://www.guardian.co.uk/world/2011/feb/22/four-americans-killed-somali-pirates. Accessed 11 November 2013.

Mackay, N. (2005) Royal Navy vows to hunt down Somali pirates. *The Sunday Herald,* 1 November, p. 13.

Mangan, S. 2011. Prosecutions advisor, counter-piracy programme, UN Office on Drugs and Crime. Interview 13 July 2011, Nairobi. In C. Singh and A.S. Bedi (eds), *'War on Piracy': The Conflation of Somali Piracy with Terrorism in Discourse, Tactic and Law.* Rotterdam: International Institute of Social Studies, 22–3.

Mohamed, A.E. 2001. *Somalia's Degrading Environment.* Available at: http://www.banadir.com/a.htm. Accessed 12 December 2013.

Muhumed, M.M. and Kemenade, L.V. 2011. Somali drought is 'worst Humanitarian crisis': U.N. *Huffington Post*, 10 July. Available at: http://www.huffingtonpost.com/2011/07/10/somalia-drought-worst-humanitarian-crisisn_894072.html. Accessed 28 November 2013.

Mullins, C.W. and Rothe, D.L. 2008. *Blood, Power, and Bedlam: Violations of International Criminal Law in Post-Colonial Africa.* New York: Peter Lang.

Murphy, M.N. 2011. *Somalia: The New Barbery?: Piracy and Islam in the Horn of Africa.* New York: Columbia University Press.

Noor, M. 2011. President, Puntland Non-State Actors' Association, Interview in Nairobi, 15 July. In C. Singh and A.S. Bedi (eds), *'War on Piracy': The Conflation of Somali Piracy with Terrorism in Discourse, Tactic and Law.* Rotterdam: International Institute of Social Studies, 25–6.

Norton-Taylor, R. 2008. Reader's page: questions, questions: how can piracy be stopped? *The Guardian*, 4 October, p. 40.

Oceans Beyond Piracy. 2011. *The Economic Cost of Somali Piracy 2011.* Available at: www.oceansbeyondpiracy.org. Accessed 11 November 2013.

O'Sullivan, J. 1999. Riddle of Scottish traveller 'shot dead by a gang of Somali pirates'. *The Independent*, 18 September, p. 3.

Panjabi, R.K.L. 2010. The pirates of Somalia: opportunistic predators or environmental prey? *William and Mary Environmental Law and Policy Review* 34(2): 377–491.

Potter, G.R. 2012. Pushing the boundaries of (a) green criminology: environmental harm as a *cause* of crime. *The Green Criminology Monthly* 3(November).

Rice, X. 2008. Focus: ocean terror: how savage pirates reign on the world's high seas. *The Observer*, 27 April.

Rinehard, B. 2012. *Horn of Africa: Land & Sea.* Norfolk, VA: Civil-Military Fusion Centre North Atlantic Treaty Organization.

Ross, M. 2003. The natural resource curse: how wealth can make you poor. In I. Bannon and P. Collier (eds), *Natural Resources and Violent Conflict: Options and Actions.* Washington, D.C.: The World Bank, 17–42.

Rothe, D.L. and Mullins, C.W. 2006. International community: legitimizing a moral consciousness. *Humanity and Society* 30(3): 253–76.

Rothe, D.L. and Collins, V.E. 2011. Got a band-aid? Political discourse, militarized responses, and the Somalia pirate. *Contemporary Justice Review* 14(3): 329–43.

Rothe, D.L. and Collins, V.E. 2013. The circle of state violence and harm. In B. Arrigo and H. Bersot (eds), *The Routledge Handbook of International Crime and Justice Studies.* Abingdon: Taylor & Francis, 494–515.

Rothe, D.L. and Collins, V.E. 2014. International financial institutions as facilitators of environmental crimes. In E. Orlando and T. Bergin (eds), *A Socio-Legal Approach to Environmental Crimes: An International Perspective.* Cambridge: Cambridge University Press.

Rothe, D.L. and Ross, J.I. 2010. Private military contractors, crime, and the terrain of unaccountability. *Justice Quarterly* 27(4): 593–617.

Schwartz, D.M. 1998. Environmental terrorism: analyzing the concept. *Journal of Peace Research* 35(4): 483–96.

Shuqin, Y. 2010. The polluting behavior of the multinationational corporations in China. In R. White (ed.), *Global Environmental Harm: Criminological Perspectives.* Cullompton: Willan, 150–60.

Silverstein, P. 2005. The new barbarians: piracy and terrorism on the North African frontier. *The New Centennial Review* 5(1): 179–212.

Singh, C. and Bedi, A.S. 2012. *War on Piracy: The Conflation of Somali Piracy with Terrorism in Discourse, Tactic and Law.* The Hague: International Institue of Social Sciences.

South, N. and Brisman, A. (eds) 2013. *Routledge International Handbook of Green Criminology.* New York: Routledge.

Tharoor, I. 2009. How Somalia's fishermen became pirates. *Time,* 18 April. Available at: http://content.time.com/time/world/article/0,8599,1892376,00.html. Accessed 13 December 2013.

The White House. 2007. *Policy for the Repression of Piracy and Other Criminal Acts of Violence at Sea.* Washington, D.C.: The White House.

United Nations Children's Fund. 2012. *Safe Water Remains Scarce in Somalia, Contributing to Disease and Malnutrition.* Available at: http://www.unicef.org/infobycountry/somalia_62048.html. Accessed 12 December 2013.

United Nations Environment Programme. 2005a. *Rebuild Differently after Tsunami: United Nations Environment Programme Advises in New Report (Press Release UNEP/268).* Available at: http://www.un.org/News/Press/docs/2005/unep268.doc.htm htm. Accessed 12 November 2013.

United Nations Environment Programme. 2005b. *Somalia.* Available at: http://www.unep.org/tsunami/reports/tsunami_somalia_layout.pdf htm. Accessed 12 November 2013.

United Nations Environment Programme. 2006. *After the Tsunami: Rapid Environmental Assessment.* Available at: http://www.unep.org/tsunami/tsunami_rpt.asp htm. Accessed 12 November 2013.

United Nations General Assembly. 2005. *Oceans and the Law of the Sea (Document Number: A/60/63).* Available at: http://daccess-dds-ny.un.org/doc/UNDOC/GEN/N05/257/59/PDF/N0525759.pdf?OpenElement. Accessed 28 November 2013.

United Nations Office for the Coordination for Humanitarian Affairs. 2012. *'Drought Strikes the Horn of Africa,' Voices of America.* Available at: http://www.voanews.com/english/news/special-reports/world-and-regional/Famine-in-Somalia-126248473.html htm. Accessed 12 November 2013.

United Nations Office on Drugs and Crime. 2010. *Eastern Africa.* Available at: http://www/unodc.org/easternafrica/en/piracy/background.html. Accessed 7 January 2015.

United Nations Security Council. 2000. *Report of the Secretary-General on the Situation in Somalia.* Available at: http://daccess-dds-ny.un.org/doc/UNDOC/GEN/N00/785/22/PDF/N0078522.pdf?OpenElement.htm. Accessed 12 November 2013.

United Nations Security Council. 2001. *Report of the Secretary-General on the Situation in Somalia (Document Number: S2001/963).* Available at: http://daccess-dds-ny.un.org/doc/UNDOC/GEN/N01/566/75/PDF/N0156675.pdf?OpenElement.htm. Accessed 12 November 2013.

United Nations Security Council. 2007. *Report of the Secretary-General on Children and Armed Conflict in Somalia (Document Number: S/2007/259).* Available at: http://daccess-dds-ny.un.org/doc/UNDOC/GEN/N07/298/52/PDF/N0729852.pdf?OpenElemen htm. Accessed 12 November 2013.

United Nations Security Council. 2008a. *Report of the Secretary-General on the Situation in Somalia.* Available at: http://daccess-dds-ny.un.org/doc/UNDOC/GEN/N08/413/59/PDF/N0841359.pdf?OpenElement.htm. Accessed 14 November 2013.

United Nations Security Council. 2008b. *Resolution 1816: UN doc. S/RES/1816 (2008).* Available at: http://daccess-dds-ny.un.org/doc/UNDOC/GEN/N08/361/77/PDF/N0836177.pdf?OpenElement.htm. Accessed 14 November 2013.

United Nations Security Council. 2010. *Resolution 1950: UN doc. S/RES/1950 (2010).* Available at: http://daccess-dds-ny.un.org/doc/UNDOC/GEN/N10/649/02/PDF/N1064902.pdf?OpenElement.htm. Accessed 12 November 2013.

United Nations Security Council. 2011a. *Letter Dated 24 January 2011 from the Secretary-General to the President of the Security Council. S/2011/30.* Available at: http://daccess-dds-ny.un.org/doc/UNDOC/GEN/N11/206/21/PDF/N1120621.pdf?OpenElement htm. Accessed 11 November 2013.

United Nations Security Council. 2011b. *Report of the Secretary-General on the Protection of Somali Natural Resources and Waters S/2011/661.* Available at: http://daccess-dds-ny.un.org/doc/UNDOC/GEN/N11/540/51/PDF/N1154051.pdf?OpenElement.htm. Accessed 11 November 2013.

Van Ginkel, B. and Landman, L. 2012. In search of a sustainable and coherent strategy: assessing the kaleidoscope of counter-piracy activities in Somalia. *Journal of International Criminal Justice* 10(4): 727–48.

Walters, R. 2006. Crime, bio-agriculture and the exploitation of hunger. *British Journal of Criminology* 46(1): 26–45.

Walters, R. 2010. Toxic atmospheres air pollution, trade and the politics of regulation. *Critical Criminology* 18(4): 307–23.

Walters, R., Westerhuis, D. and Wyatt, T. (eds) 2013. *Emerging Issues in Green Criminology: Exploring Power, Justice and Harm.* New York: Palgrave Macmillan.

Wellsmith, M. 2010. The applicability of crime prevention to problems of environmental harm: a consideration of illict trade in endangered species. In R. White (ed.), *Global Environmental Harm: Criminological Perspectives.* Cullompton: Willan, 132–49.

White, R. (ed.) 2010a. *Global Environmental Harm: Criminological Perspectives.* Cullompton: Willan.

White, R. 2010b. Globalisation and environmental harm. In R. White (ed.), *Global Environmental Harm: Criminological Perspectives.* Cullompton: Willan, 3–19.

White, R. 2013. Eco-global criminology and the political economy. In N. South and A. Brisman (eds), *Routhledge International Handbook of Green Criminology.* New York: Routledge, 243–60.

World Food Programme. 2007. *Coordinated Action Urged: Piracy Threatens UN Lifeline to Somalia.* Available at: http://www.wfp.org/node/328.htm. Accessed 28 November 2013.

PART III
Conflict that Destroys Environments

Chapter 8
Resource Wars, Environmental Crime, and the Laws of War: Updating War Crimes in a Resource Scarce World

Aaron Fichtelberg

The purpose of this chapter is to examine a gap in current war crimes law in relation to environmental crime. The laws of war, and in particular those laws that describe *war crimes*, fail to adequately protect the environment from the sort of pillaging that has become a central component of recent warfare. In this chapter, I will argue that many, indeed, perhaps most wars, can be characterised as *resource wars* – as wars where a group of states or rebels are intent upon securing control over a country's natural resources – and that the exploitation of natural resources is intimately bound up with the conduct of the war itself. Despite the prevalence of resource wars over at least the last two centuries, however, the systematic exploitation of natural resources during the course of conflict or conquest is not adequately conceived as a war crime under modern international humanitarian law. This gap leaves much of the globe's natural resources vulnerable to the vagaries of war and provides few significant legal protections for them. I argue that this lacuna makes international war crimes law particularly ill-suited for the realities of modern war, and I suggest that this should be remedied by revising the laws of war in particular ways, including the creation of a new international crime of war that I will refer to as *the criminal exploitation of natural resources in wartime* (Brisman and Nigel 2013; Hulme 2004, 2010). Such a category of criminality would both protect nature in times of armed conflict as well as potentially reduce the length of conflicts by limiting access to resources that could prolong conflict. In addition, I will argue that the concept of *joint criminal enterprise* (JCE) can be deployed to further protect the environment from profiteers in the private sector.

I will begin by briefly describing the concept of a *resource war* and its relevance for understanding modern warfare. Then, I will examine the regime of environmental protection within international humanitarian law, paying specific attention to the criminal aspect of this legal regime: those laws which determine war crimes for which individuals and groups can be prosecuted and punished. After this, I will discuss the nature of the gap between war crimes law and the reality of wartime environmental pillage, highlighting several important features of modern resources wars that are not adequately covered under the current international legal regime. Finally, I will end by suggesting some ways whereby the gap between war crimes law and pillaging the environment might be filled. In particular, I will argue that the crime of criminal exploitation will help protect the natural resources of countries in times of war, as well as helping to disincentivise recourse to war as a means for acquiring control over natural resources.

Resource Wars

Nations go to war for a variety of reasons. National security, humanitarian intervention and patriotic pride are just a few of the common *causus belli* that have been proffered in the history of war. But clearly even the most credulous account of military history will suggest that the impetus for the vast majority of wars is ultimately economic, broadly speaking. In most cases, nations have resorted to armed conflict to better their overall economic situation, either by seizing and exploiting the assets of others or by eliminating an economic rival that threatens their own prosperity. Wars to expand the frontiers of states, wars to seize colonies, and wars to expand empires were almost always first and foremost wars about bring natural resources under the sway of a particular state or a slice of its citizenry. Even when manifestly 'legitimate' reasons (such as self-defence) are given for going to war, fighting states commonly seek to assert direct or indirect control over another country's natural resources to use them for their own benefit over both the short and long term.

As alluded to earlier, wars that are fought over the control of natural materials such as oil, gold, or similar goods are often described as *resource wars*. Klare defines such wars as 'conflicts that revolve, to a significant degree, over the pursuit or possession of critical materials' (Klare 2001: 25) – usually consisting of food or fuel, but may also include goods that can be converted into cash. Nations enter into resource wars in order to gain access to minerals, oil, diamonds, and coltan to improve their economic situation and their general standard of living. The notion of a *resource war* has served as a guide for a great deal of scholarship on the subjects of international politics and armed conflict, providing insights into the *origin* of conflict, as well as the *conduct* of the war itself (Cilliers 2000; Dangl 2007; Le Billon 2004). This concept can be used to understand 'hot wars' in Africa, as well as 'cold wars' between great powers over diverse territories around the globe as they seek to ensure that their allies remain in control of valuable resources (Lee 2009).

Of course, there are problems with the concept of a resource war. Insofar as most wars (some may say *all* wars) are in some sense wars over material, rather than symbolic, goals, almost every war can be characterised as in some sense a resource war. History bears this claim out: Rome conquered Gaul not only to protect its northernmost borders from barbarian invasion, but also to establish control over gold mines in Gaul and slave labour. The United States invaded a host of countries in order to preserve access to oil, fruit, and other goods that are considered essential to American well-being, though clearly national security and humanitarian goals also figured into its calculations. Germany sought dominion over the breadbasket of Europe in the Second World War, as well as the oil fields of the Middle East in order to feed its people and ensure their economic viability and political hegemony. Independent of the rhetoric provided by political leaders to justify wars to a sceptical public, warfare in almost all cases has been focused on control over material goods – the vast majority of which are natural resources. The viability of Klare's concept, however, will not be essential to my arguments as I will claim that there are features of modern resource wars that distinguish them from their predecessors and require novel forms of legal regulation.

Despite the pervasiveness of resource wars in human history, this concept is not necessarily an accurate depiction of the exploitation of natural resources as it takes place in many modern armed conflicts. In the traditional analysis of resource wars, the goal of war is the control over resources – a state wishes to gain dominion over a site that produces valuable resources so that they can be exploited directly by the state. In its modern variant, however, the exploitation of natural resources in wartime is much more intimately connected to the conduct of the war itself and not simply a product or cause of it – war is conducted and resources are exploited simultaneously. Furthermore, in modern warfare, the exploitation of natural resources is often committed by the same people who do the fighting. Military units are deployed in gathering natural resources and securing them from enemy attack in such conflicts. To use an example: in order to fight against the Revolutionary United Front (RUF) in Sierra Leone, Executive Outcomes, the private security company, was not only paid cash, but was given title to several diamond mines within Sierra Leone. With the privatisation of much of modern war fighting (Singer 2007), the economic incentives, often in terms of control over natural resources, have become a common feature of many wars.

While the pursuit of raw materials is almost always a pervasive part of war, in traditional warfare the domination over and exploitation of natural resources is usually independent of the conduct of warfare itself. War is often considered to be the clash of armed forces and the control over resources to be an outcome of this conflict: the 'spoils' that go to the winner. That is to say, when scholars theorise about war, control and exploitation of natural resources is considered to be either a *causus belli* or a *reward for victory*, not a *part of the war itself*. In this traditional model of resource wars, a state develops a desire for another state's natural resources, invades that state, and once it has defeated this government, it establishes dominion over it and begins to exploit these coveted resources. 'Resource wars' are thus taken to be 'wars over resources'.

At the same time, in many modern resource wars, the exploitation of natural resources is not only the *causus belli*, but this exploitation is often deeply integrated with the war itself. Smaller poorer states or militias fund their war making through the exploitation of the resources that they are fighting over. In Sub-Saharan Africa, 'protracted internal and interstate armed conflicts have been triggered, sustained, and funded by the economic imperative of capturing and monopolising territorial control over the lucrative diamond producing areas' (Orogun 2004). In Sierra Leone's conflict, control over the mining of diamonds was not only the reason that the RUF was fighting against the government of Sierra Leone, but in addition, the RUF (and to a lesser extent, the Sierra Leonean government) funded their war through these same diamonds – in other words, using the diamonds to buy weapons. Clearly then, resources are more than simply the object of struggle; in many modern wars, they are deeply integrated within war itself.

There are several reasons why resource wars have most likely changed in recent history. On the one hand, the increasing speed of the global economy and transportation has made it possible to exploit resources in close to 'real time'. That is, the time required to access resources, particularly those that are quickly exploited (e.g., diamonds, gold) and sell them on the global market makes these resources a lucrative source during the conduct of hostilities. Diamonds can be mined and sold on the global diamond exchange in a fraction of the time that it would have taken to gather and sell these same resources in preceding centuries. This means that militaries, in particular guerrilla movements, need not fully finance their endeavours at the outset. Such forces can fight a war 'on spec' – they can begin fighting with the expectation that the resources captured can be quickly exploited in order to further fund the conflict. Without such a market, modern resource wars would be impossible.

On the other hand, modern technology requires that some natural resources, oil and gasoline in particular, be exploited quickly in order, in many cases, to allow military war machines to continue to operate. During the Second World War, for example, oil resources were not a primary goal for the German military because they would make Germany prosperous over the long run. Rather, these resources were integral to the ability of the *Wehrmacht* to continue to fight the allies. Without the oil fields in the south of the Soviet Union or in the Middle East, the German military would have ground to a halt. In such wars, natural resources, fuel in particular, is intimately linked to the conduct of warfare and therefore the hunt for such resources is integrated into the strategy and tactics of the war itself.

Other resources that support modern conflicts are frequently tied into global markets and are coveted more for their exchange value than their use value. Some goods take a circuitous route through global markets before returning to benefit the military and political actors involved in this resource war. Diamonds, for example, have little actual utility in war time, but may easily be traded with foreign entities for cash, military assistance or weaponry that can be deployed in the conflict. Even the acquisition of oil, arguably a motive for the 2003 US invasion of Iraq, was not for the immediate consumption of US consumers, but rather was diffused through the global market and thus had an impact on all global energy consumption which in turn benefited the US economy as the heaviest energy user in the world. Modern resource wars, then, are caught up in a much broader international economy which in turn brings in international economic actors such as multinational corporations, international energy cartels (e.g., OPEC), individual traders, acting alongside conventional governments and their militaries.

Many resource wars are international in character, but need not be. Returning to the example of Sierra Leone, the decade long civil war there has been characterised as a resource war because the conflict was motivated by the exploitation of Sierra Leone's raw materials, primarily diamonds. While foreign agents were clearly involved in the war (principally Liberian president Charles Taylor), and the rebel RUF deployed a discourse of liberation, the central theme of the war was diamonds, which clearly sustained and altered the war in a way that corrupted what ideals (if any) the RUF had at the outset of the war. As Gberie points out, the war in Sierra Leone was more complex than simple plunder, but diamonds were an essential ingredient in a protracted, bloody conflict:

> Diamonds may not have been the cause of the of the war; the question of 'causes' can often seem wholly misdirected – Taylor, the real mastermind, aimed at both revenge and pillage, as we will see, and his protégé Sankoh's grudges against the ruling All Peoples Congress (APC) party went beyond a simple wish to steal, with many among the country's despairing poor sharing his incoherent political sentiments. (Gberie 2005: 6–7)

As with all wars, the role of nature in the overall conflict in Sierra Leone is very complex, but fundamentally, the Sierra Leonean civil war was not simply a war for diamonds, it was a war *about* diamonds: possession of these gems was both part of the goal of seizing power, as well as the means by which political power was to be achieved by the rebel forces.

Other conflicts over natural resources include 'conflict timber' – the exploitation of timber resources, trees, in order to fund war (Milburn 2014; see also Wyatt, and Milburn, this volume). In its report on the illegal timber industry, 'The Logs of War', the UN affiliated organisation, Global Witness, reports 22 different countries that have engaged in illegal logging activities, and many of these do so in relation to an armed conflict (Global Witness 2002). As Global Witness observes:

> Compared to most forms of resource extraction, logging is a relatively easy activity, requiring low investment for quick return. A few soldiers with chainsaws and trucks can generate hundreds of thousands of dollars in a relatively short time … As a result, senior commanders and politicians begin to bypass such national laws as may be in place to control forest exploitation. In more extreme cases military intervention in another country is based around the attempt to control that country's resources. For a warring faction in control of forest land, logging is one of the quickest routes to obtain significant funding with which to continue the conflict. (Global Witness 2002: 8)

Other prominent natural resources that are the product of resource wars are coltan, titanium, and of course, gold – all resources that are often located in the developing world, but are in high demand in the developed world. In each case, the war was waged for, and funded by the exploitation of natural resources that are sold on an international market to the greedy advanced economies of the world.

While it would go beyond the scope of this chapter to dwell on this issue in any more depth, it is clear that the means used for exploiting natural resources in wartime are, in many ways, highly damaging to the environment. Because of the nature of war, it is most surely the case that these resources are often harvested in a hurried fashion that is harmful for the environment, more damaging to the resources themselves, and less sustainable than would be a more thoughtful exploitation conducted in a more careful and deliberate fashion. Because the resources must be harvested with a great deal of speed, there is a clear incentive to use damaging methods to extract the resources quickly. Soldiers provide a ready work force for this work, regardless of whether they have any training in the work that they are doing and whether or not they have any care for the land that they are exploiting, meaning that they are disinclined to consider the impact of their work. Furthermore, slave labour is another resource that is often used in resource wars, as local civilians or prisoners are dragooned into harvesting the riches that are sold to buy weapons and materiel for war. Exploiting resources is often a zero-sum game in wartime: if the resources are not harvested by one side, the other side will surely not hesitate to do so when they are granted access to them following a change of fortunes between the combatants. Not only the context of the exploitation of natural resources, but the means by which they are gathered are unique in warfare.

War Crimes and International Humanitarian Law

Resource wars call for combining two areas of law: international humanitarian law and international environmental law. International law, conceived most broadly, is the set of legal norms that are intended to guide the interactions of states, as well as, with increasing frequency, non-state actors such as the United Nations, non-governmental organisations and individual human beings. Under this umbrella legal category lies international humanitarian law (often referred to more colloquially as 'the laws of war') – a legal field that encompass a wide array of norms set with the task of 'humanising' armed conflict. That is, these rules are aimed at minimising the harm done to non-combatants in warfare and limiting the unnecessary suffering endured by those involved in the conflict. A select group of these norms, in turn, are criminal norms a violation of which is considered to be a war crime. These norms are often referred to as 'grave breaches' of the laws of war and their precise character are set out in a number of different documents.[1] Thus, the Fourth Geneva Convention stipulates that the

---

1   We should note that though there is a great deal of overlap between grave breaches of the laws of war and war crimes as such, in some contexts, such as the statute of the International Criminal Court, they are categorically distinct.

'wilful killing, torture or inhuman treatment, including biological experiments, wilfully causing great suffering or serious injury to body or health, and extensive destruction and appropriation of property, not justified by military necessity and carried out unlawfully and wantonly' of prisoners of war constitutes a grave breach of international law, and hence, can be prosecuted as a war crime.[2] Other domestic and international legal documents, such as the Torture Convention[3] and the Genocide Convention[4] define other acts as international crimes. Thus, war crimes law is the set of international legal norms that proscribe certain acts in armed conflict, acts that could lead to prosecution before a domestic or in extreme cases, an international criminal tribunal.

Environmental crime includes crimes that are usually committed by private individuals (though they need not be) and primarily for economic gain (again, though not exclusively). Clifford's influential definition of an environmental crime, for example, as 'an act committed with the intent to harm or with a potential to cause harm to ecological and/or biological systems and for the purpose of securing business or personal advantage', (Clifford and Edwards 2012: 104) limits those who can commit environmental crimes largely to private industry and self-interested individuals, although an exception could be made state-corporate crime (Kramer, Michalowski and Kauzlarich 2002). Other treaties dealing with the environment, such as the Convention on International Trade in Endangered Species of Wild Fauna and Flora (CITES) (1974) and the Montreal Protocol on Substances that Deplete the Ozone Layer (1987), do not provide explicit criminal provisions but help provide a legal context for the criminalisation of environmental destruction (White 2011). Most often the crimes listed as environmental crime include improperly disposing of toxic waste, illegal extraction of natural resources, and the trade in endangered wildlife (though this list is not exhaustive). The central image of environmental crime is a private corporation involved in illegal and destructive dumping, logging, or mining in order to advance their own profit margin.

This split between the legal traditions means these two fields of law come from very different perspectives. War crimes norms are primarily aimed at protecting humans from other humans who are acting in the putative interests of a government or other political institution such as a militia. Individual or 'private sector' actions only come under the scrutiny of war crimes law secondarily – in the actions of private security companies and other private organisations acting in a military capacity (Emanuela-Chiara 2006). Though there is a growing interest on the close interconnections between state crime

---

2   Convention (IV) relative to the Protection of Civilian Persons in Time of War. Geneva, Article 147.

3   Convention against Torture and Other Cruel, Inhuman or Degrading Treatment or Punishment, Article 4.

4   Convention on the Prevention and Punishment of the Crime of Genocide, 1951. Article 1.

and corporate crime in the destruction of the environment (Kramer 2010; Kramer 2013; Lynch and Stretesky 2010; Michalowski 2012),[5] environmental crime, as legally constituted and officially prosecuted, is primarily concerned with 'private' behaviour of actors in the business sphere, making it primarily a form of corporate or white collar crime. Some scholars of environmental crime have pointed to the complicity of the government in the rape of the environment, but most environmental crime is committed by private actors for private gain. While the field of green criminology has examined the complicity of the state in the rape of the environment, legal scholars have not kept up with them (Rothe 2009; South 1998). Thus, in many ways war crimes and environmental crimes represent two completely different paradigms of criminality, standing on opposite ends of the public/private crime spectrum.

Despite these important differences, there is a great deal in common between environmental crime and war crimes, and the notion of a resource war helps bring this into relief. Most wars involve some form of collusion between the public and the private sectors and almost all international legal scholars agree that private citizens can be prosecuted if they have played a significant role in the violations of the laws of war. Similarly, government officials clearly have a unique role to play in the preservation of the environment – they are the primary stewards of their own resources and have a special duty to protect them. Both environmental destruction and war pose existential threats to a state: one threatens the survival of the state as a political entity, the other threatens the people who live within the confines of the state (Frank, Hironaka and Schofer 2000). Thus, despite their significant differences, there remains a significant overlap between the destruction of a state in war and the destruction of the state through the pillaging of its natural resources.

The Protection of the Environment in Wartime

As the 1992 Rio Declaration on Environment and Development (from the United Nations Conference on Environment and Development,) put it, 'Warfare is inherently destructive of sustainable development'.[6] Pre-modern warfare, with its strategic burnings of forests, destructive campsites, and strategies of 'salting the earth' had an environmental impact, but these consequences were mild when compared to the environmental damage perpetrated in twentieth- and twenty-first century war. For example, the destruction of the French and Belgian countryside during the trench warfare in the First World War left scars in the soil that linger till today. The use of the atomic bomb at the end of the Second World War, to offer another example, was a catastrophic humanitarian and environmental tragedy that left its mark on both human and non-human survivors. To offer a third example, in the wake of the widespread use of the herbicide Agent Orange during the

---

5   I am indebted to the editors for pointing out the important work in these fields to me.
6   Rio Declaration on Environment and Development, Principle 24.

Vietnam War, and its destructive environmental and health damage, international humanitarian law sought to develop a legal regime to protect the environment in wartime.

Given that the environmental impact of modern warfare cannot be ignored, international humanitarian law does make some provisions for the protection of the environment in wartime. Earlier generations of international humanitarian law dealt largely either with the elimination of specific weapons or with the protection of certain categories of individual (prisoners, the wounded, civilians) during war. The environment as a separate issue was addressed only in Optional Protocol to the Geneva Convention of 1977 (the 'Protocol'). Under its basic rules, the Protocol stipulates that, 'It is prohibited to employ methods or means of warfare which are intended, or may be expected, to cause widespread, long-term and severe damage to the natural environment'. More specifically, however, Article 55 ('Protection of the natural environment') states:

1. Care shall be taken in warfare to protect the natural environment against widespread, long-term and severe damage. This protection includes a prohibition of the use of methods or means of warfare which are intended or may be expected to cause such damage to the natural environment and thereby to prejudice the health or survival of the population.
2. Attacks against the natural environment by way of reprisals are prohibited.

To further this point, the Rome Statute of the International Criminal Court (ICC) lists excessive environmental damage as a potential war crime. Thus, Article 8(b) (iv) stipulates that, 'Intentionally launching an attack in the knowledge that such attack will cause … widespread, long-term and severe damage to the natural environment which would be clearly excessive in relation to the concrete and direct overall military advantage anticipated' is a war crime. When it comes to the destruction of the environment as part of combat operations, either as a target of warfare or as a byproduct of warfare, international humanitarian law clearly delimits the bounds of acceptable damage (if there can be said to be such a thing).

The 1976 Convention on the Prohibition of Military or Any Other Hostile Use of Environmental Modification Techniques (the '1976 Convention'), stipulates that, 'Each State Party to this Convention undertakes not to engage in military or any other hostile use of environmental modification techniques having widespread, long-lasting or severe effects as the means of destruction, damage or injury to any other State Party'.[7] While the Optional Protocol to the Geneva Convention of 1977 protects excessive damage done by weapons of war, the 1976 Convention prevents what Bouvier describes as 'geophysical warfare', that is, actions that involve 'the deliberate manipulation of natural processes and may trigger "hurricanes, tidal waves, earthquakes, and rain or snow"'. (Bouvier 1991) Furthermore, the Fourth

---

7   Convention on the Prohibition of Military or Any Other Hostile Use of Environmental Modification Techniques, Article 1(1).

Geneva Convention protects private and public property in warfare: 'Any destruction by the Occupying Power of real or personal property belonging individually or collectively to private persons, or to the State, or to other public authorities, or to social or cooperative organisations, is prohibited, except where such destruction is rendered absolutely necessary by military operations'.[8]

Whether or not these regulations provide sufficient environmental protection in conventional warfare, when they are placed in the context of modern resource wars, is a different matter and there are several noticeable gaps. First, they emphasise the *destruction* of the environment. Article 55 of the Protocol discusses 'severe damage' to the environment and attacks *against* the environment. Similarly, the ICC statute is concerned with *excessive* damage to the environment in wartime. Even the 1976 Convention emphasised modification techniques that cause 'destruction, damage, or injury'. Protecting the environment in these treaties is taken to be protecting the environment from harm. The problem of this universal emphasis on destruction is that it is not clear that the looting of natural resources constitutes destruction under international humanitarian law. 'Destruction' in this context generally means elimination and rendering unusable – making the environment unusable. Black's Law Dictionary defines 'destruction' as 'The act of destroying or demolishing; the ruining of something. 2. Harms that substantially detract from the value of property, esp. personal property' (Garner and Black 2004: 479). It is not at all clear that the looting of a country's natural resources through environmental exploitation constitutes destruction in this legal sense. If 'exploitation' were to be considered tantamount to 'destruction', it would undermine a great deal of the world's economy – and it can be surmised that few states would support such a definition. As Dam-de Jong (2008: 42–3) points out, 'The cumulative criteria 'widespread, long-term and severe' seem to require more than incidental damage resulting from the exploitation or plundering of natural resources'. It is not always clear that the methods used to harvest diamonds, timber, gold, or oil are destructive in any meaningful (much less legal) sense of the word, or are sufficiently destructive to warrant a violation of international law, much less prosecution. This means that the exploitation of natural resources cannot be adequately conceptualised as a form of destruction under international humanitarian law.

Second, another viable source for protecting natural resources during wartime is the laws protecting the environment that come from prohibitions against looting and plunder in wartime. Article 47 of the Laws and Customs of War on Land of 1907 states explicitly that 'Pillage is forbidden', as does Article 33 of the Fourth Geneva Convention. The aforementioned Article 53 of the Fourth Geneva Convention protects private property from looting, which is conceived of as destruction or theft. Article 54(2) of the Additional Protocol I of the Geneva Conventions states that in an international armed conflict:

---

8   Convention (IV) relative to the Protection of Civilian Persons in Time of War. Article 53.

> It is prohibited to attack, destroy, remove or render useless objects indispensable to the survival of the civilian population, such as foodstuffs, agricultural areas for the production of foodstuffs, crops, livestock, drinking water installations and supplies and irrigation works, for the specific purpose of denying them for their sustenance value to the civilian population or to the adverse Party, whatever the motive, whether in order to starve out civilians, to cause them to move away, or for any other motive.[9]

As with the emphasis on destruction, however, these legal norms emphasise issues that are not relevant for modern resource wars. Dam-de Jong (2008: 39) argues that 'the term 'indispensable' is largely left to the discretion of the parties to an armed conflict. This has the major advantage of creating flexibility to adapt the provision to local circumstances. Thus, the provisions may even cover some valuable natural resources such as oil'. It is hard to see diamonds or coltan as the equivalent of food stuffs or drinking water, however. Moreover, it is difficult to see how the provisions of Article 54 would meet the standard of a 'grave breach' suitable for prosecution unless the plunder of natural resources was intended to harm civilians. Furthermore, the International Criminal Court explains that 'Destroying or seizing the enemy's property, unless such destruction or seizure be imperatively demanded by the necessities of war' is a war crime – perhaps the clearest example of environmental exploitation as a potentially criminal act.[10]

One clear case where the international legal regime has found the exploitation of natural resources in wartime to be a violation of international law is in the *Armed Activities on the Territory of the Congo (Democratic Republic of the Congo v. Uganda)* case before the International Court of Justice. In this case, the Democratic Republic of the Congo (DRC) argued that, 'the Ugandan troops 'illegally occupying' Congolese territory, acting in collaboration with Congolese rebel groups supported by Uganda, systematically looted and exploited the assets and natural resources of the DRC',[11] and that such looting 'constitute[s] violations by Uganda of "the sovereignty and territorial integrity of the DRC, more specifically of the DRC's sovereignty over its natural resources"'.[12] Therefore, the Court concluded that, 'Uganda is internationally responsible for acts of looting, plundering and exploitation of the DRC's natural resources'.[13]

This case goes the furthest in determining that there is a legal obligation to protect natural resources from plunder in wartime. While it clearly marks progress in providing legal accountability for the rape of natural resources that takes place in wartime, there are some additional important gaps in this legal field that remain

---

9   Article 14(2) of the Second Additional Protocol makes an identical rule for non-international armed conflicts.

10   ICC Statute, Article 8(2)(b)(xiii).

11   Judgment of December 2005, Paragraph 223.

12   Paragraph 226.

13   Paragraph 250.

to be addressed. Most importantly, the laws governing pillage restrict the context when exploitation of natural resources is unlawful to cases where such acts are not a necessity of war and where they are committed largely for private gain. As Dam de-Jong (2009: 54) puts it, '[T]he prohibition against pillage only applies to the plundering of natural resources for personal gain, thereby excluding the exploitation of natural resources by or under the authority of the government for the purpose of financing the armed conflict'. Because most rebel groups style themselves as governments, it is difficult to see how many cases of the exploitation of natural resources could fall under these laws. As I argued above, in many cases, the exploitation of natural resources is integrated into the war itself and the pillaged resources are not distinct from the conduct of the war. The RUF's exploitation of diamonds was absolutely necessary for the rebels to continue its brutal campaign and thus is probably not a war crime under the ICC statute. As such, modern resource wars, where the exploitation of natural resources is a necessary component of war, and where they are being perpetrated alongside the conduct of hostilities, would most likely not fit under the ICC statue or the other sources cited here – and certainly not in any clean, unambiguous way.

Developing New Norms for Resource Wars

In the final part of this chapter, I will suggest two ways by which some of the problems that I have outlined here may be ameliorated. First, I will argue that the international community should develop a new international crime of war that I have dubbed criminal exploitation. Along with this, I will suggest that international prosecutors should seek to target international businesspeople who traffic in natural resources that are gathered in resource wars. While these developments will clearly not stop the criminal exploitations in wartime, they may help limit their destructive capacity.

While contemporary international humanitarian law is, in some ways, ill-suited for modern resource wars and their terrible environmental and humanitarian toll, there are a few possibilities for developing new norms for this new type of conflict or adapting existing laws to new ends. While arms-dealing and other ancillary activities related to warfare have been prosecuted in various domestic tribunals, the exploitation of nature in warfare has been under-prosecuted at both the international and domestic level.[14] In this final section, I will discuss two different means by which international humanitarian law might seek to control and limit this damage. These proposals centre on developing a new category of war crime – *criminal exploitation* – and expanding the scope of criminal liability for those who buy and sell natural resources in the global

---

14   Two cases where individual have been prosecuted for violating Article 8(2)(b) (xiii) of the ICC statute are *The Prosecutor v. Germain Katanga, The Prosecutor v. Mathieu Ngudjolo Chui*.

marketplace using the legal concept of 'Joint Criminal Enterprise'. Many of these proposals could be developed in a new 'Convention for the Protection of Natural Resources during Wartime'.

Criminal Exploitation

Rather than focusing on 'damage' or 'pillage' in international humanitarian law – terms that I have already suggested do not adequately account for the forms of exploitation that takes place in modern resource wars – international treaties should consider *criminal exploitation*. Such an offence would be distinct from the traditional categories of pillage, looting, or destruction that were discussed in the previous section of this chapter. For this reason, expanding the list of substantive crimes punished as war crimes to include the criminal exploitation of nature for military purposes would both fill a gap in international humanitarian law and help protect important natural resources from wanton destruction. Such crimes could be defined something to the effect of: 'The extraction or harvesting of the natural resources located in an occupied territory by the occupying forces or their affiliates along with knowingly buying or selling such natural resources is a grave breach of the laws of war'. Such an offence, conceived of as a war crime, would adequately cover much of the destructive activity that takes place in modern resource wars in a way that existing law does not.

By focusing both on the 'harvesting' of natural resources and their transfer in the market place, this approach covers a great deal of what happens to natural resources during conflicts and their relationship with the broader wartime context without relying on the language of destruction, seizure or pillage. By emphasising that the perpetrators may be those in the 'occupying forces' *or* their affiliates, such an approach acknowledges that resources are sometimes exploited by military officials and sometimes by others involved in a conflict *including international actors*. It does not require, however, that the environment be 'destroyed' or 'seized' as a part of this illegal extraction, because as we have discussed, this is often not the case. 'Extracting' and 'harvesting' are terms that reflect the logging, drilling, or mining of natural resources that takes place in resource wars without commenting on their ultimate use. Even if such exploitation was for public, rather than for private gain, it would be criminalised under such a provision.

Expanding Liability

Beyond the addition of criminal exploitation to the corpus of international humanitarian law, several additional measures can be used to limit the environmental harm done by occupying forces. As noted above, one of the characteristics of resource wars is the inseparability of those who fight and those who exploit nature in a conflict – they are both essential to the conduct of the war. From the perspective of war crimes prosecutors, this situation presents both opportunities and challenges. On the one hand, this means that those who commercially exploit nature as a part of war are cogs in a war machine that falls under the jurisdiction of international humanitarian law. On the other hand, some individuals who are not ordinarily considered to be combatants under international humanitarian law, that is to say, they do not actively engage in armed combat or serve in military or paramilitary organisations, may be subject to prosecution under international humanitarian law. Businesses that trade in illicit goods, like diamonds, fuel, and lumber, are ostensibly 'civilians', but are closely connected to the conduct of war by providing the funds that make war possible. While some individuals have been prosecuted for illegally trading arms or buying and selling products that have been banned (such as conflict diamonds), none of these crimes have been prosecuted under international criminal law or, most importantly for us, under the laws of war. One tool which may help fill this gap is the international law concept of *Joint Criminal Enterprise (JCE)*.

JCE developed out of the jurisprudence of the International Criminal Tribunal for the Former Yugoslavia and has since become progressively integrated into international criminal law (Danner and Martinez 2005). In its landmark *Tadić* decision, the International Criminal Tribunal for the Former Yugoslavia ruled that under certain circumstances criminal liability for international crimes may adhere to an individual 'through participation in the realisation of a common design or purpose' (*Prosecutor v. Tadić*, Judgment 188).[15] This can include 'assistance in, or contribution to, the execution of the common plan or purpose' (Prosecutor v. Tadić, Judgment 227)[16] or joint criminal enterprise. According to the Tribunal, JCE can be established in three separate ways:

JCE I: '[I]ntent to perpetrate a certain crime'.
JCE II: [P]ersonal knowledge of the system of ill-treatment ... as well as the intent to further this common concerted system of ill-treatment.
JCE III: '[T]he intention to participate in and further the criminal activity or the criminal purpose of a group and to contribute to the joint criminal enterprise or in any event to the commission of a crime by the group'. (*Prosecutor v. Tadić*, Judgment 228)[17]

Each of these modes allows for the individual defendant to be responsible for criminal activity that he himself did not commit with his own hand. In this sense, JCE is akin to conspiracy or command responsibility, both offences that have also been used in international criminal law where crimes are often committed in the context of larger organisations.

---

15   *Prosecutor v. Tadić*, Judgement, ICTY Appeals Chamber, Case No. IT-94–1-A, ¶ 183 (15 July 1999) at ¶ 188.
16   *Prosecutor v. Tadić*, Judgement, ICTY Appeals Chamber, Case No. IT-94–1-A, ¶ 183 (15 July 1999) at ¶ 227.
17   *Prosecutor v. Tadić*, Judgement at 228.

While it was initially developed for dealing with crimes committed by military and paramilitary organisations in the Balkans, JCE provides an excellent framework for prosecuting those who participate in the exploitation of natural resources in wartime. While a complete account of the legal nuances of JCE would go beyond the scope of this chapter, clearly if private organisations, political leaders, and military command collude to wage war in order to gather and sell the natural resources of a particular country, there are good grounds for establishing criminal liability. At a minimum, purchasing resources from groups who have exploited natural resources in war time falls under 'JCE III' as they intend (in the legal sense of the term)[18] to further the criminal activity of those who sell diamonds, coltan, or wood, by providing them with money and continuing to do business with these groups. Such individuals clearly meet the intent requirement for being a part of JCE and therefore can be prosecuted for war crimes or with the (presently hypothetical) crime of criminal exploitation.

Conclusions

Of course, there are limits to the use of criminal law to protect the environment in wartime or in the prosecution and related punishment of individuals and corporations that are involved in exploitation. Along with the development of new crimes in the domain of war crimes law, new forms of monitoring can help to effectively limit the unjust exploitation of natural resources in wartime. Particularly instructive here is the movement to stop the importation of conflict diamonds during the Sierra Leonean civil war. The humanitarian cost of the precious stones triggered an international response that led to the global public's rejection of these diamonds and the development of the Kimberley Process Certification Scheme (KPCS) (Clark 2013). Such monitoring schemes, along with the pressure of activist organisations both from the human rights community and from the environmental community, can help to protect the environment and prevent some of the worst excesses of contemporary resource wars.

It would be naïve to suggest that the criminalisation of the exploitation of natural resources would put a stop to such reprehensible practices. There is too much at stake in these conflicts for the agents to simply put their quest for natural resources aside during wartime. As a deterrent, international criminal law in general is, at best, a secondary consideration among participants in an international conflict – the extra-legal price of failure in war is often death and so, strictly from a self-interested perspective, actors have good reasons to break the law now and deal with the ramifications of their crimes at a later date.

---

18   Under criminal law, an individual intends 'the natural consequences of his actions'. It is not simply a matter of wanting or wishing the result, but simply being aware of the results of your actions is adequate to establish intent. See: *Enigster Yehezkel Ben Alish, Israel*, District Court of Tel Aviv, judgment of 4 January 1951 in (Cassese 2003: 162–3).

Nonetheless, criminalising the illegal exploitation of natural resources during armed conflict can have a determined impact on the conduct of war in ways that are environmentally beneficial.

Criminalising the exploitation of natural resources in wartime brings together two disparate but powerful international movements: human rights and environmentalism. There have been remarkable strides in each of these fields over the last several decades (along with some notable setbacks), and the political and cultural discourse around the protection of the environment, along with the legitimate horror at the atrocities associated with the diamond mines and other aspects of resource wars, has created the possibility of new legal regulations. By limiting the reliance on natural resources in war using the tools of international law, it may be possible to both protect the environment and limit some of horrors of war by cutting off lines of resources.

The laws of war and the laws of war crimes are, in many ways, behind the times and do not adequately confront the realities of modern war. The slow development of legal norms contrasts with the lightning fast pace by which warfare adapts to new situations and contexts. This means that international criminal justice scholars must seek to develop new tools for confronting these new situations – even if these tools must first be developed in the purely abstract discourses of academia. In the case of environmental crimes, this is particularly important because the environment cannot speak for itself and because, when taken on its own, preserving the natural environment is often at the bottom of any public list of concerns, particularly in war time. By seeking both to protect nature and limit the destructive capacity of warfare, international criminal justice can play an important role in both humanising and 'naturalising' the most inhuman and unnatural human activity: war.

References

Bouvier, A. 1991. Protection of the natural environment in time of armed conflict. *International Review of the Red Cross*, No. 285. Available at: http://www.icrc.org/eng/resources/documents/misc/57jmau.htm. Accessed 7 January 2015.

Brisman, A. and South, N. 2013. Resource wealth, power, crime, and conflict. In R. Walters, D.S. Westerhuis and T. Wyatt (eds), *Emerging Issues in Green Criminology: Exploring Power, Justice and Harm*. London: Palgrave Macmillan, 57–71.

Cassese, A. 2003. *International Criminal Law*. Oxford: Oxford University Press.

Cilliers, J. 2000. Resource wars: a new type of insurgency. In J. Cilliers and D. Christian (eds), *Angola's War Economy*. Pretoria: Institute for Security Studies.

Clark, R.D. 2013. The control of conflict minerals in Africa and a preliminary assessment of the Dodd-Frank Wall Street Reform and Consumer Act. In N. South and A. Brisman (eds), *Routledge International Handbook of Green Criminology*. London and New York: Routledge, 214–29.

Clifford, M. (ed.) 2012. *Environmental Crime: Enforcement, Policy, and Social Responsibility*, 2nd edn. Burlington, MA: Jones & Bartlett.

Dam-de Jong, D. 2009. International law and resource plunder: the protection of natural resources during armed conflict. In O.K. Fauchald, D. Hunter and W. Xi (eds), *Yearbook of International Environmental Law*, vol. 19. Oxford: Oxford University Press.

Dangl, B. 2007. *The Price of Fire: Resource Wars and Social Movements in Bolivia*. Oakland, CA: AK Press.

Danner, A.M. and Martinez, J.S. 2005. Guilty associations: joint criminal enterprise, command responsibility, and the development of international criminal law. *California Law Review* 93(1): 75–169.

Enigster Yehezkel, B.A. 2003. Israel, District Court of Tel Aviv, judgment of 4 January 1951. In A. Casese (ed.), *International Criminal Law*. Oxford: Oxford University Press, 162–3.

Frank, D.J., Hironaka, A. and Schofer, E. 2000. The nation state and the natural environment over the twentieth century. *American Sociological Review* 65(1): 96–116.

Garner, B. and Black, H.C. 2004. *Black's Law Dictionary*. St. Paul, MN: Thomson/West.

Gberie, L. 2005. *A Dirty War in West Africa: The RUF and the Destruction of Sierra Leone*. Bloomington, IN: Indiana University Press.

Gillard, E.-C. 2006. Business goes to war: private military/security companies and international humanitarian law. *International Review of the Red Cross* 88(863): 525–72. Available at: http://www.icrc.org/eng/assets/files/other/irrc_863_gillard.pdf. Accessed 16 October 2014.

Global Witness. 2002. The logs of war: the timber trade and armed conflict. *Programme for International Cooperation and Conflict Resolution, Fafo-report, 379*. Available at: http://www.unglobalcompact.org/docs/issues_doc/Peace_and_Business/Logs_of_War.pdf. Accessed 7 January 2015.

Hulme, K. 2004. *War Torn Environment: Interpreting the Legal Threshold*, vol. 7. Leiden: Martinus Nijhoff.

Hulme, K. 2010. Environmental protection in armed conflict. In M. Fitzmaurice, D.M. Ong and P. Merkouris (eds), *Research Handbook on International Environmental Law*. Cheltenham: Edward Elgar, 586–604.

Inglehart, R. and Baker, W.E. 2000. Looking forward, looking back: continuity and change at the turn of the millennium. *American Sociological Review* 65: 19–51.

Klare, M. 2001. *Resource Wars: The New Landscape of Global Conflict*. New York: Macmillan.

Kramer, R.C. 2013. Carbon in the atmosphere and power in America: climate change as state-corporate crime. *Journal of Crime and Justice* 36(2): 153–70.

Kramer, R.C. and Michalowski, R.J. 2012. Is global warming a state-corporate crime? In R. White (ed.), *Climate Change from a Criminological Perspective*. New York: Springer, 71–88.

Kramer, R.C., Michalowski, R.J. and Kauzlarich, D. 2002. The origins and development of the concept and theory of state-corporate crime. *Crime & Delinquency* 48(2): 263–82.

Le Billon, P. 2004. The geopolitical economy of 'resource wars'. *Geopolitics* 9(1): 1–28.

Le Billon, P. 2005. *Geopolitics of Resource Wars: Resource Dependence, Governance and Violence*. London: Routledge.

Lee, J.R. 2009. *Climate Change and Armed Conflict: Hot and Cold Wars*. London: Routledge.

Lynch, M.J. and Stretesky, P.B. 2010. Global warming, global crime: a green criminological perspective. In R. White (ed.), *Global Environmental Harm: Criminological Perspectives*. Cullompton: Willan, 62–84.

Milburn, R. 2014. Gorillas and guerrillas: environment and conflict in the Democratic Republic of Congo (Chapter 3 in this volume).

Orogun, P. 2004. Blood diamonds and Africa's armed conflicts in the post-Cold War era. *World Affairs* 166(3): 151–61.

Rothe, D.L. 2009. *State Criminality: The Crime of All Crimes*. Lanham, MD: Lexington Books.

Singer, P.W. 2011. *Corporate Warriors: The Rise of the Privatized Military Industry*. New York: Cornell University Press.

South, N. 1998. Corporate and state crimes against the environment: foundations for a green perspective. In V. Ruggiero, N. South and I. Taylor (eds), *The New European Criminology: Crime and Social Order in Europe*. London: Routledge, 443–61.

White, R. 2011. *Transnational Environmental Crime: Toward an Eco-Global Criminology*. London and New York: Routledge.

Legal Materials Cited

Armed Activities on the Territory of the Congo (Democratic Republic of the Congo v. Uganda) (2005) International Court of Justice. Judgment.

Convention (IV) relative to the Protection of Civilian Persons in Time of War. (1949). Geneva.

Convention against Torture and Other Cruel, Inhuman or Degrading Treatment or Punishment. (1984). New York.

Convention on International Trade in Endangered Species of Wild Fauna and Flora (CTIES) (1974).

Convention on the Prevention and Punishment of the Crime of Genocide (1948). Paris, 9 December.

Enigster Yehezkel Ben Alish. (1951). Israel, District Court of Tel Aviv. Judgment of 4 January 1951.

Montreal Protocol on Substances that Deplete the Ozone Layer (1987).

Prosecutor v. Germain Katanga. (2012). ICC-01/04-01/07.

Prosecutor v. Mathieu Ngudjolo Chui. (2014). ICC-01/04-02/12.

Prosecutor v. Tadić, Judgement, (1990). ICTY Appeals Chamber, Case No. IT-94-1-A.

Protocol Additional to the Geneva Conventions of 12 August 1949, and relating to the Protection of Victims of International Armed Conflicts (Protocol I). (1977).

Rio Declaration on Environment and Development. (1992) Principle 24. Convention on the Prohibition of Military or Any Other Hostile Use of Environmental Modification Techniques, 1976.

Rome Statute of the International Criminal Court, 17 July 1998.

Chapter 9

The Poaching Paradox:
Why South Africa's 'Rhino Wars' Shine a
Harsh Spotlight on
Security and Conservation

M.L.R. Smith and Jasper Humphreys

The primary focus of this chapter is to examine the effectiveness of the counter-poaching strategy in the 'rhino wars'. In the process key social and political issues surrounding rhino poaching in South Africa will also be discussed, these prominently coalescing around the campaign to legalise the sale of rhino horn in an increasingly bitter and polarising debate about its merits.

The Roots of Rhino Poaching

The beginning of the modern rhino poaching crisis in South Africa began with the 'Apartheid Wars' of the 1970s and 1980s (Reeve and Ellis 1995) when elements within the former South African Defence Force (SADF) used the fighting and the draconian security laws promulgated by the Nationalist Party as cover to organise a vast network of smuggling operations involving mainly ivory, rhino horn, drugs and diamonds, particularly in conjunction with UNITA, the former Angolan resistance organisation led by Dr Jonas Savimbi (Rademeyer 2012).

According to Colonel Jan Breytenbach, conservationist and commander of the renowned 32nd 'Buffalo Soldiers' Battalion in Angola, who witnessed the slaughter of wildlife in Angola: 'the hundreds of thousands of elephants became thousands, the thousands became hundreds and the hundreds only a very few' (Potgieter 1995).

An integrated southern African smuggling trade that was effectively sanctioned by the state, with Johannesburg as the hub, had even wider strategic implications, the most immediate of which was that the smuggling enabled South African military intelligence to leverage influence over both friends, such as UNITA in Angola, and enemies such as FRELIMO in Mozambique, who were also involved in the illicit trade (Ellis 1994).

Over the long term, however, the state's involvement in smuggling had two even more powerful consequences. First, the lengthy period of fighting allowed the smuggling cartels to establish themselves with little fear of disruption, claiming that they were allied with the security forces in the fight against Communism. Over time, the roots of the smuggling networks grew deeper and wider, bringing greater corruption, evasion and non-compliance.

The second consequence was that no senior military figures were indicted for their part in this enterprise, despite a major investigation carried out soon after the end of Apartheid. A rebranding and reorganisation of the defence forces from the heavily compromised SADF to the current South African National Defence Force (SANDF) which took place after the end of Apartheid, put further closure on the past (Ellis 1998).

Thus, during the course of the 1970s and 1980s, rhino horn and ivory smuggling became institutionalised within the fabric of the South African state through the collusion of the defence forces, whose participation in smuggling activities and evasion of prosecution sent a powerful political message that the agencies of the state could be compromised and would likely be ineffective in the face of forceful vested interests.

The Counter-Poaching Response

Counter-poaching is becoming part of an increasing global trend of 'militarising' conservation, a process that securitises the protection of biodiversity and involves not just greater use of weapons, but also military and paramilitary personnel, training, technologies and partnerships. There is, however, a dilemma in South Africa relating to counter-poaching and how it should be delivered. The debate concerns whether poaching should be regarded as an insurgency and combated in a military fashion, or as a crime and broadly handled by the police.

South Africa has become the world's rhino poaching number one 'hotspot' on account of having by far the largest rhino population globally. A large percentage of the rhino population belongs to the southern sub-species of the white rhino, these living either in state-run parks or in privately owned ranches that host hunting parties or wildlife viewing safaris. It is predominately from within this latter group that the controversial campaign to legalise the trade in rhino horn has been advocated.

While rhino poaching is commonly linked with transnational crime, the act of poaching is only one distinct part of the chain, being essentially a tactic that relies on stealth and evasion as opposed to confrontation (unless under attack).With poaching there is an assumption that the resource being poached is under either custodianship or ownership. But entwined with the definition of 'poaching' are historical definitions and perceptions of what is legal and what is illegal hunting which are rooted in the question of land ownership (Eliason 2012).

The South African authorities have responded to rhino poaching in the long-established and historical tradition within the country of relying upon 'hard power' in response to threats, rather than the 'soft power' of discussion, dialogue or negotiation. Reacting to a huge surge in rhino poaching the South African authorities in 2010 drew up a counter-poaching strategy that involved both elements of the South African Police Service (SAPS) and the South African National Defence Force (SANDF). Johan Jooste, a retired major-general from SANDF, was subsequently employed by South African authorities in 2012 to put an end to rhino poaching. In the view of General Jooste the escalation in rhino poaching meant that South Africa was under 'attack' from 'armed foreign nationals' and 'armed foreign criminals' (South African National Parks 2012).

Jooste's counter-poaching strategy – the 'Jooste War' – created a rhino poaching narrative that combined highlighting the destructiveness of the poaching with broader issues of national security. This linked immigration and transnational crime as key drivers of rhino poaching, and this fusion of rhino poaching with wider security issues is described here as the 'rhinofication' of South African security. In addition, the increasingly securitised approach to counter-poaching bears a notable resemblance to similar trends in late-modern warfare of closely targeting individuals or groups, known as 'man-hunting', which in its most extreme form involves 'shoot to kill', or in the more precise military wording, 'targeted killing'. In these ways and others, counter-poaching operations are presented with new operational, legal and philosophical opportunities and challenges.

Underlying the controversies in what are colloquially called the 'rhino wars', resides not only the problem of defining the security threat posed by rhino poaching but also an often unspoken yet pervasive political subtext that comes from the dark shadow of the years of Apartheid. Rhino poaching in South Africa provides a highly visible indicator of the country's brittle internal security that reflects a stuttering economy, environmental problems and declining agricultural yields, along with high unemployment levels, industrial unrest and a land restitution programme that is a long way behind schedule.

In addition, given that poaching is generally not socially threatening, with no implicit intention to murder, rape or kidnap and does not involve any other human-centric crime, the poacher might be viewed by some sections of society, especially the poor, not as a criminal but as an opportunist driven by a normal human desire for economic survival. If that is the case, without the support of the rural population who live alongside the rhinos, counter-poaching risks merely being seen as an exercise in paramilitary 'pacification' and thus might be viewed as supporting the interests of a minority elite, which in the case of rhinos in South Africa is related to the ranches and the tourism industry that is predominately run by the white population.

It is the complicated South African mixture of national and international history, politics and economics that frames the backdrop of the 'rhino wars'. Furthermore, South Africa has a long history of 'pacification' by different groups, which follows in the country's historic tradition of reacting to threats, present or potential, with increased violence as leaders invoke images of 'backs-to-the-wall' confrontation and isolation (Potgieter 1995).

Poaching: Categorisation

Because of their incredibly high value the targeting of rhinos and other mega-fauna can be categorised as 'mega-poaching' – a supra category separate from other wildlife. The value attached is driven by strong and rising demand from the Far East for body parts, which has increased the involvement of sophisticated crime syndicates. Poaching, as Brockington et al. (2008) suggest, refers broadly to two main categories governed by historical definitions and perceptions of legal and illegal hunting.

The first category, 'subsistence' poaching, meets the needs of local communities, and frequently relies on traps and snares because the target is often small game (Brockington et al. 2008; Duffy 2010; Leakey 2001). The second category is 'commercial' poaching, operated by organised groups that target valuable species, such as rhinos and elephants; these commercial poachers use different technologies to hunt, ranging from differing calibres of firearms, to GPS and mobile-phones (Milliken and Shaw 2012). Poaching in simple terms is defined as the hunting of any animal not permitted by the state or private owner. Even so, in practice it is anything but simple because as a commercial enterprise poaching involves many people, organisations and networks. These various categories tend to be thrown together under the heading 'poachers' and thus, by implication, all participants are all deemed to be illegal hunters. However, there is a difference between the 'shooter' who might receive just a few hundred dollars for a successful kill and those people further up the 'supply-chain' receiving thousands of dollars: this distinction is evidenced in practice with 'shooters' often being lightly punished compared to transnational criminals (Rademeyer 2012).

The debate over poaching as a criminal process pivots on the very subjective definition of ownership of both the wildlife and the land on which they live, framed by Roman law concerning *res nullius* (nobody's property) or *res publicae* (the property of everyone). Poaching has evolved via a process of land enclosure and criminalisation, which intersects with a range of motivations: subsistence, financial gain, and resistance to wildlife protection laws. The lines between differing poaching identities are eroding, however: for instance there is now a version of 'subsistence' poaching that overlaps with commercial poaching in response to the global demand for bush-meat that is more and more accessible as roads and transportation networks expand in terrain previously considered impenetrable.

'Jooste War' Declaration

Following two years of a rapid escalation in rhino deaths, the South African government in early October 2010 held a 'rhino summit' in Pretoria (South African Government Information Service 2010). The then Minister of Water and Environmental Affairs, Buyelwa Sonjica of the Department of Water and Environmental Affairs (DEA), convened the summit; however, as a demonstration of the dysfunctional response to the rhino poaching, Sonjica was replaced by President Jacob Zuma just days after the meeting amid reports of poor bureaucracy and financial irregularities in the DEA (http://washafrica.wordpress.com 2010).

Two important decisions, nevertheless, were made at the summit. The first was for investigations to be undertaken into South Africa's internal rhino horn market and another into the international market. The second decision was that a Biodiversity Enforcement Directorate would be established within DEA to bring cohesion to the government's counter-poaching efforts Pretoria (South African Government Information Service 2010). Soon after the summit counter-poaching was upgraded further with overall oversight handed to the National Joints Committee (NatJoints), South Africa's highest authority for the coordination, joint planning and implementation of high priority security measures, including cooperation against smuggling across national borders (South African Government Information Service 2010). NatJoints consists of senior members of the South African Police Service (SAPS), the National Prosecuting Authority (NPA) and the South African National Defence Force (SANDF).

In 2012, the scope and depth of counter-poaching initiatives grew when General Jooste was appointed strategic overlord of all anti-poaching operations within the 22 national parks controlled by SANParks (South Africa National Parks), arguably, making General Jooste the most important person countering rhino poaching in South Africa, if not the world. Immediately General Jooste threw down the gauntlet to the poachers: 'we are going to take the war to these armed bandits and we aim to win it', and with his 'bush war' experience gained while fighting during Apartheid, General Jooste seemed to be the ideal choice (South African National Parks 2012).

Crackdown

In 2013, Western governments demonstrated a new commitment to dealing with wildlife poaching and trafficking (of both live animals and dead animal byproducts, such as rhino horn, ivory and shark-fin), which had become the third highest category of illegal trading, after drugs and guns (Coalition Against Wildlife Trafficking (CAWT)). In July 2013, President Obama launched the Wildlife Trafficking Taskforce, followed later in the year by the announcement that British Army paratroopers would train the Kenyan Wildlife Service (KWS) (https://www.gov.uk/government/news/uk 2013). United States Secretary of State, John Kerry, subsequently offered a $1 million reward for information leading to the break-up of the Laos-based, but operationally global, Xaysavang Network of wildlife traffickers. The most significant project was the $80 million three-year Clinton Global Initiative to train 3,100 park rangers in 50 trafficking/poaching 'hotspots' in Africa, as well as to increase the use of sniffer-dogs. This development followed from an announcement in 2012 from Hillary Clinton, then the United States Secretary of State: 'this is a global challenge that spans continents and crosses oceans, and we need to address it with partnerships that are as robust and far-reaching as the criminal networks we seek to dismantle' (Braun 2012).

The rhetoric of 'war' relating to counter-poaching, however, points to an inherent security puzzle posed by rhino poaching as to whether it should be viewed as *crime* or as an *insurgency* that might involve kinetic responses beyond the strictly judicial realm. While the identity of rhino poaching involves external penetration and with it an implication of an insurgent identity, the problem is also internal and with it an implication of a more criminal identity given the loss of property in the form of rhinos, a highly valuable commodity both in financial and natural resource terms. Tactically, the focus on hunting down the individual poacher categorises counter-poaching within emerging trends in late-modern combat that have been identified by political geographer, Derek Gregory, as 'the individuation of warfare': 'targets are no longer whole areas of cities – like Cologne or Hamburg in the Second World War – or extensive target boxes like those ravaged by B-52 'Arc Light' strikes over the rainforest of Vietnam. The targets are individuals' (Gregory 2013). High-profile examples of this 'individuation' of war would be the hunting down of Osama bin Laden or drone 'strikes' such as that killed radical Muslim cleric, Anwar al-Awlaki: not only does 'individuation' represent the most elemental and primal form of group violence, namely 'the hunt', but it also connects with a deep atavistic human impulse to protect and control property, both as a resource (in this case being wildlife) and the land containing the resource.

Rhinofication

The growing 'arms race' between the rhino owners (whether state or private) and poaching gangs has run alongside the growing international trend of fusing wildlife conservation issues with wider security concerns (Humphreys and Smith 2011). In this way, rhino poaching and conservation in South Africa have become enveloped within the 'rhinofication' wider security narrative. This strand of national security involving the overlap of state security and mega-fauna poaching was clearly demonstrated in the early 1980s by the intervention of the Botswana Defence Forces (BDF) against well-armed poaching gangs who were taking advantage of widespread conflict and instability across southern Africa stemming from the 'Apartheid Wars' (Henk 2006). At stake was both Botswana's internal security and substantial wildlife tourism industry. BDF operations initially employed a specialised commando squadron, which comprised small-unit foot patrols of skilled trackers from Botswana's hunter-gatherer society backed up by helicopter-borne rapid-reaction forces. Within months, the poaching gangs had been beaten back (Henk 2006).

It was during years of Apartheid that the concept of privately owned wildlife conservancies/reserves being integrated into a grand security plan was developed in South Africa by parks administrator, Nick Steele. For his 'Farm Patrol Plan', Steele convinced white ranchers during the 1970s to form joint protection forces against poaching, stock-theft and political turmoil, with rangers trained in paramilitary style. In this way, the 'Farm Patrol Plan' copied counter-insurgency's classic policy of 'inkspots' by creating islands of resistance and power that expanded over time (Draper 1998).

To understand the importance of rhino conservation, one must understand the historic place of the rhino in the political economy of pre- and post-colonial South Africa. While rhinoceros hide has been principally used in South Africa for a variety of leather goods, such as the all-purpose *sjambok* whip, the horn was exported to satisfy the ancient traditional Chinese medicine market and, in more recent years, to Yemen to create handles for *jambiya* ceremonial daggers (http:// www.pbs.org/wnet/nature/episodes/rhinoceros/rhino-horn-use-fact-vs-fiction). In pre-colonial days, hunting was important to the economy and diet of the indigenous people providing meat, domestic items and trade goods. The large-scale hunt was also an important element in establishing social and political relations. The Nguni tribe in Natal traditionally placed great emphasis on hunting, both on a small and large scale, which for the chief or king would serve as a means of keeping his soldiers employed in peacetime (MacKenzie 1997).

Hunting could be loosely categorised as either 'defensive', in order to protect humans, crops or stock, as a 'domestic resource', to supply meat, skins and receptacles, or undertaken for 'trading purposes', mainly ivory but also horns, hides and pelts (MacKenzie 1997). With the arrival of colonial rule, however, the use of wildlife by indigenous people for quotidian purposes was replaced by the 'store' or itinerant traders, while the colonists harnessed the killing of wildlife as a crucial resource in their expansion across Africa, whether for food, trade or as a means of paying for labour, while also giving the colonisers the impetus to expand frontiers.

'Few regions of the world' according to John MacKenzie (1997), 'had richer and more exploitable game resources than southern Africa. Even fewer witnessed such a dramatic decline in the space of half a century'. Mackenzie added that hunting was 'the essential concomitant of missionary endeavour and the initial survival mechanism of the frontier' (1997: 116). The killing of wildlife, especially the elephant and rhinoceros, has always sat prominently in the crosshairs of politics and history in South Africa. Here, the fortunes of wildlife have been closely bound to a battle between protective legislation versus hunting, raiding and poaching, set against a backdrop of political change and external threats.

South Africa's wildlife–national security nexus began when it was a colony of the British Empire that competed with two neighbouring empires, the Portuguese one located in today's Mozambique and Angola, and the German one in today's Namibia. It is here that the roots of 'rhinofication' lie since while these borders were mostly meaningless to the ivory and rhino horn traders. The First World War demonstrated the need for security buffer areas following uncertainty about Portuguese intentions and a series of battles fought between German and South African forces in and around the Kalahari Desert. In 1936 the Kalahari Gemsbok Park was set up, abutting both German South West Africa/Namibia and

Bechuanaland/Botswana; 10 years earlier the old Sabie park on the South African-Mozambique border had been expanded and renamed the Kruger National Park after prominent politician, Paul Kruger. The key security element of the national parks was that human occupation and movement was severely controlled within the boundaries, while the security buffering process went even further in the Kruger park with a fence erected in 1959 along the Mozambique border.

The first game legislation in South Africa was introduced as early as 1657 by the Dutch East India Company; by the mid nineteenth century, both the Orange Free State and the South African Republic had also introduced game laws (MacKenzie 1997). With global concern growing about the decline in wildlife populations, a split began to emerge at the end of the nineteenth century between the 'preservationist' supporters at the time who wanted to preserve wildlife for sport and the 'conservationists' who wanted to conserve wildlife for its own sake; over time, however, 'conservation' became dominant (MacKenzie 1997). This struggle gave rise in Britain to the Society for the Preservation of the Fauna of the Empire (SPFE), a socially and politically well-connected group and predecessor of today's equally influential Fauna and Flora International, that spearheaded two fundamental pieces of legislation: (1) the Convention for the Preservation of Wild Animals, Birds and Fish in Africa, which was signed in London in 1900 (the 'London Convention'); and (2) the Agreement for the Protection of the Fauna and Flora of Africa of 1933 (MacKenzie 1997).

The London Convention showed its 'preservationist' roots, creating 'reserves' as areas for game management and hunting with humans largely excluded; the later piece of legislation is viewed as being 'conservationist', orientated to conserving wildlife and prohibiting any hunting (MacKenzie 1997). Overall, both pieces of legislation had three broad impacts: firstly, they handed over the administration and enforcement of wildlife either to white settlers or colonial authorities, often in these designated reserves. Secondly, indigenous Africans were stopped from hunting, and in the process transforming wildlife from a direct resource for food and trade into a secondary resource for sport and tourism (MacKenzie 1997). The third impact was that the legislative process not only turned these indigenous hunters into 'poachers' but also served as another way for white settlers to establish control over land (which over time became inalienable), as well as developing a 'code' that established Western attitudes and etiquette to hunting as appropriate and correct.

By the end of the nineteenth century, the range of White and Black rhino in South Africa had been reduced to a small area at the junction of the Black and White Umfolozi rivers in Natal, an area that was later turned into the Umfolozi and Hluhluwe Game Parks. Today in South Africa, large numbers of rhinos live on land owned privately. A survey undertaken by the Department of Rural Development and Land Reform in 2013 found that 79 per cent of South African land is privately owned in a variety of forms as opposed to 14 per cent owned by the state. In the Northern Cape district for example, 1.8 million hectares were in state ownership, with 35.2 million hectares in private hands. A sizeable percentage of this private land is owned by the White population even though it constitutes just 8.9 per cent of the overall population.

Rhinos in South Africa are protected under both national and international legislation. Domestically, the protection of the rhino is enshrined in the National Environmental Management: Biodiversity Act (NEMBA) for which the maximum penalty for illegal possession of rhino horn is five years imprisonment and a fine (*Government Gazette* 2004). On the international level, the trade in rhino parts has been subject to Appendix I of the Convention on International Trade in Endangered Species of Wild Fauna and Flora (CITES) since 1975. CITES both prohibits and controls the export of threatened species and is legally binding on its 170 signatories: Appendix 1 denotes the a species that is considered among the most endangered on Earth and must not be commercially traded except under special circumstances, such as for scientific purposes (www.cites.org).

'Armed Social Work'

The dilemma of the South African authorities over how to reconcile the policing versus militarised approaches to counter-poaching seemed closer to resolution with General Jooste's appointment: this suggested a more sophisticated approach to the problem, an understandable assumption given Jooste's past record. Prior to his appointment as SANParks Commanding Officer (Special Projects), Jooste held the commercially significant position of Director of International Business Development for BAE Systems (Land Systems South Africa); swapping his salesman's suit for olive-green fatigues and an office in the Kruger National Park was a change that General Jooste seemed to relish (Jooste, www.linkedin.com).

In 1971, while in his early 20s, Jooste had joined the former South African Defence Force (SADF) just as the country's war with neighbouring 'front-line states' was entering its bloodiest and most bitter phase. The Apartheid 'total strategy' operated by the governing National Party mixed classic counter-insurgency field tactics with a policy of de-stabilisation both internally and externally and a home-front mantra of 'total onslaught' that portrayed white society as under siege (Davies and O'Meara 1985). Out of the jagged landscape of 'total onslaught' one can hear the 'rhino war' rhetoric of General Jooste, which is not surprising given that he had over 20 years of close involvement in the 'Apartheid Wars' having fought much of the time in the combat 'cockpit' of South West Africa/Namibia (Potgieter 2007).

With the end of Apartheid, Jooste continued in the newly constituted SANDF until retiring in 2006, later gaining degrees in Commerce and in Business Administration, demonstrating his knowledge of a wider non-military world (Jooste, www.linkedin.com). During Apartheid, the counter-insurgency strategy of South Africa and neighbouring Zimbabwe/Rhodesia was heavily influenced by the Malaya Emergency and the British response. General Peter Walls, commander of the Rhodesian Army, and one of his top commanders, Lieutenant-Colonel Ron

Reid-Daly, founder of the Selous Scouts, both fought in the SAS 'C' Squadron in Malaya (de Visser 2011). The most influential South African soldier with experience in Malaya was Lieutenant-General Charles 'Pop' Fraser, a veteran also of the Second World War. Fraser's influence came both from his operational rank, firstly as Chief of the South African Army in 1966 and then as General Officer Commanding Joint Combat Forces (1967–73), as well as from a series of key writings (de Visser 2011). Fraser's text, *Lessons Learnt from Past Revolutionary Wars*, was published in the early 1960s and followed up with another influential study, *Revolutionary Warfare: Basic Principles of Counter-Insurgency* (de Visser 2011). Both works distilled lessons not only from the Malaya experience but also from the more ideologically hard-line 'French School' of counter-insurgency embodied in works such as by David Galula (1964), and Roger Trinquier (1964).

Modern counter-insurgency thinking emphasises a distinction between 'enemy-centric' measures that call for hard kinetic operations aimed at eliminating insurgents versus the 'population-centric' approaches that encourage the general population to think that their best form of protection and social advancement is in supporting the government. The latter version of counter-insurgency has famously been called 'armed social work' by expert, David Kilcullen, for whom 'hearts and minds' meant: 'hearts' means persuading people their best interests are served by your success, 'minds' means convincing them that you can protect them and that resisting you is pointless. Note that neither concept has to do with whether people like you. Calculated self-interest, not emotion, is what counts' (Kilcullen 2006).

One of the key difficulties in applying any version of a 'hearts and minds' strategy to counter-poaching is how to devise an effective plan based on the 'enemy-centric' and 'population-centric' formula, which in turn is related to the separation of the law enforcement role of the police from the more kinetic approach of military operations. Moulded by the long historic traditions of border wars, punitive expeditions and the suppression of civil disturbance, the division of roles between South Africa's Army and the police have increasingly become blurred. During Apartheid these roles often became interchangeable or even reversed, which was clearly demonstrated in the Namibia/South West Africa campaign: while the Army was mounting 'hearts and minds' campaigns alongside combat operations, the paramilitary Koevoet 'Crowbar' force of the then South African police followed a separate agenda that included 'hit and run' raids, interrogation with torture, and other efforts to generally sow discord (de Visser 2011).

Today, policing in South Africa is underpinned by the tactical inter-changeability between domestic policing and paramilitary roles; additionally the increased operational integration between SAPS and SANDF includes joint 'security operations' and the exchange of equipment. Paramilitary SWAT-type units, most notably the Special Task Force (STF) and the Tactical Response Team (TRT), also bridge the gap between the police and the military. The police forces of Africa were created by the colonial powers with an emphasis on maintaining law and order, ensuring the protection of property and pacifying the local population. These are still the defining elements of policing in Africa, as the post-colonial rulers of all stripes have maintained a powerful grip on police operations, and in return, the police have been allowed to operate with considerable autonomy (Shearing 2007).

For the South African police, the inherited pacification tradition combined with a lack of training to police increasingly complex societies and 'ungoverned spaces', has led to a tendency to use of force in tense situations. Such incidents, notably in the 2012 confrontation between striking workers at the Marikana mine that resulted in 44 deaths, have led to diminishing public trust in the capacities of the police (Sosibo 2012). A graphic illustration of this has been the growth of the private security industry in South Africa, which is the largest in the world with some 9,000 registered businesses, employing 400,000 registered security guards – more than the combined strength of the South African police and armed forces (Eastwood 2013). According to the Minister of Police, Nathi Mthethwa, private security firms increasingly perform 'functions which used to be the sole preserve of the police. This has, and will continue to have a serious influence on the functioning of the criminal justice system as a whole' (www.defenceweb.co.za). Developments such as these take place against the backdrop of daunting crime statistics for murder, robbery and sexual assault (www.saps.gov.za/statistics).

To summarise, in 'classic' interpretations of counter-insurgency a line is drawn – however obliquely – between counter-insurgency and policing, which marks the precise calibration of the use of force and legality. The former is based on the application of hard military power, sometimes outside the constraints of civil law, whereas in the latter this is not sanctioned – or not supposed to be – given that it is not only the law that confines police forces, but also the need to maintain the support of the population.

Man-hunting

With the erosion of distinctions, however, both in terms of defining conflict and the application of armed force, come new patterns of violence which we can see in the evolving counter-poaching dynamic in South Africa. Most notable in this dynamic is the 'hunt' and more specifically, 'man-hunting'. Gregory links the widening use of drone strikes in anti-terrorist operations with the 'individuation of warfare', a strategy of 'man-hunting', which is 'a new form of networked (para) military violence' (Gregory 2013). According to Marks, Meer and Nilson (2012), 'man-hunting' departs from established practices in war in that there are no battles or need to meet the enemy face-to-face, except briefly 'in the competition between two enemy combatants, [where] the goal is to win the battle by defeating the adversary – both combatants must confront [each other] to win'. The authors continue: 'a man-hunt scenario differs in that each player's strategy is different. The fugitive always wants to avoid capture, while the pursuer always wants to engage and capture the target – the pursuer must *confront* to win, whereas the fugitive must *evade* to win' (Marks et al. 2012).

In 2009, George A. Crawford (2009) published a paper that proposed to make 'man-hunting a foundation of US national strategy'. Crawford's widely circulated report addressed not only drones and 'targeted assassinations', but the wider implications of operations specifically focused on human beings. For Crawford, the aim of 'man-hunting' is 'to detect, deter, disrupt, detain, or destroy networks'. Similarly, for Grégoire Chamayou (2012) the threat 'is not determined by the seriousness of an act committed, but by the estimated danger of an individual'. The concept and practice of 'man-hunting' was highlighted with the killing of Osama bin Laden by American 'special forces' in May 2011, characterised in popular commentary as 'the hunt for bin Laden' (Blair 2012). Thus, the essential 'hunting' element within counter-poaching, which this chapter has pointed to with respect to efforts to protect the South African rhino, conforms to developments within modern armed violence.

Any doubts about the ethical rationale within 'man-hunting' in relation to rhino counter-poaching are generally subsumed by the relentless media coverage showing the brutal results of poaching. However, as a sociological counter-narrative there is Eric Hobsbawm's (1965) classic analysis of 'bandits' and 'social bandits'. The 'bandit' is someone who 'simultaneously challenges the economic, social and political order by challenging those who hold or lay claim to power, law and the control of resources'; 'social bandits' are 'peasant outlaws whom the lord and state regard as criminals, but who remain within peasant society' (Hobsbawm 1965). Hobsbawm added that 'social bandits' were viewed in rural areas as 'men to be admired, helped and supported'; here Hobsbawm noted the case of the eighteenth century poacher, Mathias Klostermayer from Bavaria: he terrorised hunters, game-keepers and anyone associated with game, while all the time Klostermayer's own poaching was 'an activity peasants always regarded as legitimate, (and) he was admired and helped' (Hobsbawm 1965).

Ungoverned Space

'Ungoverned spaces' do not axiomatically have to be violent because some may be economically productive, either through tourism or agriculture, where the lack of human interference is beneficial. This is the case for the Kruger National Park which has not only become an 'ungoverned space' on South Africa's border but also the world's number one rhino poaching 'hotspot' with images of gunned down and hacked rhinos that in turn draw attention to the high levels of general violence in the country (Herskovitz and Stoddard 2012). In this way, rhino poaching and conservation in South Africa have become part of the country's wider security picture, referred to earlier as 'rhinofication'.

As an indicator and lightning-rod of the country's brittle internal security rhino poaching is highly visible as the sheer scale of the statistics of murder and unemployment have a symbolic symmetry with the number of rhino deaths. Rhino poaching also provides a critical examination of the ability of the South

African to protect the country's borders, its citizens and its biodiversity heritage. Furthermore, a series of disputes in the armed forces over pay and discipline have cast doubts about their state of preparation and operational ability, crystallised in the humiliating 'battle of Bangui' in 2013, when South African peace-keeping forces in the Central African Republic (CAR) were overwhelmed by the Seleka rebels with severe loss of life and injury (www.bbc.co.uk/news/world-africa-20889136).

In the background of events of this kind has been a continuously reinforcing feedback loop consisting of a faltering economy, growing environmental problems and declining agricultural yields, along with high unemployment levels, industrial unrest and political factionalism within the ruling African National Congress (Molele and Naidoo 2013). These problems have been connected to and exacerbated by the perennial challenge of widespread illegal immigration into South Africa. The great majority of the job-hungry have come from Zimbabwe and Mozambique, with many of the illegal incomers making their way through the porous borders around the Kruger National Park (Vale 2003) and what Clunan and Trinkunas (2010) refer to as 'ungoverned spaces'.

Rhino Wars

The intense focus on rhinos in South Africa stems from the ever-expanding 'commodification' of the animals, which lie at the heart not only of the illegal horn selling networks, but also the tourist industry – whether for sport hunting or wildlife viewing – on which more and more parts of South Africa are becoming heavily reliant economically. Furthermore, 'rhino wars' have become a global brand of sorts, supporting and harnessing a vast array of organisations that in turn are synchronised with graphic media representations, such as the adrenaline-pumping TV series *Battleground: Rhino Wars* (Animal Planet 2013) filmed in the Kruger National Park with former United States 'special forces' personnel intercepting poaching gangs, or books ranging from the award-winning reportage of Julian Rademeyer's (2012) *Killing for Profit* to Deon Meyer's (2011) gritty crime thriller *Trackers*.

The whiff of combat and 'high octane' action in rugged terrain has attracted both former soldiers with experience in Afghanistan, Iraq and 'special operations' (Taylor 2012), as well as veterans of South Africa's own Apartheid 'bush wars' (Marshall 2013). These operatives work across a wide counter-poaching spectrum, touting field-craft courses, high-tech equipment and active patrolling. The extent to which the 'rhino wars' narrative has penetrated the security discourse of southern Africa was illustrated by the discovery of a bogus rhino counter-poaching camp in northern South Africa which had been created for an attempted coup against Joseph Kabila, president of the Democratic Republic of the Congo (Govender 2013). The camp demonstrated how much the militarisation of rhino counter-poaching through the use of non-governmental organisations has filled the security void in parts of South Africa, as well as the degree to which paramilitary vigilantism and mercenary activities still flourish in Africa's semi-ungoverned spaces (Govender 2013).

The social causes and operational elements of the 'rhino wars' were forensically laid bare in 2012 by Julian Rademeyer's (2012) lengthy investigation. According to Rademeyer, the 'rhino wars' actually involve three inter-locking 'wars': one involves the protection of an historic and high-profile animal, even though the actual motivations of individuals are a variety of conservation, combat, political and economic; a second 'war' involves competing groups and individuals engaged in brutal, cynical and logistically complex strategies to cash in on a valuable resource; and a third 'war' involves an increasingly bitter 'war of words' between pro and anti-rhino horn legalisation supporters. What also emerges from Rademeyer's analysis is the existence of an almost limitless number of people offering their services as a 'shooter' for comparatively little pay. The demographic and organisational profile of the individual rhino shooter is almost always that of an impoverished black from South Africa and Mozambique. While the principal trigger-pullers are predominantly black, they are organised by middlemen some of whom are white, often with a sport hunting background and occasionally even in veterinary science. Thus the political economy of rhino wars merges with a legal process that would seem capricious and erratic at best, aided by official corruption and incompetence, as well as with some self-serving interests such as a pay strike by the Kruger National Park rangers in February 2012 which was viewed by the public as unwarranted (Broadhead 2012).

With these multiple and contrasting elements the phrase 'rhino wars' have become a useful semiotic 'floating signifier': while the moral case against rhino poaching is clear enough the reasons behind rhino poaching, along with the range of outcomes and strategies employed, and how all these mesh into the 'rhino wars' narrative are exceedingly opaque.

Counter-poaching

Since the 2010 'rhino summit', the overarching governmental response to rhino counter-poaching comes under 'Operation Rhino', the name deriving from a successful operation in 1960 that involved a mass translocation and distribution of White rhinos from the Umfolozi Game Reserve in today's KwaZulu Natal (Boynton 2013). In 1994 Ken Maggs became the Kruger National Park's one-man anti-poaching operation; within four years Maggs built up a team who were responsible for all SANParks' counter-poaching (www.sanparks.org/conservation/investigations). Today, while General Jooste directs SANParks' counter-poaching strategy, other regional organisations that control parks and reserves, such as Ezemvelo KZN in KwaZulu Natal, have started their own teams (www.projectrhinokzn.org). All these official counter-poaching teams lean heavily on private organisations for additional support.

Currently, all rhino poaching-related crimes are investigated by the Endangered Species section of the SAPS elite Directorate of Priority Crimes Investigations unit, known as the 'Hawks' (www.saps.gov.za) and the National Wildlife Crime Investigation Unit (NWCIU) (www.rhinos.org/africa-regional-programs) both of which are overseen by NatJoints. Meanwhile, security in the Kruger National Park is split into 22 different sections, each managed by a Section Ranger who is supported by a staff compliment of Field Rangers. Counter-poaching in the park is led by SANParks Corporate Investigation Services (CIS), which was developed to provide support to the Section Ranger and the Park manager (www.sanparks.org/conservation/investigations). Jooste's role has been to bring greater coherence to these counter-poaching efforts. This has included the task of integrating the role of SANDF, which since 2009 has been assisting 'Operation Rhino', with its counter-poaching activities restricted to patrolling the problematic border areas around the Kruger National Park (www.rhinos-irf). To illustrate the challenge facing Jooste, 42 rhinos were killed in Kruger National Park during January 2013 alone – the area that General Jooste had identified as the main priority of focus (Helfrich 2013).

Getting Tough

General Jooste was not alone in voicing strong declarations of a 'war' against poaching, with Dr David Mabunda, chief executive of SANParks, declaring that the poachers 'days were numbered' and that 'we are on their trail and closing quickly on them' (Strauss 2012). Ironically, the escalating death-count of rhinos was used to justify the case for legalisation of rhino horn sales; at the Conference of the Parties (CoP) of the 2013 CITES meeting held in Bangkok, Minister Molewa, the Water and Environmental affairs minister, stated that 'South Africa cannot continue to be held hostage by the syndicates slaughtering our rhinos', and thus rhino hunting could be curbed by the 'establishment of well-regulated international trade '(Cohen and Burkhardt 2013).

The relentless campaign to legalise rhino horn sales bore fruit in July 2013 when the South African Cabinet announced that it would support legalisation when the issue would be debated at the crucial CITES meeting in 2016. Proposals included permitting a one-off sale of confiscated rhino horn in order to lower the price to make poaching less economically attractive, as well as seeking a regulatory mechanism similar to the Kimberley Process that seeks to control diamonds from conflict areas (Clark 2012). As a signal of a heightened 'war' against rhino poaching the appointment of such a senior figure as General Jooste seemed to represent a *coup*, sending a message that there would be no lack of effort, commitment and expertise in the crackdown on illegal poaching. A further sign of increased counter-poaching activity was the donation of a drone by Denel, South Africa's state-owned arms corporation (Helfrich 2013) as well as a spotter-plane by the Ichikowitz Foundation, run by Ivor Ichikowitz, whose Paramount Group is a key organisation in the local defence industry (Balt 2012).

Additionally, a series of financial rewards were instituted for information leading to poaching arrests (Crawford 2013).

There were also several other politically coded messages contained within General Jooste's appointment. First, since both the conservationist and ranching lobbies in South Africa are White-dominated but have an extremely low percentage within the country's demographics, it meant that Dr Mabunda could claim that he had made a significant gesture towards the White population's anxieties with the appointment of General Jooste. Secondly, conservation groups and people within SANParks had been alleging widespread mismanagement and corruption within the organisation that had permitted poachers to gain access to the Kruger National Park by bribing rangers (McLeod 2012). Choosing someone who had been at the very top of the South African security establishment was a forceful response to these accusations, with rhino conservation groups both in South Africa and abroad calling for a much tougher approach to poaching, using tactics such as shoot-to-kill, stop-and-search, drones and other technology to halt the poachers (Joy 2013). Underpinning the intensified approach to the counter-poaching was the uninhibited and repeated use of words such as 'war', 'fighting' and 'insurgency' (South African National Parks 2012). Dr Mabunda described this counter-poaching campaign as a 'low intensity war', while General Jooste suggested the poaching constituted an 'insurgency war' (Helfrich 2013), such language according with the time-honoured mantra throughout South African history that the very fabric of society is under dire threat (Potgieter 1995).

Horn Sale Legalisation

Arguably, Dr Mabunda was promoting the rhino counter-poaching strategy along classic counter-insurgency lines by expanding the political element of the campaign along twin lines supported by the 'Jooste War'. On the one hand, there was the chance that General Jooste's efforts might reduce the rhino poaching tally; if that failed, then the concurrent government campaign to open up debate about legalising rhino horn sales could turn into outright support on the grounds that the 'hard power' solution had been tried and failed. Indeed, it would seem that during the run-up to the 2013 CITES meeting that the South African Cabinet was coming round to supporting legalisation, with Minister Molewa stating in Bangkok: 'our rhinos are killed every day and the numbers are going up. The reality is that we have done all in our power and doing the same thing every day isn't working. We do think that we need to address this issue of trade in a controlled manner so that we can at least begin to push down this pressure' (Smith 2013).

Moving towards a legalised rhino horn trade would certainly satisfy the economic interests of the White ranchers, professional hunters (such as the Professional Hunters Association of South Africa) and park managers (Lamprecht 2013). It also addressed the concern of those few conservationists, like Duan Biggs (2013), who believed that an outright ban only resulted in 'a situation where rhinos are being killed unnecessarily'. Biggs had argued that the anti-poaching effort was 'taking resources away from other conservation efforts, and is leading to the situation where there's a pseudo-war taking place in the Kruger National Park' (Bosworth 2013). Biggs proposed legalised mass breeding of rhinos to allow regular trimming of 'live' rhinos for their horn. Here the argument is that legalisation of rhino horn sales would create a safe and humane response to the demand for rhino horn (Bosworth 2013).

Tangentially, the issue of rhino poaching has provided a convenient political screen for the South African authorities to raise the politically vexatious but sensitive issue of cross-border security with Mozambique, for which an ideal solution for the South Africans would be the complete restoration and upgrading of the existing border-line fence (Marshall 2013). To do this, however, would not only be very expensive but would in theory counteract the rebuilding of post-Apartheid regional collaboration; however, according to Dr Mabunda cooperation between South Africa and Mozambique over poaching had been 'dismal'. 'A poacher will run across the border and fire victory shots. He will sit in sight of the ranger and smoke because rangers dare not cross that line ... should a SANParks official or a soldier shoot a poacher across the border it would create a serious international incident and might be seen as an act of war', said Dr Mabunda (Helfrich 2013).

Legalisation Arguments

At the Bangkok CITES meeting Minister Molewa asked for the legalisation of rhino horn sales at least to be discussed; after some heated talk it was resolved to defer any resolution until the next CoP meeting in 2016, coincidentally to be held in South Africa (Rademeyer 2013). Here the question of legalising rhino horn sales will inevitably loom large and provoke stormy debate. One of driving factors behind the South Africa's proposal at the previous CoP meeting was an awareness of the 'rhinomics' at stake, being not only the rising cost of rhino protection but also that the authorities and ranchers were missing out on the enormous financial returns of rhino horn, fetching in late 2013 between $US10,000 and $US40,000 per kilo (Platt 2013). Both the South African ranchers, heavily reliant on rhinos for sport hunting and wildlife tourism, and the park authorities, who had already been raising funds through auctioning off captured rhinos, had seen the ever-increasing financial rewards amassing to the illegal poaching networks (Platt 2013). In fact, so certain have the South African ranchers been that the ban would be lifted that they have developed extensive rhino breeding and selling programmes, along with 'horn harvesting' to create stock-piles in advance, as well as being spurred on by reports of rhino breeding in China (Stoddard 2013).

However, those against legalisation of the rhino horn trade have pointed out that there was little evidence suggesting that legalising the trade, or even allowing a one-off sale to flood the market, would do anything more than encourage poaching. As evidence, they have pointed to the one-off sale of elephant ivory sanctioned by CITES in 2008 (www.cites.org). Far from thwarting the market, the sell-off has since been seen as stimulating a huge spike in ivory prices, leading to further pressure on endangered elephant populations (Knights 2013). Another primary concern has been that a legalised trade would not be policed effectively while poaching networks would still flourish given the financial incentives. The most fundamental moral objection, though, has been that a legalised trade would grant spurious credibility to the 'misconception that this keratinous body part has medicinal qualities'. For Peter Knights of the charity WildAid, 'legitimising and promoting demand for rhino horn would inevitably create a far larger consumer base and once this genie is out we could never re-cork the bottle if the experiment went wrong' (*Wildlife Extra* 2013).

Rhino horn has been widely touted in Asia as a cure for cancer, prompting Will Travers, of the Born Free Foundation, to suggest: 'so what are they saying by legalising the rhino horn trade? Here is a product that every sensible scientist says has no significant impact and they are going to sell it at huge cost to a public that is ill-informed. I wouldn't go to sleep at night' (Rademeyer 2013). If the rhino horn trade ban is lifted it is quite possible that some conservationists from South Africa and around the world would call for tourists and the sporting world to boycott South Africa, as happened during the Apartheid years (Maromo 2012). Furthermore, attacks on rhino horn stockpile locations, as well as on ranchers and their families, are also possible, whether by committed wildlife supporters or criminal opportunists. As such these are echoes of South Africa's long history of social uncertainty that are woven into the country's 'rhino wars', particularly the economic insecurity for both the white ranchers and rural blacks – though for differing reasons – against a background of violence as domestic insecurities and instabilities are coupled with external threats, whether on the border or from foreign organisations embedded within South Africa, which today are the transnational crime networks lying at the heart of the 'rhino wars'. In addition, the heightened rhetoric of threat has traditionally resonated with the white rancher population and a fear of a political and racial 'total onslaught': historically, this has created a 'laager mentality', or 'backs-to-the-wall' isolation that prolonged the Apartheid regime into the late twentieth century.

However, despite well-publicised murders and attacks on individual ranchers, the main threat to the White rancher population continues to be economic: while current yields in products like wheat have been rising slowly at about 2.4 per cent per annum (Ray et al. 2013) data showing an increasing 'desertification' process of land that was never fertile, requiring either intensive irrigation or large areas for cattle to roam and feed, makes the cost-effectiveness of agricultural production a progressively marginal business (http://soils.usda.gov). Increasingly, South African ranchers have turned to harnessing wildlife as their key economic resource, either for differing types of tourism or for breeding; in both cases, the role of the rhino has been pivotal, while the horn is a lucrative added incentive (Lindsay et al. 2013).

Conclusion

A meaningful 'hearts and minds' strategy in the context of rhino poaching would involve a high-profile, widespread programme focused on South Africa's rural population, using conservation as the centre-piece to address chronic economic and social problems. Without an effective 'hearts and minds' strategy, the 'Jooste War' could therefore only amount to no more than replicating the time-honoured paramilitary 'pacification' dynamic in South African history in the protection of minority interests, while also being viewed by some sections of society as a 'war on the poor'. The poacher clearly presents a political challenge – albeit one without an overt agenda – to the vested interests belonging to both the state and the private sector. This unscripted political element of the poacher's identity is highlighted in Hobsbawm's (1965) evaluation of the 'social bandit', who exposes not only the vulnerabilities of state security, but also faltering governance by the state. From this perspective, even if rhino poaching is merely condoned by rural inhabitants as against being actively supported, then counter-poaching runs the risk of losing its moral standing and of being viewed as a strategy that supports the interests of a minority elite, in this case the whites who run the wildlife ranches and allied tourism industry.

2013 – the first year of the 'Jooste War' – ended with an 'official' total of 1,004 rhino poaching deaths (McGrath 2014) the worst total in the modern times and continuing the sky-rocketing upward trend. In fairness there were factors outside General Jooste's control, such an insatiable demand for rhino horn, ineffective international anti-wildlife trafficking strategies, and corruption at various levels. However, despite all the 'war-like' rhetoric of counter-poaching neither General Jooste nor Dr Mabunda had articulated a coherent counter-poaching strategy that mixed their preference for 'hard power' with the social engagement of 'hearts and minds'; instead all their *modus operandi* offered was 'more of the same', being a mixture of patrolling and policing as part of simple paramilitary enforcement in the fashion of 'man-hunting'. Therefore, the 'Jooste War' has replicated the same deeply flawed counter-insurgency strategy employed in South West Africa/ Namibia during the 'Apartheid Wars': through this strategy failure the 'Jooste War' not only escalated the rhino poaching crisis in South Africa during 2013 but shortened the odds for even higher rhino death tallies in the future.

References

Animal Planet. 2013. Rhino wars: taking down the bad guys. *Battleground: Rhino wars*. Online 19 February. Available at: http://animal.discovery.com/tv-shows/ battleground-rhino-wars. Accessed 13 November 2013.

Balt, M. 2012. Anti-poaching campaigns take to the sky. *Looklocal.com*, 4 December. Available at: http://www.looklocal.co.za/looklocal/content/en/ lowveld/lowveld-news-general?oid=6599495&sn=Detail&pid=490165/. Accessed 13 November 2013.

BBC News Africa. 2013. Central African Republic rebels halt advance on Bangui. *BBC News*, 2 January. Available at: http://www.bbc.co.uk/news/world-africa-20889136/ Accessed 13 November 2013.

Blair, D. 2012. The hunt for bin Laden. *Daily Telegraph*, 20 May.

Bosworth, B. 2013. Would a legal rhino horn trade stem poaching? *Guardian*, 18 April.

Boynton, G. 2013. Illegal poaching and the endangered rhino. *Traveller*, January.

Braun, D. 2012. U.S. pursues global strategy to end trafficking in wildlife. 8 November. Available at: http://newswatch.nationalgeographic.com/2012/11/08/u-s-pursues-global-strategy-to-end-trafficking-in-wildlife/ Accessed 13 November 2013.

Broadhead, I. 2012. Rhinos threatened by SAF ranger strike. *Voice of America*, 6 February 2012. Available at: http://www.voanews.com/content/rhinos-threatened-by-saf-ranger-strike-138848174/151697.html/. Accessed 13 November 2013.

Brockington, D., Duffy, R. and Igoe, J. 2008. *Nature Unbound: Conservation, Capitalism and the Future of Protected Areas*. London: Earthscan.

Chamayou, G. 2012. *Manhunts: A Philosophical History* (trans. Steven Rendall). Princeton, NJ: Princeton University Press.

Clark, R.D. 2012. The control of conflict minerals in Africa and a preliminary assessment of the Dodd-Frank Wall Street Reform and Consumer Act. In N. South and A. Brisman (eds), *Routledge International Handbook of Green Criminology*. Abingdon: Routledge.

Clunan, A.L. and Trinkunas, H.A. (eds) 2010. *Ungoverned Spaces: Alternatives to State Authority in an Era of Softened Sovereignty*. Stanford, CA: Stanford University Press.

Coalition Against Wildlife Trafficking (CAWT). 2009. *Illegal Wildlife Trade*. Available at: http://www.cawtglobal.org/wildlife-crime/. Accessed 13 November 2013.

Cohen, M. and Burkhardt, P. 2013. South Africa backs proposal to legalize rhino horn trade. *Bloomberg*, 3 July. Available at: http://www.bloomberg.com/news/2013-07-03/south-africa-backs-proposal-to-legalize-rhino-horn-trade.html/. Accessed 13 November 2013.

Crawford, A. 2013. South Africa rhinos under threat from poaching. *Sky News*, 11 April. Available at: http://news.sky.com/story/1076589/south-africa-rhinos-under-threat-from-poaching/. Accessed 7 January 2015.

Crawford, G.A. 2009. *Manhunting: Counter-Network Organization for Irregular Warfare*. Joint Special Operations University report. Hurlburt, FL: JSOU Press.

Davies, R. and O'Meara, D. 1985. Total strategy in southern Africa: an analysis of South African regional policy since 1978. *Journal of Southern African Studies* 11: 2.

Draper, M. 1998. Zen and the art of garden province maintenance: the soft intimacy of hard men in the wilderness of KwaZulu-Natal, South Africa 1952–1997. *Journal of South African Studies* 24: 4.

Duffy, R. 2010. *Nature Crime: How We're Getting Conservation Wrong*. New Haven, CT and London: Yale University Press.

Eastwood, V. 2013. Bigger than the army: South Africa's private security forces. *CNN*, 8 February. Available at: http://edition.cnn.com/2013/02/08/business/south-africa-private-security/. Accessed 13 November 2013.

Ellis, S. 1994. Of elephants and men: politics and nature conservation in South Africa. *Journal of Southern African Studies* 20: 1.

Ellis, S. 1998. The historical significance of South Africa's 'third force'. *Journal of Southern African Studies* 24: 2.

Galuala, D. 1964. *Counter-Insurgency Warfare: Theory and Practice*. London: Pall Mall.

Govender, P. 2013. South Africa charges Congo rebels with planning coup. *Reuters*, 7 February. Available at: http://www.reuters.com/article/2013/02/07/us-safrica-congo-idUSBRE9160RP20130207/. Accessed 13 November 2013.

Gregory, D. 2013. The individuation of warfare? *Geographical Imaginations, War, Space and Security*, 26 August. Available at: http://geographicalimaginations.com/2013/08/26/the-individuation-of-warfare/. Accessed 13 November 2013.

Helfrich, K. 2013. *More Militaristic Approach to Kruger Poaching Problem*. *Defenceweb*, 4 February. Available at: http://www.defenceweb.co.za/index.php?option=com_content&task=view&id=29312&Itemid=188/. Accessed 13 November 2013.

Henk, D. 2006. Biodiversity and the military in Botswana. *Armed Forces and Society* 32: 2.

Herskovitz, J. and Stoddard, E. 2012. South Africa rhino poaching hits new record in 2012, *Reuters*. Online 12 December. Available at: http://www.huffingtonpost.com/2012/12/27/south-africa-rhino-poaching-2012_n_2369000.html. Accessed 13 November 2013.

Hobsbawm, E.J. 1965. *Primitive Rebels: Studies in Archaic Forms of Social Movement in the 19th and 20th Centuries*. New York: W.W. Norton.

Humphreys, J. and Smith, M.L.R. 2011. War and wildlife: the Clausewitz connection. *International Affairs* 87(1): 121–42.

Joy, O. 2013. Helicopters versus drones: the cost of the war on rhinos. *CNN*, 16 October.

Kilcullen, D. 2006.Twenty-eight articles: fundamentals of company level counter-insurgency. *Small Wars Journal*. Online 29 March. Available at: http://smallwarsjournal.com/documents/28articles.pdf. Accessed 13 November 2013.

Lamprecht, D. 2013. South Africa to propose legalising rhino horn trade at CITES meeting in 2016. *Wildlife Extra*, 10 August. Available at: http://www.wildlifeextra.com/go/news/rhino-cites.html#cr/. Accessed 13 November 2013.

Leakey, R. 2001. *Wildlife Wars: My Battle to Save Kenya's Elephants*. London: Pan.

Lindsay, P.A., Havermann, C.P., Lines, R.M., Price, A.E., Retief, T.A., Rhebergen, T., Van der Waal, C. and Romañach, S.S. 2013. Benefits of wildlife-based land uses on private lands in Namibia and limitations affecting their development. *Oryx* 47(1): 41–53.

McGrath, M. 2014. Worst year ever for SA rhino poaching. *BBC News*, 14 January. Available at: http://www.bbc.co.uk/news/science-environment-25781746/. Accessed 7 January 2015.

MacKenzie, J.M. 1997. *The Empire of Nature: Hunting, Conservation and British Imperialism*. Manchester: Manchester University Press.

McLeod, F. 2012. SANParks tenders probed. *Mail & Guardian*. Online 17 February. Available at: http://mg.co.za/article/2012-02-17-sanparks-tenders-probed. Accessed 13 November 2013.

Marks, M., Shearing, C. and Wood, J. 2008. Who should the police be? Finding a new narrative for community policing in South Africa. *Police Practice and Research* 10(2): 145–55.

Marks, S., Meer, T. and Nilson, M. 2005. *Manhunting: A Methodology for Finding Persons of National Interest*. Monterey, CA: Naval Postgraduate School.

Maromo, J. 2012. Rhino activists threaten global boycott on SA products. *Mail & Guardian*. Online 22 February. Available at: http://mg.co.za/article/2012-02-22-rhino-activists-threaten-global-boycott-on-sa-products. Accessed 13 November 2013.

Marshall, L. 2013. Worsening rhino war strains countries' relations. *National Geographic News Watch*, 30 April. Available at: http://newswatch.nationalgeographic.com/2013/04/30/worsening-rhino-war-strains-countries-relat ions%E2%80%A8%E2%80%A8%E2%80%A8/. Accessed 13 November 2013.

Meyer, D. 2011. *Trackers* (trans. K.L. Seegers). London: Atlantic Monthly Press.

Milliken, T. and Shaw, J. 2012. *The South African – Viet Nam Rhino Trade Nexus*. Johannesburg: TRAFFIC.

Molele, C. and Naidoo, S. 2013. Zuma declares war on ANC's 'demon of factionalism'. *Mail & Guardian*, 8 January. Available at: http://mg.co.za/article/2012-01-08-zuma-speaks-of-ancs-future-at-centenary-celebrations/. Accessed 13 November 2013.

Platt, J.R. 2013. As rhino poaching surges South Africa proposes legalized trade in precious horns. *Scientific American*. Online 12 July. Available at: http://blogs.scientificamerican.com/extinction-countdown/2013/07/12/rhino-horn-south-africa-legalized/. Accessed 13 November 2013.

Potgieter, D.W. 1995. *Contraband: South Africa and the International Trade in Ivory and Rhino Horn*. Cape Town: Queillerie.

Potgieter, D.W. 2007. *Total Onslaught: Apartheid's Dirty Tricks Exposed*. Cape Town: Zebra Press.

Rademeyer, J. 2012. *Killing for Profit: Exposing the Illegal Rhino Horn Trade*. Cape Town: Zebra Press.

Rademeyer, J. 2013. South Africa pushes for legal trade in rhino horn. *Mail & Guardian*. Online 22 March. Available at: http://mg.co.za/article/2013-03-22-00-sa-pushes-for-legal-trade-in-rhino-horn. Accessed 13 November 2013.

Ray, D.K., Mueller, N.D., West, P.C. and Foley, J.A. 2013. Yield trends are insufficient to double global crop production by 2050. *PLoS ONE* 8: 6.

Reeve, R. and Ellis, S. 1995. An insider's account of the South African security forces' role in the ivory trade. *Journal of African Studies* 13: 3.

Shearing, C. 2007. Policing our future. In A. Henry and D.J. Smith (eds), *Transformations of Policing*. Aldershot: Ashgate.

Smith, D. 2013. South African minister backs legalisation of rhino horn trade. *Guardian*. Online 25 March. Available at: http://www.theguardian.com/environment/2013/mar/25/south-africa-rhino-horn-trade. Accessed 13 November 2013.

Sosibo, K. 2012. NUM: lethal force ahead of Marikana shootings was justified. *Mail & Guardian*. Online 22 October. Available at: http://mg.co.za/article/2012-10-22-lonmin-caused-problem-at-marikana-say-police. Accessed 13 November 2013.

South African Government Information Service. Rhino summit. 2010. Keynote address by minister Buyelwa Sonjica, MP, Reserve Bank conference, South African Government Information, 5 October. Available at: http://www.info.gov.za/speech/DynamicAction?pageid=461&sid=13442&tid=21086/. Accessed 13 November 2013.

South African National Parks. 2012. *SANParks Enlists Retired Army General to Command Anti-poaching.* 12 December. Available at: http://www.sanparks.org/about/news/default.php?id=55388/. Accessed 13 November 2013.

Stoddard, E. 2013. Africa money: legalising rhino horn, ivory trade in focus. *reuters.com*, 26 April. Available at: http://www.reuters.com/article/2012/04/26/africa-money-idUSL6E8FP0XC20120426/. Accessed 13 November 2013.

Strauss, L. 2012. Kruger National Park steps up fight against poachers. *Kruger Park*. Available at: http://www.krugerpark.co.za/krugerpark-times-e-4-fight-against-poachers-25091.html/. Accessed 13 November 2013.

Taylor, D. 2012. Iraq war veteran battles rhino poachers in Africa: special forces operative teaches military tactics to wildlife rangers. *Voice of America*, 29 January. Available at: http://www.voanews.com/content/iraq-war-veteran-battles-rhino-poachers-in-africa-138338229/159563.html/. Accessed 13 November 2013.

Trinquier, R. 1964. *Modern Warfare: A French View of Counter-Insurgency*. London: Pall Mall.

UK gives support to Kenya in fight against wildlife poaching. 2013. *gov.uk*. Available at: https://www.gov.uk/government/news/uk-gives-support-to-kenya-in-fight-against-wildlife-poaching. Accessed 1 November 2013.

de Visser, L.E. 2011. Winning hearts and minds in the Namibian border war. *Scientia Militaria, South African Journal of Military Studies* 39: 1.

Washafrica.wordpress. 2010. South Africa. Edna Molewa replaces Buyelwa Sonjica as Water and Environmental Affairs minister, top officials suspended. *Washafrica.wordpress*, 2 November. Available at: http://washafrica.wordpress.com/2010/11/02/south-africa-edna-molewa-replaces-buyelwa-sonjica-as-water-and-environmental-affairs-minister-top-officials-suspended/. Accessed 7 January 2015.

Xolani, M. 2013. Most SA land in private hands: survey. *City Press*, 5 September. Available at: http://www.citypress.co.za/politics/sa-land-private-hands-survey/. Accessed 13 November 2013.

Chapter 10

Weaponising Conservation in the 'Heart of Darkness': The War on Poachers and the Neocolonial Hunt

Tyler Wall and Bill McClanahan

Introduction: A 'War on Poachers'

The 'war on poaching', as it is often called, is one of the most visible and concerted campaigns magnifying the contested politics of eviction and exclusion imbuing African conservation and ecology. Anti-poaching efforts are ostensibly aimed at protecting a variety of species, but the most intensive efforts focus on the illegal hunting of elephants and rhinos due to their ivory tusks and horns, which are highly valued commodities on the black market as there are currently no legal markets for these items.[1] Park rangers and anti-poaching scouts, using police and military tactics and technologies, play important roles in the war on poaching as they go about hunting, quite literally, human prey who themselves are hunters, or 'poachers', of wildlife (see also Jasper's chapter, this volume). Although estimates vary and are said to be unreliable, it is believed that hundreds of poachers have been killed by anti-poaching units in the last few years, with some instances of poachers bodies being mutilated (Lombard 2012). A comment made by Jonathan Adams and Thomas McShane in their book, *The Myth of Africa*, written over 20 years ago, has proven prophetic: 'If current trends continue, the war on poaching may soon resemble the war in Vietnam: a massive, well-armed force struggles in vain against a poor but unyielding foe' (1992: 130). Ivor Ichikowitz, chairman of Paramount, Africa's largest private defence firm has stated, 'this [poaching] is a war. You cannot take a stick to a gunfight' (Govender 2012). This quotation, one of many using the language of war, tellingly demonstrates how anti-poaching efforts are most often framed as a justifiable and necessary response to increasingly well-armed, brutal poachers – while simultaneously framing this war against poachers as primarily a narrow issue that can only be approached through coercive security measures. Yet importantly, as Rosaleen Duffy (2000) points out in *Killing*

---

1 There is, however, a legal market for these items that assumes a provenance of over 100 years.

for Conservation, her book on the violence of conservation in Zimbabwe, military and police forces have long been poachers of wildlife themselves.

The common refrain is that poachers are increasingly militarised in their tactics and technologies and therefore can be countered only with anti-poaching efforts that are structured by military and police practices that are technologically advanced and as equally harsh as the so-called poachers. Hence, anti-poaching efforts are animated by the technologies of war power and police power, such as scouting and armed patrols, spatial exclusions such as fences, shoot-to-kill policies, military vehicles, tracking equipment, and aerial surveillance with helicopters, airplanes, and most recently, aerial drones, which are now emerging as the latest anti-poaching technology. The 'war on poachers' then is not merely a rhetorical tool – although it is that, too – but an actual security offensive that is circumscribed by the mutually reinforcing architectures of war and police power, much like the infamous wars on crime, drugs, and terrorism. The war on African poachers is not solely state directed, but also includes NGOs, private land ranchers, and private corporations – and these actors often come into conflict over methods, jurisdictions, and politics.

As the most direct and visible form of 'wildlife crime', what has become known as 'poaching' is inseparable from colonial history and what anthropologist Dan Brockington (2002) has called 'fortress conservation' – a 'powerful, persistent, and popular vision' animating much of Western conservation approaches. A central practice of fortress conservation is the development and maintenance of 'protected areas' such as wildlife parks and game reserves – public, private, and NGO initiatives that are contingent on the eviction and persistent efforts of expunging thousands of local peoples from their ancestral homes. As particular landscapes of defence, wildlife parks and game reserves are actively 'secured' through a variety of strategies and tactics of security. The first line of defence, so to speak, is the physical barrier of the fence, sometimes with electric shock capabilities, which demarcates the boundaries of particular 'protected areas', while simultaneously enclosing wildlife within a geography defended by keeping undesirable humans out.

Fortress conservation is reinforced by a variety of taken-for-granted logics, such as problematic and hegemonic scientific discourses on environmental change, the appealing myth of an untouched and unpeopled 'wilderness', and the widespread circulation of popular representations of gorgeous landscapes (see Cronon 1995). Largely associated with Africa, but in no way confined to this continent, this colonial logic hinges on the exclusion of local indigenous peoples from their own land in the name of saving elephants or lions or rhinos or fauna or more broadly 'the wilderness' or 'nature', ironically, from the locals themselves. One serious problem, then, of fortress conservation is that this (neo)colonialist project often obscures the ways in which, in the name of saving ecology, it simultaneously perpetuates, and is in fact premised on, the organised production of great social harm for local peoples, such as the loss of land and subsistence, cultural customs and identity, and self-determination and economic and political power.

Indeed, this pervasive and insidious approach to conservation understands the 'environment' as being harmed primarily by local peoples, and hence the environment needs to be saved and therefore secured in order to preserve or conserve the ecology in a 'pristine' condition. Key here is the notion that those indigenous to a particular land do not properly respect, appreciate, and care for the ecological brilliance of their own habitat. Locals, themselves, are in fact part of the problem, this logic goes, and therefore conservation efforts must be directed at regulating the cultural and economic customs of natives since these are deemed harmful and threatening to local ecologies. Therefore, as a particular sociopolitical construction delimiting the parameters of what is 'conservation' and 'the environment', fortress conservationist frames often serve the interests of powerful states (African or otherwise), multinational corporations and rich white ranchers that own vast proportions of African land, at the expense of the dispossessed and poor indigenous wage labourers or surplus populations. As Adams and McShane (1992: xvii–xviii) contend, 'The entire modern conservation edifice rests on the ideals and visions of people other than Africans ... Conservation has long operated on the comfortable belief that Africa is a paradise to be defended, even against the people who have lived there for thousands of years'. Conservation efforts that adopt the fortress model ignore the vast inequalities that characterise the causes and impacts of environmental and ecological harm; while 'wealthy countries have contributed disproportionately to a variety of environmental problems' and 'poor countries bear most of the harm' associated with ecological degradation (Gonzalez 2013: 78). If conservation is to be an equitable and effective practice, then, it must focus its efforts on the most effectual contributors to environmental harm – the powerful corporate and state actors of the Global North – rather than on those cultures, peoples, and geographies that contribute less but suffer more, the Global South.

If the war on poaching and its guiding architecture of fortress conservation is to be approached critically, the labels of 'poaching' and its umbrella term 'wildlife crime' should not be normalised and taken as apolitical labels. These terms must be understood as first and foremost inherently political in nature – as they are constructions produced and nearly solidified as normalised 'fact' through various histories and political economies of violence and accumulation. As a criminalised category created through the historical violence of colonisation, the Eurocentrism of fortress conservation, and the capitalist hunt for markets, 'poaching' has been and continues to be a vital political technology that serves to separate indigenous populations from their traditional means of subsistence. Put another way, the cultural and political economies of the war on poaching strike at the heart of what Marx (1867/1976) famously called 'primitive accumulation'.[2] As Edward Steinhart (2006) shows in *Black Poachers, White Hunters*, his social history of

---

2　In *Capital, Vol. I*, Marx defines primitive accumulation as the 'historic process[es]' of capital that seek to alienate and 'divorce the producer from the means of production' (p. 502). For an extended discussion on primitive accumulation, see Perelman (2000).

hunting in Kenya, it was originally European colonisers, and then imperialist 'safari' hunters, and later white conservationists that transformed indigenous hunters into – to borrow a contemporary phrase – eco-criminals that needed to be policed and punished. This criminalisation of local hunters quite literally framed *them* as the beasts needing to be hunted. Of course, this history is still enforced in the colonial present, as the capitalist markets circumscribing the safari hunt for big cats, elephants, and rhinos, catering to mostly rich Western 'hunters', remain legal and are flourishing. The contemporary war on African poachers often obscures and enforces the important history of organised hunting on the continent by white European hunters, as well as the long tradition of subsistence, economic, and sport hunting by many African peoples (Steinhart 2006). Refusing to take seriously the historical and political construction of 'poaching' not only serves to dumb down thinking about this particular form of 'wildlife crime', but also to obscure the fact that this colonial history haunts contemporary understandings of what constitutes 'proper hunting' and who might be the 'proper hunters' in Africa.

In what follows, we unpack the cultural and political dynamics of the war on poachers in Africa by paying particular attention to the relatively new non-profit anti-poaching organisation of the International Anti-Poaching Foundation (the 'IAPF'). We contend that a critique of the IAPF provides a limited but useful example of how the war on poachers is often underpinned by both colonial mythologies of white saviour manhunters in the 'dark continent' and by the logic of security which exhibits an insidious ability to attach itself to virtually any issue (see Neocleous 2008; see also Zedner 2009). By discussing the IAPF and its attendant representations of poaching and anti-poaching efforts in various parts of Africa, our goal is to inquire into the social construction of the (neo)colonial common sense that naturalises popular notions of legitimate 'hunting' and illegitimate 'poaching'. Furthermore, our narrative also strives to provoke questions concerning the coupling of security logics and conservation logics through the practice of the hunt for human prey. We broadly ask: to what extent is 'conservation' circumscribed by a logic of security and the neocolonial 'manhunt', at least as depicted by the manhunting IAPF? Similarly, if fortress conservation reproduces the fetish of security, what might this mean for the status or viability of 'conservation' efforts that aim to reduce or eliminate ecological harm? To what extent is 'conservation' a category emerging out of the violence of primitive accumulation? How might a critical political ecology further problematise the ways that conservation efforts are often intertwined with the logics of war and police? Unsurprisingly, we raise more questions than provide answers, but our hope is that our narrative provokes some reconsideration of the weaponisation of conservation that has historically been and persists as a guiding animus of the war on African poachers.

Importantly, for our purposes here, Perelman situates the historical construction of 'the game law' directly at the heart of primitive accumulation.

A Great White Hunter of Black Skins: Teaching Natives Security

After serving several military tours in Iraq, Damien Mander, whom *National Geographic* describes as a 'hard-muscled former Australian Special Forces sniper with an imposing menagerie of tattoos, including 'Seek and Destroy' in gothic lettering across his chest' (Gwin 2012), travelled to Africa in 2009 and soon thereafter formed the IAPF in October of 2010. According to the IAPF website, the organisation's Mission Statement is to 'protect and preserve wildlife in volatile regions' by working in conjunction with Zimbabwean authorities to provide education, research, leadership, and awareness regarding global conservation. Although a new non-profit anti-poaching organisation, all indications point to the IAPF as growing and increasingly popular and recognised within conservation circles and popular media. As the CEO and Founder of IAPF, Mander himself has gained a sort of cult celebrity status in regards to his campaign of saving African wildlife, having been featured in countless media reports from international newspapers and magazines to international television, perhaps most notably *National Geographic* and the Australian version of the popular news broadcast *60 Minutes*. One newspaper has described Mander as a 'wildlife war zone hero' and a 'personal bodyguard' to rhinos (Keeton 2011). He is increasingly becoming an influential human face of anti-poaching efforts in Africa – and specifically, a single white humanitarian face among multitudes of black faces. Borrowing a phrase from Sherene Razack (2004), we might say Mander understands himself and the IAPF, at least as represented in journalistic accounts and the IAPF website, as a 'white knight' combating the 'dark threats' that are African poachers.

The power of colonial mythology is highlighted in the story on the origin of the IAPF. While in Zimbabwe, Mander had what he has told numerous news outlets was nothing short of a transformational life experience that ultimately served as the catalyst for him forming the IAPF. *Voice of America*, the official external broadcast institution of the United States federal government, reports: 'Mander had come to Africa to escape the death and destruction he'd seen in the Middle East. Instead, he found himself staring at more horror – in the form of the bloodied, rotting carcass of an elephant, riddled with bullets and its tusks hacked off' (Taylor 2012). Hence, the origins of the IAPF developed not out of intentional design, but through an unplanned encounter with the brutalising horror that is Africa – Conrad's (2010) 'heart of darkness'. Of course, this narrative of the white traveller encountering the violence and depravity of dark 'Others' has long served to dehumanise foreign peoples while simultaneously fabricating a political economy of domination and resistance (Razack 2004).

The story goes that after his life-transforming event of witnessing a slaughtered elephant, Mander realised he had the security skills and experience needed to fight poachers, and therefore tried to get involved in anti-poaching units across Africa. Due to his whiteness and nationality, however, he was turned away. In response, Mander liquidated all of his assets and developed the IAPF in Victoria Falls, Zimbabwe. The IAPF, Mander reasoned, would best serve the animals of Africa by educating and training local scouts and rangers, both state and private varieties, on the 'proper' way to wage a war on African poachers – specifically, by tracking and hunting. Therefore, the IAPF was premised on what Mander perceives as the inadequacy and failure of already established anti-poaching units – that is, Africans simply do not know what they are doing and therefore need to learn the advanced military and policing skills of a Western trained, combat proven soldier and hunter of men.[3] In fact, it is Mander's 'lessons from Baghdad' that he learned in 'liberating' the Iraqi people from a vicious Hussein regime that must now be repurposed to 'save' wildlife from an equally vicious regime of African poachers – regardless of the type of poacher. As he states, 'Baghdad is very different to the bush of Africa but many of the principles of security and policing that we applied there can be applied against poachers in Africa' (quoted in Taylor 2012).

The narratives of Mander and the IAPF fail to recognise that the cultural, material and personal reasons for poaching vary (see Duffy and St John 2013; White 2013). Instead of acknowledging this, Mander and the IAPF lump all poachers together and claim that they all share an unethical 'mindset' and 'a distinct lack of conservational and ethical thinking' (IAPF website 2014). Indeed, Mander and the IAPF frequently and simplistically frame African poachers as callous, calculating and heartless individuals or members of advanced criminal organisations, who simply do not care about the welfare of Africa's 'exotic' wildlife. In countless journalistic accounts and IAPF documents, poachers exist in a state of discursive liminality between juridical subjects, such as 'criminals' and 'offenders', and 'warring subjects', such as enemies, targets, and insurgents. As the central discursive context of IAPF, Mander's previous military career and war experiences paint a picture of faceless but ruthless and highly securitised poachers that emanate from outside the surroundings of the 'protected area' or Zimbabwe entirely. Poachers, for the IAPF, are nothing less than an enemy of war. Mander embraces and actively helps to cultivate this image of the militarised and highly organised poaching groups, arguing that the IAPF provides the best approach and should be a welcomed anti-poaching strategy:

> If we're to save the rhino, we really have no choice other than employ these kinds of tactics against the poachers. Rangers can no longer function like a bunch of boy scouts in the bush. We're no longer dealing with amateurs here; we're dealing with professional criminals who have access to the latest technology. They've militarized their assault on rhino so we must militarize our response against them. (Taylor 2012)

---

3   Currently, the IAPF has at least two training schools intended not only to provide 'better' anti-poaching tactics, but also to professionalise the field of anti-poaching by providing various certifications and qualifications. In addition, the IAPF partners with a variety of other conservation organisations, including Conservation Guardians and Eco-Rangers – a group similar to the IAPF that was formed by Johan 'JC' Strauss, one of the controversial pioneers of militarised anti-poaching tracking in Africa.

Yet, the IAPF also maintains an image of subsistence poachers as criminal offenders living within local communities, and the organisation takes great pride in the fact it actively tries to 'rehabilitate' and 'reeducate' subsistence poachers and then 'redeploy' them as anti-poaching rangers. But, as mentioned above, Zimbabwe's military and police forces and park rangers have long been associated with their own fair share of wildlife poaching (Duffy 2000) – at least, as recently as 2010. This well-documented fact is not included in IAPF narratives, however – something that is not at all surprising considering the IAPF's close, but at times contentious, partnerships with the Zimbabwean government. Thus, from the IAPF's perspective, the local communities surrounding the parks and reserves where the IAPF operate represent threats to wildlife and therefore need close attention through pedagogical policing – a perspective made apparent by Mander's statement concerning IAPF plans to co-manage the Chizarira National Park with Parks and Wildlife: 'Today, Chizarira stands at a critical point; it is on the brink of being consumed by the communities that surround it. A proven, yet externally oriented approach to implementing and managing a park plan for Chizarira is required immediately'.

Regardless of the particular figure of the African 'poacher' constructed by the IAPF and other fortress conservationists, the IAPF is, first and foremost, a manhunting organisation. Whether the poacher is deemed a local individual or a member of an organised poaching unit is irrelevant to the IAPF. For the IAPF, the best way to combat poachers and hence save African wildlife is through the practice of pursuit. IAPF-trained scouts and rangers are said to be highly skilled manhunting professionals turning the pursuit of the hunt back onto the criminalised poachers. In January 2014, the IAPF was featured in the inaugural episode of The Discovery Channel's new series, *Lone Target*, where IAPF manhunters put their skills to the test by tracking an ex-Navy Seal through the African safari. Bestowing the Western trained man-hunter with a beastliness surpassing the violence of the lion, an IAPF-trained ranger has stated, 'It is better for the poachers if they meet a lion than if they meet us' (Gwin 2012). Hence, the IAPF, with its neocolonial sensibilities, promotes the belief that the best way to save and preserve African wildlife from poaching is through a weaponisation of conservation that is dependent on the predatory technology of the manhunt.

Mander has even suggested that his supreme empathy for African wildlife, such as elephants and rhinos, comes directly from his own experiences of being hunted in war: 'I know what it feels like to be hunted by humans and so I'm able to sympathise with animals that are hunted by poachers' (Taylor 2012). Here, Mander engages in a sort of zoomorphism, wherein his personal history as a veteran of war provides, what he feels to be, not only a strategic advantage stemming from empathic advantage, but also a unique insight into the *feelings* of hunted animals. What is particularly interesting in Mander's conceptualisation of the interplay in the hunt between humans and non-human animals is the way that his assumed insights into the feelings of prey allow him to understand himself as something uniquely other than the 'Great White Hunter' trope common in Western art, literature and popular discourse produced in the early–mid twentieth century. The great white hunters romanticised in the fiction of Haggard, Hemingway, and Household,[4] of course, primarily hunted animals on the African plains, while Mander's IAPF, when viewed with an awareness of colonial power, privilege, and aggression, becomes a reformulated version of the great white hunter – one that turns the hunter's eye away from the lion, rhino, and elephant and toward the black and brown human bodies of subaltern Africa.

In *Manhunts: A Philosophical History* (2012), Grégoire Chamayou discusses the powerful role that pursuit and capture has played throughout history, from antiquity to the capitalist order. Indeed, the 'world historical importance of the manhunt' (Neocleous 2013: 14) is demonstrated in the ways that capitalist order has quite literally been built on and continues to be built through the logic of pursuit. As a technology of predation, Chamayou shows the ways that the hunt extends and perpetuates relations of domination, as the notion of the chase implies a dominant hunter tracking a fleeing and weaker prey.[5] The practice of the hunt is premised, though, on theories of the selected prey that also work to classify and demarcate those who can/should or cannot/should not be hunted.

The powerful allure of the manhunt, then, is important in situating the IAPF within the larger historical context of colonial domination and capitalist accumulation – a violent history that was often premised on the practice of hunting down the indigenous people, slaves, migrants, and other dispossessed, 'disorderly' subjects. In his discussion on the 'chief moments of primitive accumulation', Marx mentions how Africa became a 'warren for the commercial hunting of black skins …' (1867/1976: 915). With this in mind, Mander's IAPF becomes a perfect contemporary illustration. Of course, the IAPF is certainly not hunting African 'poachers' for the profit of their 'black skins', which was the case with the political economy of chattel slavery. Yet, the hunt for poachers is directed at fabricating and protecting the market of 'legitimate' big game forged mostly by the white wealthy of the Global North, as well as the fortress conservationist industry of wildlife parks and safari tourism. If at the heart of primitive accumulation is the separation of local peoples from traditional means of subsistence that exist outside capitalist relations, the IAPF perpetuates this historical structure of domination in the present through the hunting logics and practices of the contemporary war on poachers. Capital seeks this separation, of course, to construct social order and further capitalist control of resources and to transform labourers into wage workers.

---

4   The trope of the 'great white hunter' made its first notable appearance in Hemingway's *The Short Happy Life of Francis Macomber* (1936). The archetype reappeared three years later in Geoffrey Household's *Rogue Male* (that the first film adaptation of the novel was titled *Man Hunt* makes a compelling case for the historic conflation of the great white hunter archetype with that of the man-hunter). H. Rider Haggard made a career out of the trope, placing his great white hunter/hero, Allan Quartermain, in a series of novels, beginning with *King Solomon's Mines* (1950).

5   On this point, see also Neocleous (2013b).

Hunting from Above

Ultimately, Mander is optimistic about the possibility of the IAPF successfully eradicating poaching by drawing parallels to the 'successes of Iraq': 'People said Iraq would never get better, and that's happening. I'm taking the long view here too' (Gwin 2012). Yet, Mander and the IAPF also admit a certain level of immediate defeat – they tell a story that depicts poachers as simply too technologically advanced as well as determined and ruthless and the African bush too thick with foliage and brush and too geographically vast for IAPF scouts to adequately hunt and capture poachers. The IAPF, then, is constantly hunting for donations to support 'technological fixes' to what they admit are, yet simultaneously seem to disregard, complex problems of political economy, cultural tradition, and state power. One such technological fix that has put the IAPF 'on the map', so to speak, and has garnered the organisation much media attention, has been the aerial drone or Unmanned Aerial Vehicle (UAV).

If the fenced obstruction fails to adequately protect wildlife, and if the underfunded security tactics of anti-poaching hunts are only moderately successful, the IAPF contends that African wildlife can be best secured by 'repurposing' and 'redeploying' military-style aerial drones that have proven so central and controversial in the occupations of Iraq, Afghanistan, and Pakistan, as well as the occupation of Gaza. Mander (2013: 55) has stated that his 'vision is that one day, soon, wildlife everywhere will have a watchful eye flying overhead, just as our soldiers have on the battlefield'. As one increasingly influential conservationist group, the 'IAPF intends to make these advances available to conservation' (Mander 2013: 54). A piece Mander penned for the magazine *Africa Geographic*, is instructive. We quote at length:

> Heavily armed Tanzanian poachers cross the border illegally to take advantage of the remoteness that engulfs us. Our lack of resources makes me want to scream with frustration and I start to wonder: why could a drone protect me in Iraq, but these ancient creatures can't drink from a water-hole without the threat of a heavy-calibre bullet ripping through soft tissue, skull and eventually brain matter? I no longer wear a uniform, carry the gear that would give an attack on an insurgent position a better-than-average chance of success, or have access to a helicopter gunship. I'm barefoot, my hair has grown out and there is an old Czech-made AK-47 with worn wooden grips at my side. I haven't been deployed by any army and no longer take home a wage. This is a war being fought by a select few and there are no joining papers to sign. All that exists is a deep understanding of what needs to be done. Right now that means bringing to conservation the technology that has transformed the regular battlefield. (Mander 2013: 53)

Mander (2013: 54) writes how the morning after they ran their first test flights, a new IAPF drone 'located the embers of a poacher's campfire' and an anti-poaching unit of the Lugenda Wildlife Reserve was dispatched, located the poachers, and then arrested them. According to media reports, the IAPF currently possesses three small aerial drones, custom built by Simon Beart, a former Royal Navy helicopter technician and now IAPF member. But Mander (2013: 55) writes that this is only the start, since a:

> longer-range UAV would be especially helpful in patrolling the reserve's vast areas ... Envisage a drone with a 20-hour endurance flying time patrolling endless grids across the bush. Live feedback is channeled through software that distinguishes between human and animal shapes and movement, and alerts the staff to any incursions. The drone locks onto the target and guides ground teams into position while the entire incident is recorded. Now imagine this technology injected into the rhino wars raging further south ...

Yet, as the good soldier, Mander understands that the anti-poaching drones must always be tethered to the ground – as all air power is – so that the anti-poaching patrols can become 'specialised reaction units' that would be 'on constant standby to interpret and respond to real-time intelligence', effectively bolstering the hunt for African poachers on the ground. Whereas pre-aerial drone days were characterised by rangers patrolling and 'waiting to bump into something (a two-day-old footprint or worse, the mutilated carcass of an animal)', the conservation drone allows the IAPF to 'peek over the horizon' and allow the manhunters on the ground to be more efficient (Mander 2013: 54).[6]

The weaponisation of conservation, coupled with the nascent anti-poaching drone, extends and perpetuates not only the practice of the hunt, but the relations of domination that the hunt depends upon and exploits. The aerial drone, whether the 'hunter-killer drone' of the military or the emerging domestic police drone that as of now most resembles the IAPF drone, is a technology that is structured and animated by the logic of pursuit and predation (see Chamayou 2011; Wall 2013). That is, security drones are quintessential hunting technologies. Here, the hunt for individual bodies or small groups takes flight into what Weizman (2007) calls the politics of verticality, itself a logic undergirding relations of domination and occupation. The drone is often framed as technology of both precision and legibility, and the IAPF vision of the drone stays true to this by implying that the anti-poaching drone will make more legible the African landscape and those who traverse it illegally.

More substantively, drone advocates, including Mander, suggest that these aerial hunting systems provide visual truth, accuracy, and objectivity. But the scopics of drones are highly partial and inaccurate systems in that they enact what

---

6   The anti-poaching drone is said to alleviate strained resources and make for more efficient patrols. Of course, the emergence of the anti-poaching drone is loaded with problems, just as the military drone in combat has proven to be: they often lose contact with their controllers and crash unexpectedly.

Derek Gregory (2011: 173) dubs the 'techno-cultural production of targets'. That is, drones are always limited by their technical capacities and the cultural scripts that identify what is a legitimate and illegitimate target, and they often identify subjects-as-objects on the ground. In drone warfare proper, this is most clearly seen in the accumulating atrocities associated with dead civilians. It is too early to tell how the problems of the scopic register might exactly play out in anti-poaching efforts, but there is a better-than-good chance that the drone war on poachers will resemble the more standard drone war with its own fair share of mistaken identities, 'collateral damage', and racialised targeting logics.[7]

While the IAPF drones are smaller and unarmed and hence seemingly unlike the larger Predator and Reaper 'hunter-killer' drones that are armed with missiles, we must not see this as evidence that anti-poaching drones are somehow less political and less problematic technologies than military drones. Due to their constant link to those hunters on the ground, the pure surveillance drone remains at once a hunter of humans. In addition, most military drones are micro-drones – unarmed and used primarily for intelligence-gathering and surveillance, and to support ground troops – a fact that does not absolve them of complicity in state violence, but actually bolsters said violence. Moreover, militaries are no longer happy with surveillance-only micro-drones and are now working towards arming micro-drones. We can also point to the efforts already underway to arm US and British domestic law enforcement micro-drones with both lethal and non-lethal technology, such as shotguns and stun guns (Wall 2013).

Just as much as the IAPF is in no way the only example of the weaponisation of conservation, the IAPF drone programme is but one example where conservationists are trying to repurpose drones for anti-poaching efforts. Recently, it was announced that Google awarded the World Wildlife Fund (WWF) $5 million to purchase several aerial drones to be used for anti-poaching efforts in various locations in Africa and Nepal (Rosen 2012; Ungerleider 2012). 'Conservation drones' are also being used over forests and wildlife in Thailand (Gray 2012). The emergence of the anti-poaching, conservationist, drone is not all that surprising when situated within the history of using airplanes and helicopters, and even hang gliders, in the war on poachers. This history includes not only the use of aerial surveys to map and count carcasses, but also for the surveillance of poachers, and at times death from above. Here, we are specifically thinking of these controversial conservation tactics as used by researchers Mark and Delia Owens (Goldberg 2010), along with the World Wildlife Fund's controversial donation of an anti-poaching helicopter that ended with a poacher being killed from above (Duffy 2000). Interestingly, yet unsurprisingly, most of the media reporting we have come across, including coverage of the IAPF's drone program, as well as the WWF's planned use of

---

7 Military planners and technology development firms frequently respond to criticisms of these – and other – 'bugs' in current drone technology with a bit of tautology that advocates for increased investment in these technologies in order to 'work out the bugs'.

drones, takes anti-poaching drones as an unqualified good largely due to a blind acceptance of the terms circumscribing the popular imaginary of poaching. This also serves as a powerful demonstration of the allure and force of, and connections between, conservationist discourse and discourses of security.

A Civilised Project: Police, War, Pacification

Even though there is a clear militarised aspect to the IAPF, it is also an organisation invested in the logic of police – and by police we mean not only what is usually thought of as *the* police, but also the broader and historically older notion of police that is concerned with the governing of the welfare and health of populations (Foucault 2007) and the fabrication of capitalist social order (Neocleous 2000). And even though the IAPF defines anti-poaching units as a 'law enforcement element that has the direct responsibility of wildlife protection in a designated area' and the IAPF teaches courses on crime scene preservation and other standard law enforcement procedures, they are guided by both understandings of police. Similarly, even though the IAPF trains students on military tactics and lethal force, Mander is quick to point out that he does not advocate for the shoot-to-kill policies adopted in some African countries, including Zimbabwe. Instead, he prefers negotiation tactics and police search and seizure procedures – that is, he subscribes to the liberal narrative of rule of law and Western exceptionalism. As Mander explains, 'We are teaching the *correct* escalation of lethal force. This is preserving human life as well as wildlife. In many African countries they have orders to shoot poachers on sight' (quoted in Keeton 2011). As Mander has stated, 'we are re-training rangers in a [*sic*] ethical way ... we push home ... things like human rights and prohibition against torture and use of force' (*Sixty Minutes* 2010). When his rangers are forced to confront the violence of poachers, they can be approached, as he says, 'humanely (like in the Western culture), which is something completely new to the people we are training, but I think it is essential' (*Sixty Minutes* 2010). This notion that the IAPF is just as much invested in police power and the accountability of law as they are militarised power serves the IAPF by allowing it to frame its project as a more 'civilised' and democratic – albeit militarised – anti-poaching project. Here, we see how the weaponisation of conservation is not simply about a militarisation, but also about the insidious ways liberalised policing logics play their own distinct role in normalising and legitimating poaching as predominately an issue of security and order.

On this point, we should also be careful not to think of the conservation drone in IAPF and other anti-poaching efforts as only a militarisation – that is, as *solely* a manifestation of a military logic. Rather, the anti-poaching drone is just as much circumscribed by the logic of police power that is linked to war power through the logic of security and that aims to actively fabricate a social order. Indeed, air power has long been a police power (Neocleous 2013a). As Neocleous (2013a: 582), has recently argued, 'More or less from its very inception air power has been structured around the police concept'. Put another way: although most histories of air power trace its origins to military power, often speaking of the Second World War as the crucial historical moment, air power was originally conceived by its earliest proponents in Britain and the US as an explicit police technology to be used to govern – to police – the colonised. More specifically, Neocleous shows how in the 1920s, many of the debates taking place in metropoles concerning colonial populations framed air power as a police technology deployed to pacify indigenous peoples and fabricate order by crushing rebellions and policing minor resistances, separating the indigenous from traditional means of production, conducting aerial surveillance including land surveys and censuses, and winning hearts and minds through moral effect. And importantly, air power as police power was not only discussed, but actually exercised, by metropoles in the securing of a slew of colonised territories. Indeed, from what we can tell, this argument of air power as police power has merit when considering the ways helicopters and airplanes, and recently hang gliders and now drones, have been used in anti-poaching efforts.

In addition, our earlier argument about the logic of the hunt is buttressed by the IAPF as police power. Indeed, at its foundation, police power is the power to hunt – to track, pursue, chase, seize, and capture and often kill human prey (Chamayou 2012). Thinking of police power as a hunting power intervenes in the common practice of conflating law with police. That is, the IAPF appeals to a legal discourse of 'human rights' and restraints on 'use of force', yet when the IAPF's police power is situated within the movements of the hunt, this legal trope can be called into question. As Chamayou (2012: 90) argues, 'because the police, as a power of pursuit, does not deal with legal subjects but rather bodies in movement, bodies that escape and that it must catch, bodies that pass by and that it must intercept', police power is first and foremost a hunting power that often understands law as an external limit on its power to hunt. 'To be an efficient hunter', Chamayou (2012: 90) continues, 'one must pursue prey despite the law, and even against it'. If the police are inherently about order, then the hunt – the police pursuit – has long been a prime way in which disorderly subjects are ordered, despite the constraints of the law. The state of ambiguity in which the IAPF seems to operate – as either a paramilitary or police organisation – is reconciled through the logic of the hunt. The technology of the hunt animates both war power and police power (Neocleous 2013; Wall 2013), and in this sense, the IAPF can be seen as hunters of men who hunt four-legged animals. To successfully hunt 'poachers' to the fullest extent, the powers of war and police are, so to speak, 'fair game'.

Yet, regardless of the civilising police discourse, much of the IAPF's initiatives and tactics are clearly political and controversial. Although receiving less media attention than the security hunts for 'poachers', especially the drone programme that has received significant press in its own right, the IAPF has initiated campaigns aimed at governing the health and welfare of locals by educating local and global citizens on the importance of conservation and promoting conservation volunteerism. Indeed, it is important to point out that although the IAPF is modelled after security training, tactics, language and aesthetics, this organisation maintains other 'community conservation' initiatives less overtly securitised and aimed at winning the 'hearts and minds' of both local Africans and those in the Global North. These initiatives include a beading necklace project to empower local women, school resource materials for educating children on wildlife conservation, a 'philanthropy challenge' for children, and fundraisers, such as the 'Rock and Ride for Rhinos' concert and motorcycle event. Moreover, one of the central goals of the IAPF website is to educate the global community, while also soliciting needed items, such as backpacks, night vision, computers, knives, GPS devices, and various administrative materials.

In addition, the IAPF has created a volunteer programme called the 'Green Army' designed for individuals from near and far to 'come ... to the frontline and be a part of this mission' and 'be integrated into the lifestyle of an anti-poaching ranger' (IAPF website 2014). Although these Green Army volunteers are unarmed, due to state laws against foreign gun possession, part of their duties is to assist the anti-poaching units during patrols, wildlife monitoring, and fence checks. Yet, Green Army members are also asked to help the IAPF's efforts by providing their own form of expertise, whatever that might be, such as fundraising, animal medicine, conservation research, or community education expertise. These 'softer' tactics of the IAPF fit within a larger move within fortress conservationist organisations to help decentre the 'harder' approaches of this weaponised conservation and therefore the consent of local peoples. As Brockington (2002: 3) states, recent fortress conservation approaches are taking more efforts 'to provide for peoples' needs around protected areas in order to win local support'.

Considering the security fetishism of the IAPF and its patronising neocolonialism, this organisation's educational campaigns can usefully be understood as a 'more friendly' form of weaponisation geared towards the production of consent and smoother administration of both local and global actors. We might say, then, that fortress conservationist approaches to anti-poaching, of which the IAPF is but one contemporary example, constitute a project of pacification – if pacification is understood as it was historically developed by colonial regimes (see Neocleous 2011) – as a practice simultaneously deploying coercive strategies, such as policing and military tactics, and those more 'peaceful' strategies, such as providing education and food to locals in order to 'win hearts and minds' so that larger goals are secured, such as accumulation and territorial control, and ostensibly in this case, the securing of ecology.

Conclusion

Adams and McShane (1992: 130) have written that, 'The war on poachers will always fall just a little short of its goals, for no matter how well equipped the game scouts may be, with high-tech tents and camping equipment, radios, helicopters, and airplanes, it will never be enough'. Although we think this sentiment is correct in terms of the war on poachers ultimately failing to effectively stop the problems of poaching, Adams and McShane presume that the eradication of poaching is in fact the actual goal of anti-poaching efforts. Perhaps this is so, but it seems to us that the war on poaching in Africa is less about 'poaching' per se, and more about the fabrication of a social order where local social relations are transformed to meet the mandates of capitalist order as constructed by elite 'conservation consumers', local and state authorities, and fortress conservationists. In this sense, anti-poaching projects are part and parcel of capitalist political economy.

A *National Geographic* journalist has suggested that since Mander is no longer a professional soldier, but a conservationist, his 'Seek and Destroy' tattoo should instead read 'Seek & Save' (Gwin 2012). Yet, as we have attempted to suggest above, the IAPF demonstrates that the 'saving' of wildlife, along with the policing of 'natives', is itself understood as first and foremost a neocolonial security offensive, where saving rhinos and elephants from on the ground or in the air threats means nothing less than the hunting of those deemed unruly, unethical, and illegitimate 'hunters'. Similarly, the IAPF and Mander starkly demonstrate how the cultural capital associated with the manly, racialised security offensives in 'geographies of horror' such as Iraq – another war of accumulation – is so easily converted into the practice and representation of conservation that its weaponisation in Africa is seen as the best and only way to preserve not only 'wildlife', but 'human life'.

It is also important to note that many of the anti-poaching efforts underway in Africa – particularly those of the IAPF – reflect a decidedly anthropocentric ecophilosophical positioning. The language and logics deployed by the IAPF rarely – if ever – illustrate an organisational recognition of the inherent and natural value of non-human lives, instead focusing on the value of conservation for human interests; these are not efforts undertaken to advance or instantiate an egalitarian ideal of inter-species protection, but rather to delineate and reify the social divisions that dictate *who* can kill these animals without fear of a militarised reprisal. In a contemporary Africa that sees revenue streams estimated as high as $200 million annually from legal 'trophy hunting' (*Economists at Large* 2013), a 'sport' popular with wealthy American and European hunters, the manhunting approach of the IAPF that ignores the deaths of countless legally killed animals – focusing instead solely on 'poaching' – cannot be said to be motivated by ecocentric or biocentric philosophical concerns (Halsey and White 1998). Instead, such an approach should be seen as an anthropocentrically minded securitising scheme to enforce a sociolegal and socioeconomic order developed in the shadow of colonial occupation and accumulation. Put simply, the IAPF does not concern itself so much with the senseless and violent deaths of non-human animals, provided that those doing the killing reflect the assumed conservationist nobility of European and American hunters, rather than the assumed ignorance and savagery of African poachers. Considered through the lens of the historical and securitising power of the 'manhunt', the IAPF is itself a hunting organisation, albeit one premised on the hunting of human prey rather than non-human animals – a distinction that seems to allow Mander and the IAPF to view itself as legitimate hunters, while simultaneously delegitimising the hunting practices of indigenous 'poachers'. If the IAPF are, in fact, (man)hunters in a concrete sense, the IAPF fails to fully legitimise itself discursively as an organisation that is 'anti-hunting'. Of course, the mandate of the IAPF is not or has never been 'anti-hunting' per se, but 'anti-poaching', and attention to the political construction of these two categories is key to understanding the IAPF project as one that problematically helps to demarcate lines between the legitimate hunter and the criminalised 'poacher'. The violent contradictions of this formation become clear with the words of one man captured for killing an elephant: 'How can you tell me I don't belong in a place where I've lived my whole life?' (quoted in Adams and McShane 1992: 122).

The central operating logic, then, in the war on poachers is security – where both military and police measures fabricate a social order set on securing not only the conservation of wildlife, but also a regime of accumulation based on wildlife tourism and 'legitimate' safari hunting. The central technology in operation here is the hunt for human prey, whereby certain human animals are singled out and tracked down along coercive lines of classification and demarcation. The security offensive that is the war on poachers then is not merely *against* poachers – it is simultaneously *for* accumulation. The hunt for poachers is a hunt for accumulation. The architectures of conservation are so compatible with the architectures of security that the logics of both conservation and security, at least it seems to us, must be rethought, and perhaps rejected outright. Hence, if Marx's proclamation that 'security is the supreme concept of bourgeois society' is particularly apt, as we believe it is, then we might find it useful to think through the ways that *security has become the supreme concept of conservation*. All of this begs the following question: What might a political ecology look like that is explicitly *against security* and *against conservation*?

References

Adams, J.S. and McShane, T.O. 1992. *The Myth of Wild Africa*. New York: W.W. Norton.

Brockington, D. 2002. *Fortress Conservation: The Preservation of the Mkomazi Game Reserve, Tanzania*. Bloomington, IN: Indiana University Press.

Chamayou, G. 2011. The manhunt doctrine (trans. Shane Lillis). *Radical Philosophy* 169: 2–6.

Chamayou, G. 2012. *Manhunts: A Philosophical History* (trans. Steven Rendall). Princeton and Oxford: Princeton University Press.

Conrad, J. 2010. *Heart of Darkness*. London: Macmillan.

Cronon, W. 1995. The trouble with wilderness; or, getting back to the wrong nature. In W. Cronon (ed.), *Uncommon Ground: Rethinking the Human Place in Nature*. New York: W.W. Norton, 69–90.

Duffy, R. 2000. *Killing for Conservation: Wildlife Policy in Zimbabwe*. Oxford: James Currey.

Duffy, R. and St. John, F. 2013. *Poverty, Poaching and Trafficking: What are the Links?* Report prepared for Evidence on Demand. Available at: http://eprints. soas.ac.uk/17836/1/EoD_HD059_Jun2013_Poverty_Poaching.pdf/. Accessed 7 January 2015.

Economists at Large. 2013. *The $200 Million Question: How Much Does Trophy Hunting Really Contribute to African Communities?* A report for the African Lion Coalition, prepared by Economists at Large, Melbourne, Australia.

Foucault, M. 2007. *Security, Territory, Population: Lectures at the Collège de France, 1977–1978*. New York: Picador.

Goldberg, J. 2010. The hunted. *The New Yorker*, 5 April. Available at: http://www. newyorker.com/reporting/2010/04/05/100405f.a_fact_goldberg/. Accessed 7 January 2015.

Gonzalez, C.G. 2013. Environmental justice and international environmental law. In S. Alam, Md Jahid Hossain Bhuiyan, T.M.R. Chowdhury and E.J. Techera (eds), *Routledge Handbook of International Environmental Law*. London: Routledge, 77–97.

Govender, P. 2012. South Africa deploys high-tech plane for rhino poaching fight. *Reuters, U.S. Edition*, 4 December. Available at: http://www.reuters.com/ article/2012/12/04/us-safrica-rhinos-idUSBRE8B30NI20121204/. Accessed 7 January 2015.

Gray, D.D. 2012. Conservation drones protect wildlife, spot poachers and track forest loss. *The Huffington Post*, 19 August. Available at: http://www. huffingtonpost.com/2012/08/19/conservation-drones_n_1806592.html/. Accessed 7 January 2015.

Gregory, D. 2011. From a view to a kill: drones and late modern war. *Theory, Culture, & Society* 28(7–8): 188–215.

Gwin, P. 2012. Rhino wars. *National Geographic Magazine*, March. Available at: http://ngm.nationalgeographic.com/print/2012/03/rhino-wars/gwin-text/. Accessed 7 January 2015.

Halsey, M. and White, R. 1998. Crime, ecophilosophy and environmental harm. *Theoretical Criminology* 2(3): 345–71.

International Anti-Poaching Foundation Website. 2014. Available at: http://www. iapf.org. Accessed 7 January 2015.

Keeton, C. 2011. Wildlife war zone hero. *Times Live*. Available at: http://www. timeslive.co.za/lifestyle/2011/10/02/wildlife-war-zone-hero/. Accessed 7 January 2015.

Lombard, L. 2012. Dying for ivory. *New York Times*, 20 September. Available at: http://www.nytimes.com/2012/09/21/opinion/elephants-dying-for-ivory. html?_r=0/. Accessed 7 January 2015.

Mander, D. 2013. Rise of the drones. *Africa Geographic*, February. Available at: http://www.iapf.org/images/documents/riseofthedronesjan2013.pdf/. Accessed 7 January 2015.

Marx K. 1867/1976. *Capital: A Critique of Political Economy*, vol. 1, trans. B Fowkes. Harmondsworth: Penguin.

Neocleous, M. 2008. *Critique of Security*. Montreal: McGill-Queen's University Press.

Neocleous, M. 2011. 'A brighter and nice new life': security as pacification. *Social & Legal Studies* 20(2): 191–208.

Neocleous, M. 2013a. Air power as police power. *Environment and Planning D: Society and Space* 31(4): 578–93.

Neocleous, M. 2013b. The dream of pacification: accumulation, class war, and the hunt. *Socialist Studies/Études Socialistes* 9(2): 7–31.

Perelman, M. 2000. *The Invention of Capitalism: Classical Political Economy and the Secret History of Primitive Accumulation*. Durham, NC: Duke University Press.

Razack, S. 2004. *Dark Threats and White Knights: The Somalia Affair, Peacekeeping and the New Imperialism*. Toronto: University of Toronto Press.

Rosen R.J. 2012. Google gives $5 million to drone program that will track poachers. *The Atlantic*, 11 December. Available at: http://www.theatlantic.com/technology/archive/2012/12/google-gives-5-million-to-drone-program-that-will-track-poachers/266133/. Accessed 7 January 2015.

Sixty Minutes. 2010. Chat: Damien Mander. *Sixty Minutes*, 5 October. Available at: http://sixtyminutes.ninemsn.com.au/article.aspx?id=8098935/. Accessed 7 January 2015.

Steinhart, E.I. 2006. *Black Poachers, White Hunters: A Social History of Hunting in Colonial Kenya*. Oxford: James Currey.

Taylor, D. 2012. Iraq War veteran battles rhino poachers in Africa. *Voice of America*, 19 January. Available at: http://www.voanews.com/content/iraq-war-veteran-battles-rhino-poachers-in-africa-138338229/159563.html/. Accessed 7 January 2015.

Ungerleider, N. 2012. The Google-funded drones that hunt illegal hunters. *Fast Company*, 10 December. Available at: http://www.fastcompany.com/3003870/google-funded-drones-hunt-illegal-hunters/. Accessed 7 January 2015.

Wall, T. 2013. Unmanning the police manhunt: vertical security as pacification. *Socialist Studies / Études socialistes* 9(2): 32–56.

Weizman, E. 2007. *Hollow Land: Israel's Architecture of Occupation*. London: Verso.

White, R. 2013. *Environmental Harm: An Eco-Justice Perspective*. Bristol: Policy Press.

Zedner, L. 2009. *Security*. London: Routledge.

PART IV
Conflict over
Natural Resources
Extraction Processes

Chapter 11

The Hidden Injuries of Mining: Frontier Cultural Conflict

Kerry Carrington, Russell Hogg and Alison McIntosh

This chapter addresses a topic of growing significance to green criminology – the harmful effects of mining on local communities and the environment (Long et al. 2012; Ruggiero and South 2013; Stretesky and Lynch 2011; White 2013a). While mining has long been recognised as an agent of environmental harm (White 2013a), less recognised is that its global expansion also has harmful effects on localised patterns of violence, work and community life in mining towns. Australia provides an excellent case study for exploring some of these mining impacts.

In recent decades, mining has been Australia's fastest growing industry sector, a function of the continent's rich endowment of natural resources and surging demand from China and other Asian nations for the resources needed to support their rapid economic development. Australia is currently the world's largest exporter of iron ore and is second only to Indonesia in the export of coal (BREE 2012; http://www.dfat.gov.au/publications/stats-pubs/australias-coal-and-iron-ore-exports-2001-to-2011.pdf). Mineral resources are non-renewable in that they do not renew themselves at sufficient rates for sustainable economic extraction in meaningful human time frames; as such, they can only be mined once. But their extraction (as well as their subsequent use) has manifold and enduring social and environmental effects. The idea that nothing should stand in the way of pursuing the short-term economic benefits of a relentlessly expanding mining sector is therefore problematic. Yet, this is the prevailing logic in Australian public policy; such is the economic and political might of the mining sector. Even the immediate national benefits are often illusory, exaggerated, very unevenly distributed and deeply uncertain given the notorious volatility of global resource markets. Nonetheless, mining has been allowed to cut a swathe through the Australian physical, social, economic and political landscape. Its processes have distorted economic development and created a 'two speed' economy in which other industries are disadvantaged (e.g., agriculture, education, manufacturing, tourism); biodiversity destroyed; waterways contaminated and cherished ecosystems and iconic natural heritage areas (like the Great Barrier Reef) threatened; government undermined in the public interest; other rural land uses (farming, vineyards) encroached upon; and nature reserves, state forests and even entire small communities swallowed up or otherwise destroyed (Pearse et al. 2013). This list of localised effects does not include the stark fact that the mining and burning of coal, in particular, pumps vast amounts of greenhouse gases into the atmosphere which, according to the Intergovernmental Panel on Climate Change (2013), is the dominant cause of anthropogenic global warming, making coal mining and use a major contributor to the long-term catastrophic threats of climate change.

Even as governments have mostly bowed before the power of the mining industry, significant new economic, social and cultural fissures and political battlegrounds have emerged in Australia: between resource-rich Australian states and others; between different land uses and economic sectors (agriculture and tourism on the one hand and resource extraction on the other); between corporate mining interests and novel alliances of farmers and environmentalists (Cleary 2012; White 2013a); between resident workers in traditional mining communities and new non-resident workforces; and, overarching all these, between competing and conflicting conceptions of the national interest and the role of government. This chapter will show, in particular, how non-resident resource sector workers have become emblematic of the destruction of communal solidarities caused by post-industrial mining regimes (Carrington et al. 2011). Many who otherwise feel powerless in the face of the might of the mining sector have taken the opportunity afforded by the Australian Federal Government's parliamentary inquiry into the use of fly in/fly out workforce practices which was launched in 2011 to vent their resentments and frustrations concerning the impact of post-industrial mining regimes on their communities. The resulting Windsor Inquiry Report, based on submissions received and public hearings conducted throughout Australia's mining regions and major cities, was tabled in February 2013 but the Federal Government is yet to act upon any of the report's 21 recommendations. The chapter draws on submissions to and findings of that inquiry, our earlier empirical research (i.e., Carrington, Hogg and McIntosh 2011) and case study material drawn from Bowen Basin mining communities in Queensland, to explore some of the harmful impacts of mining on local communities in Australia.

Mining, 'Supercapitalism' and Globalisation

According to US economist, Robert Reich, the age of democratic capitalism has given way to the age of 'supercapitalism', a phase in which economic power invades every domain of life, empowering people as investors and consumers, whilst weakening forms of collective life, public institutions and citizenship. As most countries – including those formerly belonging to the communist world – have become integrated into global capitalism, inequalities have widened, democracy has weakened, and private economic power threatens to eclipse the public good (Reich 2008: 4).

The resource sector is presently operating at the frontier of supercapitalism's transformative reach over not only Australia's economy, society, politics and intellectual life, but also economies in South America, Asia, Canada, Africa and the Pacific. Ruggiero and South (2013: 13) argue that neo-liberal discourses rationalise 'harm against humans and the environment' as the inevitable outcome of economic growth, such that effectively 'the entire planet is given to those who are most capable of exploiting it'. Examples include oil despoliation of the environment and the oceans (such as the 2010 BP oil spill in the Gulf of Mexico) and other criminogenic connections between oil and crime such as smuggling, oil theft and the corruption of officials (Ruggiero and South 2013: 15). Increasing global resource extraction has led to the dispossession of traditional owners from their lands and livelihoods in places like Brazil, Laos, Mozambique, Papua New Guinea, Peru and Sudan. In Western Australia, one of the big Australian iron ore miners, Fortescue Metals Group (FMG), funded an alternative Aboriginal advocacy group, the Wirlu-Murra, to contest the legitimacy of the Yindjibarndi Aboriginal Corporation's successful land rights claim on land that FMG wanted to mine (Cleary 2012: 123). The global mining corporations involved have no long-term commitment to any state or society. Strategic investment decisions are often made a hemisphere away from the operations and societies affected, but their power overwhelms the voices and interests of local communities, whether in Africa or Australia. Although power imbalances, lack of regulation and transparency and their malign effects are more extreme in the 'developing' world, these problems are manifest wherever corporate miners operate (Tombs and Whyte 2010). To deal with such conflicts, some have urged the establishment of an International Environment Court, to operate under United Nations Conventions in the same way as the International Criminal Court (White 2013b). Others have suggested that Australia sign the Extractive Industries Transparency Initiative (EITI), strengthen regulation of the industry and independently monitor the conditions attached to mine approvals (Cleary 2012). While many 'developed' nations, including Australia, contribute funds to the EITI through aid, none – with the exception of Norway – are signatories (Department of Foreign Affairs and Trade 2012).

Forces may be grossly unevenly matched, but this does not preclude local resistance, greater (rather than less) socially responsible corporate activity, and practical social and legal policy interventions that might more effectively regulate the mining industry. The operation of global power is riddled with contradictions and vulnerabilities that carry heterogeneous and sometimes unpredictable effects (Thayer 2010: 4). Transnational social movements such as Amnesty International, Greenpeace, Human Rights Watch and a range of NGOs supported by the United Nations have been growing in number and influence, as have local forms of resistance such as Mining Communities United (MCU) in Queensland and Lock the Gate, a broad alliance of landholders and environmentalists established to fight the spread of the coal seam gas industry in Australia (see Manning 2013). To travel the mining frontier in Australia is to uncover myriad expressions of resistance: from farmers, residents of small, vulnerable rural towns, horse breeding associations, winegrowers, commercial fishers and others new to the ranks of protest against the post-industrial model of rapid, unconstrained development represented by the big corporate miners. Mining is even dispensing with the very communities spawned by the modern mining industry and which have constituted such a distinctive and vital part of its history until recently.

The Mining Boom/Bust Cycle

Australia is no stranger to mining booms. From the gold rushes of the 1850s, which brought with it the first big wave of free immigrant settlers to the colonies, mining booms have punctuated Australian history and made a significant contribution to population growth, economic development, and the establishment of towns, transport networks and other infrastructure in the sparsely populated interior (Blainey 1969). Nor is Australia a stranger to the dangers of the mining industry, which have not only periodically led to terrible human tragedy but also underlined the unique traditions and solidarities of mining communities. Mine collapses causing mass deaths in small, tightly knit communities have been a recurrent feature of the coal industry over its history in Australia (Murray and Peetz 2010: 36–8). The shift to open-cut mining alongside a safer mining culture has done much to reduce the incidence of these workplace harms, but the advent of post-industrial mining regimes has created new risks, whilst also contriving to externalise them in what is a fiercely competitive global sector. This has seen the current Australian mining boom contribute to the record profits enjoyed by the very big companies (like BHP Billiton and Rio Tinto) and by many second order miners, although economic performance remains prey to the boom/bust cycle endemic to the industry. The boom has also delivered high incomes to resource sector workers (on average in excess of A\$100,000 per annum), which are necessary to attract labour in a tight market and to compensate for increasingly precarious conditions of employment. Federal government policies – in areas like taxation, workplace legislation and immigration – have bowed to the imperative of resource sector expansion. This probably just further encourages impatient industry demands to, inter alia, 'cut red tape' and provide 'certainty' (code for gutting approvals processes); reduce costs (i.e., curtail union power and further de-regulate the labour market); abolish climate change measures that impinge industry profits (notably the Labor Government's tax on carbon); and alter immigration laws to permit the industry to employ increased numbers of overseas workers. The 'rush to be rich', to cash in on Australia's mineral and energy wealth, is leaving many questions about the darker side of the resource boom unasked and unanswered in the public domain (Cleary 2011). The tendency to treat this as just the latest in a long line of mining booms (bigger and better than earlier ones) has deflected attention from the fundamentally changed character and effects of mining development or what we have termed the advent of 'post-industrial mining regimes'.

Post-industrial Mining Regimes

Australia is the most sparsely populated continent in the world. Roughly the physical size of China, it has a population of only 23 million people, 85 per cent of whom live within 50 kilometres of the coast, mostly on the eastern seaboard and in a pocket in the south west of the country. Until the 1970s, it was an accepted principle of national development policy that Australian state governments would only issue mining leases subject to conditions that companies build or substantially finance local community infrastructure, including housing, streets, transport, schools, hospitals and recreation facilities. Townships and communities went hand in hand with mining development. During the boom of the 1960s and early 1970s, some 25 new mining settlements were established in various regions of Australia (Houghton 1983) to accommodate workers and their families. But the 1980s saw the establishment of the last of these towns, Roxby Downs in South Australia (Storey 2001). Initially the use of non-resident workers (NRW) was mostly confined to remote gold mining in Western Australia (Houghton 1993). Then in 1991, Queensland removed the requirement for companies to provide homes for workers when developing new mines (ABC 2006). By 2000, many types of mining operations (including iron ore and nickel projects in Western Australia and coal in Queensland) had adopted non-resident workforce arrangements (Storey 2001).

Under the growing influence of global economic forces, mining companies have moved increasingly to adopt an expeditionary strategy with respect to all aspects of their mining operations. This intensifies reliance on NRWs and contract labour in place of traditional employment relationships that in the past bound companies and workers together to form a socially cohesive industry, even if it was characterised by intermittent industrial conflict. Non-resident, contract workforces are now routinely used not only for construction and maintenance but also for mining operations. Western Australian data for 2009 indicate that contractors comprised 56 per cent (around 40,000) of mining personnel. Contractors have represented the majority of this sector's workers since 2001–02 (Western Australian Department of Mines and Petroleum 2009). In Queensland, the percentage of contractors rose from 6 per cent in 1996 to almost 50 per cent in 2005 (Murray and Peetz 2010: 18). The steep rise in use of contractors in the resources sector was in part spurred by new workplace relations laws introduced by the former Howard conservative government (Murray and Peetz 2010: 22).

Accurate data in relation to the mining workforce are hard to come by, as the Windsor Inquiry (2013) found with respect to the number of workers directly employed by the resources sector, let alone the numbers of NRWs and their patterns of work and modes of travel. Data are not collected about NRWs in any form by the Australian Bureau of Statistics (ABS) or any other federal government body. Forecast work numbers are equally elusive (McIntosh and Carrington 2014). Moreover, the mining industry workforce as identified by the ABS using the Australian and New Zealand Standard Industrial Classification (ANZSIC) does not include tens of thousands of others directly employed by the resources sector for activities such as surveying, construction of new and expansion projects, transportation, processing, maintenance, and work camp accommodation (e.g., catering, cleaning, management, security). We estimate that there were around 348,500 workers (including mining-allied workers) in the resources sector in 2012 (see Table 11.1, Appendix 1). The ratio for mining-allied workers to mining industry workers (using ABS 2013a: Cat. No. 6291.0 four-quarterly averages) is 1:3. We also estimate that nearly two out of three (64.5 per cent or 224,700 workers) of those directly employed by the sector in 2012 were NRWs. These figures are based on ABS statistics and also on assumptions informed by our long-term analysis of other publicly available data.

Notwithstanding claims in relation to the employment opportunities provided by the industry, mining does not employ large numbers of workers, accounting for only around 3.3 per cent of the full-time Australian workforce (ABS 2013a). Nevertheless, resource sector employment has grown sharply in recent years. Indeed, full-time mining industry employment increased by over 80 per cent in the five years from February 2007 (132,900 workers) to February 2012 (243,385 workers). Latest available ABS data to November 2013 show further growth to 268,900 full-time workers (ABS 2013a). Although the number of females in the industry has risen in recent years, mostly in clerical and administrative positions, it remains dominated by men. In February 2012, 85 per cent of full-time employees were males (ABS 2013a).

The advantages to industry and government of non-resident workforces have been well documented. They include the physical isolation and short project life of some mines, difficulties of sourcing labour, avoiding costs of construction and maintenance of purpose-built towns, and reducing industrial disputes (BHP Billiton 2009; Gillies et al. 1991; Jackson 1987; Kinhill Engineers 1991; Storey 2001, 2008; Storey and Shrimpton 1989). Alongside radical structural shifts in employment practices, the organisation of work itself – the 7-day, 35-hour working week won by coal miners in a historic 1970 industrial victory (Murray and Peetz 2010: 13) – has been transformed into multiple-week block rosters of 12-hour shifts to support continuous 24/7 production processes. From 1985 to 2012, the proportion of mining industry employees working a 'standard' week of 30–39 hours (or less) declined from 50 per cent of the industry's workforce to 30 per cent (ABS 2013a). During the same period, the proportion working 50 hours or more rose from 20 per cent to 53 per cent. By November 2012, 70 per cent of the mining industry workforce worked 40 hours or more per week (ABS 2013a).

More flexible work arrangements are part of a larger global trend in the pattern of employment in a post-industrial world (Louis et al. 2006: 456). Often flexible work conditions translate into precarious employment that can adversely impact worker health and well-being, occupational health and safety, union membership, job satisfaction, gender equity and skills development (Louis et al. 2006: 466–7).

In crude terms, the mining industry has been at the forefront of a trend to encourage trading of rights, security and conditions in exchange for higher wages. A longer term, more holistic view of the role of work in relation to well-being, personal identity, family and community is giving way to a narrower, shorter-term focus on immediate economic benefits. Precarious work practices may have a range of diffuse, often hidden consequences for individuals and communities, even if work is generously rewarded in economic terms (Offe 1985; Sennett 1998).

The organisation of production and employment in the mining industry has been recast over the last two decades. The term 'post-industrial' captures these qualitative shifts and their attendant ramifications for the structures of economy, work, family, community and governance, involving transition from relative stability and predictability in these domains of life to increasing uncertainty, insecurity and risk. In a short time, the mining sector has gone from being one of the most highly unionised and regulated in Australia to one now heavily reliant on contractors, precarious employment practices and industry self-regulation (Murray and Peetz 2010). These changes affect individual workers but they also have major consequences for families and the structure, associational life and social capital of communities. Kelly Vea Vea (2013), the founding President of Mining Communities United, describes the impact of 12-hour shifts:

> Sporting clubs and community volunteering have been hit hard. The rosters and shift length leave little free time for any activities during your 'tour' [the work cycle of the roster]. Days off [in the leave cycle] are inconsistent, so it's rather difficult to make commitments to organisations.

The impact of block rosters and 12-hour shifts are exacerbated for fly in, fly out (FIFO) and drive-in/drive-out (DIDO) workers, their families and communities. The extended roster system has hugely disruptive effects on source communities, where women in the main are left to single-handedly raise families while their partners spend large blocks of time at worksites hundreds or thousands of kilometres away. The impacts on individual workers, partners and families in these source communities are even more under-researched than those relating to host mining communities. Doubtless it is simply assumed that workers choose this lifestyle due to the economic incentives and with an understanding of the trade-offs involved. This may be true for many, although increasingly, mining workers are not given the choice of living in the communities in which they work. Even existing residents of mining towns are often excluded as a matter of policy from employment in local mines, so that their only choice if they are to work in the industry is to leave and return as NRWs. Very high labour turnover rates suggest that many find this mode of employment unsustainable but the reasons for this – and the costs, risks and harms involved – are submerged in what are taken to be the private economic decisions of individual workers.

Turnover rates for the industry have swollen in recent years. Reasons cited for this include the ageing of the mining workforce (Beach et al. 2003; Kinetic Group 2012; NRSET 2010) and chronic health problems compared with other industries (Shannon and Parker 2012). A turnover rate in excess of 20 per cent is detrimental to productivity and is estimated to cost around $140 million annually for direct costs of recruitment, induction and training. The probability of job separation (turnover and replacement) in the mining industry is relatively high compared with other industries and substantially higher for NRWs. According to the Kinetic Group's 2012 survey of 35,371 Queensland mining industry workers, the annual turnover rate during 2010–11 was 17 per cent overall and 24 per cent if contracted workers are included. If estimated costs to the Queensland industry are extrapolated to the national industry and the same turnover rates applied, then (based on ABS May 2012 labour workforce statistics) the national turnover burden for the resources sector would be at around $500 million annually for the direct costs of recruitment, induction and training alone. This does not account for indirect costs associated with managing loss of skills, productivity and experience. The average gross replacement rate (those who leave the sector or retire) has been assessed at around 10 per cent a year and is higher for blue- than white-collar workers. The turnover rate for NRWs, at 61.5 per cent, was more than double that of other industry workers, a telling sign that there are major problems and stresses involved in being a NRW, which remain largely unexplored despite the huge costs they impose on the industry as well as individuals, families and communities.

NRWs may have choices but there is no choosing for the mining towns and communities that 'host' non-resident workforces. Without local consultation, the effective resident population can surge overnight as a mobile, predominantly male labour force moves in. In typically small, established towns, the effects are enormous, highly contentious and can lead to conflict. Where these practices dominate, they have led to 'a hollowing out of established regional towns' (Windsor Inquiry 2013: viii). In the 'towns of the mining boom' (ABS 2013b), typically 20–40 per cent of the population recorded on census night in 2011 were non-residents (and this undercounted by 50–100 per cent the numbers of NRWs that were moving in and out over full roster cycles). Growing NRW numbers also influence more masculine and youthful demographic characteristics in these towns (ABS 2013b). NRWs typically work long hours when in their work cycle, typically 12 hour shifts. But this means that there are always large contingents of NRWs off-shift and looking for ways of spending their time and money in towns that provide few diversions for cashed-up, rootless young men other than the universal 'vices' of drinking, drugs, sex and gambling. Workers mostly live in mining camps or claim available accommodation in motels, hotels and caravan parks. Local rents and house prices soar sometimes beyond even capital city prices, creating a windfall for some while pricing many non-mining sector workers (teachers, health care workers and other service providers) out of local housing markets.

Submissions to the Windsor Inquiry (2013) bear testimony to the extent of divisiveness and conflict that impacts on quality of life in mining towns (including effects on the cost of living – particularly housing affordability – on infrastructure and services, and on levels of violence and disorder). Government funding of services and infrastructure has historically been based on permanent resident populations with no allowance for the inflated demands, costs and impacts caused by the sudden influx of large NRW populations, although the Royalties for Regions policy in Western Australia has recently mitigated this for some mining centres in that state. The burdens of the mining boom are heavily concentrated in a significant number of small, dispersed localities, and remain largely invisible to the predominantly metropolitan Australian population, whilst the benefits flow elsewhere, mostly to the large cities. NRWs are the most palpable symbol of this chronic imbalance in the eyes of local communities. Post-industrial mining regimes take neo-liberal logic to an extreme, one perhaps encapsulated in the figure of the FIFO worker – contracted, non-unionised, with a generous pay packet, compressed work roster, fragile job security and truncated family and community life.

Research into social impacts of post-industrial mining regimes on mining communities, although limited, has been increasing both in Australia (Carrington et al. 2010, 2011, 2012; Carrington and Pereira 2011; Cheshire 2010; Haslam McKenzie et al. 2008; Lockie et al. 2009; Murray and Peetz 2010; Petkova et al. 2009; White 2013a) and elsewhere, including Canada (Doukas, Cretney and Vadgama 2008; Ruddell 2011; Storey 2001, 2008; Ruddell 2011) and the United States (Bell and York 2010; Long et al. 2012, Stretesky and Lynch 2011). The Windsor Inquiry (2013) received many submissions expressing concern about social disorder and violence associated with FIFO workforces. These confirm findings from our own research on frontier masculinities and violence and conflict in Australian mining communities (Carrington et al. 2010, 2011; Carrington and Hogg 2011; Scott et al. 2012). In communities undergoing rapid socio-demographic redefinition (and distortion) due to these new work regimes, there is enormous social and cultural conflict. The local camps and pubs become 'zones of exception', that operate outside normative forms of social control where brawling and alcohol-related violence are commonplace (Carrington et al. 2010). NRWs are the classic 'outsiders' (Becker 1966; Elias and Scotson 1994) who have become emblematic of the social dislocation, disorder, and loss being experienced by residents who feel themselves overpowered by these new mining developments (Carrington et al. 2012).

The increasing reliance on non-resident workforces, shrinking permanent resident workforces and the related 'fly-over' effects of the boom threaten the sustainability of some mining towns. They become less attractive places to live owing to a combination of soaring living costs, erosion of community amenities and – ironically at the geographical epicentre of a boom – shrinking economic opportunities due in part to mining company preferences for NRWs over local workers.

None of this should really surprise. Maintenance of the traditions, employment relationships and communal solidarities that formed and sustained large sectors of the mining industry in the modern era is antithetical to the logic of post-industrial mining regimes and their prevailing modes of economic calculation, which are global, pertain to the short-term only and are ideally purified of any non-economic contaminants. This logic is as apparent in the higher echelons of the industry in, for example, the short-term performance-based remuneration of senior mining executives and their rapid turnover, as it is in mining labour processes and attitudes to mining communities, although senior executives who are passed over do not quite suffer in the same way as mining workers and communities. This is rational in a very limited sense, as mining corporations, perhaps more than most, are prey to what behavioural economists (invoking Keynes) see as the rather blind psychological and emotional forces (the 'animal spirits', or irrational exuberance) that drive market decision-making, as a recent report on the Australian coal industry, *Stranded Down Under?*, appears to confirm (Hannam 2013). Viewed through a different prism and within a longer time frame, practices regarded as imperative or expedient as ways of responding to boom conditions may inflict sizeable unnecessary costs such as those associated with high labour turnover, replacement and loss of skills and experience as discussed above.

In the remainder of this chapter, we take case studies from the Bowen Basin in Queensland to explore more closely the impacts of post-industrial mining regimes on established mining communities.

Mining in the Bowen Basin, Queensland

Coal was first mined in the Bowen Basin in Central Queensland in the late nineteenth century. The industry underwent rapid expansion in the second half of the twentieth century, emerging as one of the two largest Australian coal mining regions, attracting a growing permanent population and spawning towns and communities whose lifeblood was the industry. By Australian standards, the Bowen Basin has never been regarded as geographically remote. It had an estimated *resident* population (ERP) of 82,065 in July 2012 (OESR 2012) (down from a previous high of 84,850 in 2011 (OESR 2011b)). Major mining townships include Blackwater, Collinsville, Coppabella, Dysart, Glenden, Middlemount, Moranbah, Moura, and Tieri, several of which are among the biggest growth 'towns of the mining boom' (ABS 2013a). The mining industry is the Bowen Basin's single largest employer (OESR 2011a: 2). The non-resident mining workforce was estimated at 25,035 workers on shift (i.e., excluding those away in the leave cycle of their rosters) in July 2012 or 53 per cent of the mining workforce; more than two thirds (68 per cent) were employed in the Isaac Local Government Area (OESR 2012). A large proportion of NRWs, however, are not captured in point-of-time population statistics because up to half of this population may be in the leave cycle of their roster and thus elsewhere at the time of the count. Thus NRW numbers are likely to be under-estimated for this among other reasons, but notably the region had long-established resident mining workforces and communities. Nevertheless, in the five years from July 2007, a 3.7 per cent growth in the population (2,958 additional residents) has been overwhelmingly outstripped by a 126 per cent growth in NRWs (up by 13,960).

In the Bowen Basin, unlike some remote regions that have been newly opened up to mining, post-industrial mining regimes and the growing reliance on NRWs confront deeply rooted mining traditions and communities. In 2011, one of the authors conducted an online survey on the impacts on these communities of mining projects reliant on NRWs (see Carrington and Pereira 2011). Most of the respondents (out of the total of 559) were from localities in the Bowen Basin. The overwhelming majority (between 79 per cent and 59 per cent depending on locality in the Basin) felt non-resident workforces had an adverse impact on their communities, in particular on housing availability and affordability, local infrastructure and services, employment, business and the local economy, and community safety, crime and justice (Carrington and Pereira 2011).

A further major problem with the frenzy of mining development in the Bowen Basin relates to road trauma. In addition to the massive increases in large mining vehicles travelling on already over-loaded local roads, there is the heavier reliance on drive-in/drive-out NRWs. In fact, 72 per cent of the NRWs counted on shift in July 2012 were DIDOs; the remaining 28 per cent were FIFOs (OESR 2012). DIDO workers travelling at the beginning or (especially) at the end of demanding work cycles are at increased risk of death or injury to themselves and/or others on the roads. The Windsor Inquiry heard evidence that 'the accident rate in Queensland's Bowen Basin is particularly high' (2013: 56) and this is supported by other sources (Queensland Courts, Office of the State Coroner 2011; Murray and Peetz 2010: 36, 192–3, 218–21). Based on their research, Di Milia and Bowden (2007) suggested that fatigued NRWs are more likely to be killed or injured as they commute at either end of work cycles than in the workplace. This is a classic instance of how post-industrial mining regimes serve to externalise risk and responsibility for work related harms. The Windsor Inquiry recommended that mine operations ban car parking and DIDO practices and replace them with other safer means of transport, such as buses, to alleviate traffic congestion and reduce car accident rates (2013: 57). The report refers to companies in Canada that have successfully adopted this practice to improve road, worker and community safety.

We now turn to recent events in two mining communities in the Bowen Basin – Collinsville and Moranbah – to show why these communities, although pro-mining, have such negative experiences of Australia's largest ever mining boom and were led to form an organisation to resist many of its effects.

Collinsville

In 2010, Mining Communities United Incorporated (MCU 2011) was formed to improve the social and economic well-being of the Collinsville and Scottville communities in the Bowen Basin and ensure their long-term prosperity. In the following year, a broader coalition of Bowen Basin towns (Blackwater, Clermont, Collinsville, Dysart, Moranbah and Moura) formed the Queensland Mining Communities (QMU) alliance. These groups' principal source of dispute with the mining companies and the Queensland Resources Council (QRC), the body representing the industry, was the growing reliance on NRWs for local mining projects. NRWs were seen as undermining the sustainability of most small regional mining communities and some towns, Collinsville and Moranbah in particular. MCU, a non-profit community organisation, is led by women from Collinsville, echoing the long tradition of female-driven organisations in mining communities. The Collinsville MCU website proudly states:

> *Collinsville is a community, not a commodity.* The people of Collinsville and
> Scottville have a strong sense of community identity, and the members of
> MCU act as ambassadors on their behalf to ensure that the unique and valuable
> character of our town is protected and enhanced through future development and
> investment. A proud and welcoming town, Collinsville has been a 'mining town'
> since 1912. With generations of mining families still living in Collinsville, it is
> important that we do not allow the modern trend of DIDO and FIFO to ravage
> the country lifestyle that still exists in Collinsville today. (MCU 2011)

According to interview-based research undertaken by Murray and Peetz
(2010: 4) in these towns, the women 'fought long battles to make conditions
liveable in the coal towns, established women's auxiliaries, distributed food to
strikers and their families, and stood on picket lines'. In the 1952 coal strike in
Collinsville, a women's auxiliary was established with assistance from the Union
of Australian women (Murray and Peetz 2010: 39). The women's auxiliary
engaged in a wide range of community building activities. According to one of
their interviewees from Collinsville, this included 'a child minding centre, milk
for school children, a swimming pool, kindergarten equipment, a full-time dentist
(and) books for the school library' (Murray and Peetz 2010: 97).

Donna Bullock and Kelly Vea Vea are contemporary examples of women
actively engaged in local struggles in mining communities. Vea Vea, the
founding President of Queensland Mining Communities, was recently elected
as a councillor in local government elections. Bullock is the founding President
of the Collinsville Mining Communities United. In March 2013, Vea Vea and
Bullock gave presentations on the experiences of '*Women, Families and Mining
Communities*' at the Crime and Justice Research Centre, QUT, public seminar
series and we draw on material from these presentations in this section of the
chapter. As they see it, the growing reliance by mining companies on NRWs
is aimed at breaking the traditionally strong influence of trade unionism in the
Bowen Basin and undermining the rich traditions of community solidarity of
mining towns. Collinsville already has a 400-bed camp on the outskirts of the
town which has an ERP of around 1,500 (ABS 2011) and there are plans to build
another 300-bed camp in the town's centre. Bullock (2013) has stressed that
mining development is welcome, but:

> MCU strive to ensure that the developments will improve the social and economic
> environment of Collinsville. While they have a legitimate place in remote areas
> with no other available facilities, in our experience workers accommodation camps
> placed in existing towns negatively affect local businesses and enhance the 'US vs
> THEM' mentality which plagues mining towns by segregating the drive-in, drive-
> out (DIDO) and fly-in, fly-out (FIFO) workers from the rest of the population.

In August 2013, Glencore Xstrata, one of the world's largest resource companies
and a majority joint venture operator of the Collinsville open-cut coal mine, laid-off

400 workers, around half of whom lived in Collinsville, and set about replacing them with NRWs 'with more flexible working practices' (ABC *7.30* television programme report: 31 October 2013). The mass lay-off of workers invoked comparisons with the 1998 waterfront dispute in Australia when a large stevedore company conspired to break the traditionally powerful and militant waterfront union by locking out its union workforce in the four major ports of Melbourne, Brisbane, Fremantle and Sydney and replacing it with non-unionised labour, recruited from former members of the armed forces and trained in Dubai for the new role on the waterfront (Trinca and Davies 2000).

The controversial merger of Glencore with Xstrata in 2012 created a super resources company worth US$90 billion, with 101 mines, over 50 metallurgical facilities, and 130,000 workers in 33 countries (*Sydney Morning Herald* 2012). Reporters from the ABC current affairs programme, *7.30*, obtained company documents which revealed Glencore Xstrata harboured (or perhaps were seeking to foster) fears of a violent confrontation with sacked Collinsville workers, with a 'risk assessment' from July 2013 alluding to the dangers of sabotage, death, criminal damage and intimidation, and recommending that company staff avoid the local pub. Collinsville, like many established mining communities, has a long tradition of unionism, social solidarity, and radicalism (Murray and Peetz 2010: 4), reflected in its local museum, which documents its past struggles and triumphs and is also a monument to 26 workers killed in a 1954 coal mine disaster. The company apparently knew little and cared less about the roots of community solidarity in Collinsville but possibly found in the demonisation of the town a further convenient rationalisation for its ruthless dismissal of the workforce. The dismissal of the 400 workers in late August 2013 prompted a disciplined public campaign, but nothing to confirm the predictions of violence contained in the company 'risk assessment'.

As Christmas 2013 approached, Collinsville MCU President Donna Bullock issued a public plea for donations to buy presents and organise a Christmas party for the 400 families who lost their jobs; this raised many thousands of dollars. They had their Christmas party and the children of laid-off workers received generous gifts. This is exemplary of the resilience historically shown by the women of mining communities.

Moranbah

Moranbah was purposely built as a mining town in the 1970s under Joh Bjelke-Peterson's conservative National Party government policy of issuing mining leases only to companies committed to developing regional townships. That policy was abandoned in the 1990s. Moranbah now has one of the highest ratios of NRWs to residents in Australia – 4,585 NRWs to 8,990 ERPs in July 2012 (or 1 NRW to 2 ERPs) (OESR, 2012) – and has become the site of considerable conflict between mining companies and the union and community. Vea Vea (2013), who, as noted above, founded Queensland Mining Communities and now serves as Isaac LGA Councillor, explains why:

> When Queensland's biggest coal miner, BHP Billiton Mitsubishi Alliance (BMA), announced their plans for 100% fly in fly out workforce for the new 4 billion dollar Caval Ridge Mine in 2010, Moranbah was drawn into the political and industrial debate … To be employed in this mine situated just 6kms from town, you must relocate to Brisbane and work fly in, fly out (FIFO). You can't be a local and apply for a job there and you will be discouraged from moving to the community once you are employed.

After the BMA announcement, the Moranbah Action Group Inc., an incorporated body run by women from a broad cross-section in the community, held community meetings, organised a rally, and met with politicians, including the Labor Party's State Premier and Prime Minister at that time. They won the support of regional mayors, all of whom united against the BMA proposal. The group emphasised in their submission to the Queensland State Government's Coordinator General, who was to decide on BMA's request for a change to previously agreed workforce arrangements, that 'The community of Moranbah passionately supports the expansion of industry and the opportunities that come with it. But our community and indeed our region deserves the right to grow sustainably …' (Moranbah Action Group 2012).

The debate over relocation to Moranbah and expansion of a camp to house hundreds of NRW workers for the Caval Ridge Mine was central to a long-running public dispute with BMA. BMA was ultimately granted approval to recruit 100 per cent of its workforce as NRWs (Moranbah Action Group 2011). The Moranbah Action Group then led a long campaign to prevent the approval of the related work camp. Similar to its campaign against the 100 per cent FIFO application, the group campaigned against the proposed 1,945 room worker's camp, Buffel Park that was associated with the Caval Ridge Mine development. According to the MCU (2011) website:

> Moranbah Action Group Inc. has been formed in response to the mining industry's decision to develop new mine projects with no offer of residential housing for their employees. We feel this strips working families of the freedom to make living decisions with their families, and shows blatant disregard to the communities in which they develop. Camp accommodation needs to be carefully balanced with residential housing to ensure the community will progress alongside industry.

The campaign was widely supported by local unionists, councils, community groups and businesses. The only two doctors practicing in Moranbah made a submission to the Windsor Inquiry (2013) in which they highlighted some of the implications:

> the doctor patient ratio is estimated to be around 1: 2750 – an unsustainable and unsafe level for doctors and patients alike. This shortage is further exacerbated by the effects of the resources boom and the influx of population into the area … too often industry comforts themselves with the delusion that a non-resident workforce

has no impact on the town's soft infrastructure such as medical services, police, ambulance and other emergency services. (Scholtz and Nieuwoudt 2011: 2)

The Moranbah community did not oppose the use of NRWs outright, but merely argued that workers at the BMA mine should have a choice as to whether they lived locally with their families or commuted as NRWs. At the time of the proposal to relocate and expand the work camp, BMA distributed a new draft enterprise agreement to all employees signalling that '… the company may make commute arrangements a precondition of employment for new employees' (BMA multi-site Enterprise Agreement Draft 2011 in Moranbah Action Group 2011). While long and hard fought, the campaign failed.

Then, in June 2012, the Queensland State Government granted approval for an additional 3,258 person work camp to be erected by BMA near Moranbah, not associated with the Caval Ridge Project, but with another development. Moreover, a 100 per cent FIFO workforce arrangement was also approved for the BMA owned and operated Daunia mine near Moranbah which was officially opened in September 2013. Buffel Park is the camp associated with the Caval Ridge Mine development. As noted above, the application was for 1,945 rooms. The former Bligh Labor Party government set the condition that 900 rooms were to be decommissioned after the construction phase. That condition has since been overturned by the Newman Liberal National Party State Government. As we write, submissions are due for BMA's Red Hill Mine project, and again they are applying for 100 per cent FIFO and another 3,000 room onsite camp. The boom continues unabated.

Without taking into account these additional camps and NRWs, assuming rosters with even-time work and leave cycles, the additional number of NRWs approved by this subsequent decision would increase the total number of NRWs moving through Moranbah in the switch between roster cycles from 9,170 to 14,676. This would mean an increase in NRWs in the workforce as a proportion of the estimated resident population from 87 per cent to 163 per cent (see Table 11.2 in Appendix 1). In other words there would be 1.6 NRWs on cycle in Moranbah for every resident – and this is an under-statement of those projected.

Another indicator of the growth in NRWs (FIFOs in this case) is the increase in local air traffic. As of 2009, the Moranbah airport provided one flight a day in and out of town. It now has 22 flights per day (Passmore, *The Courier Mail*, 16 September 2013). Data from the Brisbane Airports Corporations show that the average number of intra-state flights to regional centres in Queensland has increased by 60 per cent over the three years to 2013 (Passmore 2013).

In many of these communities, the FIFO acronym has been creatively adapted to reflect the deeper concerns, rifts and resentments symbolised by the growing size of the non-resident workforce: problems fly in whilst benefits fly out and, less politely, 'fit in or fuck off' (Carrington et al. 2012).

Concluding Comments

Elected governments have a responsibility to protect the public interest. Yet there is abundant evidence that Australian governments which bear the responsibility for safeguarding collective well-being are cowered by the mining sector. Both Labor and Liberal governments at state and commonwealth levels have substantially abdicated their responsibility to regulate the mining industry by not compelling compliance with laws and standards that are there to safeguard the long-term public interest. Paul Cleary, in his two very fine books on the mining boom (2011, 2012), points to the 'do it yourself (DIY)' character of much regulation. Environmental impact statements are essentially left to companies and growing corps of freelance consultants who are on company payrolls. According to Cleary (2012: 97), 'DIY regulation involves submitting reports to the state government that often include breaches of conditions, with no consequence'. There is also a paucity of independent, transparent monitoring of mining industry practices by state regulatory agencies (see Carrington 2013), whose staff are increasingly subject to industry poaching.

Too little policy attention has been given to planning for the boom/bust cycles of resource extraction. Maintaining economic diversification is fundamentally important for the long-term viability and prosperity of localities, regions and the national economy, but has been sacrificed to the immediate benefits believed to flow from the boom. At a local level, there is something profoundly perverse about economic incentives that encourage health workers and teachers to abandon their professions in favour of working in the mines so that they can afford the exorbitant cost of living in their towns.

It is clear that any regard for the overall human, social and environmental impacts of the mining boom are being subjugated to short-term economic considerations, primarily those of industry profits and State Government greed for mining royalties. Although projects are proliferating across the country, there is no effective mechanism for assessing cumulative environmental, social or economic impacts even in the short- let alone the long-term. Three examples illustrate recent State Government changes which favour development proponents apparently at the expense of frontline communities. Firstly, in 2013, not long after being elected to office, Queensland's conservative Newman Government removed the requirement for social impact assessments to accompany applications for resource developments. These social impact statements were regarded as the sole policy instrument that permitted communities to express their views about resource developments. While the concepts of social licence and corporate social responsibility have been co-opted into audit compliance and corporate language (Kirsch 2010: 88; Sadler and Lloyd 2009), such statements appear to be little more than hollow rhetoric. An emerging body of research contests the industry's claims to really support negotiating a 'social licence' or to act responsibly (Carrington et al. 2011; Carrington, Hogg and McIntosh 2011, Carrington Pereira and Cleary 2011, 2012). The case studies of Collinsville and Moranbah certainly appear to support this contention.

Secondly, after the NSW Land and Environment (L&E) Court invoked the social and environment impact to reject a development application for the extension of an open-cut coal mine that would have swallowed a small Hunter Valley community, Bulga, the NSW Government changed the law to ensure economic considerations were paramount in the approvals process. Although the Supreme Court unanimously dismissed, with costs, the appeal by proponent Rio Tinto against the L&E Court decision, this is likely to prove to be a temporary victory as the mining company has signalled its intent to resubmit its application to take advantage of the change in legislation. Lastly, at the behest of the mining lobby, NSW and Queensland governments have cut off funding to Environmental Defenders Offices (EDOs), often the only financially feasible source of professional advice and advocacy for communities and organisations wishing to contest mining developments. Moreover, in December 2013, the newly elected Commonwealth Government without warning ended $10 million worth of funding to EDOs across the country, threatening many with closure.

Private corporations seeking to maximise their share prices and their competitive position on the global stage are not natural stewards of national and local community interests. They lack the expertise, let alone the incentive, to elevate such considerations over those of the profitability of their operations. It is the task of government to reflect and safeguard the public interest and compel adherence to it. The oxymoron of corporate social responsibility simultaneously masks the private self-interest driving corporate sector demands for deregulation, whilst diverting public institutions from their essential responsibilities.

Indications are that the mining boom in Australia still has a way to go, although this could be interrupted by a slowing of the Chinese economy. One phase of the boom, the price boom, in which record commodity prices delivered record company profits, is giving way to another phase, the volume boom. This shift aligns with many new projects coming out of the construction phase and into production. The few projects that have been shelved have had only a limited impact on the overall investment pipeline at this stage. The principal response of peak mining bodies and executives to dips in demand or commodity prices has not been to examine their own practices and priorities, but to launch ever louder complaints about declining productivity and the high cost of doing business in Australia, with the ever present threat that they will take their investment elsewhere. The scene may be set for a further intensification of the trends described in this chapter: the complete subjugation of social to economic considerations, of long-term impacts to short-term gains, and of the public interest to private corporate interests.

Acknowledgement

The empirical research project was funded by ARC Discovery Project DP0878476.

APPENDIX 1

Table 11.1 Estimation of Australia's resources sector workforce, 2012

ANZSIC mining industry workers			
Number, 12 months to February 2013 (4-quarter average) (a)		261,400	
Mining-allied workers – using ratio of 1:3 industry worker			
Number, 12 months to Feb 2013		87,100	
Total industry + allied workers, 2012			**348,500**
Resources sector non-resident workers (NRWs) – FIFOs, DIDOs, and so on:			
ANZSIC Mining industry workers			
Number, 12 months to February 2008 (4-quarter average) (a)	135,300		
Conservatively estimate 50 per cent were NRWs		67,650	
Number, 12 months to Feb 2013 (4-quarter average)	261,400		
Increase over last 5 years (2008–13)	126,000		
Estimate NRWs 80 per cent of this increase		100,880	
Mining industry NRWs Feb 2013			168,530
Mining-allied NRWs – using ratio of 1:3 industry workers (b)			56,170
Total industry + allied NRWs, 2012			**224,700**

Source: ABS 2013a.

Note: This is substantially less than the recommended KPMG (2013) ratio of 1:1.

Table 11.2   Proportions of non-resident workers to the Moranbah resident population

Moranbah	NRWs in work cycle of roster	In leave cycle (even-time roster)	Total NRWs moving through population
July 2012:			
Estimated resident population (ERP) July 2012	8,990		8,990
Number of NRWs	4,585	4,585	9,170
Total persons	13,575		18,160
per cent NRWs additional to July ERP of 8,990	51 per cent		102 per cent
Including approved camps			
Additional number of NRWs	3,258	3,258	6,516
Total number of NRWs	7,843		14,676
Total persons	16,833		23,666
per cent NRWs additional to July 2012 ERP of 8,990	87 per cent		163 per cent

Source: OESR, 2012: note that including the applications currently up for approval, if approved the number of NRWs would increase to more than 9,500.

References

ABC (Australian Broadcasting Corporation). 2006. Mining boom blamed for basin housing shortages. *ABC News*, 6 November. Available at: www.abc.net.au/news/stories/2006/11/06/1781965.htm. Accessed 18 October 2010.

ABC (Australian Broadcasting Corporation). 2013. Rio Tinto half year profit plunges by 71%. *ABC News*, 8 August. Available at: http://www.abc.net.au/news/2013–08–08/rio-tinto-profit-result/4874382. Accessed 1 February 2014.

ABC (Australian Broadcasting Corporation). 2013. BHP Billiton's profits fall 30 per cent to $12 billion on back of lower commodity prices. *ABC News*, 20 August. Available at: http://www.abc.net.au/news/2013-08-20/bhp-profits-fall-30-per-cent/4900332. Accessed 1 February 2014.

ABC (Australian Broadcasting Corporation). 2013. Mining town fears for future after 'demonisation' by mine. *ABC News*, *7.30*, 31 October. Available at: http://www.abc.net.au/7.30/content/2013/s3881587.htm. Accessed 1 February 2014.

Australian Bureau of Statistics (ABS). 2011. *2011 Census QuickStats, Collinsville UCL*. Available at: http://www.censusdata.abs.gov.au/census_services/getproduct/census/2011/quickstat/UCL315024?opendocument&navpos=220. Accessed 1 February 2014.

Australian Bureau of Statistics (ABS). 2013a. *Labour Force, Australia, Detailed, Quarterly*, Cat. No. 6291.0.55.003. Canberra: ABS.

Australian Bureau of Statistics (ABS). 2013b. Towns of the mining boom. *Australian Social Trends, April 2013*, Cat. No. 4102.0. Canberra: ABS. Available at: http://www.abs.gov.au/AUSSTATS/abs@.nsf/Lookup/4102.0Main+Features1 0April+2013. Accessed 1 February 2014.

Beach, R., Brereton, D. and Cliff, D. 2003. *Workforce Turnover in FIFO Mining Operations in Australia: An Exploratory Study*. Brisbane: Centre for Social Responsibility in Mining & Sustainable Minerals Institute, University of Queensland.

Becker, H. 1966. *Outsiders: Studies in the Sociology of Deviance*. New York: The Free Press.

Bell, S.E and York, R. 2010. Community economic identity: the coal industry and ideology construction in West Virginia. *Rural Sociology* 75(1): 111–43.

BHP Billiton. 2000. *Olympic Dam Expansion: Draft Environmental Impact Statement*. Melbourne: BHP Billiton.

Blainey, G. 1969. *The Rush that Never Ended*. Carlton: Melbourne University Press.

BREE. 2012. *Resources and Energy Quarterly, June 2012*. Canberra: Bureau of Resources and Energy Economics.

Bullock, D. 2013. Paper presented at the symposium: women, families and mining communities. QUT Garden Point campus, 1 March 2013.

Carrington, K. and Hogg, R. 2011. Benefits and burdens of the mining boom for rural communities. In *Human Rights Defender*. Sydney: UNSW Law Faculty.

Carrington, K. and Pereira, M. 2011. Assessing the impact of resource development on rural communities. *Rural Society* 21(1): 2–20.

Carrington, K., Hogg, R. and McIntosh, A. 2011. The resource boom's underbelly: the criminological impact of mining development. *Australian and New Zealand Journal of Criminology* 44(3): 335–54.

Carrington, K., McIntosh, A. and Scott, J. 2010. Globalization, frontier masculinities and violence: booze, blokes and brawls. *British Journal of Criminology* 50: 393–413.

Carrington, K., Hogg, R., McIntosh, A. and Scott, J. 2012. Crime talk, FIFO workers and cultural conflict on the mining boom frontier. *Australian Humanities Review* 53: 1–14.

Cheshire, L. 2010. A corporate responsibility? The constitution of fly-in, fly-out mining companies as governance partners in remote, mine-affected localities. *Journal of Rural Studies* 26(1): 12–20.

Cleary, P. 2011. *Too Much Luck: The Mining Boom and Australia's Future*. Collingwood: Black.

Cleary, P. 2012. *Minefield: The Dark Side of the Mining Boom*. Collingwood, Victoria: Black.

Department of Foreign Affairs and Trade. 2012. *Mining for Development: Extractive Industries Transparency Initiative*. Available at: http://aid.dfat.gov. au/aidissues/mining/Pages/initiative-extractive-industries-transparency.aspx. Accessed 1 February 2014.

Di Milia, L. and Bowden, B. 2007. Unanticipated safety outcomes: shiftwork and drive-in, drive-out workforces in Queensland's Bowen Basin. *Asia Pacific Journal of Human Resources* 45: 110–12.

Doukas, A., Cretney, A. and Vadgama, J. 2008. *Boom to Bust: Social and Cultural Impacts of the Mining Cycle*. Calgary, AB: The Pembina Institute.

Elias, N. and Scotson, J. 1994. *The Established and the Outsiders: A Sociological Enquiry into Community Problems*. London: Sage.

Gillies, A.D.S., Just G.D. and Wu, H.W. 1991. *The Success of Fly-in Fly-out Australian Mining Operations*. Melbourne: Proceedings of the Second Gold Forum on Technology and Practice, April.

Hannam, P. 2013. Doubts cast on major works as demand sags. *Sydney Morning Herald*, 16 December, 10.

Hopkins, A. 1989. Crime without punishment: the Appin Mine disaster. In P. Grabosky and A. Sutton (eds), *Stains on a White Collar*. Sydney: Hutchinson Australia.

Houghton, D.S. 1993. Long-distance commuting: a new approach to mining in Australia. *The Geographical Journal* 159(3): 281–90.

Intergovernmental Panel on Climate Change. 2013. *Fifth Assessment Report: Climate Change 2013*. Available at: http://ipcc.ch/report/ar5/wg1/#. Uug9aRK4ZpA. Accessed 1 February 2013.

Kinetic Group. 2012. *Heartbeat Report 2012: Annual Workforce Report of the Resources Industry*. Brisbane: Kinetic Group.

Kinhill Engineers. 1991. *Remote Mining Projects Fly-in Fly-out Study*. Perth: Report prepared for the Department of State Development.

Kirsch, S. 2010. Sustainable mining. *Dialect Anthropology* 34: 87–93.

KPMG. 2013. *Analysis of the Ling Distance Commuter Workforce across Australia*. Canberra: Minerals Council of Australia. Available at: http://www.minerals.org.au/news/analysis_of_the_long_distance_commuter_workforce_across_australia. Accessed 18 March 2013.

Lockie, S., Franettovich, M., Petkova-Timmer, V., Rolfe, J. and Ivanova, G. 2009. Coal mining and the resource community cycle: a longitudinal assessment of the social impacts of the Coppabella Coal Mine. *Environmental Impact Assessment Review* 29: 330–39.

Long, M.A., Stretesky, P.B., Lynch, M. and Fenwick, E. 2012. Crime in the coal industry: implications for green criminology and treadmill of production. *Organization & Environment* 25(3): 328–46.

Louis, A., Ostry, A., Quinlan, M., Keegel, T., Shoveller, J. and LaMontangne, A. 2006. Empirical study of employment arrangements and precariousness in Australia. *Relations Industrielles* 61(3): 465–89.

McIntosh, A. and Carrington, K. 2014. Challenging mining workforce practices: implications for frontline rural communities. In R. Dufty-Jones and J. Connell (eds), *Rural Change in Australia: Population, Economy, Environment*. Farnham: Ashgate.

Manning, P. 2013. *What the Frack? Everything You Need to Know about Coal Seam Gas*. Sydney: NewSouth Publishing.

MCU (Mining Communities United Inc.). 2011. Available at: http://miningcommunities.com.au. Accessed 20 January 2014.

Media Release, Bureau of Resources and Energy Economics (BREE). 2013. *Australian Resources and Energy Production to Boom*. 27 November. Available at: http://www.bree.gov.au/media-releases/20131127. Accessed 7 January 2015.

Media Release, Bureau of Resources and Energy Economics (BREE). 2013. *Transition to Production Phase to Underpin Increased Export Earnings*. 18 December. Available at: http://www.bree.gov.au/media-releases/20131218. Accessed 7 January 2015.

Murray, G. and Peetz, D.R. 2010. *Women of the Coal Rushes*. Sydney: University of New South Wales Press.

NRSET (National Resources Sector Employment Taskforce). 2010. *Resourcing the Future*. Canberra: Commonwealth of Australia.

OESR (Office of Economic and Statistical Research). 2011a. *Demographic Analysis of the Bowen Basin, 2010*. Brisbane: OESR, Queensland Government.

OESR (Office of Economic and Statistical Research). 2011b. *Bowen and Galilee Basins Population Report, 2011*. Brisbane: OESR, Queensland Government.

OESR (Office of Economic and Statistical Research). 2012. *Bowen Basin Population Report, 2012*. Brisbane: OESR, Queensland Government.

Offe, C. 1985. *Disorganized Capitalism*. Cambridge: Polity Press.

Passmore, D. 2013. Brisbane Airport offers to help competitors take customers away from congested hub. *The Courier Mail*, 16 September. Available at: http://www.couriermail.com.au/news/queensland/brisbane-airport-offers-to-help-competitors-take-customers-away-from-the-congested-hub/story-fnihsrf2-1226719498738. Accessed 1 February 2014.

Pearse, G., McKnight, D. and Burton, B. 2013. *Big Coal: Australia's Dirtiest Secret*. Sydney: NewSouth.

Petkova, V., Lockie, S., Rolfe, J. and Ivanova, G. 2009. Mining developments and social impacts on communities: Bowen Basin case studies. *Rural Society* 19: 211–28.

Queensland Courts, Office of the State Coroner. 2011. *Finding of Inquest into the Deaths of Malcolm McKenzie, Graham Brown, and Robert Wilson*. Coroner's Court, Rockhampton, 23 February.

Reich, R. 2008. *Supercapitalism: The Transformation of Business, Democracy, and Everyday Life*. Melbourne: Scribe.

Ruddell, R. 2011. Boomtown policing: responding to the dark side of resource development. *Policing* 5(4): 328–42.

Ruggerio, V. and South, N. 2013. Toxic state-corporate crimes, neo-liberalism and green criminology: the hazards and legacies of oil, chemcial and mineral industries. *International Journal for Crime, Justice and Social Democracy* (2): 12–6.

Sadler, D. and Lloyd, S. 2009. Neoliberalising coporate social responsibility: a political economy of corporate citizenship. *Geoforum* 40: 613–22.

Scholtz, J. and Nieuwoudt, R. 2011. Submission No. 2, House of Representatives Standing Committee on Regional Australia Inquiry into the Use of 'Fly-in, Fly-out' (FIFO) Workforce Practices in Regional Australia, Canberra, Australian Parliament.

Scott, J., Carrington, K. and McIntosh, A. 2011. Established-outsider relations and fear of crime in rural towns. *Sociologia Ruralis* 52(2): 147–69.

Sennett, R. 1998. *The Corrosion of Character: The Personal Consequences of Work in the New Capitalism*. New York: W.W. Norton.

Shannon, H. and Parker, T. 2012. Sustaining a healthy workforce. *Australasian Mine Safety Journal* 3(8): 76–81.

Storey, K. 2001. Fly-in, fly-out and fly-over: mining and regional development in Western Australia. *Australian Geographer* 32(2): 133–48.

Storey, K. and Shrimpton, M. 1991. Fly in mining: pluses and minuses of long-distance commuting. *Mining Review* 15: 27–35.

Storey, K. 2008. The evolution of commute work in Canada and Australia. In F. Stammler and G. Eilmsteiner-Saxinger (eds), *Biography, Shift-Labour and Socialization in a Northern Industrial City: The Far North*. Novy Urengoy, Russia: 23–32.

Stretesky, P.B. and Lynch, M.J. 2011. Coal strip mining, mountain top removal and the distribution of environmental violations across the United States, 2002–2008. *Landscape Research* 36(2): 209–30.

Sydney Morning Herald. 2012. Glencore Xstrata seal the world's biggest mining merger. *Business Day*, 7 February. Available at: www.smh.com. au/business/world-business/glencore-xstrata-seal-worlds-biggest-mining-merger-20120207–1r58c.html. Accessed 1 February 2014.

Thayer, M. 2010. *Making Transnational Feminism*. New York: Routledge.

Tombs, S. and Whyte, D. 2010. Crime, harm and corporate power. In J. Munice, D. Talbot and R. Walters (eds), *Crime: Local and Global*. Milton Keynes: Open University and Willan.

Trinca, H. and Davies, A. 2000. *Waterfront: The Battle that Changed Australia*. Milson's Point: Doubleday.

Vea Vea, K. 2013. Paper presented at the symposium: women, families and mining communities. QUT Garden Point campus, 1 March 2013.

Western Australian Department of Mines and Petroleum (WADMP). 2009. *Western Australian Mineral and Petroleum Statistics Digest 2008–09*. Perth: WADMP.

Windsor Inquiry (House of Representatives Standing Committee on Regional Australia). 2013. *Cancer of the Bush or Salvation for our Cities? Fly-in, Fly-out and Drive-in, Drive-out Workforce Practices in Regional Australia*. Canberra: Commonwealth of Australia. Available at: http://www.aph. gov.au/parliamentary_business/committees/house_of_representatives_ committees?url=ra/fifodido/report.htm. Accessed 13 February 2013.

White, R. 2013a. Resource extraction leaves something behind: environmental justice and mining. *International Journal for Crime, Justice and Social Democracy* 2(1): 50–64.

White, R. 2103b. Environmental crime and problem solving courts. *Crime, Law and Social Change* 59(3): 267–78.

Chapter 12

On Harm and Mediated Space:
The BP Oil Spill in the Age of Globalisation

Nels Paulson, Kim Zagorski and D. Chris Ferguson

Introduction

This chapter focuses on international media coverage surrounding the 2010 Deepwater Horizon oil spill in the Gulf of Mexico. In doing so it provides insight into the framing of conflict over natural resource extraction processes, including who benefits, who does not, and, most significantly, who is considered a legitimate actor in relation to such processes. Although the damage caused by the oil spill was largely contained to US sovereign territory, the owner of the well – BP plc (BP) – is a multinational corporation, with its headquarters in the United Kingdom. Given this international dimension, we investigate the ways in which disaster and harm are couched in the media, how this in turn is shaped by globalisation and national context, and ultimately what types of responses in risk management are most likely occur as a result of media framing.

In the interest in evaluating conflict over natural resources, we focus on globalisation as a force that shapes and exacerbates conflict over natural resource extraction processes in spaces ranging from oil in Nigeria to frac sand mining in Wisconsin (a special type of silica sand is used in hydraulic fracturing technologies for natural gas extraction; such sand mining is producing significant socio-ecological conflict, for example, Pearson 2013). Given globalisation's propensity to influence conflict, we explore whose voice may enter that contestation over resources. In what follows, we summarise the Gulf oil spill itself, review previous scholarship on the relationship between disasters and media, and then describe the usefulness of green criminology and global fields theory in understanding the media framing of the Gulf oil spill. From there we describe the research methods used, the results of the analysis, and offer a discussion of potential implications for this research on public policy, green criminology, and future research on the management of disasters and hazards.

Conflict within a disaster context is exposed through variation in media framings of the disaster's origins, damages, solutions, and risks, and some voices in such conflict are legitimated over others in those framings. These media frames further illustrate different types of conflict: over ownership of land, water, and resources, between national governments, within media outlets over selling papers and serving as a watchdog, and most prominently in this analysis conflict between capital protection surrounding the oil industry and environmental protection. While these conflicts direct us to identify winners and losers, we find the overriding pattern of reporting is the lack of identification of, and with, those people most vulnerable to disasters.

The Deepwater Horizon Oil Spill

The spill began on 22 April 2010 after the drilling rig, Deepwater Horizon, suffered a catastrophic explosion while running last minute tests on the Macondo well, an oil and gas prospect 40 miles off the coast of Louisiana and owned by BP in the Mississippi Canyon Block 252 (ironically named after a cursed town from Gabriel Garcia Marquez's novel *One Hundred Years of Solitude*). Subsequent investigations pinpoint the cause of the explosion as a combination of technology failures and poor decision-making by both BP, the owner of the Macondo well, and TransOcean, the contractor hired to place the well and owner of the Deepwater Horizon drilling rig. Over a period of four months, billions of barrels of crude oil gushed from the bottom of the Gulf of Mexico, creating environmental and economic damages that reverberated along a stretch of the coastline from Louisiana to the western shores of Florida (Achenbach 2011; Juhasz 2011).

At the time of the oil leak, United States federal law under the Oil Pollution Act of 1990 mandated that well owners bore the responsibility for cleaning up any damage caused by their drilling activities. This responsibility included both the operational and financial sides of the reclamation efforts. On-the-ground interpretation and enforcement of this act, however, was largely dependent on the outcome of ongoing conflicts between different stakeholders surrounding such potential efforts. This Act is still in effect today. Another component of this Act was the mandate requiring the federal government to provide logistical assistance to facilitate clean-up efforts. As a result, the US government was an active player from the outset, with the US Coast Guard assisting in everything from press conferences to containing the oil slick spreading from the well head. Within a few days of the explosion, it became apparent that the spill could potentially exceed that of the Exxon Valdez disaster of 1989 (Bergin 2011), leading to heightened concern by the US Congress and the Obama Administration by mid May. Congress launched a series of investigations designed to tease out paths of accountability. One set of hearings looked at the conditions leading up to the explosion, focusing specifically on the role of regulation and oversight (or lack thereof) by the Department of Interior's Minerals Mining Service, as outlined in previous research on the oil spill (Spencer and Fitzgerald 2013). The second set of hearings was held in June 2010 and centered on BP and the oil industry itself. At issue was the decision-making process in the exploration industry that allowed the explosion and subsequent spill to take place.

While Congress focused on culpability, efforts by the Obama Administration focused on stopping the oil spill. By May, the Obama Administration was applying pressure on BP to devise an action plan to not only contain the oil spill, but also to provide financial restitution to stakeholders in the Gulf impacted by the oil spill and to ensure environmental restoration of the Gulf shoreline. By mid June, conflict between the Obama Administration and BP spiked, when efforts at forcing BP to take swifter action drew in the British Government and threatened to turn an environmental disaster into an international crisis. While Obama took an aggressive stance towards BP, the company and its chairman had allies within the British political and financial establishment. Prime Minister Cameron was at first reluctant to get involved. Only when Obama floated the idea that BP use its profits to pay for the spill did the British Government intervene. Cameron called Obama to protest this option, and statements from the House of Commons publically opposed it as well (Achenbach 2011; Bergin 2011). Meetings between Obama and BP CEO Tony Hayward eventually resolved the issue, with BP taking complete financial responsibility for the oil spill. Operational efforts to cap the well were designated as shared between the US government and BP. In reality, however, progress on capping the well and cleaning the oil spill moved slowly. It was not until late July that a temporary cap was placed on the well, and full closure was not achieved until early September 2010. All along the way, this conflict between British and US governments was only one of many conflicts at play associated with disaster of this magnitude. This paper tries to reveal underlying patterns of conflict within the media framing beyond the most obvious one between governments.

Disasters and the Media

When disasters strike, the media are central players in the production and dissemination of information and, in so doing, can prompt action by responsible and affected parties. Media outlets frame the nature of disasters – what is being done about them, what should be done, and help to even determine whether something is a disaster at all. In doing so they offer a space for understanding conflicts surrounding disasters and they can provide an important function as conflict mediators. For example, previous research reveals the media role as a watchdog entity (Brisman 2010). In these cases, the media opens avenues for conversations about disaster problems and can provide a forum for marginalised people to express their voice(s) (Buettner 2009; Pantti and Wahl-Jorgensen 2011; Stabile 2007; Widner and Gunter 2007). However, the opportunity may be most obvious and generous in alternative media outlets, and thus may reach fewer people and carry less influence over attitudes and behaviors regarding any given disaster than the mainstream media (Widner and Gunter 2007). Even so, the media in general can provide an emancipatory channel for disaster victims insofar as questions of relief are concerned.

In fact, many previous studies illustrate how relief for disasters is greatly shaped by the media (Besley and Burgess 2002; Eisensee and Stromberg 2007; Stromberg 2004; Widner and Gunter 2007). A given perspective over the disaster, as well as the overall coverage of a disaster, depends upon the salience of news, in terms of whether the audience feels a given story is relevant enough to their lives to act upon it (Drury, Olson and Van Belle 2005), and the dependency of the audience on news (which varies by age and perception of threat, according to Lowrey 2004). Additionally, actual media coverage of a disaster, in terms of context of what is reported, depends upon proximity of the media outlet to that disaster (Colstra 2010; Van Belle 2000). However, within the confines of whether a disaster is a salient and extensively covered story, further problems exist with the type of relief that is promoted and, to some extent, produced by the media.

Problems with disaster portrayals often occur in the form of watered-down stories that offer little insight into the complexity of disasters (Moeller 2006; Stabile 2007). For example, during Hurricane Katrina in 2005 African Americans (those most severely impacted by the disaster) were framed in the media as complicit and, in some reporting, at fault for their suffering, which ignored the more complex sociological forces of marginalisation and vulnerability that more accurately explain why they were disproportionately affected by the disaster (Stabile 2007). In addition, media outlets typically portray minorities incorrectly as solely victims and not in positions of expertise. For example, Voorhees, Perkins Vick, and Pearson (2007) argued in part of their research of Hurricane Katrina that those in poverty likely coped with the disaster just as well as others, but in different ways due to different resources available to them. The media, however, overwhelmingly represented whites and males (89.5 per cent and 86.1 per cent respectively) as people of authority and expertise (Voorhees, Perkins Vick, and Pearson 2007: 424). Furthermore, instead of offering a portrayal of actual problems with government/corporate relationships, anti-government rhetoric is frequently provided that actually limits media and other concerned citizens' collaboration with public health and other government agencies in relief efforts (Barnes et al. 2008; Littlefield and Quenette 2007). The media likewise frequently criticise non-governmental organisations' effectiveness in providing relief, and thus they undermine trust and thereby limit the ability of NGOs to work with media to address disasters (Benthall 2008). In general, the commercial media could provide an important avenue to effectively respond to disasters and address the systemic problems that produced the disasters in the first place, but typically do not do so.

Furthermore, other research shows that close relationships between government regulators and corporations are a primary cause of inequitable risk and vulnerability (and many subsequent disasters) in the first place. These relationships are problematic in that they produce groupthink, where individual group members tend to follow the norms of the group rather than offer contrarian ideas, more often than not (Barsa and Dana 2011), informed by neoliberal policy themes. For example, calls for a minimalist state create 'hollow' governments whereby government power in regulating risk and vulnerability (among other things) is eroded in the US and elsewhere. This can be seen as a result of the 'incessant drumbeat for less regulation and smaller government [that] has dominated political discourse for the last thirty years and remains stronger than ever with the push for drastic federal spending cuts' (Flournoy 2011: 299). A 'hands off' government approach to environmental regulation was a particularly prominent contributor to the Deepwater Horizon disaster. However, these stories remain underreported by the media due to the perception of disaster stories, like others, as a consumer commodity. Neoliberal ideology and policies are not easily criticised in those stories nor is complexity provided, as this would not create an opportunity for selling stories (Benthall 2008; Eisensee and Stromberg 2007; Moeller 2006; Petrucci 1997; Stabile 2007). This conflict between market realities of the news business and mission of telling a story is a common dichotomous struggle for media outlets and individual reporters.

As a result of those constraints to criticising neoliberal ideologies and policies and the conflict between telling a story and selling a story, previous researchers argue that origins and solutions to disasters are often not properly framed in the media. Disaster response and recovery is emphasised over mitigation and preparation (Barnes 2008) and aid to relieve victims is emphasised instead of disaster preparedness (Bethnall 2008; Flournoy 2011). Such portrayals are problematic because disasters are often the result of a failure to previously and properly evaluate problems with risk and vulnerability in a given community or nation-state, especially in poorer places (Wisner et al. 2004). Barsa and Dana, (2011) convincingly argue that portrayals of systemic, institutional vulnerability are particularly important to acknowledge in moving forward on deep water drilling regulation after the Deepwater Horizon disaster. Specifically, they argue that institutional vulnerability was high due to insufficient permitting processes by the Minerals Management Service (MMS), prevalent occurrences of groupthink among governmental agency and industry actors, and overt downplaying of environmental risks by BP through calculated cost-benefit analyses regarding its own profits.

Further exploration is needed regarding different media framings of disasters that go beyond discrete geographic and political boundaries, such as with the Deepwater Horizon disaster. In an era of globalisation, we can perhaps expect that conflict over natural resources and insufficient portrayals of disaster vulnerability will become increasingly common. Some suggest more uniformity in reporting may exist – or at least increase – across media outlets with the expansion of similar economic processes globally (Bojanic and Budimi 2011). Others find that there is significant variation in portrayals of disasters in the media across nation-states due to processes of globalisation. For example, Letukas and Barnshaw (2008) offer an intriguing way of seeing how disaster portrayals in the media vary as a consequence of global processes. They use world systems theory to explain variations in portrayals and how those varied portrayals lead to problematic results in disaster relief. Specifically, countries like Indonesia and Thailand received assistance in recovering from the Indian Ocean Tsunami of 2004, but that assistance was not sufficient or directed in the ways most effective for the given nation-state (in this example, Indonesia actually desired support for basic services and financial assistance; Thailand tourism and financial assistance).

This reflected the wishes of the core states, informed by media portrayals, over the reliant periphery states (Letukas and Barshaw 2008: 1079). We expand on their approach to show how globalisation makes media portrayals even more complex than world systems theory can explain. Globalisation does not just at times adversely impact disaster mitigation, preparation, relief, and recovery according to a periphery-core dichotomy. It instead may also allow for and produce tremendous variability in reporting of disasters between core states alone, *except* with regards to representation of human populations most at risk to environmental harm.

Globalisation and Green Criminology

This chapter uses a green criminology perspective to understand the dynamics of globalisation and the effects of social, political and economic management of nature. Green criminology offers an opportunity to focus on harm to humans, nonhuman animals and ecosystems as a result of human activities (e.g., Brisman 2009; South et al. 2013; White 2013). This interdisciplinary perspective provides a critical way to evaluate the relationship between culture and nature (White 2010, 2013). One area of particular focus to which green criminology lends itself is in the evaluation of media framings of environmental crime, harm, and disaster (Brisman and South 2013). Through this approach, we can understand the challenges to informing public discourse and policy construction that might most directly and longitudinally affect the greatest risks posed to people, animals, and ecosystems. For example, Fitzgerald and Baralt (2010) show how media depictions of mercury-contaminated fish normalised the risks posed by that environmental hazard and placed the locus of responsibility on individual choices of consumers rather than on mercury releasing industries, the commercial fish industry, or supermarkets and restaurants. This, therefore, limits the likelihood of any systemic changes in how the broadest and most problematic environmental harm might be mitigated in a long term, effective manner. A green criminology perspective has also been used to evaluate the Gulf oil spill, illustrating how BP was able to shape the way harm was illustrated in the disaster through vigorous public relations efforts (Brisman and South 2014; Safina 2011; Walters 2010).

One avenue where green criminology can expand to offer a better understanding of the media and environmental harm and risk is with a focus on global processes. Much environmental harm occurs across borders and cultures (Carrabine et al. 2004; White 2013). This obfuscates chances to mitigate such harm in light of how scalar politics make it less visible (Smith 1996). Very simply, as systems of exchange increase in scale, relational disconnect among those both within and outside any given supply chain increase. People cannot always see (or, perhaps consequently, understand) the suffering of people and nature in other places, and therefore such lack of visibility makes their concern less likely. This contributes to larger negative externalities, where people who exist outside the supply and demand curves for any given product take on the costs of that product.

Scalar politics also complicate our ability to fully know the most pressing risk and harm that does occur (Barak 1995; Wisner et al. 2004). This chapter attempts to further bring this focus on globalisation into green criminology by using a 'global fields' theoretical approach, first articulated by Bourdieu (1991), to evaluate the framing of environmental harm across time and space.

Globalisation has very real impacts and can both cause and mitigate harm to humans and nature. Beyond that, individuals and groups that shape globalisation do so in ways that constrain legitimacy of discourses in the media. This is of course understandable insofar as all voices cannot be represented at once. However, as suggested above, the voices of those people most vulnerable to disasters are also potentially those least likely to be represented in the media in the era of globalisation. There are various ways of understanding how globalisation works theoretically. While an in-depth exploration of these is outside the scope of this chapter, we note several approaches here. One way is to focus on the global economy as a system (Letukas and Barnshaw 2008). Focusing on the global economy as one system can help us to explain core state and periphery state commodity chain relationships (Wallerstein 2004) as well as deregulation and the effect of neo-liberalisation on the welfare state (Harvey 2007). Another approach is to conceptualise globalisation as a cultural process whereby certain isomorphic and universal ways of structuring our behaviours and values provide constraints and opportunities to address global and local problems, often labelled 'world culture theory' (Meyer et al. 1997). This is dependent on following certain legitimised scripts and schemas that are codified by global institutions, such as the United Nations and the World Bank. For example, if a nation-state were established on a previously unidentified island today, the identification of that nation-state as legitimate to the global community would depend on certain characteristics that are isomorphic of established nation-state. That island nation-state would likely institute a democratic system of governance, create centrally managed organisations to protect individual human rights, commoditise and privatise many of the available resources for exchange in the global market, and establish a standardised mass education system, among other legitimised scripts and schemas.

By way of blending those two theoretical approaches, a 'global fields' theory on globalisation (Go 2008) argues that global 'fields' shape how we evaluate our social world in similar ways across space and time. A 'field', for Bourdieu (1991), is a taken for granted social system with rules for access, rules for action, and rules for improving one's position of power. This is similar to how world culture theory focuses on norms, but a global fields approach allows that actors exhibit agency in redefining rules of a field, thus shifting the framing for a field over time. This explanation of globalisation is especially useful for green criminology insofar as it focuses on conflicting frames. That is, we use cultural schemas across time and space that consolidate our ways of identifying problems and processes, and these fields are shaped by power dynamics that are reinforced by continual capital accumulation and consolidation. This theoretical approach emphasises a more dynamic process at play whereby feedback loops may alter legitimating schemas and illuminate both the extant power relationships at play at a global scale and the recognition of environmental risks and harm.

The remainder of this chapter evaluates how global fields shape media framing of environmental harm and illuminates the apparent legitimacy of conflicts over natural resource extraction. In addition, we seek to identify how 'feedback' could potentially reinforce or alter those fields. By identifying the global fields at play in shaping media framings of the BP oil spill, we argue that future mitigation will likely disproportionately protect some from harm more than others, reinforcing conflict between capital protection and environmental protection while minimalising other more systemically problematic disaster vulnerabilities in natural resource extraction processes.

Methods

In our research we asked, how do media outlets frame a multinational disaster across nation-states? And, just as importantly, what does this tell us about globalisation and the framing of conflict over natural resource extraction processes? To address these questions, we conducted a series of analyses on media coverage from the US and the UK over the first 100 days after the Deepwater Horizon explosion. Our data consisted of newspaper articles from two US and two British daily newspapers. In an effort to overcome potential political biases in the media, we selected one left-mainstream and one conservative-financial newspaper from each country. For the United States, this was *The New York Times* and *The Wall Street Journal*. The British selections were *The Guardian* and *The Financial Times*. Using the *Lexis-Nexus* database, we searched for all stories published between 20 April and 30 July 2010. Editorials, op-eds, and letters to the editor were excluded from the analysis in an effort to limit stories to just the most general and purportedly objective framings offered by each media outlet.

The stories were first subject to an inductive coding analysis, where the intent was to determine the types of frames all four newspapers employed when covering the oil spill. Four major frames were utilised in teasing out legitimacy in conflict over natural resource extraction: *origins, damages, risk,* and *solutions*. The *origins* frame centred on the events leading up to the explosion of the Deepwater Horizon, especially those designated as causal within the story. *Damages* focused on the impact the oil spill had on the environment, people, the economy and/or business with ties to the Gulf Coast. The *risk* frame concentrated on the idea of uncertainty. Examples of risk included discussions over the final cost of the oil spill, the extent of environmental damage, and the outcomes of congressional investigations. The fourth frame, *solutions*, included discussions of ways to cap the well and stop the spill, environmental clean-up, and future government regulations. A story was coded as possessing a given frame if its narrative fit any of the above criteria. Coding was not mutually exclusive, and we found that some stories contained multiple frames.

After coding, we created a dataset to reflect the number of times each frame was used each day across all four newspapers. We compared the overall levels of coverage among the four newspapers, and compared the use of frames in the newspapers over time. Correlations were conducted across media outlets and across the four codes, using two tailed tests for significance and controlling for number of stories and whether a 'main event' occurred within two days prior to the reporting of the story. 'Main events' were determined according to a *Time* magazine timeline of the first 100 days after the explosion (*Time* N.d.). These major events range from political announcements by governmental leaders in the US or UK (for example, Obama making his first visit to the Gulf Coast) to significant shifts in socio-environmental conditions relating to the disaster (for example, when the first oil washed ashore in Louisiana).

A second round of codes evaluated qualitative variation, focusing on important remaining questions (with regards to our interest in globalisation and green criminology) from correlations found in the first round of codes. Within that second round of codes, a qualitative analysis of reporting of the voices of the most vulnerable populations was evaluated in order to identify the opportunities given to those most harmed by the disaster to articulate ways forward for the mitigation of future risk. We use the definition of vulnerability from Wisner et al. (2004), in which vulnerable groups are those who find it hardest to reconstruct their livelihoods following a disaster, with livelihoods defined as 'the command an individual, family, or other social group has over an income and/or bundles of resources that can be used or exchanged to satisfy its needs' (Wisner et al. 2004: 12). This process of developing a coding protocol is essential to media analysis (Altheide 1996) as it involves a careful process of 'reflexive or dialectical interplay between theory and data whereby theory enters in at every point, shaping not only analysis but how social events come to be perceived and written up as data in the first place' (Emerson et al. 1995: 167). Therefore, while this process was largely inductive, the theoretical approach described above in terms of globalisation and green criminology was integral to the coding process. In the end, this study analysed 811 documents.

Results

Little homogeneity in reporting was found across the media outlets, suggesting there is space for conflicting frames. While total counts of stories correlated highly with the number of events that occurred during the first 100 days following the explosion (see Table 12.1), the emphases on damages, origins, solutions, and risk varied considerably (see Table 12.2). That is, the numbers of stories were highly correlated, but the themes within those stories were not. For example, controlling for the occurrence of major events in the Gulf Spill timeline, there was only one significant positive correlation between *The Guardian* and *The New York Times* (regarding damages). In other words, conflicting frames of the disaster were more common than agreement.

Table 12.1   **Correlations among papers for reporting on a given day, controlling for the occurrence of a 'major event' in the first 100 days after the Deepwater Horizon explosion**

		T	**NT**	**FTCOUNT**	**GDCOUNT**
WSJ COUNT	Correlation	1	**0.276	***0.381	**0.25
	Sig. (2-tailed)	.	0.006	0	0.013
	df	0	97	97	97
NYT COUNT	Correlation	**0.276	1	**0.27	***0.324
	Sig. (2-tailed)	0.006	.	0.007	0.001
	df	97	0	97	97
FT COUNT	Correlation	***0.381	**0.27	1	**0.29
	Sig. (2-tailed)	0	0.007	.	0.004
	df	97	97	0	97
GUARD COUNT	Correlation	**0.25	***0.324	**0.29	1
	Sig. (2-tailed)	0.013	0.001	0.004	.
	df	97	97	97	0

Other general patterns in Table 12.2 include significant correlations between British papers regarding origins and solutions, and significant correlations between the British papers and *The Wall Street Journal* regarding origins. *The New York Times* reported quite differently from each of the other newspapers. The most interesting relationships pertained to the very heterogeneous reporting of risk among the four papers. Not only is there only one significant relationship, but also that relationship (between *The New York Times* and *Financial Times*) was *negative*. This means that when one paper reported on risk the other paper was significantly less likely to report on risk that day.

With 'risk' presenting such an interesting category of variation in reporting, we further teased out a positive, albeit not statistically significant, correlation among the two UK papers regarding risk, *The Guardian* and *Financial Times* (Table 12.3). When speculation of the extent of spill coverage was high, both papers discussed that risk. When litigation began regarding culpability, coverage of financial risk and risk to the oil industry was high in both papers. However, within these patterns there was notable qualitative variation in terms of type of risk between the two newspapers. *Financial Times* focused more on industry risk. *The Guardian* focused more on spill coverage/spread risk.

Table 12.2 Correlations among papers for damages, origins, solutions, and risk, controlling for total number of articles on a given day and the occurrence of a 'major event' in the first 100 days after the Deepwater Horizon explosion

		WSJDAM	NYTDAM	FTDAM	GDDAM
WSJ DAMAGES	Correlation	1	0.085	-0.025	*0.224
	Sig. (2-tailed)	.	0.405	0.81	0.027
	df	0	96	96	96
NYT DAMAGES	Correlation	0.085	1	0.153	*0.211
	Sig. (2-tailed)	0.405	.	0.133	0.037
	df	96	0	96	96
FT DAMAGES	Correlation	-0.025	0.153	1	0.049
	Sig. (2-tailed)	0.81	0.133	.	0.631
	df	96	96	0	96
GUARD DAMAGES	Correlation	*0.224	*0.211	0.049	1
	Sig. (2-tailed)	0.027	0.037	0.631	.
	df	96	96	96	0

		WSJSOL	NYTSOL	FTSOL	GDSOL
WSJ SOLUTIONS	Correlation	1	0	0.132	0.148
	Sig. (2-tailed)	.	0.998	0.195	0.146
	df	0	96	96	96
NYT SOLUTIONS	Correlation	0	1	0.004	0.094
	Sig. (2-tailed)	0.998	.	0.97	0.358
	df	96	0	96	96
FT SOLUTIONS	Correlation	0.132	0.004	1	**0.251
	Sig. (2-tailed)	0.195	0.97	.	0.013
	df	96	96	0	96
GUARD SOLUTIONS	Correlation	0.148	0.094	**0.251	1
	Sig. (2-tailed)	0.146	0.358	0.013	.
	df	96	96	96	0

		WSJORG	NYTORG	FTORG	GDORG
WSJ ORIGINS	Correlation	1	0.066	**0.276	**0.256
	Sig. (2-tailed)	.	0.518	0.006	0.011
	df	0	96	96	96
NYT ORIGINS	Correlation	0.066	1	0.056	-0.006
	Sig. (2-tailed)	0.518	.	0.586	0.951
	df	96	0	96	96
FT ORIGINS	Correlation	**0.276	0.056	1	**0.257
	Sig. (2-tailed)	0.006	0.586	.	0.011
	df	96	96	0	96
GUARD ORIGINS	Correlation	**0.256	-0.006	**0.257	1
	Sig. (2-tailed)	0.011	0.951	0.011	.
	df	96	96	96	0

		WSJRIS	NYTRIS	FTRIS	GDRIS
WSJ RISK	Correlation	1	-0.14	0.037	-0.027
	Sig. (2-tailed)	.	0.168	0.719	0.795
	df	0	96	96	96
NYT RISK	Correlation	-0.14	1	*-0.218	0.02
	Sig. (2-tailed)	0.168	.	0.031	0.847
	df	96	0	96	96
FT RISK	Correlation	0.037	*-0.218	1	0.1
	Sig. (2-tailed)	0.719	0.031	.	0.326
	df	96	96	0	96
GUARD RISK	Correlation	-0.027	0.02	0.1	1
	Sig. (2-tailed)	0.795	0.847	0.326	.
	df	96	96	96	0

Table 12.3   Risk reporting between the *Guardian* and *Financial Times* by per cent of stories

	Industry/BP Risk	Financial Risk	Environmental Risk	Spill Coverage/ Spread Risk
Financial Times	53.97%	15.87%	15.87%	14.29%
Guardian	29.69%	19.53%	16.41%	34.38%

In spite of very few similarities in terms of reporting on risk, damages, solutions, and origins, one overriding pattern appeared across media outlets. Direct or personalised references to the most vulnerable groups in this disaster setting (according to how Wisner et al. (2004) define such vulnerability, described above), especially when exploring risk (the category where one would most expect such references to emerge), were very rare. Those framed as 'at risk' were the oil companies and general industry, marine life and Gulf ecosystems, rig workers, and people whose lives depend on stable preservation of Gulf ecosystems (such as the tourism industry). All combined, this analysis yielded only 24 references to vulnerable populations, like shrimp fishermen. These 24 references existed primarily in *The New York Times* (14 of the total references to vulnerable populations), and early in the reporting of the disaster (13 of the references were in May 2010). These references are quite small compared to the overall 583 general references to risk. This means that only 4 per cent of the total reporting on risk made reference to vulnerable populations; the rest focused on marine life, oil companies, and capital protection (and even those 4 per cent were to a certain extent *connected to* risk surrounding marine life, oil companies, or capital protection). This category of risk was also evaluated as the most relevant to a green criminology perspective on media reporting in that vulnerable groups are likely those most in *actual* conflict with processes of extracting oil resources, and they are most in conflict with dominant depictions of what or who is at risk.

The most dominant way of framing at risk populations was in terms of marine life, from both the oil spill itself and the dispersants meant to reduce the impact of the spill. Here is one example from the *Financial Times*:

> Myriad industries are threatened by the pollution: tourism, including the multibillion-dollar game fishing business, and oyster, shrimp and deep-sea commercial fishing. Environmentalists say the disaster has struck an ecosystem already vulnerable from overfishing, dredging and offshore oil exploitation. Mike Beck, a marine scientist with the Nature Conservancy, said dispersants, some injected at the broken wellhead, could limit the impact of the spill on the coastline, partially sparing rich oyster and shrimp beds.

However, sub-surface pollution would enter the food chain from plankton up to big game fish. 'It is virtually certain that fish, shrimp and many other vital cogs in the web of life are dying underwater, unseen,' said Frank Gill, president of Audubon, a US conservation charity. (*Financial Times*, May 2010)

In terms of at risk groups and oil companies, the concern was occasionally framed in terms of stakeholders within oil companies. This is one of the ways capital protection was presented as a dominant concern. For example, one report in *The New York Times* discussed the far-reaching impact a market tradable company like BP has on people not living in the Gulf region:

> There are certainly some mutual funds and pension funds that will be affected on both sides of the Atlantic. Nebraska's retirement fund, for instance, reportedly will lose $1.3 million each quarter that BP suspends its dividend. The erasure of about $100 billion in BP stock value has translated into big losses for several funds. The California Public Employees' Retirement system has lost more than $284 million in value, Bloomberg News reported … at the moment BP's woes are shared widely, especially among companies that would like to drill more in the Gulf of Mexico. The current drilling moratorium will hurt the majors and service companies. Oil companies will almost certainly face more regulatory hurdles and safety expenses in the future. (*The New York Times*, June 2010)

Risk to vulnerable human populations as a result of the activities of the oil industry was primarily framed across media outlets as a problem for rig workers. Specifically, the lack of oversight in protecting the rig workers was presented as most problematic regarding vulnerabilities of oil exploration in the Gulf. Here is one report from *The Guardian*:

> You can have all the health and safety regulations you like, but you cannot legislate for human error. And 12 hours' daily hard labour for a minimum of two weeks straight, often in atrocious weather, means mistakes happen. The MMS reports that there have been 69 deaths, 1,349 injuries and 858 fires and explosions on offshore rigs in the Gulf of Mexico alone since 2001. In almost every case, the finger has been pointed at a lack of communication and failure to observe correct procedures, rather than equipment malfunction. And that's just the Gulf. According to The Complete Offshore Rig Employment Handbook, there were 766 rigs drilling in all parts of the globe – more often than not the most dangerous and inhospitable parts – in January 2010, and accidents are a part of life. Major disasters, such as Piper Alpha in 1988 in which 165 men died, and Deepwater Horizon may grab the headlines, but working on a rig is always attritional. (*Guardian*, April 2010)

The human populations framed as vulnerable in terms of their connection to marine life across media outlets were the fishermen and shrimpers, people within industries closely tied to the identity of the Gulf communities. *The New York Times* also specifically identified the 'Cajun' communities:

> For the Cajuns of South Louisiana – exiled in the 1700s from French settlements in Acadia, now part of eastern Canada, for refusing to swear allegiance to the British – life along the bayous has been bittersweet, with the constant threats of lightning-quick destruction from hurricanes and floods on top of the slow-motion agony of coastal erosion. What they got in return for their tolerance of living in what early cartographers called No Man's Land was a world-class bounty of seafood and freedom in an environment of striking natural beauty. Now that is in jeopardy. The oil spill has delivered a dose of misery for all those who live intimately with the land here. But for the Cajuns, whose rustic French-American culture is almost wholly dependent on the natural bayous that open to the Gulf of Mexico, it has forced the question of whether they can preserve their way of life – and if so, at what cost? (*The New York Times*, July 2010)

One report in the *Financial Times* did speak to a *general* human health risk posed by both oil spills and dispersants to address the oil spill on vulnerable populations. This came closer to specifying those who may experience the greatest environmental harm in the BP oil spill. Who those populations are is not articulated, however, nor are the voices of those people offered.

> Public health officials do not have enough information about the impact oil exposure has on human health and are becoming increasingly concerned about the safety of 'vulnerable populations' in the Gulf of Mexico region impacted by the BP spill, writes Stephanie Kirchgaessner in Washington. The lack of knowledge puts public health 'at a disadvantage,' said Lisa Kaplowitz, deputy assistant secretary for policy at the Department of Health and Human Services. Testifying at a congressional hearing on the issue, Dr Kaplowitz said health officials had difficulty countering claims by other interests – including those with environmental concerns – as decisions were made on how to handle the spill and clean-up. John Howard, the director of the National Institute for Occupational Safety and Health, said he was 'not a fan of dispersant' used in the clean-up from a health and public safety viewpoint, and there was a correlation between its use and nine fishermen falling ill. (*Financial Times*, June 2010)

There was one instance where the National Association for the Advancement of Colored People (NAACP) took the initiative to clarify the populations most vulnerable in disasters like the Gulf oil spill, and this appeared in *The New York Times*:

> The N.A.A.C.P. has sent a letter to BP expressing concerns that minority members helping with the Gulf of Mexico cleanup tend to be assigned tougher, lower-paying jobs than whites. Benjamin T. Jealous, the civil rights organization's

president, said in the letter dated Friday that he wanted to meet with BP's chief executive. The N.A.A.C.P. also says minority contractors are not receiving equal consideration for work. And it claims that contractors are busing in workers from out of state instead of hiring local residents who have lost their livelihoods because of the spill. (*The New York Times*, July 2010)

This example illustrates how the *voices* of the populations most vulnerable to the environmental risk posed by the oil industry and offshore drilling may be conspicuously absent from almost all reporting. In one article from *The Guardian*, the voice raised on behalf of those most vulnerable comes from an attorney:

> Then there is the general population, which is facing a lengthy exposure to tiny airborne particles of crude oil. 'A lot of people are thinking that if the well stops flowing, these issues are going away, but they are not going to go away for a very long time,' she [attorney Wilma Subra] said. (*Guardian*, June 2010)

Discussion

To summarise the results of this analysis, environmental harm is mediated in ways that reflect two global fields of risk: environmental protection and capital protection, and not necessarily in that order. This is the primary conflict represented within the media over natural resource extraction processes. The framing of stories varied tremendously across nation-states and newspapers supporting prior research into similar issues (Lynch, Nalla and Miller 1989). Occasionally, similar reporting occurred across media outlets. Even then, the types of risk framed by the report varied. The *one* overriding pattern of similarity was the lack of recognition of those human populations most vulnerable to environmental harm from the BP disaster across media outlets.

What does this tell us about globalisation? First, globalisation allows (or perhaps even facilitates) variation in the framing of disasters across time and space. Such variation reflects some conflict surrounding disasters in framing, not the least of which between capital and environmental protection as two dominant global fields in media frames of disaster. This conflict will likely continue to fracture preparedness across polities and industries of other forms of risk beyond those fields, allowing additional fortification of power relationships within the extant status quo. Structural changes to reduce vulnerabilities for people most marginalised in society are unlikely to occur without their recognition in the context of disasters; we can expect those vulnerabilities may increase with foci in the media on either environmental protection or capital protection. In other words, these media framings may further exacerbate problems with the environmental harm that is disproportionately experienced by those most vulnerable across time and space as they are least represented as at risk in the media.

However, because of the variability in how and when media outlets report origins, damages, solutions, and risk surrounding disasters, we see potential avenues of raising awareness of more critical conflicts over natural resource extraction processes, and the largest and most problematic vulnerabilities in these processes, through different conceptions of risk in the media. A challenge that remains for green criminology (and other applied socio-environmental research) is to identify exact mechanisms for such avenues of an expanded conception of risk that may, in turn, create a global field that simultaneously (1) connects the media's audience with vulnerable groups and (2) makes space for visualising more proportionate future mitigation of risk and harm.

The hope is that this chapter provides a way of seeing how media frames environmental harm and conflict, how globalisation shapes such frames, and whether opportunities exist for re-framing environmental harm, conflict, and vulnerability in the age of globalisation. This is an important avenue for resolving conflicts and improving our risk allocation and public awareness of environmental vulnerability, central to concerns in green criminology.

Bibliography

Achenbach, J. 2011. *A Hole at the Bottom of the Sea: The Race to Kill the BP Oil Gusher*. New York: Simon & Schuster.

Altheide, D. 1996. *Qualitative Media Analysis*. Thousand Oaks, CA: Sage.

Barak, G. 1995. Media, crime, and justice: a case for constitutive criminology. In J. Ferrell and C. Sanders (eds), *Cultural Criminology*. Boston, MD: Northeastern University Press, 142–66.

Barnes, M.D., Hanson, C.L., Novilla, L.M.B., Meacham, A.T., McIntyre, E. and Erickson, B.C. 2008. Analysis of media agenda setting during and after Hurricane Katrina: implications for emergency preparedness, disaster response, and disaster policy. *American Journal of Public Health* 98: 604–10.

Barsa, M. and Dana, D.A. 2011. Reconceptualizing NEPA to avoid the next preventable disaster. *Environmental Affairs* 38: 219–35.

Benthall, J. 2008. The disaster-media-relief nexus. *Anthropology Today* 24: 4–5.

Bergin, T. 2011. *Spills and Spin: The Inside Story of BP*. London: Random House.

Besley, T. and Burgess, R. 2002. The political economy of government responsiveness: theory and evidence from India. *The Quarterly Journal of Economics* 117: 1415–51.

Bojanić, I.B. and Budimir, M. 2011. Globalization and information-communication technology development impact on the new world order. *Contemporary Legal and Economic Issues* 201–10.

Bourdieu, P. 1991. *Language and Symbolic Power*. Cambridge, MA: Harvard University Press.

Brisman, A. 2009. The indiscriminate criminalisation of environmentally beneficial activities. In R. White (ed.), *Global Environmental Harm: Criminological Perspectives*. Cullompton: Willan, 161–92.

Brisman, A. 2010. 'Creative crime' and the phytological analogy. *Crime Media Culture* 6: 205–25.

Brisman, A. and South, N. 2013. A green-cultural criminology: an exploratory outline. *Crime, Media, Culture* 9: 115–35.

Brisman, A. and South, N. 2014. *Green Cultural Criminology: Constructions of Environmental Harm, Consumerism and Resistance to Ecocide*. Oxford: Routledge.

Buettner, A. 2009. Skeletal figures: presence and the unrepresentable in images of catastrophe. *Continuum: Journal of Media and Cultural Studies* 23: 351–66.

Carrabine, E., Iganski, P., Lee, M., Plummer, K. and South, N. 2004. The greening of criminology. In E. Carrabine, P. Iganski, M. Lee and N. South, (eds), *Criminology: A Sociological Introduction*. London: Routledge, 313–30.

Colstra, R. 2010. The rumble and the dark: regional newspaper framing of the Buffalo Creek Mine disaster of 1972. *Journal of Appalachian Studies* 16: 79–100.

Drury, A.C., Olson, R.S. and Van Belle, D.A. 2005. The politics of humanitarian aid: U.S. foreign disaster assistance, 1964–1995. *The Journal of Politics* 67: 454–73.

Eisensee, T. and Stromberg, D. 2007. News droughts, news floods, and U.S. disaster relief. *The Quarterly Journal of Economics* 122: 693–728.

Emerson, R.M., Fretz, R.I. and Shaw, L.L. 1995. *Writing Ethnographic Fieldnotes*. Chicago, IL: University of Chicago Press.

Fitzgerald, A.B. and Baralt, L.B. 2010. Media constructions of responsibility for the production and mitigation of environmental harms: the case of mercury-contaminated fish. *Canadian Journal of Criminology and Criminal Justice* 52: 341–68.

Flournoy, A.C. 2011. Three meta-lessons government and industry should learn from the BP deepwater horizon disaster and why they will not. *Environmental Affairs* 38: 281–303.

Go, J. 2008. Global fields and imperial forms: field theory and the British and American empires. *Sociological Theory* 26: 201–29.

Harvey, D. 2007. *A Brief History of Neoliberalism*. Oxford: Oxford University Press.

Juhasz, A. 2011. *Black Tide: The Devastating Impact of the Gulf Oil Spill*. Hoboken, NJ: John Wiley & Sons.

Letukas, L. and Barnshaw, J. 2008. A world-system approach to post-catastrophe international relief. *Social Forces* 87: 1063–87.

Littlefield, R.S. and Quenette, A.M. 2007. Crisis leadership and Hurricane Katrina: the portrayal of authority by the media in natural disasters. *Journal of Applied Communication Research* 35: 26–47.

Lowrey, W. 2004. Media dependency during a large-scale social disruption: the case of September 11. *Mass Communication and Society* 7: 339–57.

Lynch, M.J., Nalla, M.K. and Miller, K.W. 1989. Cross cultural perceptions of deviance: the case of Bhopal. *Journal of Research in Crime and Delinquency* 26(1): 7–35.

Meyer, J., Boli, J., Thomas, G.M. and Ramirez, F.O. 1997. World society and the nation-state. *American Journal of Sociology* 103: 144–81.

Moeller, S.D. 2006. 'Regarding the pain of others': media, bias, and the coverage of international disasters. *Journal of International Affairs* 59: 173–96.

Pantti, M.K. and Wahl-Jorgensen, K. 2011. 'Not an act of God': anger and citizenship in press coverage British man-made disasters. *Media, Culture & Society* 33: 105–22.

Pearson, Th. 2013. Frac sand mining in Wisconsin: understanding emerging conflicts and community organizing. *Culture, Agriculture, Food and Environment* 35: 30–40.

Petrucci, M. 1997. Television environments and the fourth scopic epoch. *Social Alternatives* 16: 47–51.

Safina, C. 2011. *A Sea in Flames: The Deepwater Horizon Oil Blowout*. New York: Crown.

Smith, N. 1996. Spaces of vulnerability, the space of flows and the politics of scale. *Critique of Anthropology* 16: 63–77.

South, N., Brisman, A. and Beirne, P. 2013. A guide to a green criminology. In N. South and A. Brisman (eds), *Routledge International Handbook of Green Criminology*. Oxford: Routledge, 27–42.

Spencer, D.C. and Fitzgerald, A. 2013. Three ecologies, transversality and victimization: the case of the British petroleum oil spill. *Crime, Law and Social Change* 59: 209–23.

Stabile, C.A. 2007. No shelter from the storm. *South Atlantic Quarterly* 106: 683–708.

Stromberg, D. 2004. Radio's impact on public spending. *Quarterly Journal of Economics* 119: 189–221.

Time. N.d. Available at: http://content.time.com/time/interactive/0,31813,2006455,00.html. Accessed 7 January 2015.

Van Belle, D.A. 2000. *New York Times* and network TV news coverage of Foreign disasters: the significance of the insignificant variables. *Journalism and Mass Communication Quarterly* 77: 50–70.

Voorhees, C.C.W., Perkins Vick, J. and Pearson, D.D. 2007. 'Came hell and high water': the intersection of Hurricane Katrina, the news media, race and poverty. *Journal of Community & Applied Social Psychology* 17: 415–29.

Wallerstein, I. 2004. *World-Systems Analysis: An Introduction*. Durham, NC: Duke University Press.

Walters, R. 2010. Toxic atmospheres air pollution, trade and the politics of regulation. *Critical Criminology: An International Journal* 18: 307–23.

White, R. 2010. *Global Environmental Harm: Criminological Perspectives*. Cullompton: Willan.

White, R. 2013. *Environmental Harm: An Eco-Justice Perspective*. Bristol: Policy Press.

Widner, P. and Gunter, V.J. 2007. Oil spill recovery in the media: missing an Alaska native perspective. *Society and Natural Resources* 20: 767–83.

Wisner, B., Blaikie, P., Cannon, T. and Davis, I. 2004. *At Risk: Natural Hazards, People's Vulnerability and Disasters*. New York: Routledge.

Chapter 13

Environment and Conflict: A Typology of Representations[1]

Avi Brisman

Introduction

As an emerging perspective, *green cultural criminology* seeks to bring together green criminology and cultural criminology, and to identify points of overlap (Brisman and South 2013a, 2014).[2] More specifically, *green cultural criminology* endeavours to illuminate how cultural criminology's attention to space is central to green criminology (and thus that cultural criminology is, at some levels, 'already doing' green criminology). In addition, *green cultural criminology* attempts to highlight means by which green criminology might adopt a cultural criminological lens: (1) by assigning greater consideration to the way(s) in which environmental crime, harm and disaster are constructed and represented by the news media and in popular culture forms; (2) by dedicating increased attention to patterns of consumption, constructed consumerism, commodification of nature and related market processes; and (3) by devoting heightened concern to the contestation of space, transgression, and resistance, in order to analyse the ways in which environmental harms are opposed in/on the streets and in day-to-day living (Brisman and South 2013a, 2014; see also McClanahan 2014).

This chapter looks to further the *green cultural criminological* undertaking by examining fictionalised representations of environment and conflict. It begins

---

1 An embryonic version of this chapter was presented to the Department of Security and Crime Science, University College London (London, United Kingdom) on 21 May 2013. I am grateful to Ms Joanna F. Hill and Professor Shane D. Johnson for providing me with the opportunity to speak to their department. I thank them and other members of the audience for their questions, comments and suggestions.

2 'Green criminology' is concerned with crimes and harms affecting the natural environment, the planet as a whole, and the associated impacts on human and non-human life. It considers both acts and omissions prohibited by law, as well as those environmental disruptions that are legal and take place with the consent of society (see, e.g., Brisman and South 2013a: 115–17, 2014: 2–6; South et al. 2013, 2014; White and Heckenberg 2014). 'Cultural criminology' explores the convergence of cultural and criminal processes in contemporary social life and seeks to comprehend how crime and crime control are constructed, enforced, represented and resisted (see, e.g., Brisman and South 2013a: 117–18, 2014: 9–19).

by briefly describing four post-apocalyptic or dystopian novels and teasing out some commonalities and key differences between them in their depictions of the relationship between environment and conflict. With this representative literature as a point of comparison, this chapter then identifies four different categories of environment-conflict relationships in film, before turning to a consideration of the dangers and problems inherent in the messages communicated by these films. This chapter concludes by articulating the need for studying, examining and critiquing the depictions, representations and narratives in fiction and film of humans' relationship to the Earth and to each other.

Environment and Conflict Relationships in Literature: A Sample

In Nevil Shute's *On the Beach* (1957), set primarily in and around Melbourne, Australia, in 1963, World War III has wiped out most of the populated world, polluting the atmosphere with nuclear fallout and killing all human and nonhuman animal life in the Northern Hemisphere. Global air currents are slowly carrying the lethal nuclear fallout to the Southern Hemisphere, and the only parts of the planet still habitable are Australia and New Zealand, South Africa, and the southern parts of South America, although these areas are slowly succumbing to radiation poisoning as well. Life in Melbourne continues in a reasonably normal fashion, although there is a paper famine, the near-complete lack of petrol makes travel difficult, and there is some looting. As the characters in Shute's novel await the fallout from the Northern Hemisphere and their inevitable deaths, they neither express intense emotions (e.g., anger, fear), nor do they mope about, indulging in self-pity. Rather, they make their best attempts to enjoy their remaining time on the planet, engaging in quotidian activities (e.g., restoring a car, tending to a garden that they will never see) or undertaking new ones (e.g., taking classes in typing and shorthand). Once the radiation reaches the latitudes in which they live, most of the characters accept their fate and opt for the suicide pills that the Australian government distributed and promoted so that they can avoid prolonged suffering from radiation poisoning.

In David Graham's *Down to a Sunless Sea* (1981), which takes place in January 1983, the United States has plummeted into the equivalent of a bankrupt Third World and borderline-starving country (where the average person struggles to survive on 1,200 calories/day, the standard relief ration), after having exhausted nearly all of its oil reserves and a resultant collapse of the dollar. Without oil and with a collapsed dollar, food cannot be distributed, leading to widespread hunger and looting. A planeload of people, flying from New York to London, learn that Israel has attacked Beirut, Damascus, and Cairo with nuclear weapons in retaliation for their poisoning of Tel Aviv's water supply. Israel's strike triggers a worldwide nuclear holocaust, with the USSR and China attacking the US and its allies. The survivors eventually land at McMurdo Station in the Antarctic, where they begin to rebuild a world of peace and cooperation and an absence of nationalism.

James Howard Kunstler's *World Made By Hand* (2008) takes place in upstate New York in the fictional town of Union Grove, where citizens must negotiate a world devoid of all modern comforts – a world ravaged by terrorism, epidemics, and the economic upheaval of 'peak oil', all of which have been exacerbated by anthropogenic climate change.[3] The setting for Kunstler's novel resembles the scenarios he depicts in some of his nonfiction (see, e.g., Kunstler 2005, 2007). Here, in his novel, readers learn that Union Grove is not an anomaly: much of the rest of the United States is splintering and falling apart, with nuclear explosions obliterating Los Angeles and Washington, D.C., and cities across the country devolving. The novel focuses on several contrasting groups which are meant to represent the different directions society could head after a breakdown of modern social norms: the citizens of Union Grove, who try to carry on living as they had done before (attending church, playing music, and trying to balance community concerns and town needs with individualism and autonomy); scrappers and thugs who salvage and steal from around the county and live in a group of trailers known as Karptown, led by Wayne Karp; a religious group called the New Faith Church led by Brother Jobe; and a self-sufficient English manor set up by Steven Bullock, a landed farmer. In varying ways and to varying degrees, the groups struggle to respect life in a way that was taken for granted before events changed and to build pragmatically for a new future. There is often tension and violence within and between the groups, although in the end, the groups that emphasise cooperation and community fare better than those organised around exploitation. The novel is intended to provide a look into the future at the dire consequences of the poor American system of urban planning – in particular, the impracticality of the contemporary suburban arrangement without the continuous flow of inexpensive and abundant energy to maintain its infrastructure.[4]

Finally, Douglas Coupland's *Player One: What Is to Become of Us* (2010) follows four characters in the lounge of an airport bar. While they are there, crude oil prices go up – first to \$251.16/barrel then to \$290/ barrel then to \$350/barrel and then to \$900/barrel, although by this point, 'it's no longer for sale' (2010: 91). Chaos ensues – riots, explosions, assaults, murder. But, in the end, order is restored.

---

3   'Peak oil' refers to the point in time when the maximum rate of petroleum extraction is reached, after which the rate of production is expected to enter irreversible and terminal decline. As Mooallem (2009: 31) explains, '[t]he theory of peak oil concludes that the productivity of the earth's oil wells will soon peak – if it hasn't already – and, once production falls short of demand, the market for our fundamental resource will rapidly spiral into chaos, potentially pulling much of society down with it'. For more on 'peak oil', see Aleklett 2012; Kunstler 2005, 2007; see also Urry 2010: 196–7.

4   Kunstler (2007) is more explicit and more forceful in his indictment of urban planning in the United States in his article, 'Making Other Arrangements', proclaiming that 'American suburbia represents the greatest misallocation of resources in the history of the world. The far-flung housing subdivisions, commercial highway strips, big-box stores, and all the other furnishings and accessories of extreme car dependence will function poorly, if at all, in an oil-scarce future'.

As the narrator states, 'It will begin to rain, and the chemicals outside the lounge will crackle and fizz and drain away. Gas will be rationed and doled out by the government, and it will never go below $350 a barrel again' (2010: 212).

Treating *On the Beach* (1957), *Down to a Sunless Sea* (1981), *World Made by Hand* (2008), and *Player One: What Is to Become of Us* (2010) as a group (and recognising that many other novels fall within this rich, enduring (sub)genre), I would like to make two observations about the ways in which these novels engage a common theme – that 'we are about to face destruction from some terrible, awesome enemy' (Chomsky 2014). First, as Chomsky (2014) explains, '[t]he United States is an unusually frightened country. And in such circumstances, people concoct either for escape or maybe out of relief, fears that terrible things happen'. Other commentators do not consider this collective fear to be a uniquely American trait. According to Murphy (2013: 50), '[h]umans have been preparing for the worst for millennia', while Rosenthal (2000: 16) remarks that 'every generation in our Western culture has had its version of the Apocalypse, usually stimulated by war, famine or revolution, those leitmotifs of human history'.[5] Dunne (2009: 46) offers a variation on Murphy's and Rosenthal's points:

> Every age seems to invent a master narrative about its own demise. At the turn of the 20th century, the fear was of a violent struggle between races and civilisations. In the post-1945 world, the nightmare was of a nuclear holocaust. The narrative of demise that haunts us today is the threat that environmental harm holds for the planet and its ability to support human and other life forms.

Similarly, cultural theorist Andrew Ross has observed that with the fall of the Soviet Union, 'apocalyptic fears about widespread droughts and melting ice caps have displaced the nuclear threat as the dominant feared ... disaster' (Ross 1991: 8, quoted in Hulme 2009: 63).[6] As I hope my synopses have demonstrated, we have moved from a story in which conflict in the form of nuclear war brings about environmental degradation and scarcity of natural resources (*On the Beach*) to one in which exploitation of the Earth and our collective ecocide (including that from anthropogenic climate change) bring about violence, death, murder, war (*Down to a Sunless Sea*, *World Made by Hand*, and *Player One: What Is to Become of Us*). In a sense, the narrative has not shifted; rather, it has been flipped: environmental harm *now leads to* nuclear explosions and disaster, not vice versa.

---

5   Much of this is built into religious teachings as a matter of course, such as in the Book of Revelation, and Christian eschatology, more generally, where reward in 'heaven' is often premised upon 'hell on earth' and/or an impending 'judgement day'.

6   A 'survivalist' theme often runs parallel to and occasionally intersects with American or Western preoccupation with endgame scenarios. For example, one of the characters in Barbara Kingsolver's novel, *Flight Behavior*, asserts: 'Humans are in love with the idea of our persisting ... We fetishise it, really. Our retirement funds, our genealogies. Our so-called ideas for the ages' (2012: 282).

Second, with the exception of *On the Beach*, all of these post-apocalyptic or dystopian novels leave us with *some degree of hope* – an image of precarious worlds different from our own and without certain material comforts, but ones void of the selfishness, greed, competition and myopia responsible for humanity's downfall. In other words, they are *cautionary* tales and the message is clear: WE HUMANS are to blame for environmental degradation – which either results from conflict (*On the Beach*) or leads to it (*Down to a Sunless Sea*, *World Made by Hand*, *Player One: What Is to Become of Us*). In Hollywood, the dynamics are a bit different, and in the next section, I map out four different categories of environment-social conflict relationships in film.

Environment and Conflict Relationships in Film: A Four-Part Typology

In this section, I present a four-part typology of representations of environment and conflict in film. The typology moves from (1) films in which environment and conflict play a minor role to (2) films in which the environment- conflict relationship is more significant to the plot to (3) films where environment and conflict leads to a search for a new planet (or where conflict over the environment ensues upon humans' arrival upon a new planet) to (4) films where alien life forms invade Earth for its natural resources. After delineating and describing this four-part typology, I discuss the messages conveyed by the films in this typology and the problems that these lessons – and films – pose.

In the first category of films, the environment-conflict relationship is rather subsidiary. For example, in *Die Another Day* (2002), the twentieth film in the James Bond spy film series and the fourth and final film to star Pierce Brosnan as James Bond, the fictional M16 agent, Bond infiltrates a North Korean military base, where Colonel Tan-Sun Moon (Will Yun Lee) is illegally trading African 'conflict diamonds' for weaponry. But we learn very little in the film about the dynamics of conflict diamonds (also referred to as 'blood diamonds') – diamonds mined in war zones and sold to finance insurgencies, invading armies' war efforts, or warlords' activities (see, e.g., Brisman and South 2013c; Clark 2013; Milburn this volume; Santora 2006; Wyatt this volume). Similarly, in *Lord of War* (2005), Nicholas Cage stars as an illegal arms dealer, whose character (Yuri Orlov), is based on the real-life Russian arms smuggler, Viktor Anatolyevich Bout. At one juncture in the film, Yuri trades weapons for diamonds with Andre Baptiste Sr. (played by Eamonn Walker), a ruthless dictator waging a never-ending civil war in Liberia. As the trade unfolds, we witness a militia force allied with Baptiste Sr. preparing to destroy a refugee camp and hack to death with a machete a woman and child trying to escape. But elsewhere in the film, Yuri trades weapons for cocaine and sells them for cash. Conflict diamonds are thus portrayed as just one component of the illegal global arms trade and, indeed, Amnesty International hailed *Lord of War* for highlighting the atrocities caused by arms trafficking as a whole, rather than for its specific depiction of conflict diamonds (see http://www.

amnestyusa.org/events/young-professionals-amnesty-international-ypai-presents-dinner-a-movie).

In the second category of films, the environment-conflict relationship plays a more prominent role, where a resource or aspect of the environment is the *reason* for conflict or helps drive (fund) conflict. For example, the plot of *Quantum of Solace* (2008), the twenty-second film in the James Bond spy series and the second film starring Daniel Craig as Bond, centres around Dominic Greene (Matthieu Amalric), a wealthy businessman and member of the villainous Quantum organisation, who intends to stage a coup d'état in Bolivia to seize control of the country's water supply (see generally Brisman and South 2013b; Scott 2008; South 2010) – somewhat of a nod to the privatisation of water supply and sanitation in Bolivia under then-President Hugo Banzer (see McClanahan In Press for a discussion). Just as the environment-conflict relationship is more crucial to the plot of *Quantum of Solace* than *Die Another Day*, we learn more about the horrors associated with conflict diamonds in *Blood Diamond* (2006), the political war thriller film starring Leonardo DiCaprio, than in *Lord of War*. *Blood Diamond* takes place in 1999 during the Sierra Leone Civil War and depicts a country torn apart by the struggle between government loyalists and rebel factions, such as the Revolutionary United Front, who intimidate Mende locals and enslave many to harvest the diamonds that fund their increasingly successful war effort. The film portrays both the RUF's practice of hacking off limbs to instill fear and spread terror among the civilian population, and its widespread use of child soldiers; it ends with a conference on blood diamonds being held in Kimberly, South Africa – a reference to the development of the Kimberley Process Certification Scheme (KSPC) in 2003, which was established to identify the origin of rough diamonds and prevent blood diamonds from entering the market.

To varying degrees, the films in these two categories describe or portray human-induced environmental degradation and the conflict that ensues, prompts, or surrounds it. None of these films, however, are *cautionary* tales – and certainly not to the same extent as the novels discussed earlier in this chapter.[7] Rather, diamonds and water are almost incidental – employed to drive the plot; they are not the source of consternation nor do they really raise consciousness about a particular environment-conflict dynamic.

Moreover, the films in both categories all seem to contain what Sparks (1995: 62) refers to as, a 'dialectical play' between anxiety and reassurance that exists in 'crime fiction' – whereby stories in television and film 'often begin from a premise of anxiety, though many of them go on to impose a pleasing order and coherence on a shifting and troubling world'. Sparks suggests crime television and

---

7   *Bling: A Planet Rock* (2007) examines how 'blinging' – flaunting one's material wealth – in the flashy world of commercial hip-hop played a part in the Sierra Leone Civil War. One could make the argument that the film offers a cautionary story about the dangers of excess but it is a documentary film, rather than an action film or drama, and thus one of the intentions behind it is (presumably) instruction.

film crime drama appeal to our personal and social anxieties – they distract, move, and frighten us – and then present imagery of restoration, repair, and social order. Sparks contends that the 'inherent tension between anxiety and reassurance ... constitutes a significant source of ... appeal to the viewer' (1995: 62).[8] A similar element of 'order restoration' occurs in these environment-conflict films – one that is quite different from the tenuous (but slightly hopeful) endings to the novels discussed earlier.[9]

Despite claims that *Blood Diamond* (2006) called attention to the relationship between natural resource extraction and violent conflict (Duffy 2010; Stevens 2006),[10] the films in the first two categories desensitise us to the particular problem (illegal trade of diamonds, conflict over control of and access to water); they suggest that the villains have been vanquished (as in the two James Bond films – *Die Another Day* and *Quantum of Solace*) or that whatever harm that has transpired is a 'necessary evil' (as in *Lord of War*)[11] or that whatever atrocities have occurred will cease (as in KPCS scene at the end of *Blood Diamond*), when, in actuality, this is not the case. Or, to borrow from Susan Sontag, in her classic account of photography, representations of atrocity both 'transfix' and, at the same time, 'anesthetise' (1977: 20; see also Carrabine 2011: 8, 2012a: 464). Film, perhaps more so than still photography, can just as easily 'deaden conscience' – and consciousness – as well as 'arouse it' (Sontag 2001: 21;

---

8   In a variation on this idea of 'order restoration', Stephen King, the best-selling horror writer, has argued that the rural slasher film (and many other horror films, more generally) 'is really as conservative as an Illinois Republican in a three-piece suit; that its main purpose is to reaffirm the virtues of the norm by showing us what awful things happen to people who venture into taboo lands. Within the framework of most horror tales we find a moral code so strong it would make a Puritan smile' (1981: 395; see also DeKeseredy et al. 2014: 182–3; Donnermeyer and DeKeseredy 2014: 19).

9   Cultural criminologists have engaged in significant analysis of media constructions of crime. For an overview of this literature, see Brisman and South (2013a: 123, 2014: 12–14).

10   As Stevens (2006) concludes her review: '*Blood Diamond* is a by-the-numbers message picture, to be sure. When in dire need of some exposition on the international jewel trade, it's not above cutting to a discussion around a G8 conference table. But ... the pace never slackens, the chase scenes thrill, and the battle scenes sicken. And if it makes viewers think twice about buying their sweethearts that hard-won hunk of ice for Christmas, so much the better'.

11   As Yuri tells Interpol agent, Jack Valentine (Ethan Hawke), after the latter has apprehended him:

The reason I'll be released is the same reason you think I'll be convicted. I *do* rub shoulders with some of the most vile, sadistic men calling themselves leaders today. But some of these men are enemies of *your* enemies. And while the biggest arms dealer in the world is your boss – the President of the United States, who ships more merchandise in a day than I do in a year – sometimes it's embarrassing to have his fingerprints on the guns. Sometimes he needs a freelancer like me to supply forces he can't be seen supplying. So. You call me evil, but unfortunately for you, I'm a necessary evil.

see also Andén-Papadopoulos 2008: 24 n. 4; Carrabine 2011: 8, 2012a: 464), with the images on the screen and their accompanying narratives descending into quotidian banality, 'sapp[ing] our capacity to react' (Carrabine 2011: 9, 2012a: 464).

If the films in the first two categories contain the 'dialectical play' between anxiety and reassurance that Sparks describes – if they are films with themes of 'order restoration', where by their end, an environmental resource (water, diamonds) is no longer a source of conflict or a catalysing/perpetuating force of/ for conflict – the third category could be considered 'Mirror Earth' or 'Planet B' films. Here, order is not restored, harm is not repaired; conflict relating to the environment does not cease because of a secret agent's intervention (as in the James Bond films) or an international political process (as in *Blood Diamond*). Instead, we abandon the Earth that we have harmed and order (as well as a new home for humanity) is sought elsewhere.

For example, *Pandorum* (2009), the German science fiction thriller, opens with the following text:

1969

Man Lands On The Moon

World Population = 3.6 Billion

2009

Kepler Telescope is Launched To Search For Earth Like Planets

World Population = 6.76 Billion

2153

Paleo 17 Space Probe Lands On Planet Tanis

World Population = 24.34 Billion

Food And Water Shortages Are Commonplace

2174

The Battle For Earths Limited Resources

Reaches Its Boiling Point

Spacecraft Elysium Is Launched

At some juncture after the 60,000-person sleeper ship, *Elysium*, is launched on its 123-year-voyage to the Earth-like planet of Tanis, members of the crew learn of Earth's destruction: 'You're all that's left of us. Good luck, God bless, and God's speed'. The rest of the film takes place on the spaceship.

Whereas in *Pandorum*, our 'ecocidal tendencies' (South 2010; see also Agnew 2013) have led to widespread environmental degradation and conflict over resources that eventually results in Earth's demise, in *Avatar* (2009), set in 2154, humans have not destroyed Earth but have severely depleted its natural resources (see Richard 2009; Toomey 2010). The Resources Development Administration

(RDA) mines for a valuable mineral – 'unobtanium' – on Pandora, a densely forested habitable moon orbiting the gas giant (a giant planet or jovian planet) Polyphemus in the Alpha Centauri star system (see Richard 2009; Toomey 2010). Pandora, whose atmosphere is poisonous to humans, is inhabited by the Na'vi, 10-foot tall (3.0m), blue-skinned, sapient humanoids indigenous to Pandora, who live in harmony with nature and who worship a mother goddess (Ewya) (see Richard 2009; Toomey 2010). Unfortunately for the Na'vi, their dwelling, Hometree, happens to sit on top of massive deposits of unobtanium (see Richard 2009; Toomey 2010). While the implication is that there are potentially peaceful methods for extracting the minerals, conflicts inevitably arise: the RDA brings in massive gunships and explosives to destroy the Na'vi's home.

Whereas in *Pandorum* (2009), conflict arises out of the battle for Earth's remaining resources (after we have destroyed much of the planet), prompting a search for a Mirror Earth or a Planet B, in *Avatar* (2009), we replicate our anthropocentric ecophilosophy (see Halsey and White 1998) on the moon, Pandora, and engage in violent conflict for *that moon's* resources. Given that we have already located planets that could theoretically support Earth-like life (see, e.g., Gannon 2014; Howell 2012; Kaufman 2011; Knapp 2011; Landau 2013; Lemonick 2012a, 2012b, 2014; Wall 2014; see generally Greenfieldboyce 2014), these films seems to reflect a collective sentiment that we can continue on our current trajectory of population growth and global resource consumption, and that when Earth can no longer support us, we can just head for Mirror Earth and our new home on Planet B. Thomas Barclay, Kepler scientist at the Bay Area Environmental Research Institute in Sonoma, California, has remarked: 'With all of these discoveries we're finding, Earth is looking less and less like a special place and more like there's Earth-like things everywhere' (quoted in Landau 2013; cf. Lightman 2014). From the perspective of an astronomer or astrophysicist, Barclay may be correct. And while we should not fault the excitement of an 'exoplaneteer' (a scientist who searches for planets circling stars beyond the Sun and studies other solar systems for planets that may be suitable for life (see Lemonick 2012: 10, 146, 174–5, 230)), one could understand how such comments might be viewed as a scientific declaration of Earth's pedestrianism, as well as a tacit endorsement of unfettered economic growth and its concomitant environmental degradation. Indeed, Newt Gingrich, the American politician and one-time candidate for the Republican Party presidential nomination, has repeatedly called for a lunar colony that could mine minerals from the moon, as well as the development of a propulsion system to send us to Mars (Broad 2011; Chang 2012) – the implication being that we need more natural resources and can despoil more planetary bodies, rather than rethink and rework our relationship and responsibility to Earth.

In the fourth category of films involving environment and conflict, humans do not embark on a celestial search for a new home. Instead, Earth is targeted as or becomes Planet B for alien life. For example, in *Battlefield Earth* (2000), the science fiction action film based upon the first half of Scientology founder L. Ron Hubbard's novel of the same name, Earth has been under the rule of the humanoid alien 'Psychlos' for 1,000 years, with humans enslaved to mine Earth's natural resources. Similarly, in *Battle: Los Angeles* (2011) (also known as *Battle: LA* and *World Invasion: Battle Los Angeles)*, and *Oblivion* (2013), hostile extraterrestrial life attack Earth for its water. In *Battleship* (2012), it is not clear why aliens from Planet G attack Earth, but as Shostak (2012) reminds us, 'Hollywood usually guesses that extraterrestrials would only be interested in one of three things: (1) They want to breed with us, because their own reproductive machinery is on the blink; (2) They want Earth's resources; or (3) They want the Earth. All of it'. In all four films, humans eventually overcome their alien enemies and as with those in the first two categories, order is restored at the end of the films. The difference, however, lies in the message delivered.

I suggested earlier that with films in the first and second categories like *Die Another Day* (2002), *Lord of War* (2005), *Blood Diamond* (2006), and *Quantum of Solace* (2008), we either overlook or become desensitised to a particular environmental problem (e.g., illegal trade of diamonds, conflict over control of and access to water) and come to believe that the perpetrator of a given environment-related conflict has been thwarted or that whatever harm that has occurred has been repaired or could be repaired – just as in 'crime fiction' where the 'bad guys' are caught and justice is served. Here in the third category, with films like *Battlefield Earth* (2000), *Battle: Los Angeles* (2011) and *Oblivion* (2013), the 'ruthless threat' to planet Earth (Hadadi n.d.) is external – and extraterrestrial. And this message, I would suggest, is problematic on a number of levels.

First, *we* are the 'bad guys'. *We, humans*, are the threat to Earth – not the Psychlos or any other alien species. Richard (2009), in his comments about *Avatar*, observes:

> In most fiction, it makes for a better narrative to have a clear antagonist, some enemy or external force to oppose the main characters. We've been trained almost from birth to find someone to blame when something goes wrong, which might explain why a lot of people aren't very good with situation [sic] where everybody's or nobody's to blame (gray areas).

> But in the real world, things aren't so clear cut with most of the current environmental problems we face. Take oil companies for example. Many consider them villains of the first order – and indeed many of them are doing unethical things (i.e. Exxon funding biased studies to confuse the public) – but fundamentally, the reason why those companies are producing 80-something million barrels of oil *each day* is because [sic] most people have cars and drive around, and buy products that have been shipped from far away, etc. Oil companies don't burn all that oil by themselves, we do. We're paying them for it, creating the demand.

Richard may be a bit too forgiving of oil companies: although his piece predates the BP oil spill of April 2010, it omits, for example, any reference to Royal Dutch

Shell's involvement in the 1995 murder of Ken Saro-Wiwa and other Ogoni, whose citizens had engaged in a nonviolent campaign against oil waste dumping in their homeland in the Niger Delta (see, e.g., Hartman 1999; Scheffran and Cannaday 2013; Williams 1996). Thus, while many oil companies are to blame for environmental degradation of land and water and for loss of human and nonhuman life either as a direct or proximate result of extraction processes, we, as individual and collective members of society, are at fault for the uninhibited and unrelenting consumption of fossil fuels and other resources and the accompanying harm. We have created the Anthropocene,[12] and the threat to Earth is from its human inhabitants, not from otherworldly ones.[13]

Second, even when we are the 'bad guys' – even when films depict human-induced environmental degradation and conflict (as in the first three categories) – we make a number of assumptions.

1. We believe that despite our 'ecocidal tendencies', we will find a technological solution to whatever environmental problem that we have

---

12   The 'Anthropocene' is a term credited to the German atmospheric chemist and Nobel Prize winner, Paul J. Crutzen, and the late biologist, Eugene F. Stoermer, to refer to the current geological epoch (beginning roughly in the latter part of the eighteenth century) 'to emphasise the central role of mankind in geology and ecology' – to the 'major and still growing impacts of human activities on earth and atmosphere, and at all, including global, scales …'. (Crutzen and Stoermer 2000: 17). Other conceptualisations and formulations have also been offered. For example, Hulme (2009: 289) defines the 'Anthropocene' as 'the era when humans first began to have a marked effect on the Earth's climate and ecosystems'. According to Coupland (2010: 217), the 'Anthropocene' is:

A term recognising that human intrusion on the planet's surface and into the atmosphere has been so extreme as to qualify our time on earth as a specific geological epoch. Along with vast increase in anthropogenic emissions of greenhouse gases, which have drastically raised the atmospheric concentration of carbon dioxide, our human footprint now covers more than 83 per cent of the earth's surface, according to the Wildlife Conservation Society.

For additional conceptions and discussions, see, Corcoran et al. 2014; DeMocker 2012: 6; Editorial 2011, 2014; Revkin 2011; Walsh 2012: 84–5; see also Urry 2010: 195.

13   I recognise that some humans are more culpable than others and that some modes of production and consumption more responsible for environmental harm than others – a point that my co-authors and I made in the first chapter of this volume. Thus, I agree with Seager (1993: 59), who writes: 'We have so degraded our environment, so stressed physical carrying capacities that the lives of millions of people on the planet (and certainly our cherished ways of life) are at risk. But, "we" – an undifferentiated humanity – have not done so. Rather, large-scale environmental problems are the result of control exercised by people within very particular clusters of powerful institutions, that include, prominently, militaries, multinationals, and governments, which often act in collusion'. My purpose in 'blaming everyone', so to speak, is not to retreat from my position in the first chapter of this volume or to adopt an essentialist notion of humanity or to make gross generalisations about all humans being equally at fault, but to underscore that the threat to planet Earth is not from some *extraterrestrial* lifeform, as depicted in various films discussed in this chapter.

caused – that some sort of technological *salvation* awaits us. As Matt Ridley wrote in his article, 'Apocalypse Not', for the September 2012 issue of *Wired*, the American magazine that reports on the ways in which emerging technologies affect culture, economics and politics:

> Ever since Thomas Robert Malthus, doomsayers have tended to underestimate the power of innovation. In reality, driven by price increases, people simply developed new technologies, such as the horizontal drilling technique that has helped us extract more oil from shale. ... Humanity is a fast-moving target. We will combat our ecological threats in the future by innovating to meet them as they arise ... (2012: 150)

Ridley, however, neglects to acknowledge that this horizontal drilling technique presents its own environmental risks (see, e.g., Bloomberg and Krupp 2014; McClanahan 2014) – a point to which I will return below.

Echoing Ridley, Peter Schwartz, in his article, 'In Gas We'll Trust', in the same issue of *Wired*, proclaimed:

> We've long been acutely aware of the geopolitical ramifications of relying on Middle Eastern oil. And the threat of climate change – along with high fuel prices – has made us all realize the need for greater energy efficiency. Thankfully, technology is coming to the rescue. New methods of extracting gas and oil, combined with efficiency gains in nearly every industry, mean that we are now minimizing demand and maximizing supply. (2012: 92, 96)

Similarly, Steven D. Levitt and Stephen J. Dubner, in their popular book, *SuperFreakonomics: Global Cooling, Patriotic Prostitutes, and Why Suicide Bombers Should Buy Life Insurance* (2009: 11) argue:

> [H]umankind has a great capacity for finding technological solutions to seemingly intractable problems, and this will likely be the case for global warming. It isn't that the problem isn't potentially large. It's just that human ingenuity – when given proper incentives – is bound to be larger. Even more encouraging, technological fixes are often far simpler, and therefore cheaper, than the doomsayers could have imagined.[14]

Likewise, Walsh (2008: 57), writing about the role that the United States should play in addressing climate change, asserts that 'the outcome of any crisis is usually determined by one dominant global player that has the innovators who can churn out the technology, the financiers who can back it and the diplomatic clout to pull the rest of the planet along. That player, of course, exists, and it is, of course,

---

14   For a scathing critique of some of the ideas and suggestions in Levitt and Dubner's book, see Kolbert (2009), who writes 'some forms of horseshit ... will always be with us'.

us'. Correspondingly, Jesse Ausubel, director of the Program for the Human Environment and senior research associate at The Rockefeller University, believes that humans are sufficiently clever and creative to steer through present and future environmental predicaments, and that our needs will spur innovation: 'Over time people find, invent and spread solutions for many environmental problems ... . Technology has liberated humans from the environment' (2009: 38, 39; see also McNall 2011: 61).[15]

We see the sentiments of Ridley, Schwartz, Levitt and Dubner, Walsh and Ausubel in films such as *Die Another Day* (2002), discussed above, and *The Dark Knight Rises* (2012). In the former film, the antagonist has created an orbital mirror satellite, 'Icarus', which is able to focus solar energy on a small area and provide year-round sunshine for crop development. But he intends to use 'Icarus' to cut a path through the Korean Demilitarised Zone with concentrated sunlight, allowing North Korean troops to invade South Korea and reunite the countries by force. In *The Dark Knight Rises* (2012), Bruce Wayne/Batman develops a fusion reactor project, but discontinues it when he learns that the core could be weaponised, turning it into a nuclear bomb.

The 'solutions' in *Die Another Day* and *The Dark Knight Rises* are presented as problematic because of their destructive capabilities when placed in the wrong hands. We leave these films thinking that such technologies are possible, inevitable (even) – what Douglas Coupland (2010: 243) refers to as 'technological fatalism', and which he defines as '[a]n attitude positing that the next sets of triumphing technologies are going to happen no matter who invents them or where or how.

---

15   Such convictions about technology are not confined to one particular political party. For example, Lee (2009: 18) notes that the Reagan Administration of the 1980s 'saw a future inherently possessing a technology fix to environmental and sustainability problems'. In the summer of 2013, President Barack Obama decried the 'fundamental lack of faith in American business and American ingenuity' (The White House, Office of the Press Secretary 2013). To resounding applause, President Obama stated, 'these critics seem to think that when we ask our businesses to innovate and reduce pollution and lead, they can't or they won't do it. They'll just kind of give up and quit. But in America, we know that's not true. Look at our history'. This is not to suggest, however, that there are not differences between American political parties with respect to the *right combination* of technological fixes and legislation. According to Krugman (2010: MM34):

This reaction – this extreme pessimism about the economy's ability to live with cap and trade – is very much at odds with typical conservative rhetoric. ... They [modern conservatives] believe that the capitalist system can deal with all kinds of limitations, that technology, say, can easily overcome any constraints on growth posed by limited reserves of oil or other nature resources. And yet now they submit that this same private sector is utterly incapable of coping with a limit on overall emissions, even though such a cap would, from the private sector's point of view, operate very much like a limited supply of a resource, like land. Why don't they believe that the dynamism of capitalism will spur it to find ways to make do in a world of reduced carbon emissions? Why do they think the marketplace loses its magic as soon as market incentives are invoked in favour of conservation?

The only unknown factor is the pace at which they will appear'.[16] As Halsey and White (1998: 349) point out, 'reliance on human ingenuity and technological invention is seen as the most appropriate way to guarantee the continued exploitation of nature (e.g. biogenetic research in relation to food production)', but as Kunstler (2007) cautions, '[t]he popular idea, expressed incessantly in the news media, is that if you run out of energy, you just go out and find some "new technology" to keep things running. We'll learn that this doesn't comport with reality'.[17] In other words, there is no guarantee that such technologies will be widely available in the future (see Gillis 2014): we may not be able to find technological solutions to the various environmental problems we have caused,[18]

---

16   A variation on Coupland's 'technological fatalism' is Lee's (2009: 154) notion of 'technological optimism' – '[t]he viewpoint is that problems can be solved through the application of new technologies in a free market system'. As Lee (2009: 154) explains, '[w]ith the promise of technology to solve climate problems [and other environmental challenges], key decisions can be perpetually delayed because the solution will arrive when it is needed'.

17   Kunstler's (2007) position here parallels Barak's (2012: 380) point that the news media perpetuates the notion that 'resolution of crime [is] dependent on technological rather than social interventions'.

18   A number of writers have commented on this kind of near-religious belief in technology. For example, Barnett (1999: 173) criticises the notion of '[t]echnological progression ... as the white knight of environmental rejuvenation'. While he recognises the potential for technology to address some environmental problems, he asserts that 'technological means and economic ends must be subservient to the characteristics, dynamics, and carrying capacity of the ecosystem' (1999: 176). In a related vein, Furness (2010: 205), promotes bicycling, but cautions that 'bicycles are not the solution to transportation problems just as any technological fix is incapable of solving problems that are hardly reducible to technology in the first place'. Similarly, Stretesky and colleagues identify two popular – and problematic – views about environmental issues: 'the false assumption that green crime can be reduced with better technology and/or alternative forms of governance that allows 'markets' to remedy environmental problems' (2014: 2–3; see generally Greife and Stretesky 2013). Likewise, Hartmann (1999: 10–11), in addressing the belief that social and technical ingenuity can help overcome the problem of resource scarcities, maintains: 'Missing from this technocratic framework is the notion of political *transformation*: democratising control over economic and natural resources and the direction of technological development'. Writing more specifically about faith in technology to meet the challenges of climate change, Bryce (2010: A31) maintains:

Lawmakers should stop perpetuating the hope that the technology [in this case, technology that removes carbon dioxide from the smokestack at power plants and forces it into underground storage] can help make huge cuts in the United States' carbon dioxide emissions ... . For some, carbon capture and sequestration will remain the Holy Grail of carbon-reduction strategies. But before Congress throws yet more money at the procedure, lawmakers need to take a closer look at the issues that hamstring nearly every new energy-related technology: cost and scale.

More forcefully, Lynch (2012:91) denounces the position that 'the innovative nature of capitalism and its corresponding technological advances will ultimately address the

and whatever technological advances we do achieve may be insufficient. While '[i]t's in our blood to tinker, and we're exceedingly good at it' (Dilworth 2010: 397), our 'addiction to technological fixes', to quote Dilworth again (2010: 397), impairs our ability to recognise that 'no combination of alternative technologies can generate enough energy, or be installed fast enough, to keep us at that height before the oil is gone' (Mooallem 2009: 30).[19]

Moreover, the solutions offered in *Die Another Day* (2002) and *The Dark Knight Rises* (2012) do not sufficiently reveal the paradox that 'the greater our scientific and technological achievements, the greater the potential for chaos' (Rosenthal 2000: 15). Thus, while some question whether technological fixes, including geoengineering – 'the deliberate, large-scale intervention in the climate system to counter global warming or offset some of its effects' (Hamilton 2013: 17; see also Davies 2012; Dickel 2013: 248–50; Maas et al. 2013: 213–14; Mooney 2010: 5; Scheffran and Cannaday 2013)[20] – is even possible, others, such as the Nobel Prize-winning atmospheric chemist, Paul Crutzen, noted above, argue that 'geoengineering should be seriously studied, but only with the understanding that it represents a risky, last-ditch attempt at averting catastrophe' (cited in Kolbert 2009). As another Nobel Prize winner – former Vice-President Al Gore – has opined, 'We care already involved in a massive, unplanned planetary experiment. We should not begin yet another planetary experiment in the hope that it will

---

problem', while Washingon and Cook (2011: xii, 137) criticise the ideological argument that 'people [a]re highly adaptable, and [that] technological innovation, flourishing under free market conditions, [will] enable us to address any adverse impacts that ar[i]se', and suggest that '[o]ne should indeed question the unbridled scientific "can do" optimism which argues that humans are masters of nature and can do anything, as this is "progress"'.

19   For a similar perspective, see, for example, Pretty (2013: 476), who contends that 'marginal improvements in efficiency and productivity through technological improvements (or worse by letting energy-intensive industries transfer offshore) obscure the scale of the necessary reductions in total resource consumption' (citations omitted).

20   Hulme (2014: 5–6), in his consideration of stratospheric aerosol injection, a type of geoengineering, employs the Royal Society's (2009) definition of geoengineering: 'the deliberate, large-scale manipulation of the planetary environment in order to counteract anthropogenic climate change'. According to Hulme (2014: 2–3), geoengineering 'technologies are united in their ambition to deliberately manipulate the atmosphere's mediating role in the planetary heat budget. They aim to do one of two things: either to accelerate the removal of carbon dioxide from the global atmosphere; or else to reflect more sunlight away from the Earth's surface and so to compensate for the heating of the planet caused by rising concentrations of greenhouse gases'. For a description of geoengineering and some geoengineering technologies, see Hulme (2014: 5–12); for a brief overview, see Dickel (2013: 248–50); Hulme (2009: 25, 315–17, 333, 335, 349, 350, 352, 259); McNall (2011: 38, 65–6); Scheffran and Cannaday (2013: 270–88); for a discussion of historical attempts at weather modification and the international treaties pertaining thereto, see Hulme (2014: 71–3); Lee (2009: 156–60); see also Zilinskas (1995); see generally Prud'homme (2011); for a discussion of geoengineering for military purposes, see Hulme (2014: 72–3); Zilinskas (1995: 236, 244, 248, 251–2).

somehow magically cancel out the effects of the one we already have' (2009: 315). Similarly, Clive Hamilton, Professor of Public Ethics at the Centre for Applied Philosophy and Public Ethics at Charles Sturt University in Canberra, Australia, asks: '[I]s it wise to play God with the climate? For all its allure, a geoengineered Plan B may lead us into an impossible morass. ... How confident can we be, even after research and testing, that the chosen technology will work as planned?' (2013: A17; see also Maas et al. 2013: 214).[21] The one cinematic exception might be *The Colony* (2013), the Canadian science fiction horror film set in 2045, where we learn that weather machines to control a warming climate have broken down, creating a cold Earth of ice and snow, forcing humans into underground colonies. Unfortunately, what could serve as a cautionary tale about the risks of geoenginneering is undercut by the ridiculousness of a marauding group of cannibals that terrorise the survivors.

2. Even when we are the 'bad guys' – even when films depict human-induced environmental degradation and conflict – we assume that we might find a Mirror Earth or Planet B. But as McNall (2011: 38) points out, currently, '[n]o one has the option of moving to Pandora'. What if there is no Tanis (as in *Pandorum*) or Nova Prime (as in *After Earth* (2013))?[22] And if there is, it may not be that easy to get to it, as in *Dark Planet* (1997), where the habitable planet is located on the far side of a dangerous wormhole. But even if there are planets with alien life, who is to say that we will treat

---

21   As an example, Hamilton (2013: A17) explains that 'ocean fertilisation – spreading iron slurry across the seas to persuade them to soak up more carbon dioxide – means changing the chemical composition and biological functioning of the oceans. In the process it will interfere with marine ecosystems and affect cloud formation in ways we barely understand'. Klein (2012: SR4) agrees: 'Ocean fertilisation could trigger dead zones and toxic tides. And multiple simulations have predicted that mimicking the [cooling] effects of a volcano would interfere with monsoons in Asia and Africa, potentially threatening water and food security for billions of people'. Hulme (2014: xii) offers in-depth argument for why stratospheric aerosol injection is *undesirable* ('because regulating global temperature is not the same thing as controlling local weather and climate'), *ungovernable* ('because there is no plausible and legitimate process for deciding who sets the world's temperature'), and *unreliable* ('because of the law of unintended consequences: deliberate intervention in the atmosphere on a global scale will lead to unpredictable, dangerous and contentious outcomes').

22   By the same token, what if we cannot create a satellite paradise, as in *Elysium* (2013), 'where advanced medical technology heals any ailment, from a hangnail to terminal cancer, in seconds' (Smith 2013: 39)? And even if we could create such a satellite, would it be paradise knowing that 'Earth has become a Third World slum' (Smith 2013: 39)? And is it not rather preposterous that human ingenuity could manipulate gravity (see Frank 2014) and create advanced medical technology that could cure terminal cancer in seconds but yet could not repair the Earth or create a satellite to house *all of humanity*, rather than a select few?

their residents with any greater respect than we do each other? We fight with the Na'vi in *Avatar* while in *District 9* (2009), we exhibit our finest xenophobia when an alien species in need of help comes to Earth, referring to them as 'prawns' and confining them in a government camp. As science writer, Marc Kaufman, author of *First Contact: Scientific Breakthroughs in the Hunt for Life Beyond Earth*, notes, 'the history of powerful beings is that when they find others who perhaps aren't as powerful, they come and exterminate them ... like ... when Europeans came to North America and elsewhere'. If our past and present are any indications, we do not seem to be particularly good at *intraspecies* inclusion. Who is to say that we will suddenly excel in *interspecies* interactions?

Along these lines, even if there is life on other planets, who is to say that they will welcome our arrival or that our new home might not also be desirable to other species? In *AE: Apocalypse Earth* (2013), humans are attacked by near-invisible humanoids almost as soon as they crash land on a new planet. In *After Earth*, humans find a new world, Nova Prime, but they come into conflict with the Skrel, alien creatures who invade Nova Prime intending to conquer it (see Greengerger 2013; see generally Puig 2013).

Such depictions, combined with news media stories about other planets that can sustain life (see above), further contribute to the notion of 'planetary obsolescence' – that just as we can discard appliances, articles of clothing, and other products when we are 'done' with them (see Eastwood 2006: 119; Ferrell 2013; Foster and Clark 2012; Furness 2010: 153; see generally Giroux 2012: 19), when we have 'used or have become dissatisfied or bored with this planet, we can simply acquire/inhabit a new one' (Brisman and South 2013: 411). As one of the environmental activists interviewed by Cianchi (2013: 214, 222) points out, 'we spend billions of dollars searching for life in outer space. For intelligent life in outer space when we have intelligent life out here on this planet and we ignore it. Look at the way we treat it. We murder it, we dismember it, we cut it into small pieces to figure out what makes it tick'. In a similar vein, Jensen (2009) reminds us, 'Nothing matters but that we stop this culture from killing the planet. It's embarrassing even to have to say this. The land is the source of everything. If you have no planet, you have no economic system, you have no spirituality, you can't even ask this question [how shall I live my life right now?]. If you have no planet, nobody can ask questions'. Or as Sass (2006: A23) warns, 'if we use up, or more realistically, greatly deplete, the resources of this earth, we have no place to go'.

Conclusion

Extending the green cultural criminological project, this chapter has discussed both literary and cinematic representations of the relationship between environment and social conflict. Numerous other examples exist in both literature and film (see generally Pérez-Peña 2014)[23] and thus I would like to close by offering two arguments for continued investigations and analyses thereof.

First, '[c]ultural criminology sees a blurring of the boundaries between image and reality in a variety of representational arenas, not least in popular culture, advertising, news, and films' (Lanier and Henry 2010: 368), and it investigates the collapsing boundaries between the mediated manufacture of news and information and popular film, popular music, and television entertainment programming (Ferrell 2003: 74; see also Carrabine 2012b: 67; Ferrell and Websdale 1999: 11). In a similar vein, Lowe and colleagues (2006: 438), in their article, 'Does tomorrow ever come? Disaster narrative and public perceptions of climate change', question 'whether *facts* (accepted scientific evidence) determine behaviour as much as *perceptions*, where the mediating factors are science, as communicated to the public through the news media, and strong visual images, communicated through a Hollywood film'. While the question of whether facts and statistics influence behavior as much as or more than perceptions communicated through or generated by various media is subject to debate (compare, for example, Witten (1993) with Friedman (2014)) and need not be resolved here, it is safe to say that public concern for environmental problems (or public belief in *the existence* of certain environmental problems, such as climate change) is influenced by many factors (see, e.g., Leiserowitz et al. 2013). Indeed, as Rosenthal (2000: 31) suggests, we must 'draw attention to images and visual metaphors, to areas of the mind that we have not yet fully penetrated – not as scientists, not to tell us how things work, but rather to tell us *what is actually at stake …*' (emphasis added). Along these lines, Nellis (2009: 130) observes that '[i]t is now generally accepted that literary and cinematic representations of criminal justice institutions play a part in shaping public consciousness of how those institutions work – or not' (citing Mason 2003; see also Barak 2012: 375; Presser 2009: 189) – and the same could be asserted about literary and cinematic representations of the environment and the dynamics, forces and structures that contribute to its harm and degradation. Thus, we need to examine and assess representations of environmentally-related harm, crime and conflict because of the role that such depictions play (or may play) in forming and moulding public consciousness about what is in jeopardy – about what lies in the balance – and in affecting individual and collective behaviour.

Second, cinematic depictions and literary narratives 'have the capacity to reveal truths about the social world that are flattened or silenced by an insistence on more traditional methods of social science and legal scholarship' (Ewick and Silbey 1995, 1999; see also Witten 1993: 105; see generally Card 1991: xxiv–xxv). In a similar vein, Nellis (2009: 144) asserts that 'fiction need never diminish truthfulness about character and circumstance; at its best, it accentuates it, and therein lies its aesthetic power'. While the perspectives of Ewick and

---

23   I leave for another day an examination of 'reality television' series that recreate or reenact 'man-against nature' epics (e.g., *Ax Men*; *Black Gold*; *Coal*; *The Deadliest Catch*; *Billy the Exterminator* (formerly *The Exterminators*); *Ice Road Truckers*).

Silbey and Nellis lend support to the claim that we need to examine and assess representations and stories of environmental harm, crime and conflict because these representations and stories may reveal or accentuate truths about our world, Presser (2009: 178) suggests that 'we know the world through and pattern our lives after stories'. Given what is at stake, it becomes incumbent on us to analyse and critique those stories that 'perpetuate a particular view of reality' and offer new ones that 'shatter complacency and challenge the status quo' (Delgado 1989: 2422, 2414 (footnote omitted)) – that 'defy and at times politically transform' (Ewick and Silbey 1995: 217; see also Presser 2009: 191; see generally Brisman 2013: 286). As Delgado contends:

> [c]ounterstories ... challenge the received wisdom ... . They can open new windows into reality, showing us that there are possibilities for life other than the ones we live. They enrich imagination and teach that ... we may construct a new world richer than [current reality]. Counterstories can quicken and engage conscience. Their graphic quality can stir imagination in ways in which more conventional discourse cannot.
>
> . . .
>
> Stories give us a glimpse of a world we have never seen ... to point the way to another better, larger, more inclusive one. (1989: 2414–15, 2439 n. 83 (internal footnotes omitted))

More specifically for this chapter – and this volume's – purposes, Moore asserts:

> Historically that's what human beings use to explore our place in the world: we tell stories about it. Sometimes they're scientific stories. Sometimes they're philosophical stories. Sometimes they're songs or movies. Sometimes they're fables or mortality tales. We need to tell stories to describe who we are in relation to the land, to honor what's been lost, to help us understand our kinships, to affirm what we care about, to explore the difference between right and wrong, moral and immoral. (quoted in DeMocker 2012: 9–10)

Those working in green cultural criminology, in green criminology (more generally) and across the natural sciences, social sciences and humanities (even more generally) must endeavour to help create new depictions, representations, and narratives that not only describe our relationship to the environment and to each other today and show us what is at stake and warn us of what is to come if we do not change our ecocidal tendencies (as the contributors in this volume have done), but that offer 'alternative stories' (Richardson 1995: 213) – ones that present an imagined future of a healthier Earth and a better world for humanity on *this* planet.

References

Agnew, R. 2013. The ordinary acts that contribute to ecocide: a criminological analysis. In N. South and A. Brisman (eds), *Routledge International Handbook of Green Criminology*. Oxford, UK: Routledge, 58–72.

Aleklett, K. 2012. *Peeking at Peak Oil*. New York: Springer.

Andén-Papadopoulos, K. 2008. The Abu Ghraib torture photographs: news frames, visual culture, and the power of images. *Journalism* 9(1): 5–30.

Ausubel, J. 2009. Ingenuity wins every time. Interview by Alison George. *New Scientist* (September 26): 38–9.

Barak, G. 2012. Media and crime. In W.S. DeKeseredy and M. Dragiewicz (eds), *Routledge Handbook of Critical Criminology*. London and New York: Routledge, 372–85.

Bloomberg, M.R. and Krupp, F. 2014. The right way to develop shale gas. *The New York Times*. April 30: A25.

Brisman, A. 2013. Not a bedtime story: climate change, neoliberalism, and the future of the Arctic. *Michigan State International Law Review* 22(1): 241–89.

Brisman, A. and South, N. 2013a. A green-cultural criminology: an exploratory outline. *Crime Media Culture* 9(2): 115–35.

Brisman, A. and South, N. 2013b. Conclusion: the planned obsolescence of planet Earth? How green criminology can help us learn from experience and contribute to our future. In N. South and A. Brisman, (eds), *Routledge International Handbook of Green Criminology*. London and New York: Routledge, 409–17.

Brisman, A. and South, N. 2013c. Resource wealth, power, crime and conflict. In D. Solomon Westerhuis, R. Walters and T. Wyatt (eds), *Emerging Issues in Green Criminology: Exploring Power, Justice and Harm*. London: Palgrave/Macmillan, 57–71.

Brisman, A. and South, N. 2014. *Green Cultural Criminology: Constructions of Environmental Harm, Consumerism and Resistance to Ecocide*. Oxford, UK: Routledge.

Broad, W.J. 2011. Among Gingrinch's passions, a doomsday vision. *The New York Times*. 12 December: A1, A4.

Card, O.S. 1991. *Ender's Game*. New York: Tom Doherty Associates.

Carrabine, E. 2011. Images of torture: culture, politics and power. *Crime Media Culture* 7(1): 5–30.

Carrabine, E. 2012a. Just images: aesthetics, ethics and visual criminology. *British Journal of Criminology* 52(3): 463–89.

Carrabine, E. 2012b. Telling prison stories: the spectacle of punishment and the criminological imagination. In L.K. Cheliotis (ed.), *The Arts of Imprisonment: Control, Resistance and Empowerment*. Surrey, UK: Ashgate, 47–72.

Chang, K. 2012. In visions of a moon colony, technology is the easy part. *The New York Times*. 28 January: A15.

Chomsky, N. 2014. Why Americans are paranoid about everything (including zombies). *AlterNet*. 19 February. Available at: http://www.alternet.org/noam-chomsky-why-americans-are-paranoid-about-everything-including-zombies. Accessed 7 January 2015.

Cianchi, J. 2013. *I Talked to My Tree and My Tree Talked Back: Radical Environmental Activists and Their Relationships with Nature*. PhD Thesis. School of Social Sciences, University of Tasmania (Australia).

Clark, R.D. 2013. The control of conflict minerals in Africa and a preliminary assessment of the Dodd-Frank Wall Street Reform and Consumer Act. In N. South and A. Brisman (eds), *Routledge International Handbook of Green Criminology*. London and New York: Routledge, 214–29.

Corcoran, P.L., Moore, C.J. and Jazvac, K. 2014. An anthropogenic marker horizon in the future rock record. *GSA Today* 24(6): 4–8. Available at: http://www.geosociety.org/gsatoday/archive/24/6/pdf/i1052–5173–24–6-4.pdf. Accessed 7 January 2015.

Coupland, D. 2010. *Player One: What Is to Become of Us?* Toronto: Anansi.

Crutzen, P.J. and Stoermer, E.F. 2000. The 'anthropocene'. *Global Change Newsletter* 40 (May): 17–18. Available at: http://www.igbp.net/download/1 8.316f1832132347017758000140l/1376383088452/NL41.pdf. Accessed 7 January 2015.

Davies, D. 2011. The high probability of finding 'life beyond Earth' [interview with Marc Kaufman]. Fresh Air. National Public Radio (NPR). 1 April. Transcript available at: http://www.npr.org/templates/transcript/transcript. php?storyId=135040012. Accessed 7 January 2015.

Davies, D. 2012. Climate 'weirdness' throws ecosystems 'out of kilter' [Interview with Michael Lemonick]. Fresh Air. National Public Radion (NPR). 14 August. Transcript available at: http://www.npr.org/templates/transcript/transcript. php?storyId=158756024. Accessed 7 January 2015.

DeKeseredy, W.S., Muzzatti, S.L. and Donnerymeyer, J.F. 2014. Mad men in bib overalls: media's horrification and pornification of rural culture. *Critical Criminology* 22(2): 179–97.

Delgado, R. 1989. Storytelling for oppositionists and others: a plea for narrative. *Michigan Law Review* 87(8): 2411–41.

DeMocker, M. 2012. If your house is on fire: Kathleen Dean Moore on the moral urgency of climate change. *The Sun* 444[December]: 4–15.

Dickel, S. 2013. Beyond cynicism: climate engineering technologies and vegan diets as alternative solutions for climate change. In A. Maas, B. Bodó, C. Burnley, I. Comardicea and R. Roffey (eds), *Global Environmental Change: New Drivers for Resistance, Crime and Terrorism?* Baden-Baden: Nomos, 243–59.

Donnermeyer, J.F. and DeKeseredy, W.S. 2014. *Rural Criminology*. London and New York: Routledge.

Duffy, R. 2010. *Nature Crime: How We're Getting Conservation Wrong*. New Haven and London: Yale University Press.

Dunne, T. 2009. How do we secure the environment: review of 'security and environmental change' by Simon Dalby, Polity, 2009, *Times Higher Education*, 8 October: 46. Available at: http://www.timeshighereducation.co.uk/books/security-and-environmental-change/408572.article. Accessed 7 January 2015.

Eastwood, L.E. 2006. Contesting the economic order and media construction of reality. In S. Best and A.J. Nocella, II (eds), *Igniting a Revolution: Voices in Defense of the Earth*. Oakland, CA: AK Press, 114–26.

Ewick, P. and Silbey, S.S. 1995. Subversive stories and hegemonic tales: toward a sociology of narrative. *Law and Society Review* 29(2): 197–226.

Editorial. 2011. The anthropocene. *The New York Times*. February 28: A22.

Editorial. 2014. Notes from the plasticene epoch. *The New York Times*. June 15: SR10.

Ferrell, J. 2003. Cultural criminology. In M.D. Schwartz and S.E. Hatty (eds), *Controversies in Critical Criminology*. Cincinnati, OH: Anderson Publishing Company, 71–84.

Ferrell, J. 2013. Tangled up in green: cultural and green criminology. In N. South and A. Brisman (eds), *Routledge International Handbook of Green Criminology*. Oxford, UK: Routledge, 349–64.

Ferrell, J. and Websdale, N. 1999. Materials for making trouble. In J. Ferrell and N. Websdale (eds), *Making Trouble: Cultural Constructions of Crime, Deviance, and Control*. Hawthorne, NY: Aldine de Gruyter, 3–21.

Foster, J.B. and Clark, B. 2012. The planetary emergency. *Monthly Review* 64(7) [December]: 1–25. Available at: http://monthlyreview.org/2012/12/01/the-planetary-emergency. Accessed 7 January 2015.

Frank, A. 2014. I was promised flying cars. *The New York Times*. June 8: SR9.

Friedman, D. 2014. Grimm is first Republican to flip on climate change: 'I don't think the jury is out'. *New York Daily News*. April 25. Available at: http://www.nydailynews.com/blogs/dc/grimm-republican-flip-climate-change-don-jury-blog-entry-1.1769112. Accessed 7 January 2015.

Furness, Z. 2010. *One Less Car: Bicycling and the Politics of Automobility*. Philadelphia, PA: Temple University Press.

Gannon, M. 2014. Alien planet-hunting telescope tool snaps 1st amazing images. *Space.com/Yahoo!News*. 4 June. Available at: http://www.space.com/26119-sphere-exoplanet-hunting-telescope-images-video.html and http://news.yahoo.com/alien-planet-hunting-telescope-tool-snaps-1st-amazing-150413968.html. Accessed 7 January 2015.

Gillis, J. 2014. Climate efforts falling short, U.N. panel says. *The New York Times*. April 14: A1.

Giroux, H.A. 2012. *Disposable Youth: Racialized Memories and the Culture of Cruelty*. New York and London: Routledge.

Gore, A. 2009. *Our Choice: A Plan to Solve the Climate Crisis*. Emmaus, PA: Rodale.

Graham, D. 1981. *Down to a Sunless Sea*. New York: Ballantine.

Greenberger, R. 2013. *After Earth: United Rangers Corps Survival Manual*. San Rafael, CA: Insight Editions.

Greenfieldboyce, N. 2014. In search for habitable planets, why stop at 'Earth-like'? [Interview with Rene Heller and Rory Barnes]. All Things Considered. National Public Radio (NPR). 16 January. Transcript available at: http://www.npr.org/templates/transcript/transcript.php?storyId=263106030. Accessed 7 January 2015.

Greife, M.B. and Stretesky, P.B. 2013. Crude laws: treadmill of production and state variations in civil and criminal liability for oil sischarges in navigable waters. In N. South and A. Brisman (eds), *Routledge International Handbook of Green Criminology*. London and New York: Routledge, 150–66.

Hadadi, R. N.d. Movie review: *Battle Los Angeles* (PG-13). Available at: http://www.chesapeakefamily.com/index.php/blog/movies-a-dvds/2032-movie-review-battle-los-angeles-pg-13. Accessed 7 January 2015.

Halsey, M. and White, R. 1998. Crime, ecophilosophy and environmental harm. *Theoretical Criminology* 2(3): 345–71.

Hamilton, C. 2013. Geoengineering: our last hope, or a false promise? *The New York Times*, May 27: A17.

Hartmann, B. 1999. Population, environment and security: a new trinity. In J. Sillliman and Y. King (eds), *Dangerous Intersections: Feminism, Population and the Environment*. London: Zed Books, 1–24.

Howell, E. 2012. Closest 'Alien Earth' may be 13 light-years away. Space.com. 7 February. Available at: http://news.yahoo.com/closest-alien-earth-may-13-light-years-away-225759935.html. Accessed 7 January 2015.

Hulme, M. 2009. *Why We Disagree About Climate Change: Understanding Controversy, Inaction and Opportunity*. Cambridge, UK: Cambridge University Press.

Hulme, M. 2014. *Can Science Fix Climate Change?: A Case Against Climate Engineering*. Cambridge, UK: Polity Press.

Jensen, D. 2009. World at Gunpoint. *Orion* 28(3) [May/June]. Available at: https://orionmagazine.org/article/world-at-gunpoint/. Accessed 7 January 2015.

Kaufman, M. 2011. *First Contact: Scientific Breakthroughs in the Hunt for Life Beyond Earth*. New York: Simon & Schuster.

King, S. 1981. *Danse Macabre*. New York: Berkley.

Kingsolver, B. 2012. *Flight Behavior*. New York: HarperCollins.

Knapp, A. 2011. Did NASA find a habitable planet? Maybe. *Forbes*, 5 December. Available at: www.forbes.com/sites/alexknapp/2011/12/05/did-nasa-find-a-habitable-planet-maybe/. Accessed 7 January 2015.

Kolbert, E. 2009. Hosed: is there a quick fix for the climate? *The New Yorker*. 16 November, 75. Available at: http://www.newyorker.com/arts/critics/books/2009/11/16/091116crbo_books_kolbert?currentPage=all. Accessed 7 January 2015.

Krugman, P. 2011. Building a green economy. *The New York Times*. April 11: MM34.

Kunstler, J.H. 2005. *The Long Emergency: Surviving the Converging Catastrophes of the Twenty-First Century*. New York: Atlantic Monthly Press.

Kunstler, J.H. 2007. Making other arrangements. *Orion Magazine*. January/February. Available at: http://www.orionmagazine.org/index.php/articles/article/7/. Accessed 7 January 2015.

Kunstler, J.H. 2008. *World Made By Hand*. New York: Grove Press.

Landau, E. 2013. 3 new planets could host life. *CNN*. 21 April. Available at http://www.cnn.com/2013/04/18/us/planet-discovery/index.html. Accessed 7 January 2015.

Lanier, M.M. and Henry, S. 2010. *Essential Criminology* 3/e. Boulder, CO: Westview Press.

Lee, J.R. 2009. *Climate Change and Armed Conflict: Hot and Cold Wars*. London and New York: Routledge.

Lemonick, M.D. 2012a. *Mirror Earth: The Search for Our Planet's Twin*. New York: Walter & Company.

Lemonick, M.D. 2012b. Super-Earths' in M-Dwarf survey: life on other planets? *Time*, 30 March. Available at: www.time.com/time/health/article/0,8599,2110388,00.html. Accessed 7 January 2015.

Lemonick, M.D. 2014. The hunt for life beyond Earth. *National Geographic* 226(1): 26–45.

Levitt, S.D. and Dubner, S.J. 2009. *SuperFreakonomics: Global Cooling, Patriotic Prostitutes, and Why Suicide Bombers Should Buy Life Insurance*. New York: HarperCollins.

Lightman, A. 2014. Our lonely home in nature. *The New York Times* May 3: A19.

Lowe, T., Brown, K., Dessai, S., de França Doria, M., Haynes, K. and Vincent, K. 2006. Does tomorrow ever come? Disaster narrative and public perceptions of climate change. *Public Understanding of Science* 15: 435–57.

Lynch, G. 2012. *Capitalism: A Structural Genocide*. New York: Zed Books.

Maas, A., Comardicea, I. and Bodó, B. 2013. Environmental terrorism – a new security challenge? In A. Maas, B. Bodó, C. Burnley, I. Comardicea and R. Roffey (eds), *Global Environmental Change: New Drivers for Resistance, Crime and Terrorism?* Baden-Baden: Nomos, 203–20.

Mason, P. (ed.) 2003. *Criminal Visions: Media Representations of Crime and Justice*. Cullompton, Devon: Willan.

McClanahan, B. 2014. Green and grey: water justice, criminalization and resistance. *Critical Criminology* 22(3): 403–18.

McNall, S.G. 2011. *Rapid Climate Change: Causes, Consequences, and Solutions*. New York and London: Routledge.

Mooallem, J. 2008. The end is near! *The New York Times Magazine* (April 19): 28–32, 34.

Mooney, C. 2010. Geoengineering our climate future. *The Westchester Guardian*. 2 September, 5, 11.

Murphy, T. 2013. Barackalypse now. *Mother Jones* 38(1) [January/February]: 49–51.

Nellis, M. 2009. The aesthetics of redemption: released prisoners in American film and literature. *Theoretical Criminology* 13(1): 129–46.

Pérez-Peña, R. 2014. College classes use arts to brace for climate change. *The New York Times*. April 1: A12.

Presser, L. 2009. The narratives of offenders. *Theoretical Criminology* 13(2): 177–200.

Pretty, J. 2013. The consumption of a finite planet: well-being, convergence, divergence and the nascent green economy. *Environmental and Resource Economics* 55(4): 475–99.

Prud'homme, A. 2011. Drought: a creeping disaster. *The New York Times*. July 17: SR3.

Puig, C. 2013. 'After Earth' leaves an uninspiring aftertaste. *USA Today*. May 31: 5D.

Revkin, A.C. 2011. Confronting the 'anthropocene'. *The New York Times*. 11 May. Available at: http://dotearth.blogs.nytimes.com/2011/05/11/confronting-the-anthropocene/?_php=true&_type=blogs&_r=0. Accessed 7 January 2015.

Richard, M.G. 2009. *Avatar*: big movie with big environmental themes. December 18. *Treehugger*. Available at: http://www.treehugger.com/culture/avatar-big-movie-with-big-environmental-themes.html. Accessed 7 January 2015.

Richardson, L. 1995. Narrative and sociology. In J. van Maanen (ed.), *Representations in Ethnography*. Los Angeles, CA: Sage, 198–221.

Ridley, M. 2012. Apocalypse not. *Wired*. September 110–15, 148, 150.

Rosenthal, N. 2000. Apocalypse: beauty and horror in contemporary art. In N. Rosenthal, M. Barcher, M. Bracewell, J. Hall and N. Kernan (eds), *Apocalypse: Beauty and Horror in Contemporary Art*. London: Royal Academy of Arts, 12–31.

Ross, A. 1991. Is global culture warming up? *Social Text* 28, 3–30.

Santora, M. 2006. Hollywood's multifaceted cause du jour. *The New York Times*. 3 December.

Sass, S.L. 2006. Scarcity, mother of invention. *The New York Times*. 10 August: A23.

Scheffran, J. and Cannaday, T. 2013. Resistance to climate change policies: the conflict potential of non-fossil energy paths and climate engineering. In A. Maas, B. Bodó, C. Burnley, I. Comardicea and R. Roffey (eds), *Global Environmental Change: New Drivers for Resistance, Crime and Terrorism?* Baden-Baden: Nomos, 261–92.

Schwartz, P. 2012. In gas we'll trust. *Wired*. September 092, 096, 098.

Scott, A.O. 2008. 007 is back, and he's brooding. *The New York Times*. 14 November: C1, C15.

Seager, J. 1993. Creating a culture of destruction: gender, militarism, and the environment. In R. Hofrichter (ed.), *Toxic Struggles: The Theory and Practice of Environmental Justice*. Philadelphia, PA: New Society Publishers, 58–66.

Shostak, S. 2012. Depth change: what do the 'battleship' aliens want from us, anyway? *Discover*. May 18. Available at: http://blogs.discovermagazine.com/crux/2012/05/18/depth-change-what-do-the-battleship-aliens-want-from-us-anyway/. Accessed 7 January 2015.

Shute, N. 1957. *On the Beach*. New York: William Morrow and Company.

Smith, S. 2013. Future shock. *Entertainment Weekly*. August 2: 36–43.

Sontag, S. 2001. *On Photography*. New York: Picador USA.

South, N. 2010. The ecocidal tendencies of late modernity: transnational crime, social exclusion, victim and rights. In R. White (ed.), *Global Environmental Harm: Criminological Perspectives*. Cullompton, Devon, UK: Willan, 228–47.

South, N., Brisman, A. and Beirne, P. 2013. A guide to a green criminology. In N. South and A. Brisman (eds), *Routledge International Handbook of Green Criminology*. Oxford, UK: Routledge, 27–42.

South, N., Brisman, A. and McClanahan, B. 2014. Green criminology. *Oxford Bibliographies Online: Criminology*. 28 April 2014. DOI: 10.1093/OBO/9780195396607–0161. Available at: http://www.oxfordbibliographies.com/view/document/obo-9780195396607/obo-9780195396607–0161.xml. Accessed 7 January 2015.

Sparks, R. 1995. Entertaining the crisis: television and moral enterprise. In D. Kidd-Hewitt and R. Osborne (eds), *Crime and the Media: The Post-Modern Spectacle*. London: Pluto Press, 49–66.

Stevens, D. 2006. Trading spaces. *The Slate*. 8 December. Available at: http://www.slate.com/articles/arts/movies/2006/12/trading_spaces.html. Accessed 7 January 2015.

Stretesky, P.B., Long, M.A. and Lynch, M.J. 2014. *The Treadmill of Crime: Political Economy and Green Criminology*. London and New York: Routledge.

Toomey, D. 2010. Avatar promotes seven profound environmental themes. 5 January. *Supergreenme*. Available at: http://www.supergreenme.com/go-green-environment-eco:Avatar-Promotes-Seven-Profound-Environmental-Themes. Accessed 7 January 2015.

Urry, J. 2010. Consuming the planet to excess. *Theory, Culture and Society* 27(2–3): 191–212.

Wall, M. 2014. Newfound alien planet has longest year known for transiting world. *Space.com/Yahoo!News*. 22 July. Available at: http://news.yahoo.com/newfound-alien-planet-longest-known-transiting-world-223514280.html. Accessed 7 January 2015.

Walsh, B. 2008. Why green is the new red, white and blue. *Time* 171(17) [April 28]: 45–50, 53–4, 57.

Walsh, B. 2012. Nature is over. *Time* 179(10) [March 12]: 82–5.

Washington, H. and Cook, J. 2011. *Climate Change: Heads in the Sand*. London and Washington, D.C.: Earthscan.

White, R. and Heckenberg, D. 2014. *Green Criminology: An Introduction to the Study of Environmental Harm*. London and New York: Routledge.

The White House, Office of the Press Secretary. 2013. *Remarks by the President on Climate Change. 25* June. Available at: http://www.whitehouse.gov/the-press-office/2013/06/25/remarks-president-climate-change. Accessed 7 January 2015.

Williams, C. 1996. An environmental victimology. *Social Justice* 23(4): 16–40.

Witten, M. 1993. Narrative and the culture of obedience at the workplace. In D.K. Mumby (ed.), *Narrative and Social Control: Critical Perspectives.* Newbury Park, CA: Sage, 97–118.

Index

Note: *italic* page numbers indicate tables and figures; numbers in brackets preceded by *n* are footnote numbers.

9/11 attacks 12, 81

Achieng, J. 157
Adams, Jonathan 221, 223, 234–5
AE: Apocalypse Earth (film, 2013) 301
Afghanistan 13(*n*8), *44*
Africa 4, *44*
   as 'dark continent' 224, 225
   diamond trade in *see* diamonds and
      conflict
   drought/famine in 160
   elephant poaching in 5, 5–6(*n*5)
   illegal logging in 47, *47*, 48, *48*, 49
   sub-Saharan 44, 179–80
   sustainable development in 15
   wars in 4–5, 178
   water scarcity in 7
   see also specific countries
'Africa's World War' 59
After Earth (film, 2013) 300, 301
Agent Orange 11, 13, 184–5
agriculture 51, 76, 87, 208, 214, 241
   industrial 76, 86
   and peace 17
   and war 12
aid 2, 52, 160
Al-Shabab 65
alien planets/species 292–3, 294, 300–301,
   301
Altamira (Brazil) 137, 138, 139, *139*, 143
Amazon region 48, 57, 126
   see also Belo Monte hydroelectric dam
Andrade Sampaio, A. 140

AngloGold Ashanti (AGA) 18, 125,
   128–31
   and Colombian authorities 129
   illegal activities of 128–9
   and murder of activists 129, 131
   public relations/CSR by 128
   subsidiaries 128, 131
   and UNGPs 129
Angola 4, *44*, *47*, 48, 197, 203
animal rights 95, 115, 118
Anthropocene epoch 294
anthropocentrism 17–18, 86, 95, 111, 116,
   118, 235, 293
apes 51, 60–61, 65, 67, 68–9
Arango, Andrés Pastrana 81
Arctic 4, 8–9, 44, 49
arms trade 49, 289, 291(*n*11)
Asia *44*, 242
   illegal logging in *47*, 48, *48*
   see also specific countries
Australia 53
   and East Timor 4, *44*
   indigenous people in 2, 243
   mining in 241–59
      boom/bust cycle in 244, 256
      in Bowen Basin *see* Bowen Basin
         mining communities
      community solidarity/unionism in
         251–3
      conflicts surrounding 242
      corporations 243, 253–4, *254*,
         256–7
      and development 245

effects on communities of 241,
243, 247, 248, 249, 254–5
employment regimes of 244–50
employment uncertainty/risk in
246–7, 252–3
industry regulation for 243, 247,
256–7
non-resident workers (NRWs)
in 242, 244, 245, 246, 247,
248–9, 251, 252, 253–5, *259*
resistance to 243
risks to workers in 244, 251
and supercapitalism 242–3
use of contractors in 245, 247
and violence 241, 248, 249, 253
Windsor Inquiry on (2013) 242,
245, 248, 251, 254–5
women and 246, 247, 251–2, 253
workforce statistics 245–6, *258*
see also Bowen Basin mining
communities
see also On the Beach
Ausubel, Jesse 296–7
Avatar (film, 2009) 292–3, 294, 301

Baer, H. 13, 14
Baralt, L.B. 270
Barclay, Thomas 293
Barnshaw, J. 269
Barre, General Siad 155–6, 158, 165
Barsa, M. 269
Bas-Congo forest (DRC) 63
Batley, G. 15
Battle: Los Angeles (film, 2011) 294
Battlefield Earth (film, 2000) 293–4
bears, killing of 8–9, 96, 100–102
court rulings on 102, 103–4, 105–8,
115
licences for 113–14
motivations for 111, 112, 113
Norwegian state policies on 96, 98,
100–102
suffering in 116
Beirne, P. 96
Belo Monte hydroelectric dam (Brazil) 18,
125, 136–43

Environmental Impact Assessment
(EIA) for 139
and indigenous people 136, *139*
forced displacement of 138, 139
rights of, neglected by state
139–40, 141, 143
threat to lifestyle of 137
licence for construction of 138, 139,
140
protests about 136, 137–8, 141
from international organisations
138, 141
threats/violence against activists
138
state support for 139–43
and Brazilian Development Bank
(BNDES) 141
environmental authority (IBAMA)
140
and judicial system 140–41
and police/military 141–3
Bern Convention 96, 100, 118
BHP Hilton/BHP Hilton Mitsubishi
Alliance (BMA) 244, 254, 255
Biggs, Duan 212–13
bin Laden, Osama 202, 208
biodiversity 42, 51, 53, 57, 60, 95, 97, 241
Law of 100, 101(*n*14), 102(*n*16), 103,
115
securitisation of 198
biopiracy 86
Blood Diamond (film, 2006) 290, 291, 292,
294
Blundell, A.G. 69
Boekhout van Solinge, T. 50
Bogotá (Colombia) 75, 78
Bolivia *44*, *47*, 48, 290
Bond, James *see Die Another Day*;
Quantum of Solace
borders 46, 64, 98, 101, 201, 203, 204, 270
and poaching 208–9, 211, 213, 214,
229
see also frontiers
Børresen, B. 114
Botswana *44*, 202
Bourdieu, P. 271

Bouvier, A. 185
Bowen Basin mining communities
    (Australia) 242, 250–55
    Collinsville township 250, 251–3, 256
    coal strike in (1952) 252
    lay-offs in 252–3
    Moranbah township 250, 253–5, 256
    NRWs in 250–51, 252, 253–5
    and road accidents 251
    overview of region/townships 250
    Queensland Resources Council (QRC)
        in 251
    women/community organisation in
        (MCU) 243, 251–2, 253, 254, 255
BP *see* Deepwater Horizon oil spill
Brazil 18, *44*, *47*, 48
    Altamira 137, 138, 139, *139*, 143
    hydroelectric power in *see* Belo Monte
        hydroelectric dam
    mining in 126, 243
    Xingu River/Peoples *132*, 136, 137
Brazilian Development Bank (BNDES)
    141
Breytenbach, Jan 197
Britain (UK) 44, *44*, 155, 156, 163, 265
Brockington, D. 200, 222, 234
Bruch, C. 2, 17
Bullock, Donna 252, 253
bushmeat 51, 58, 60, 61, 62
    sustainable 69

Cabrejas, A.H. 16
Camargo, Alfonso Lleras 79
Cambodia 4, *44*, 45, *47*, 48, 49, 50, 52
Cameron, David 267
Cameroon *44*, *47*, 48, 62–3
Canada 132, 133, 242
capitalism 19, 86, 127, 223, 224, 228, 232,
    235, 297(*n*15), 298–9(*n*18)
    super- 242–3
Castaño, Carlos 80–81
Caval Ridge Mine (Bowen Basin,
    Australia) 254–5
Central African Republic (CAR) 49, 50,
    64, 209
Cepeda, Ivan 129
Chamayou, Grégoire 208, 228, 233

charcoal trade 17, 51, 65–7, 70
chemical/biological weapons 11, 12, 13
children 160, 234
    and war 5
China *44*, 156, 213, 241, 286
    in conflict over oil/gas 3–4
    dams in 7
    ivory trade in 6(*n*5)
    and Japan 3, 4, *44*
Chizarira National Park (Zimbabwe) 227
Chomsky, Noam 288
Christie, T. 69
Christy, B. 5
Convention on International Trade in
    Endangered Species (CITES), 1974
    45, 183, 205, 211, 212, 213, 214
Cleary, Paul 256
Clifford, M. 183
climate change 2(*n*3), 7, 9, 14, 16, 57,
    241–2, 295(*n*12), 302
    and technological fixes 299–300
    and timber trade 46, 51, 66–67
climate justice 16
Clinton, Hillary 201–2
cloud seeding *see* weather manipulation
coal 16, 18, 244
    and climate change 241–42
    see also Bowen Basin mining
        communities
coca growing 84–5, 87–8, 87(*n*9)
Collinsville township *see under* Bowen
    Basin mining communities
Colombia 17, 18, *44*, *47*, 48, 75–90
    agricultural corporations in 77, 86, 87,
        88
    corruption in 79, 82, 85
    deforestation in 76, 84–5
    drug issues in 76
        land access 84–5
        mafia culture 82
        toxic fumigations 85, 88
        trafficking cartels 80–81
    forums in 75–6, 77, 83–90
        environmental sustainability
            discussed in 89–90
        food sovereignty discussed in 88
        land access discussed in 84–6

land uses discussed in 86–8
and nature parks 86
people/groups represented in 84
rural development/infrastructure
   discussed in 89
indigenous people/peasants/rural
   women in 76, 79, 84, 85–90
displacement of 80, 82
and land access 84–6
and land use 86–8
traditional knowledge of 77, 88
internal armed conflict in 77–84
and BACRIM militias 82
Caguán peace talks (1998) 81
ELN 75(n1), 131
environmental harms caused by 86
FARC-EP in 79–80, 81, 82, 84
government paramilitaries in
   80–82, 85
guerrilla activities in 78–9, 81, 85,
   131
main actors in 75
peace efforts (1998–2001) 81–2
and Peace and Justice Law (2005)
   81–2
termination agreement (2012) 75,
   82–4
victims of violence of 75, 77, 82
land access/use issues in 75, 76, 84–8
and coca growing 84–5, 87(n9)
and failure of agrarian reform 79
mining corporations in 82, 87, 126
and mining-energy committee
   (CME) 129
and paramilitaries 129, 132, 133,
   134–5
and small-scale miners 126, 130,
   133, 134
and UNGPs 129, 135, 136
see also AngloGold Ashanti; Gran
   Colombia Gold
National Front agreement in (1957) 77,
   78–9
Peasant Enterprise Zones (PEZ) in 85
sustainable development in 76–7
traditional knowledge in 77
colonialism/neocolonialism 2, 20, 203–6

and conservation 222, 223–4, 227–8,
   234, 235
Colony, The (film, 2013) 300
coltan/tantalum 5, 57, 58, 59, 66, 71, 178,
   181, 187
commodification of nature 164, 209, 285
communism 78, 79, 198, 242
conflict/conflict relationships 1, 42–5
definitions of (n2), 42–3
HIICR database of 41, 42–5, *44*, 49
and ideologies 77
intensity of 43
routes out of 2
sites of 43–5, *44*
see also environment-conflict
   relationships
Congo Basin/River 42, 47, 48, 49, 62
Congo, Democratic Republic of *see* DRC
Congolese Wildlife Service (ICCN) 61, 62,
   65, 66, 68
consensus conference 83, 83(n7)
conservation 15, 19–20, 42, 57, 59, 69–71,
   204, 222
and education 225, 226, 232(n3), 233
fortress 222–3, 224, 227, 234, 235
and indigenous people 222–4, 228
militarisation/securitisation of 68,
   69–70, 198
use of drones *see* drones
and neocolonialism 222, 223–4, 234
see also IAPF
Cooney Seisdedos, P. 125
Corbin, J. 76
Corporate Social Responsibility (CSR)
   127, 144, 256
corruption 4, 79, 82, 85, 126, 155, 198, 210
and logging 41, 46, 63
counter-insurgency 205–7
Coupland, Douglas *see Player One: What
   Is to Become of Us*
Crawford, George A. 208
criminology
and conflict relationships 1
see also green/environmentally
   sensitive criminology
Crutzen, Paul 299–300
Cuba 82, 83

Cuellar, Ramirez 135
Cullen, P. 16
cultural criminology 285(*n*2), 291(*n*9), 302
    green 20, 285–6, 301–2, 303

Dam-de Jong, D. 186, 187, 188
dams 10, 12, 16
    see also Belo Monte hydroelectric dam
Dana, D.A. 269
Darfur (Sudan) 43, 64(*n*3), 65
Dark Knight Rises, The (film, 2012) 297, 299
Dark Planet (film, 1997) 300
Deepwater Horizon oil spill (2010) 20, 265–80
    and BP's profits 267, 269
    and BP's public relations 270
    conflicts in 267
    culpability for 266
    and globalisation 265, 269, 270–72, 273, 279
    media framing of 265–6, 267, 269, 272–80
        analysis of, discussion 279–80
        analysis of, research methods for 272–3
        analysis of, results 273–9, *274, 275, 276*
        and capital
            protection–environmental
            protection conflict 266, 272, 276–7, 279
        risk reporting 274–6, *276*
        and vulnerable human populations 277–9
    and UK 267
deforestation 17, 45, 50–51, 60, 84–5, 154
    and climate change 46, 51
    and land access 76
    scale of 47, 62–3
    as weapon in conflicts 11, 13, 50, 184
del Olmo, Rosa 11–12
Delgado, R. 303
DeMocker, M. 303
Democratic Forces for the Liberation of Rwanda (FDLR) 59, 65–6

development 2, 52, 144
    and indigenous people 140
    social 17, 76
    stat-corporate actors in 126, 127
    sustainable 15, 76–7
diamonds and conflict 4, 42, 57, 58, 59, 71, 178, 180, 181, 186, 187, 188, 197
    fictionalised accounts of 289–90, 291, 292
    and Kimberley Process 191, 211, 290
Diaoyu/Senkaku Islands 3
Die Another Day (film, 2002) 289, 291, 292, 294, 297, 299
Dilworth, C. 18, 299
disease 137, 159
displaced people *see* refugees/displaced persons
District 9 (film, 2009) 301
Down to a Sunless Sea (Graham) 286, 288–9
Democratic Republic of Congo (DRC) 4–5, 17, *44, 47*, 48, 57–71, 128, 209
    Army of (FARDC) 5, 60(*n*1), 62, 65, 66, 68
    Bas-Congo forest in 63
    charcoal trade in 65–7
    conflict in 57–8, 59–67
        impact of 60–64
        and living environment 64–7
    elephants/ivory trade in 61–2, 64–5
    Garamba National Park 6, 61–2, 64–5
    gorillas in 60–61, 65, 67, 68
    Kahuzi-Biega National Park 61
    Kivu region 57, 59–60, 65–6, 68
    living environment in 57, 63–6
    logging/deforestation in 62, 62–3, 66–7
        and corruption 63
    LRA in 64–5, 70
    mining in 61, 66
    Okapi Faunal Reserve 62
    peacebuilding in 67–70
        'Peace Parks' movement 67–8
    refugees in 60, 61, 62, 67, 70
    and Rwanda 57, 59–60, 61, 65–6, 67–8, 69

and Uganda *44*, 59, 60, 60(*n*2), 64–5,
        67, 68–9
    and ICC case 187–8
    Virunga National Park 17, 60–61, 65,
        66, 67, 68, 69
    Wildlife Service (ICCN) in 61, 62, 65,
        66, 68
drive in, drive out (DIDO) workers *see*
        NRWs *under* Australia, mining in
drones, 'conservation' 15, 202, 207, 208,
        211, 212, 222, 229–32, 233
    and logic of police 233
    media representation of 231–2
    problems with 120(*n*6), 231
drought 18, 156, 159, 160–61, 164
drugs 11–12, 197
    see also under Colombia
Dubner, Stephen J. 296, 297
Duffy, Rosaleen 221–2
Dunne, T. 288

East China Sea 3
East Timor 4, *44*
eco crime 76
ecocide 11, 12, 118, 288, 292, 295, 303
ecophilosophy, *see* anthropocentrism
ecosystem health 41, 51, 157
ecosystem services 58, 59, 66
education 17, 52, 69, 76, 79, 161, 241
    and conservation 225, 226
Eichstaedt, Peter 157, 164–5, 166
elephants 61–2, 69, 197
    see also ivory trade
Emerson, R.M. 273
employment 16, 69
    uncertainty/risk in 246–7
endangered species 9, 11, 18, 96, 98, 100,
        111, 115, 157
    Convention on *see* CITES
    protection of 45, 183, 205
    trade in 154
    as environmental crime 183
energy consumption 4, 65, 180–81, 295
    see also oil/gas
energy prices 18, 125
Enough Project 64
environment-conflict relationships

fictionalised accounts of 20, 286–303
    in film/television 289–301
    novels 286–9
    typologies of 1–2, 2–3(*n*3), 17, 41, 289
environmental crime 183
environmental degradation and conflict 2,
        10–15, 18–20, 49, 61, 85–7, 90,
        154–5, 289
    fictionalised accounts of 288–9, 290,
        292, 293, 295, 302–3
    and food scarcity 8–9
    and geo-political structures 163–4
    and geographical scale 76
    and green criminology 154–5
    low priority in addressing 49–50, 53
    and media framing 265–6, 267–70
        see also under Deepwater Horizon
        oil spill
    and migration 7–8
    and 'War on Drugs' 11–12
    see also living environment
environmental/ecological justice 12, 41,
        42, 96, 164
Environmental Modification Techniques,
        Convention on (1976) 185
environmental peacebuilding theory 67–8
environmental protection laws 45
environmental rights 7, 164
environmental security 7
Escobar, Pablo 80, 81
Estonia *47*, 48
Ethiopia *44*, 155, 156, 160
ethno-religious conflict 8, 43
Europe
    illegal logging in *47*, 48, *48*, 49, 52
        see also under Russia
European Union (EU) 16, 53
Ewick, P. 302–3
Executive Outcomes 179
Extractive Industries Transparency
        Initiative (ETTI) 243

Falkland Islands 44
famine 18, 156, 159, 160–61, 164
FARC-EP (Colombia) 79–80, 81, 82, 84
farmers 96, 101–2
Fauna and Flora International 204

Ferrell, J. 77
First Gulf War (1990–91) 11
fisheries 3, 15, 51, 270, 277–8
fishing, illegal 18, 156–7, 159, 161, 164
    military protection for 163
Fitzgerald, A.B. 270
Flournoy, A.C. 268–9
fly in, fly out (FIFO) workers *see* NRW
    under Australia, mining in
food availability/scarcity 8–9
    and contamination 11
    see also bushmeat; famine
food security 8, 9, 17, 76, 137
forests 4, 18, 50, 57
    conflict as protection for 62, 63
    firewood harvesting in 60, 61, 70
    non-timber resources of 45, 51
    as renewable resource 58
    sustainable management of 45, 63, 69
    see also deforestation; logging
Forest Law Enforcement Governance and
    Trade (FLEGT) 53
Fortescue Metals Group (FMG) 243
fracking 15–16, 265, 296
France 155, 156
free market 6, 299(*n*18)
Friedman, D. 302
Friedman, M. 127
frontiers 9, 18, 49, 125, 127, 143–4
Frontino S.A. 133–4

Gabon *44*, *47*, 48, 62–3
Gacha, Gonzalo Rodriguez 80
Gaitán, Jorge Eliecer 77, 78
Garamba National Park (DRC) 61–2, 64–5
Gberie, L. 181
gender 6, 76, 114
    see also masculinity; women
Geneva Convention 10, 182–3, 186–7
    Optional Protocol (1977) 185
Genocide Convention 183
Gerber, J.F. 51–2
Germany 156, 179, 180
Gettleman, J. 64
Ghana *47*, 128
Giordano, M. 49
Glencore Xstrata 252–3
global fields theory 265, 271–2, 279–80

Global South 14(*n*9), 44, 48, 49, 223
Global Witness 41, 181
globalisation 9, 20, 242–3, 245, 265, 269,
    270, 279
    and green criminology 270–72, 273,
    280
    and power relationships 279, 280
gold 178, 180, 181, 186
    mining 4, 5, 57, 58
    see also AngloGold Ashanti; Gran
        Colombia Gold
Gómez, Laureano 78
Gonzalez, C.G. 223
Gorbachev, Mihkail 68
Gore, Al 299–300
gorillas 60–61, 65, 67, 68–9
governance 49, 52, 53
Graham, David *see Down to a Sunless Sea*
Gran Colombia Gold (GCG) 18, 125,
    132–6
    Artisanal Miner Partnership Model of
        135
    involvement in causing crime 134–6
    land grab by 133–4
    violence perpetrated by 133
greed 3, 5–6, 153
green criminology 1, 2, 57, 153
    cultural 20, 285–6, 301–2, 303
    and globalisation 265, 270–72, 273,
        280
    and illegal logging 41, 45, 49, 53
    and living environment 59
    and state complicity in environmental
        crime 184
    and theriocide 96
    and traditional knowledge 90
'Green Helmets' force (UN) 68
Green, P. 161
Gregory, Derek 202, 207, 231
grounded theory 76
groupthink 268, 269
Guterres, A. 159
Gwin, P. 225, 227, 229, 235

Halsey, M. 298
Hamilton, Clive 300
Hari, J. 162
Hartmann, B. 12, 15, 298(*n*18)

Hayward, K. 77
Hayward, Tony 267
He, Y. 3
healthcare 52, 69, 76, 79, 161
Heidelberg Institute for International
    Conflict Research (HIICR) 41,
    42–5, *44*, 49
herbicides 11–12, 85, 88
Hobsbawn, Eric 208, 215
Honduras *44*, 77, 156
Honenen, Pirko 159
human health *see* public/human health
Human Rights Council (UN) 127
Human Rights Watch 128, 243
human rights/human rights abuses 7, 84
    and multinational corporations *see*
        under multinational corporations
human-predator conflicts *see* theriocide
humanitarian assistance 14, 178, 179
humanitarian law 11, 19, 177
humanitarian organisations 59, 135
hunters 97, 212
    'great white' 227–8
    see also man-hunting
hunting 203–5
    indigenous 203, 204
    and neocolonialism 222–4, 227–8, 235
    of predatory animals *see* theriocide
    sort/safari 19–20, 209, 212, 213, 224
    see also poaching
Hussein, B.M. 158, 159
Hussen, Ahmed 164
hydropower 16, 18, 126

Ichikowitz, Ivor 211, 221
IIRSA (Initiative for the Integration of
    Regional Infrastructure in South
    America) 89
India 4, 7, 156, 163
indigenous people 2, 76, 85
    and corporations 136, 137, 138
    ILO Convention on (1989) 140
    right to consent of 139–40
    traditions/spirituality of 9, 88
    and wildlife conservation 222–4, 228
    see also traditional knowledge

Indonesia *44*, *47*, 48, 52, 62, 158, 241, 269
infrastructures 52, 62, 69, 81, 89, 137, 159,
    161
    and dystopian fiction 287
Inter-American Commission on Human
    Rights (IACHR) 138, 141
inter-tribal conflicts 43
International Anti-Poaching Foundation
    (IAPF) 19, 224, 225–36
    attitude to poachers of 226–7
    and drones 229–32, 233
    education campaigns by 226(*n*3), 232,
        233–4
    formation of (2010) 225
    and Green Army volunteers 234
    lethal forces used by 232
    and logic of police 232
    Mander and 225–6, 227–8, 229–30
    manhunting strategy of 227–8, 230,
        233, 235–6
    militarised strategy of 226
    and neocolonialism 225, 226, 234, 235
International Court of Justice 187
International Criminal Court (ICC) 10,
    182(*n*1), 185, 186, 187
International Labour Organisation (ILO)
    138
    Convention on Indigenous and Tribal
        Peoples (1989) 140
international law/agreements 11, 45
    humanitarian 11, 19, 177, 182–4
    environmental protection in 185
    new norms for 188–91
    of war *see* crimes/laws of *under* war
international political community (IPC)
    156, 157, 159, 163
International Tropical Timber Organization
    (ITTO) 41, 45, 51
Inuit people 9
Iraq 11, *44*
    invasion/occupation of 180, 226, 229
Iraq–Iran War 10–11
Israel 7, 11, *44*, 286
Italy 155, 156, 157
Ivory Coast 62
ivory trade 5, 5–6(*n*5), 17, 64–5, 70, 197,
    198, 213–14, 221, 225

Jaichand, V. 140
Janjaweed 65
Japan 3–4, *44*, 49, 156
Jasparro, C. 165
Jensen, D. 301
Johnson, R. 162, 163
joint criminal enterprise (JCE) 177, 189,
    190–91
Jones, K. 42
Jooste, Johan/'Jooste War' 199, 201, 205,
    211, 212, 215

Kabila, Laurent 59, 209
Kahuzi-Biega National Park (DRC) 61
Katrina, Hurricane (2005) 268
Katunga, J. 4
Kaufman, Marc 301
Kedahda S.A./Kedahda Secunda Ltda 128,
    131
Kenya *44*, 65, 156, 160, 224
Kenyan Wildlife Service (KWS) 201
Khmer Rouge 49
Kilcullen, David 206
Kimberley Process Certification Scheme
    (KPCS) 191, 290
Kivu region (DRC) 57, 59–60, 65–6, 68
Klare, M. 178, 179
Knights, Peter 214
Kony, Joseph 64
Kookana, R.S. 15
Korean War 10, 12
Kramer, R. 127, 135
Kruger National Park (South Africa) 204,
    205, 208, 209, 210, 211, 213
Kunstler, James Howard 298
    see also World Made By Hand

labour unions *see* trade unions
land erosion 13, 51, 63
land ownership/access/use 3, 17, 44, 75,
    76, 84–8
land redistribution policies 76
land reserve zones 76
landmines/sea mines 12, 14
Lang, Jack 163
Laos *47*, 201, 243
Latin America *see* South America
Latvia *47*, 48

law enforcement 42, 53, 114
Laws and Customs of War on Land (1907)
    186
Letukas, L. 269
Levitt, Steven D. 296, 297
Liberia 4, *47*, 49, 50, 60, 62–3, 66, 69, 181
Libya 42, *44*
licences/permits 45, 46, 127
    for predator hunting 98, 99, 100
living environment 57, 58–9
    and conflict 58, 59, 63–4, 70–71
    and ecosystem services 58, 59
    as renewable resource 58–9
    see also forests
logging 4, 16, 17, 41–53
    activities encompassed by 45–6
    and climate change 46
    and conflict 48–52, *48*
        impacts of 50–52
        importance of investigating 50
        as source for funding/cause of 43
    and corruption 41, 46, 63
    and crime 50, 51, 53
    defined 45–7
    and deforestation 45, 46
    extent of 46, 47
        difficulties in estimating 49–50
    and forest decline 41
    and governance 49, 52, 53
    initiatives on 53
    and legal logging 45, 46
    low priority in addressing 49–50, 53
    reasons for 46–7
    sites of 47–8, *47*, *48*
        remote regions 46, 49
    and timber market 46, 49
    and war 16, 181
    and women 51–2
London Convention (1900) 204
Lord of War (film, 2005) 289–90, 294
Lord's Resistance Army (LRA) (DRC)
    64–5, 70
Lovelock, J. 20
Lowe, T. 302
Lugenda Wildlife Reserve 230
Lujala, P. 2
Lula da Silva, Luiz Inácio 136, 140
lynx, killing of 96, 99–100

court rulings on 102, 105, 110–11, 115
motivations for 112, 113, 115
Norwegian state policies on 96, 98,
99–100

M23 rebellion 57, 60, 68
Mabunda, David 211, 212, 213
McNeely, J.A. 63
McShane, Thomas 221, 223, 234–5
Maggs, Ken 210
Malaya 205–6
Malaysia 4, *47*, 163
man-hunting 202, 207–8, 221, 224, 226,
227–8, 230, 233
see also drones, 'conservation'
Mander, Damien 225–6, 227–8, 229–30,
232, 235, 236
Mangan, S. 163
Marikana mine shootings (South Africa,
2012) 207
marine ecosystem 157, 158, 159, 300(*n*21)
maritime disputes 3–4
markets/market processes 6, 46, 49, 180,
182, 285, 297(*n*15)
Marks, M. 207
Marx, Karl 223
masculinity 6
and theriocide 114
and war 12
Matza, D. 127, 144
Medellin cartel 80, 81
media 20, 42, 231–2, 285, 298, 301, 302
framing *see* Deepwater Horizon oil
spill
Meer, T. 207
mercenaries 179, 183, 210
mercury pollution 133, 158, 270
Merton, R.K. 78
Mexico, Gulf of *see* Deepwater Horizon
oil spill
Michalowski, R. 127, 135
Michel, D. 6–7
Middle East *44*, 179, 180, 225
migration 7–8, 70, 139
see also refugees/internally displaced
persons

migratory corridors 69
mining 4–5, 16, 18, 20, 76, 82, 86, 154,
178
and forced displacement 129, 134, 135
industry regulation for 243, 247
localised effects of 241
and resistance/protest movements 243
small-scale *126*, *130*, 133, 134
and violence 129, 131–2, 133, 135,
241, 248
see also AngloGold Ashanti; fracking;
Gran Colombia Gold
Mining Communities United, Australia
(MCU) 243, 251–2, 253, 254, 255
Montreal Protocol on Substances that
Deplete the Ozone Layer (1987)
183
Moranbah township (Australia) *see under*
Bowen Basin mining communities
mountaintop removal (MTR) 16
Mozambique 197, 203, 204, 209, 210, 213,
243
Muffett, C. 2, 17
multinational corporations 18, 77, 82, 86
and CSR 127, 144
and environmental crime 183–4
and frontiers 125, 127, 135, 138, 139,
143–4
and governments 268–9
and human rights abuses 127, 129, 132,
134, 135, 138, 139–40, 141, 143
and judicial systems 140–41
military/police support for 88, 127,
129, 141–3
mining 243
see also under Colombia
neutralisation techniques used by 127,
144
and resource wars 180–81, 188
and state-corporate crime theory
125–7, 144
and traditional knowledge 90
and UNGPs 127, 129, 135, 136, 144
Murillo, Diego 80–81
Murphy, T. 288
Murray, G. 252

Myanmar *44*, *47*, 48

Namibia 205, 206
napalm 10, 11
National Liberation Army, Colombia
    (ELN) 75(*n*1), 131
national security 13, 14, 80, 179, 199, 202
natural gas *see* oil/gas
natural resource conflicts 2–20, 41, 43
    over declining resources 2, 6–10, 18,
        49
        and migration 7–8
        water scarcity 6–7
    over extraction 2, 15–16, 20, 269, 290,
        291
        see also mining; oil/gas
    over possession 2, 3–6, 17
        and wealth/greed 4–6, 57
    see also environment-conflict
        relationships, typologies of;
        environmental degradation and
        conflict; living environment
Nellemann, C. 41
Nellis, M. 302
Neocleous, M. 228, 232–3
neoliberalism 6, 86, 242–3, 268–9, 271
New York, Act of 133–4
Nicaragua *44*, 77
Nigeria 4, *44*, 265, 294–5
Nilson, M. 207
nødverge 99
non-governmental organisations (NGOs)
    97, 100–101, 128, 129, 138, 222,
    243, 268
non-timber forest products 45, 51
norms 96, 117, 136, 182–3, 187–91, 192,
    268, 271
Norte Energia 137, 138, 140, 141, 143
Norway 44, *44*, 83, 243
    hunting predatory animals in *see*
        theriocide
Norwegian Environment Agency 97, 98,
    99, 100
NRW (non-resident workers) *see under*
    Australia, mining in
nuclear weapons/war 14, 16, 184, 286,
    287, 288

Nurse, A. 114

Obama, Barack 201, 266–7, 273, 297(*n*15)
Oblivion (film, 2013) 294
O'Hagan, Andrew 10, 12
Oil and Natural Gas Corp (India) 4
oil/gas 3–4, 18, 44, 296
    and dystopian fiction 287–8, 294–5
    and pollution *see* Deepwater Horizon
        oil spill
    and war/military 11, 13–14, 178, 179,
        180, 186, 187
Okapi Faunal Reserve (DRC) 62
O'Keeffe, A. 9
On the Beach (Shute) 286, 288–9
organised crime 153, 162
    see also drugs; piracy
Organization of American States (OAS)
    141
Orogun, P. 179–80
Owens, Mark/Owens, Delia 231

Pakistan 7, *44*, 156, 229
Pandorum (film, 2009) 292, 293, 300
Papua New Guinea *44*, *47*, 48, 243
Paraguay *44*, *47*, 48
Passas, N. 42
peace 2, 16, 50
    and development 17
'Peace Parks' movement 67–8
peacebuilding 17, 67–70
    environmental, theory of 67–8
Pearson, D.D. 268
Peasant Enterprise Zones (PEZ), Colombia
    85
Pečar, J. 5
Peetz, G.R. 252
Perkins Vick, J. 268
Peru *44*, *47*, 48, 243
Philippines 4, *44*, *47*, 48
Pinilla, Gustavo Rojas 78
piracy 18, 153–5
    and environmental harm/economic
        need 155, 159, 161–5, 166
    and geo-political structures 163–4
    and green criminology 154–5
    holistic response required for 165

and Hollywood 153
and loss of traditional income 161–3, 165
military response to 154, 163, 164
Player One: What Is to Become of Us (Coupland) 287–8, 289, 297–8
poaching 5, 5–6(*n*5), 8–9, 15, 51, 66
    and bandits/social bandits 208, 215
    and borders 208–9, 211, 213, 214, 229
    of elephants *see* ivory trade
    and indigenous people 222–4
    and land ownership 198
    militarised/securitised response to 198–9, 201, 205, 207–9, 221–36
        capitalist goals of 235
        futility of 234–5
        'hearts and minds' strategy 206, 215, 233, 234
        man-hunting strategy *see* man-hunting
        non-state actors in 222
        rhetoric of war in 198, 199, 201, 202, 211, 212, 214, 221, 222, 224, 225, 229
        use of drones 202, 207, 208, 211, 212, 222, 229–32
        see also IAPF
    by police/military 222, 227
    as political/colonial construction 235, 236
    by refugees 17
    of rhinos *see* rhino poaching
    subsistence 200, 227
    and ungoverned space 208–9
    Western governments' response to 201–2
polar bears 8–9
Polgreen, L. 7
police 138, 206–7
    logic of 232–3
    as poachers 222, 227
pollution 9, 133, 159
    and 'war on Drugs' 11–12
    water contamination 11, 12, 15–16, 128, 241
    see also toxic waste dumping
population growth 3, 60, 97, 293
Portugal 156, 203

Potter, G.R. 154–5
poverty 6(*n*5), 70, 76, 161
power gives right 95
Presser, L. 303
primitive accumulation 223
protest movements 15–16, 17, 126, 155
    and judicial systems 141
    violence against activists 129, 131, 133, 135, 136
public/human health 13, 17, 51, 52, 159, 268, 278
    see also sanitation

Quantum of Solace (film, 2008) 290, 291, 292, 294
Queensland (Australia) 243, 245, 247–8, 256, 257
    see also Bowen Basin mining communities

Rademeyer, Julian 210, 214
radioactive waste 14, 158, 159
raizales 76, 84, 85, 89
Razack, Sherene 225
refugees/displaced persons 8, 17, 50, 60, 61, 62, 67, 70, 75
    from drought/famine 160
    in frontiers 125, 134, 135, 138, 139
Reich, Robert 242
renewable energy 14
'resource curse' 4
resource management 1–2
Reuveny, R. 7, 8
Revolutionary United Front (RUF), Sierra Leone 179, 180, 188
rhino conservation 203, 204–5, 215, 226
    and CITES 205, 211, 212, 213, 214
    horn sale legalisation 211, 212–14
    Operation Rhino 210–11
    White domination of 205, 212, 214
rhino poaching 19–20, 197–215, 221
    and corruption 198, 210, 212, 215
    and immigration/transnational crime 199
    media representations of 209
    militarised/securitised response to 198–9, 202–3, 208, 209–10, 211–12

rhetoric of war in 198, 199, 201, 202, 211, 212, 214
use of drones 202, 207, 208, 211, 212, 222
roots of 197–8, 203–5
summit on (2010) 200–201
and ungoverned space 208–9
Richard, M.G. 294
Ridley, Matt 295–6, 297
Rio Declaration on Environment and Development (1992) 184
Rio Tinto 244, 257
riparian ecosystems 51
Rivero, S. 125
Rosenthal, N. 288, 302
Ross, Andrew 288
Royal Dutch Shell 294–5
Ruggiero, V. 242–3
Russia *44*, 49, 163
illegal logging in 45, 46, 47, *47*, 48, 49, 51
Rustad, A. 2
Rwanda 5, *44*, 57, 59–60, 60(*n*2), 61, 67–68
FDLR rebel group in 59, 65–6
gorillas in 68–9

Salo, R. 46
San José del Guaviare (Colombia) 75, 84–5
sanitation 52, 161, 290
Saro-Wiwa, Ken 294–5
Sass, S.L. 301
Schwartz, Peter 296, 297
Seager, Jodi 12
seal hunting 8–9
Second World War 3, 10, 179, 180, 184, 202
security/insecurity 3, 7, 16, 19, 52, 57, 58, 59, 60, 61
as bourgeois concept 236
and climate change 66–7
see also food security; national security
Segovia (Colombia) 132–4, 135
Seneca Creek and Associates 45
shale oil/gas *see* fracking
Shostak, S. 294
Shute, Nevil *see On the Beach*
Sibley, S.S. 302–3

Sierra Leone 4, 49, 52, 60
war in 179, 180, 181, 188, 191, 290
Singer, M. 13, 14
skadefelling 99, 100
slavery/slave labour 178, 182, 228, 290, 293–4
social development 17, 76
soil resources 18, 51, 63
Somalia
environmental degradation in 18, 153
from drought/famine 18, 156, 159, 160–61, 164
from illegal fishing *see* fishing, illegal
from toxic waste dumping 156, 157–9, 161
and geo-political structures 163–4
volunteer coastguard response to 162
history of division/conflict in 155–6
and international political community (IPC) 156, 157, 159, 163
ivory trade in 65
piracy in *see* piracy
and tsunami (2004) 158, 163
Sonjica, Buyelwa 200–201
Sontag, Susan 291
Souquet, Jerome 160
South Africa
'Apartheid Wars' in 197–8, 202, 205–6, 215
as centre of poaching trade 197–8
counter-poaching in 198–99, 201, 205, 209, 210–11
economic/political issues in 199
Marikana mine shootings (2012) 207
National Environmental Management: Biodiversity Act (NEMBA) 205
national parks of (SANParks) 198, 201, 202, 203–4, 205, 208, 210, 211
and ungoverned space 208–9
police force of 206–7
see also rhino poaching
South African Defence Force (SADF) 197, 198
South African National Defence Force (SANDF) 199, 201, 205, 211

South African Police Service (SAPS) 199, 201
South/Central America 11–12, *44*, 50, 144
  illegal logging in *47*, 48, *48*
  Initiative for the Integration of Regional Infrastructure in (IIRSA) 89
  see also specific countries
South Korea 3, 163, 297
South Sudan 4, 44, *44*, *47*, 48, 64, 64(*n*3)
sovereignty 3, 87, 161, 187
  food 88
Spain 16, 49, 156, 163
Sparks, R. 290–91, 292
species justice 41, 42, 115
speciesism 95, 115, 118
state-corporate crime theory 125–7
Steele, Nick 202–3
Steinhart, Edward 223–4
Strauss, A. 76
sub-Saharan Africa 44, 179–80
Sudan 4, 44, *44*, 64, 64(*n*3), 243
supercapitalism 242–3
Sur de Bolívar (Colombia) *126*, 131–2
sustainable growth 2
Sweden 115, 117
Sykes, G.M. 127, 144

Tacconi, L. 45
Tadić decision 190
tantalum *see* coltan/tantalum
Tavernise, S. 7
taxation 52, 79, 129, 244
Taylor, Charles 49, 181
technological fixes 229, 295, 296–9
terrorism 12–13, 42, 46
  and ivory trade 65
  and piracy 153
  war on 81, 222
Thailand *47*, 49, 156, 231, 269
theriocide 17–18, 95–118
  and Animal Welfare Act 103, 105, 106, 107, 110, 115, 118
  and anthropocentrism 17–18, 95, 111, 116, 118
  of bears *see* bears, killing of
  and Bern Convention 96, 100, 118
  court rulings 95, 100–101, 102–11

  appeals court (*Borgarting lagmannsrett*) 101, 103, 106, 107, 109
  deterrent effect of 116–17
  Supreme Court (Høyesterett) 101(*n*11), 102, 103, 104, 105, 106, 107, 109, 110
  dimensions/roles/parties involved in 96–7
  and environmental justice 96
  and farmers 96, 101–2
  and green criminology 96
  lack of empathy in 112–13, 114, 115
  and Law of biodiversity 100, 101(*n*14), 102(*n*16), 103, 115
  legal/illegal 98
  licences for 98, 99, 100, 113–14
  of lynx *see* lynx, killing of
  and masculinity 114
  motivations in 111–13
    hatred 114, 115
    rationality of hunters 117
  and NGOs 97, 100–101
  and Norwegian Environment Agency 97, 98, 99, 100
  Norwegian state policies 96, 97, 98–102
    wildlife laws 96, 101, 102
  and pain/suffering/animals as individuals 115–16
  and power gives right 95
  socio-legal approach to 96
  and speciesism 95, 115, 118
  use of term 95–6
  and Wildlife law 96, 101, 102, 105, 106, 108, 111, 115, 117, 118
  of wolverine *see* wolverine, killing of
  of wolves *see* wolves, killing of
timber market 46, 49, 59, 181, 186
  see also logging
torture 132, 156, 183, 206, 232
Torture Convention 183
tourism 1, 19–20, 61, 67, 69, 86, 198, 202, 208, 209, 213, 241
toxic chemicals *see* pollution
toxic colonialism 157
toxic waste dumping 18, 154, 156, 157–9, 161, 295

as environmental crime 183
fishermen act against 163
and human health 159
and piracy 159, 164
and Somalian conflict 158
and wildlife/livestock 158–9
trade unions 84, 131, 134, 135, 138, 244,
   247, 253
traditional knowledge 77, 88
   and green criminology 90
transboundary protected areas (TBPAs)
   67–8
transnational crime 11, 198, 199, 200
transnational networks/social movements
   43, 243
tsunami (2004) 158, 163, 269

Uekart, B. 133
Uganda *44*, 59, 60, 60(*n*2), 67
   Army of 64–5, 68–9, 187–8
ungoverned space 208–9, 210
UNICEF 159
UNITA 197
United Nations (UN) 42, 49, 60(*n*1), 75,
   182, 243, 271
   Environment Programme (UNEP) 46,
      157, 158
   military of, and conservation 68, 69–70
   Security Council 162, 163, 164
United Nations Declaration on the Rights
   of Indigenous Peoples (2008) 139
United Nations Guiding Principles on
   Business and Human Rights
   (UNGPs) 127, 129, 135, 136, 144
United Self-Defense Armies of Colombia
   (AUC) 81, 82
United States (US) 3, 53, 64, 65, 163
   and Colombia 79, 85
   Drug Enforcement Administration
      (DEA) 81
   in dystopian fiction 286, 287–8
   energy consumption of 13–14, 180
   environmental disaster in *see*
      Deepwater Horizon oil spill
   fear in 288
   Fish and Wildlife Service 9
   and Korean War 10, 12

military of 13–15
   conservation efforts by 15
   oil consumption by 13–14
   training exercises, damage caused
      by 14
and 9/11 attacks/terrorism 12–13, 81
Oil Pollution Act (1990) 266
and poaching trade 201–2, 209
and Vietnam War 10, 13, 79
and 'War on Drugs' 11–12
wars waged by 178–9
uranium 14, 158
urbanization 3, 137

Vea Vea, Kelly 247, 252, 253–4
Vélez, Ílvaro Uribe 81, 133, 134
Velez, Manuel Marulanda 81
Venezuela 4, *44*, 77
Veuthey, S. 51–2
Vietnam 4, *47*, 51
Vietnam War 10, 13, 79, 184–5, 202
violence 1(*n*3), 16, 42, 43
   and frontiers 125
   greed-motivated 3, 153
   and multinational corporations 18, 20,
      129, 131–2, 137
   see also conflict/conflict relationships;
      war
Virunga National Park (DRC) 17, 60–61,
   65, 66, 67, 68, 69
Voorhees, C.C.W. 268

Walsh, B. 296, 297
war 5
   cold/hot 178
   crimes/laws of 18–19, 177, 182–4
      1976 Convention 185, 186
      criminal/commercial exploitation
         in 178, 188–92
      Fourth Geneva Convention 182–3,
         185, 186–7
      Genocide Convention 183
      humanitarian 182, 182–4, 188
      inappropriate to modern wars 177
      International Criminal Court 185,
         186, 187
      and Joint Criminal Enterprise
         (JCE) 177, 189, 190–91

pillage/looting of resources 177,
181, 186, 187–8, 189
reality gaps in 177–8, 186, 192
and *Tadić* decision 190
Torture Convention 183
as drain on natural resources 18
and environmental degradation 6–7,
10–12, 13–14, 17
and climate change 14
as crime 183, 184–8
and forestry/logging 16, 181
pillaging of resources 177, 178
and 'scorched earth' tactics 10
and environmental protection 184–8
post-conflict relief/recovery 2, 16, 17,
70–71
privatisation of 179, 183
resource 177, 178–82
and global markets 180, 182
modern, distinguishing features of
179–81
new norms for 188–91
rhetoric of, in counter-poaching
strategies *see under* poaching
see also nuclear weapons/war
'War on Drugs' 11–12
Ward, T. 90, 161, 162
water resources 6–7, 290, 291, 292
contamination of 11, 12, 15–16, 128,
241, 286
weather manipulation 10, 13, 185,
300(*n*21)
Western Australia 243, 245, 248
whales 14, 157
white-collar crime 76, 184
wildlife 4, 8–9, 15, 42, 51, 57
illegal trade in 76
intrinsic value of 97, 106, 115, 116
ownership of 200
as resource 18, 114
rights/ownership of 97
see also endangered species; hunting;
poaching; species justice
wildlife crime, construction of 223–4
Wildlife law (Norway) 96, 101, 102, 105,
106, 108, 111, 115, 117, 118

wildlife parks 222
see also national parks *under* South
Africa
Wildlife Trafficking Taskforce 201
Windsor Inquiry (2013) 242, 245, 248,
251, 254–5
Wisner, B. 273
Witten, M. 302
wolverine, killing of 96, 100
court rulings on 102, 105, 109
licences for 113–14
motivations for 112–13
Norwegian state policies on 96, 98, 100
wolves, killing of 96, 97, 98, 100–101,
117, 118
court rulings on 102, 103, 106–7, 115
motivations for 111–12, 113
Norwegian state policies on 96, 97,
98–9
women 76, 84, 85, 234, 246
hunters 114
and illegal logging 51–2
and mining 246, 247, 251–2, 253, 254
as war casualties 5
world culture theory 271
World Made By Hand (Kunstler) 287, 288,
289
world systems theory 269, 271
World Wildlife Fund (WWF) 231–2
Wyatt, J. 10–11

Xaysaving Network 201
Xingu River/Peoples (Brazil) *132*, 136, 137
Xu, B. 3, 4

'Yellow Berets' force 68–9
Young, J. 77
Yugoslavia, Former, International Criminal
Tribunal for 190

Zilinskas, R.A. 13, 299(*n*20)
Zimbabwe 4, 205, 209, 222, 225, 227, 232
zoomorphism 227
Zuma, Jacob 201

PGSTL